FOUNDATIONS
OF CODING

FOUNDATIONS OF CODING

Compression, Encryption, Error Correction

JEAN-GUILLAUME DUMAS
Université de Grenoble

JEAN-LOUIS ROCH
Université de Grenoble

ÉRIC TANNIER
Inria, Université de Lyon

SÉBASTIEN VARRETTE
Université du Luxembourg

Published by John Wiley & Sons, Inc., Hoboken, New Jersey
Published simultaneously in Canada

For general information on our other products and services or for technical support, please contact our
Customer Care Department within the United States at (800) 762-2974, outside the United States at
(317) 572-3993 or fax (317) 572-4002.

Wiley also publishes its books in a variety of electronic formats. Some content that appears in print may
not be available in electronic formats. For more information about Wiley products, visit our web site at
www.wiley.com.

Library of Congress Cataloging-in-Publication Data:

Dumas, Jean-Guillaume.
  Foundations of coding : compression, encryption, errorcorrection / Jean-Guillaume Dumas, Jean-Louis
Roch, Eric Tannier, Sebastien Varrette.
      pages cm
  Includes bibliographical references and index.
  ISBN 978-1-118-88144-6 (cloth)
  1. Coding theory. I. Roch, Jean-Louis (Mathematician) II. Tannier, Eric. III. Varrette, Sebastien.
IV. Title.
  TK5102.92.D86 2015
  003′.54–dc23

                                                                                              2014039504

Printed in the United States of America

10 9 8 7 6 5 4 3 2 1

CONTENTS

LIST OF FIGURES, TABLES, ALGORITHMS AND ACRONYMS

List of Figures

List of Tables

List of Algorithms

Acronyms

FOREWORD

This work has been initiated in spring 2000 with the creation of the joint ENSIMAG-ENSERG Telecommunication department at the National Polytechnic Institute of Grenoble (INPG – France) and the setting up of a general course (last year French Licence level in the Licence-Master-Doctorate scheme) providing an introduction to codes and their applications.

Although it was initially published as a handout, it evolved and became reference material for several courses in Grenoble universities – both in the INPG and in the Joseph Fourier University (UJF) at the master level.

We take this occasion to thank our colleagues who participated in these courses and helped us improve our material with their remarks: Gilles Debunne, Yves Denneulin, Dominique Duval, Grégory Mounié and Karim Samaké.

In 2007, a book was published in French by Dunod editions in their mathematics and computer science collection. It was then reprinted, with a few amendments, in the beginning of 2009, and edited in an augmented version in 2013.

Éric Bourre, Cécile Canovas-Dumas, Mélanie Favre, Françoise Jung, Madeline Lambert, Benjamin Mathon, Marie-Aude Steineur, and Antoine Taveneaux participated to these first two editions by reading the drafts and spotting some mistakes.

This English edition was started in 2009, when our colleagues Rodney Coleman and Romain Xu undertook the task of translating the 352 pages of the French edition in English. Let them be gratefully thanked here.

Compared to this translation, this book has been revised and significantly augmented (20% additional pages and 27 new exercises). We now cover modern and frequently used techniques, as elliptic curves, low density codes, or matrix bar-codes as well as new standards like the ESTREAM portfolio, Galois hashing and counter mode, and the new standard hashing algorithm 3, Keccak. In addition, we have updated several parts, including steganography and watermarking, maximum likelihood decoding, saturation attacks (on AES), and postquantum cryptography.

"Foundations of Coding: Compression, Encryption, Error Correction" comes now with a companion website http://foundationsofcoding.imag.fr. This web site provides access to tools, resources, and news about the book, and, more generally, about security. In particular, we propose interactive solutions to several exercises via worksheets, using the free mathematical software Sage.

GRENOBLE, LYON, LUXEMBOURG
JEAN-GUILLAUME DUMAS, JEAN-LOUIS ROCH,
ÉRIC TANNIER, SÉBASTIEN VARRETTE.

INTRODUCTION

This work is aimed at providing a textbook for master students in applied mathematics or computer science. It can be used as a reference book by teachers, researchers, or companies involved in telecommunication or information security. The book is, to a certain extent, self-contained, that is, all used concepts are introduced. However, some training in algebra, algorithmics, and probability theory will be helpful. Indeed, the originality of this book is to present fundamental structures and applications, covering all coding operations, in a single framework.

The subject is the automatic transmission of numerical information. We will focus on the structure of information, without regarding the type of transmission support. Information can be of any kind as long as we can give a numerical representation of it: for example texts, images, sounds, and videos. Transmission of this type of data is ubiquitous in technology, especially in telecommunications. Hence, it is necessary to rely on solid bases for that transmission to be reliable, the term "reliable" having several different meanings depending on the objectives that will guide us throughout this book.

Transmission channels can also be of any kind (wirenets or wavenets), possibly through data storage. We will not consider the physical issues coming with transmission, which are the subjects of the theory known as "signal" theory. "Coding" deals with information itself when it is meant to be transmitted or stored.

Communication of a piece of information begins with a sender writing it, goes on with its transmission through a channel and ends with the reconstruction of the

Foundations of Coding: Compression, Encryption, Error Correction, First Edition.
Jean-Guillaume Dumas, Jean-Louis Roch, Éric Tannier and Sébastien Varrette.
© 2015 John Wiley & Sons, Inc. Published 2015 by John Wiley & Sons, Inc.
http://foundationsofcoding.imag.fr

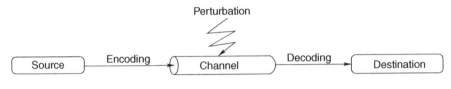

Figure I.1   Fundamental coding scheme

message by the recipient. Sometimes, the sender is also the recipient: it is the case of a processor or a person saving data in a register, a memory, or a disk and reading it later on. Information has to be fully, safely, and quickly transmitted to its recipient. However, whatever the channel may be, with variations depending on the support, it can never be considered "safe" in several ways: errors can appear during transmissions, and the message is likely to be read, and even modified, by a potentially malicious third party.

It is up to the sender to compose his messages in a form that allows the recipient to reconstruct them – considering potential alterations during the transfer or confidentiality of some information – while minimizing the size of data.

These constraints are the starting points of several fields in mathematics and computing that are often developed separately although they deal with the same subject. The purpose of this book is to gather them into one volume and to present a single theory whose subject is the form given to information during its transmission, namely a general *coding* theory.

In 1948, Claude Shannon laid the foundation stone of what he called a "mathematical theory of communication." It is said that his theory began with his comments on natural languages: Shannon used to hide some parts of the text he was reading and to recover them from the visible part. When removing a few words, he was able to determine the meaning of a sentence with absolute certainty. Actually, the hidden words were *redundant*, they did not add anything to the meaning of the message. If he removed too many words, he was unable to guess the message with certainty. Then Shannon developed a theory that would allow one to calculate the "amount of information" of any kind of message, hence the determination of a redundancy rate.

Nowadays, the operation of reducing redundancy is called *compression* or "information theory." Here, we are not only looking for efficiency in terms of optimization of the storage space but mainly in terms of transmission speed: we are interested in having the shortest message by keeping only what is necessary, or even better, reformulating it without redundancy.

Another and older concern in the transmission of a piece of information is confidentiality. Assuming that roads (as well as numerical channels) are not safe – and that a message can be intercepted during the transmission – the text has to be transformed, uncorrelated from its signification, while guaranteeing that only its recipients are given the decryption keys. The history of societies and nations is full of secret code stories and battles between code inventors and code breakers (who wanted to recover the meaning of the message without knowing the key). Shannon also contributed in this field by giving the first theoretical proof of confidentiality in 1949.

Today, a scientific discipline is dedicated to secret codes – *cryptology*. Not only do current techniques guarantee the *secrecy* of a message, but they also allow one to *sign* documents and *identify* a sender.

In addition to ill-intentioned third parties, all channels that are used in transmission of numerical information can suffer from perturbations that are likely to alter some parts of the messages, hence to modify their meaning. If the information is sent without redundancy, the least significant modification can lead to misunderstandings once at destination. As for natural languages, most of the errors will not alter the perception of the reader because redundancy will allow him to recover the initial message. Once again, Shannon presented a revolutionary result in 1948: even on channels with high error rate, it is still possible to add enough redundancy so that the message will be entirely received. But the proof is not constructive and this theorem keeps motivating the development of methods including ordered and optimized redundancy for the recipient to be able to detect modifications of the message (*detection codes*) and to correct potential errors himself (*correction codes*). All these methods are customizable – flexible – depending on the kind of support considered and its error rate.

Efficiency, *security*, and *integrity* are the three concerns for developers of information transmission methods. This book tackles those issues in one single volume through their common object – *the code* – which is used to structure the information on all current technological support.

The general theory of codes is based on a background coming from linear algebra, arithmetic, probability theory, algorithmic, and combinatorial analysis. In the first chapter of this book, we will present the mathematical models and the first algorithmic developments that structure the notion of code. The presentation of these models includes some introduction to useful mathematical concepts for the manipulation of codes, as well as general notions on the efficiency of calculation methods, which will be frequently used throughout the present work. Reading this chapter will require a basic theoretical knowledge of linear algebra (a first course in this field should be sufficient). Some elements go beyond the standard knowledge of nonmathematician students and are presented in detail here. The reader will soon be aware of their real practical importance, most of the time during their very introduction. Figure I.2 clarifies the usefulness of these notions and the dependencies between them.

As linear reading is not necessary, this scheme will also allow a reader in a hurry – or only interested in a specific part of this book – to quickly find his way. Although the first chapter is meant to introduce the foundations of coding, it can also be used as a reference toolbox during the reading of the following chapters. Those chapters deal with the notions of compression, cryptography, detection, and correction codes separately. They present the fundamental theoretical results and the algorithms that follow from them. Each chapter is illustrated with concrete examples and training exercises in the field of telecommunications. We have striven to present

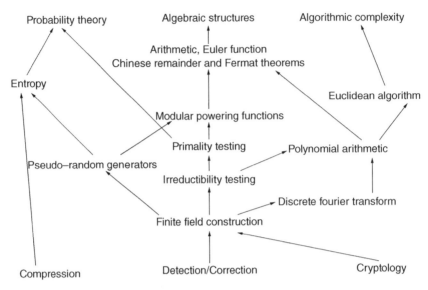

Figure I.2 Notions introduced in Chapter 1

both classical coding theories and the most recent developments dealing with them as far as such an introductory book allow us to.

Not only does this book gathers mathematical theories sharing the same subject, but its creed is also algorithmic. Here, the mathematical properties of the functions are used in order to make their calculation efficient. Computation methods are always detailed and can be immediately implemented in any programming language. Efficiency of the methods is always stated and debated. Existing implementations are compared.

These sciences are derived from both Greek mathematics – whose quality was based on their aesthetic nature – and oriental mathematics – which focused on usefulness and calculation. This is what can also bring together the foundations of coding, and one of their greatest merit is to call upon rigorous mathematics – which are appreciated by aesthetes – in order to build efficient methods applied to common communications. Hence, this book is at the confluence of these rivers and will attract technology and number theory enthusiasts, as well as all those whose imagination is still fired by stories of decryption of arcane languages, machines that correct their own errors and secret codes.

1

FOUNDATIONS OF CODING

This first chapter is an introduction to the notion of code. It contains the mathematical background, necessary to manipulate the codes, and the coding operations. Through this chapter, the reader will understand the constraints of the transmission of information, starting from historical examples and eventually learning advanced techniques. The knowledge of some historical aspects is pedagogically useful to work first on simple structures. In cryptology, history is also essential for efficient protection against the whole range of known attacks.

The principle is always to start from examples of codes, showing step by step why some mathematical notions are useful so that the codes are short, safe, and efficient. While the following chapters describe recent, elaborate, and currently used protocols for coding, this chapter provides the foundations of this activity.

Simple objects from probability theory, algebra, or algorithmic are introduced along the lines of this chapter, when they become necessary. For example, block coding calls for the definition of structures in which elements can be added, multiplied, which justifies the introduction of groups and fields. The emphasis is always put on the effective construction of introduced structures. This calls for a section on algorithms, as well as polynomials and primitive roots.

This chapter is organized in four sections. The first three allow to focus on the three important mathematical notions related to coding: algorithms and their complexity, which is at the core of coding theory; probabilities, related to stream cipher; and algebra, related to block coding. Then, the last section of this chapter is devoted to

Foundations of Coding: Compression, Encryption, Error Correction, First Edition.
Jean-Guillaume Dumas, Jean-Louis Roch, Éric Tannier and Sébastien Varrette.
© 2015 John Wiley & Sons, Inc. Published 2015 by John Wiley & Sons, Inc.
http://foundationsofcoding.imag.fr

the many facets of decoding, from ambiguity and information loss to secret code breaking.

We will denote by *code* a transformation method that converts the representation of a piece of information into another one. This definition is wide enough to include several mathematical objects (functions, algorithms, and transforms), which will be used throughout this book.

The word *code* will also apply to the result of these transformations[1], namely the encoded information and its structure. But for now, in order to find our way in these definitions and to understand what is actually a code, here is a simple example mixing technologies and eras.

1.1 FROM JULIUS CAESAR TO TELECOPY

In this section, we introduce all the fundamental properties of codes, using one of them built from real examples – currently or formerly used. It is the occasion to define and use the algorithms and their properties, which are constantly used in the whole book.

Suppose that we wish to send a piece of information by fax while guaranteeing the secrecy of the transmission. We could do it with the following code.

1.1.1 The Source: from an Image to a Sequence of Pixels

Transmission by fax enables us to pass images through a phone channel. We want this code to perform the requested transformations in order to obtain – quickly and secretly – an image similar to the original one at the end, in a format that could pass through the channel.

The first transformation process will be performed by the scanner of the device. It consists in reading the image and transforming it into a sequence of pixels that we can visualize as small squares either black or white. This is a code, according to the definition we have given, and we will write it as an algorithm, in a format we will adopt throughout this book.

Encoding algorithm

Input An image
Output A sequence of pixels

The input of the algorithm is also called the *source*, and the output is called the *code*.

The chosen method will be the following: the width of the source image is split into 1728 equal parts; the length is then split into lines so that the image is divided into

---

[1]The word *code* in natural languages can have several meanings. In our context, we will see that it applies to transformations and their results, but in computer science, it can also mean a computer program. This apparent confusion actually enables one to figure out the link between various mathematical and computer processes. That is why we will keep the word with its multiple meanings.

squares of the same size, 1728 per line. These squares will be considered as pixels. Each pixel is given either the color black if the zone of the image is dark enough or the color white if the image is bright.

This is the first part of our code. The following sections describe the other transformations; one can use to encode the information: compression, encryption, and error correction.

1.1.2 Message Compression

In order to formalize source messages and codes, we define the language in which they are formulated. We call *alphabet* a finite set $V = \{v_1, \ldots, v_k\}$ of elements (called *characters*). The *cardinal number* of a finite set V is the number of elements it contains and is denoted by $|V|$.

A sequence of characters belonging to V is called a *string* . We denote by V^* the set of all the strings over V, and V^+ the set of all the strings whose length is not equal to 0. As the alphabet of the code and the alphabet of the source may differ, we will distinguish the *source alphabet* and the *code alphabet* .

For the example of the fax, the source alphabet is the result of the scanner, that is, $\{white\ pixel, black\ pixel\}$ and the code alphabet will be the set of bits $\{0, 1\}$. We could send the sequence of pixels directly as bits, as we have an immediate conversion to 0 (for white pixels) and 1 (for black pixels).

However, we can apply some compression principles to this sequence of 0s and 1s. We can imagine that the datasheet we want to send has only a few lines of text and is mainly white – which is very common with faxes. But is there a better way of sending a sequence of, let us say a 10 000 zeros, than simply using a 10 000 zeros? Surely such a method exists, and we have just used one by evoking that long sequence of bits without writing it explicitly. We have indicated that the code is composed of 10 000 zeros rather than writing them down.

The fax code performs that principle of compression line by line (i.e., over 1728-pixels blocks). For each line, Algorithm 1.1 describes precisely the encoding algorithm.

For example, with this method, a completely white line will not be encoded with a sequence of 1728 zeros, but with the code "11011000000 0" which represents "1728 0" in the binary representation that will be sent through the channel. We have replaced a 1728-bit message by a 12-bit message. This is noticeably shorter.

We will give details of this principle of message *compression* – called Run-Length Encoding (RLE) – in Section 2.3.1.

For a better visibility, we used a space character in our representation (between 1728 and 0) but that character does not belong to the code alphabet. In practice, we will see later in this chapter what constraints that statement implies.

Exercise 1.1 *A pixelized image meant to be sent by fax contains a lot of pairs "01." What do you think of the fax code presented before? Give a more effective code.*

Solution on page 281.

Algorithm 1.1 Simplified Fax Encoding for a Line of Pixels

Input M, a sequence of 1728 pixels (from $M[0]$ to $M[1727]$)
Output C, the compressed message of M
1: $n \leftarrow 1$ // *counter of consecutive pixels with the same value*
2: $C \leftarrow ""$ // *empty string*
3: **For** i from 1 to 1727 **do**
4:    **If** $M[i-1] = M[i]$ **then**
5:      $n \leftarrow n+1$ // *increment counter of consecutive pixels with value $M[i]$*
6:    **else**
7:      Append n and the color of the last pixel $M[i-1]$ to C
8:      $n \leftarrow 1$ // *re-initialize the counter*
9:    **End If**
10: **End For**
11: Append n and the col-our of the pixel $M[1727]$ to C
12: **return** C

1.1.3   Error Detection

All the readers who have already used a phone channel will not be surprised to learn that its reliability is not infinite. Each message is likely to be distorted, and it is not impossible, assuming that "11011000000 0" was sent on the channel, to receive "11010000000 0" (modification of one bit) or "1101000000 0" (loss of one bit).

Phone channels usually have an error rate between 10^{-4} and 10^{-7}, depending on their nature, which means that they can commit an error every 10,000 bits. This is far from being negligible when you consider long messages, and it can also modify their meaning. For an image, if the value 1728 becomes 1664 because of the loss of one single bit, a shift will occur in the final image and the result will be unusable.

The fax code enables the detection of such transmission errors. If an error is detected on a line, one can ask for a second transmission of the same line to have a confirmation and – as it is unlikely to have the same error twice at the same place – the message will be corrected.

The principle of error detection in the fax code is explained as follows: predetermined sequences are appended at the beginning and at the end of each line. Such flag sequences are used to establish bit and line synchronization (and in particular detect loss of bit). In order to illustrate this principle, let us suppose that "0" (respectively "1729") is added at the beginning (respectively the end) of each line even if these are not the exact values that are used in practice. The receiver can then check that each line is in the format "0 $n_1 b_1$ ... $n_k b_k$ 1729," with n_i an integer that provides the number of consecutive bits and b_i the color of these bits. In particular, the condition $n_1 + \cdots + n_k = 1728$ must be respected and the colors b_i must be alternated. Thus, a modification or the loss of one bit is easily detected as soon as this format is not respected.

All error detection and correction principles, which will be closely studied in Chapter 4, are based on this principle: the addition of information in order to check the consistency of the received message.

1.1.4 Encryption

Now, let us suppose that, after having compressed the message and set up a format that enables error detection, we wish to keep the message secret for everybody but its recipient. The phone channel, like most channels, does not provide secrecy in itself. Every message that is transmitted through it can be easily read by a third party. The setting up of the secret consists in transforming the original message, the *plaintext*, putting it into a nonunderstandable form, the *ciphertext*, and putting it back into its original form at the end.

This is a technique that has been used by men as they started to communicate. In secret codes of Antiquity, the secret resided in the method that was used to produce the ciphertext, which is what we call the encryption algorithm nowadays. For example, historians have discovered messages encrypted by Julius Caesar's secret services. The messages were texts, and the algorithm substituted each letter of the original message M with the letter located three positions later in the alphabet. For the three last letters of the alphabet, the three first letters were used. For example, the word *TROY* became *WURB*. Hence, the text did not have any immediate signification. That is what is called *mono-alphabetic substitution*, as each letter is replaced by another one (always the same) in the message.

If Caesar had wanted to send a fax, he would have adapted his code to the numerical format, which would have given the function $f(x) = x + 3 \bmod n$ for every number sent on the channel where the number n is the size of the alphabet. Here it would have been 1730 as no number greater than 1729 would theoretically be used.

These encryption and decryption functions were then extended with a simple key K, an integer chosen secretly between the interlocutors. This is equivalent to the construction of a function $f_K(x) = x + K \bmod n$. As for the Spartans, they used a completely different encryption algorithm, called transposition encryption. Their system is based on the Scytale , a stick on which a strip was rolled. The message was written on the strip along the stick rather than along the scroll. This means that the consecutive letters of the message appeared on a circumlocution different from the one of the strip.

Figure 1.1 illustrates the encryption principle. In order to decrypt the message, the recipient would have a stick with the same diameter as the stick used for the encryption.

Other cryptographic systems, more evolved, were created afterward (affine encryption $f_{a,b}(x) = a.x + b \bmod n$ – studied in Exercises 1.2 and 3.1; substitution encryption where each letter is replaced by a symbol of another alphabet – such as the Morse code, etc...).

Exercise 1.2 *Mark Antony intercepts a message sent by Caesar, encrypted with an affine encryption. Without knowing the key (a, b), how can he decrypt the message?*

Solution on page 282.

1.1.5 Decryption

In Section 1.1.4, we have seen some methods for encrypting a message and insuring the secrecy and the efficiency of its transmission. This description would not be

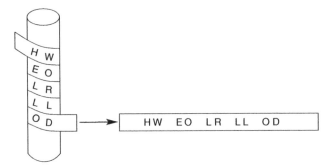

Figure 1.1   Spartan Scytale principle to transmit the text "HELLOWORLD"

complete without a short presentation of the principles of the complementary operation – decryption.

1.1.5.1 Attack and Decryption   The encrypted message arrives. It is a matter of decrypting it. If one is not given the key or the encryption method, we talk about an *attack* on the code, or a *codebreaking*. The discipline which handles the development of methods of attacking existing codes or of building more resistant codes is called *cryptanalysis*. For the recipient of the message – who knows the key – we talk about *decryption*.

We will soon talk about attacks. For now, the decryption method is very simple and consists in applying the inverse function of the encryption function, possibly customized with a key, namely $f_K^{-1}(y) = y - K \mod n$. In our case, the recipient of Caesar's fax would have to apply $f_3^{-1}(x) = y - 3 \mod 1730$ for every number received on the channel The message is now decrypted.

Now, we still have to perform the inverse of all the remaining transformations. First of all, the format of each line is checked in order to detect possible errors (in this case, we ask for a second transmission), then the decoding algorithm is performed which – given a sequence of numbers – will return the initial pixel sequence. Algorithm 1.2 formalizes this operation for each line.

Algorithm 1.2 Fax Decoding for a Decrypted and Checked Line

Input A sequence of numbers in the format "$0 \, n_1 \, b_1 \, \ldots \, n_{1728} \, b_{1728} \, 1729$"
Output A sequence of 1728 corresponding pixels
  1: **For** i from 1 to 1728 **do**
  2:    Draw n_i pixels with color b_i
  3: **End For**

1.1.5.2 Decompression and Data Loss   When we apply this algorithm to all the lines, we obtain a sequence of pixels, identical to the one we built from the original image. Now, we can recover the original image, or at least a similar image as the only information we have is the value of the pixels. Thus, the method consists in printing the sequence of corresponding black and white squares on a sheet of paper. The image resulting from this operation will be a damaged version of the initial one, as the original squares were not completely black or white. That is what gives the nonaesthetic aspect of all faxes, but the essential information is preserved.

In this case, initial information is not entirely recovered – and arrives in an approximate form – thus we talk about *encoding with (data-)loss*. One often uses codes which admit a determined level of loss, providing that important information is not distorted. It is often the case with multimedia information (see Section 2.5).

1.1.6 Drawbacks of the Fax Code

We have completely described the encoding – and decoding – processes, while respecting the major constraints we will encounter in coding (compression efficiency, error detection, and secrecy). But for several reasons, the principles used in the fax code are not very usable in practice in common numerical communications.

Compression: the way the RLE principle is applied here has several drawbacks. First of all, if the message is only composed of alternating black and white pixels, the size of the "compressed" message will be greater than that of the original. Thus, there is absolutely no guarantee of the compression of the message. Moreover, including the bits b_i is almost useless as they are alternated and the value of the first one would be enough to determine the value of the others. The fax code removes them. It then becomes a sequence of numbers $n_1 \dots n_k$. But that sequence – encoded as bits (to each number its binary representation) – is more difficult to decode. Indeed, when receiving a bit sequence "1001011010010," how do we know whether it represents a number n_i or several numbers appended ? In order to solve this issue, for example, we can encode every number with the same number of bits but then the compression algorithm is no longer optimal. We are now forced to represent "2" with the sequence "00000000010," which increases the size of the message. We will see how to insure that a message can be decoded later in this chapter. In Chapter 2, we will see how to deduce good compression methods while insuring this decoding ability.

Error detection: this principle implies that one has to ask for a second transmission of information each time an error is detected, whereas we could develop codes that automatically correct the channel errors (Chapter 4). Moreover, there is no theoretical guarantee that this code adapts to phone channel error rates. We do not know the error rate detected by the code, nor if it can accomplish the same performance adding less information in the messages. Efficiency of the transmission may depend on the quality of error detection and correction principles.

Secrecy: Caesar's code is breakable by any beginner in cryptology. It is easy to decode any *mono-alphabetic substitution* principle, even without knowing the key. A simple cryptanalysis consists of studying the frequency of appearance

TABLE 1.1   Letter Distribution in this LaTeX Script

E	13.80%	T	8.25%	I	8.00%	N	7.19%	A	6.63%
O	6.57%	R	6.37%	S	6.28%	C	4.54%	D	4.35%
L	4.34%	U	3.34%	M	3.15%	P	2.92%	H	2.81%
F	2.36%	G	1.86%	B	1.83%	X	1.35%	Y	1.07%
V	0.87%	W	0.69%	K	0.57%	Q	0.55%	Z	0.16%
J	0.14%								

of the letters in the ciphertext and of deducing the correspondence with the letters of the plaintext.

Table 1.1 presents the statistical distribution of the letters in this document written in LaTeX (LaTeX special tags are also considered). As this book is quite long, we can assume that these frequencies are representative of scientific texts in English written in LaTeX. It is obviously possible to obtain such frequency tables for literary English texts, scientific French texts, and so on.

Exercise 1.3   *Scipio discovers a parchment manuscript with the following cipher-text:* HFJXFW BTZQI MFAJ GJJS UWTZI TK DTZ! *Help Scipio decrypt this message.* Solution on page 282.

1.1.7   Orders of Magnitude and Complexity Bounds for Algorithms

We have described a code and we have presented its advantages and disadvantages. However, there is another critical point we have not yet mentioned: what about encoding and decoding speed? It depends on computer speed, but mostly on the complexity of the algorithms.

Size of numbers. We consider numbers and their size either in decimal digits or in bits. Thus, a number m will be $\lceil \log_{10}(m) \rceil$ digits long and $\lceil \log_2(m) \rceil$ bits long. For instance, 128 bits can be represented with 39 decimal digits, 512 bits with 155 decimal digits, and 1024 bits with 309 decimal digits.

Computer speed. Nowadays, the frequency of any PC is at least 1 GHz. That is to say it can execute 1 billion (10^9) operations per second. By way of comparison, the greatest speed in the universe is the speed of light: $300\,000$ km/s $= 3.10^8$ m/s. It takes only a ten thousand millionth of a second for light to cross a room of 3 m long. During this period, your computer has performed 10 operations!!! Hence, we can say that *current computers calculate at the speed of light.*

Comparison with the size and age of the universe. This computing speed is truly astronomical; yet the size of the numbers we manipulate remains huge. Indeed, one has to enumerate 10^{39} numbers just in order to count up to a 39 digit long number. In order to see how huge it is, let us calculate the age of the universe in seconds:

$$\text{Age of the universe} \simeq 15 \text{ billion years} \times 365.25 \times 24 \times 60 \times 60 \approx 5.10^{17} \text{ s.}$$

Thus, a 1 GHz computer would take more than two million times the age of the universe just to count up to a number of "only" 39 digits! As for a 155 digit number (commonly used in cryptography), it is simply the square of the number of electrons in the universe. Indeed, our universe is thought to contain about 3.10^{12} galaxies, each galaxy enclosing roughly 200 billion stars. Knowing that the weight of our sun is approximately 2.10^{30} kg and that the weight of an electron is $0.83.10^{-30}$ kg, we have

$$\text{Universe} = (2.10^{30}/0.83.10^{-30}) * 200.10^9 * 3.10^{12} \approx 10^{84} \text{ electrons.}$$

Yet such numbers will have to be manipulated. Their size will represent one of the algorithmic challenges we will have to take up, as well as a guarantee of the secrecy of our messages if it takes millions of years of computing – on the billion machines available on Earth, including the fastest ones – to decrypt them without the key. We will see how to build algorithms which can handle such numbers later.

Complexity bounds of the algorithms. There may be many different algorithms for solving the same computational problem. However despite the power of computers, an ill-conceived algorithm could turn out to be unusable. It is therefore of interest to find a way to compare the efficiency of two algorithms. This is done on the basis of a computational model and the *size* of the problem instance, which is a measure of the quantity of input data.

There exists many different computational models. For instance, one can use Turing machines, random-access machines, or Boolean circuits. Yet we will not detail them in this book (see, e.g., [1] for more details). As for the size and in order to be able to compute it in every instance, we assume that the input is a sequence of bits and the size of the input is the length of the sequence. This statement implies that we have to build a code that transforms the input of an algorithm into a sequence of bits. This is often a quite simple operation. For instance, it takes about $\log_2(a)$ bits to code an integer a (we simply write it in base 2). Thus, the size of an integer is equal to its logarithm in base 2. The size of a sequence of black and white pixels is the length of that sequence.

The number of basic computer steps needed by an algorithm expressed as a function of the size of the problem is called the *time complexity*[2] of the algorithm. This helps to define a machine-independent characterization of an algorithm's efficiency as the naive evaluation of an execution time crucially depends on the processor speed and various architecture-specific criteria.

Indeed, the notion of *basic computer step* is vague as the set of processor's instruction has a variety of basic primitives (branching, comparing, storing, performing arithmetic operations, etc.). However, all of them can be evaluated in terms of *bit operations*; Therefore, the true complexity of an algorithm is computed using this elementary unit. For the sake of simplicity, one sometimes counts only the number of arithmetical operations requested by the algorithm, typically limited to the four

---

[2]Analogous definition can be made for *space complexity* to measure the amount of space, or memory required by the algorithm.

classical operations (addition, subtraction, multiplication, and division) and some binary operations such as bit shift. In that case, it should be reminded that the conversion to bit operation depends on the base field.

As it is often impossible to count exactly all the basic computer steps performed during the execution of a program, the complexity of an algorithm is generally given with asymptotic upper bounds and lower bounds using the Big-O notation (also called Landau notation). More formally, if $f(n)$ and $g(n)$ are functions from positive integers to positive reals, then for any n large enough, it is said that

- $f(n) = O(g(n))$ if there exists a constant $c > 0$ such that $f(n) \leq c \times g(n)$. This defines g as an asymptotic upper bound for f. Intuitively, it means that f grows no faster asymptotically than $g(n)$ to within a constant multiple;
- $f(n) = \Omega(g(n))$ if there exists a constant $c > 0$ such that $f(n) \geq c \times g(n)$; This defines g as an asymptotic lower bound for f;
- $f(n) = \Theta(g(n))$ if $f(n) = O(g(n))$ and $f(n) = \Omega(g(n))$; and This defines g as an asymptotic tight bound for f;

Therefore, if an algorithm takes for instance, $14n^2 + 2n + 1$ steps on an input of size n, we simply say it runs with a time complexity bound of $O(n^2)$. Table 1.2 summarizes the typically met complexity functions and their associated names. AS Landau notation enables us to give the complexity to within a constant multiple, we can write $O(\log(n))$ without giving the base of the logarithm, knowing that the base multiplies the function by a constant (namely the logarithm of the base).

Exercise 1.4   *What is the complexity of the fax code presented in the previous section?*   *Solution on page 282.*

In practice, every algorithm should have a linear complexity $O(n)$ – where n is the size of the source message – to be "real-time" efficient, that is, usable in a transmission when a long latency is not acceptable (telephony, multimedia, etc.).

One of the fields of cryptography relies on the hypothesis that there exists some problems where no algorithm with such complexity is known. For such problems, every known algorithm requests astronomical computing time – which makes their application impossible.

TABLE 1.2   Typical Complexity Bounds Obtained from an Algorithm Analysis

Function	Complexity	Example
$O(1)$	Constant	Table lookup
$O(\log n)$	Logarithmic	Binary search on a sorted vector
$O(n)$	Linear	Traversing of an unsorted vector
$O(n \log n)$	Quasilinear	Quicksort, FFT (Section 1.4.2.4)
$O(n^k), k > 1$	Polynomial	Naive square matrix multiplication – $O(n^3)$
$O(k^n), k > 1$	Exponential	Naive Fibonacci – $O(1.6^n)$

In this book, we consider that a problem is impossible to solve (one often uses the euphemism "difficult") when there is no known algorithm which solves it in humanly reasonable time, for instance, if its resolution would request more than 10^{50} operations.

1.2   STREAM CIPHERS AND PROBABILITIES

As mentioned in Section 1.1.3, the probability of transmission error in many communication channels is high. To build an efficient code in such a situation, one can consider the message to be transmitted as a *bit stream*, that is, a potentially infinite sequence of bits sent continuously and serially (one at a time). Each character is then transformed bit by bit for the communication over the channel. Such an approach has various advantages:

- the transformation method can change for each symbol;
- there is no error propagation on the channel; and
- it can be implemented on embedded equipment with limited memory as only a few symbols are processed at a time.

This technique is notably used in cryptography in the so-called *stream cipher*. Under some conditions (Section 1.2.1), such systems can produce *unconditionally secure* messages: for such messages, the knowledge of the ciphertext does not give any information on the plaintext. This property is also called *perfect secrecy*. Thus, the only possible attack on a perfect encryption scheme given a ciphertext is the exhaustive research of the secret key (such a strategy is also called brute force attack). We also use the stream cipher model to build error detection and correction principles (see convolutional codes in Chapter 4). The *one-time-pad* (OTP) encryption scheme is an example of a cryptographic stream cipher whose unconditional security can be proved, using probability and information theory.

Some notions of probabilities are necessary for this section and also for the rest of the book. They are introduced in Section 1.2.2.

1.2.1   The Vernam Cipher and the One-Time-Pad Cryptosystem

In 1917, during the first World War, the American company AT&T asked the scientist Gilbert Vernam to invent a cipher method the Germans would not be able to break. He came with the idea to combine the characters typed on a teleprinter with the one of a previously prepared key kept on a paper tape. In the 1920s, American secret service captain Joseph Mauborgne suggested that the key should be generated randomly and used only once. The combination of both ideas led to the *OTP* encryption scheme, which is up to now the only cipher to be mathematically proved as unconditionally secure.

The Vernam cipher derived from the method introduced by Gilbert Vernam. It belongs to the class of secret key cryptographic system, which means that the secret lies in one parameter of the encryption and decryption functions, which is only known by the sender and the recipient. It is also the case of Caesar's code mentioned in Section 1.1.4, in which the secret parameter is the size of the shift of the letters (or the numbers).

Mathematically speaking, the Vernam encryption scheme is as follows: for any plaintext message M and any secret key K of the same size, the ciphertext C is given by

$$C = M \oplus K,$$

where $\oplus$ (also denoted by xor) is the bitwise logical "exclusive or" operation. Actually, it consists in an addition modulo 2 of each bit. This usage of the "exclusive or" was patented by Vernam in 1919. Decryption is performed using the same scheme due to the following property:

$$C \oplus K = (M \oplus K) \oplus K = M.$$

If K is truly random, used only once and of the same size as M i.e., $|K| = |M|$), then a third party does not obtain any information on the plaintext by intercepting the associated ciphertext (except the size of M). Vernam cipher used with those three assumptions is referred to as a OTP scheme. It is again unconditionally secure, as proved by Claude Shannon (Section 1.2.5).

Exercise 1.5 *Why is it necessary to throw the key away after using it, that is, why do we have to change the key for each new message?* Solution on page 282.

Exercise 1.6 *Build a protocol, based on the One-time-pad system, allowing a user to connect to a secured server on Internet from any computer. The password has to be encrypted to be safely transmitted through Internet and to avoid being captured by the machine of the user.* Solution on page 282.

Obviously, it remains to formalize the notion of random number generation, give the means to perform such generation and finally, in order to prove that the system is secure, make precise what "obtaining some information" on the plaintext means. For this, the fundamental principles of information theory – which are also the basis of message compression – are now introduced.

1.2.2 Some Probability

In a cryptographic system, if one uses a key generated randomly, any discrepancy with "true" randomness represents an angle of attack for the cryptanalysts. Randomness is also important in compression methods as any visible order, any redundancy, or organization in the message can be used not only by code breakers but also by code inventors who will see a means of expressing the message in a more dense form. But what do we call discrepancy with true randomness, and more simply what do we call randomness ? For instance, if the numbers "1 2 3 4 5 6" are drawn at lotto, one will doubt that they were really randomly generated, although *stricto sensu*, this combination has exactly the same probability of appearing as any other. We do not go deeply into the philosophy of randomness, but this section provides mathematical material to address randomness and its effects and to create something close to randomness.

1.2.2.1 Events and Probability Measure

An *event* is a possible result of a random experiment. For example, if one throws a six face die, getting the number 6 is an event. The set operators ($\cup$, $\cap$, $\setminus$) are used for relations between events (they stand for *or*, *and*, and *except*). We denote by Ω the set of all possible events for a given experiment. A probability measure P is a map of Ω onto $[0, 1]$ satisfying:

1. $P(\Omega) = 1$ and $P(\emptyset) = 0$;
2. For all A, B mutually exclusive events ($A \cap B = \emptyset$), $P(A \cup B) = P(A) + P(B)$.

If the set of events is a discrete set or a finite set, we talk about *discrete probability*. For example, if the random experiment is the throw of a fair six face die, the set of events is $\Omega = \{1, 2, 3, 4, 5, 6\}$ and the probability of occurrence of each one is $1/6$.

The probability function is called the *probability distribution* or the *law of probability*. A distribution is said to be *uniform* if all events have the same probability of occurrence.

Gibbs' lemma is a result on discrete distributions that will be useful several times in this book.

Lemma 1 (Gibbs' Lemma) *Let $(p_1, \ldots, p_n)$, $(q_1, \ldots, q_n)$ be two discrete probability laws with $p_i > 0$ and $q_i > 0$ for all i. Then*

$$\sum_{i=1}^{n} p_i * \log_2 \frac{q_i}{p_i} \leq 0$$

with equality if and only if $p_i = q_i$ for all i.

Proof. As $\log_2(x) = \frac{\ln x}{\ln 2}$ and $\ln(2) > 0$, it is sufficient to prove the statement using the neperian logarithm. Indeed, $\forall x \in \mathbb{R}_*^+$, $\ln(x) \leq x - 1$ with equality if and only if $x = 1$. Hence $\sum_{i=1}^{n} p_i * \ln \frac{q_i}{p_i} \leq \sum_{i=1}^{n} p_i * (\frac{q_i}{p_i} - 1)$.

Having $\sum_{i=1}^{n} p_i = \sum_{i=1}^{n} q_i = 1$, we can deduce that $\sum_{i=1}^{n} p_i * (\frac{q_i}{p_i} - 1) = \sum_{i=1}^{n} q_i - \sum_{i=1}^{n} p_i = 0$. As a result, $\sum_{i=1}^{n} p_i * \ln \frac{q_i}{p_i} \leq 0$. The equality holds if $q_i = p_i$ for all i so that the approximation $\ln(\frac{q_i}{p_i}) \leq \frac{q_i}{p_i} - 1$ is exact. $\square$

1.2.2.2 Conditional Probabilities and Bayes' Formula

Two events are said to be *independent* if $P(A \cap B) = P(A)P(B)$.

The *conditional probability* of an event A with respect to an event B is the probability of appearance of A, knowing that B has already appeared. This probability is denoted by $P(A|B)$ and defined by

$$P(A|B) = \frac{P(A \cap B)}{P(B)}$$

By recurrence, it is easy to show that for a set of events $A_1, \ldots, A_n$,

$$P(A_1 \cap \ldots \cap A_n) = P(A_1 | A_2 \cap \ldots \cap A_n) P(A_2 | A_3 \cap \ldots \cap A_n) \ldots P(A_{n-1} | A_n) P(A_n).$$

Bayes' formula enables us to compute – for a set of events $A_1, \ldots, A_n, B$ – the probabilities $P(A_k | B)$ as functions of the probabilities $P(B | A_k)$.

$$P(A_k | B) = \frac{P(A_k \cap B)}{P(B)} = \frac{P(B | A_k) P(A_k)}{\sum_i P(B | A_i) P(A_i)}$$

Exercise 1.7   *One proposes the following secret code, which encodes two charac-*
ters a and b with three different keys k_1, k_2, and k_3: if k_1 is used, then $a \to 1$ and
$b \to 2$; if k_2 is used, then $a \to 2$ and $b \to 3$. Otherwise, $a \to 3$ and $b \to 4$.
Moreover, some a priori *knowledge concerning the message M and the key*
K is assumed: $P(M = a) = 1/4$, $P(M = b) = 3/4$, $P(K = k_1) = 1/2$,   and
$P(K = k_2) = P(K = k_3) = 1/4$.
What are the probabilities of having the ciphertexts 1, 2, and 3? What are the con-
ditional probabilities that the message is a or b knowing the ciphertext? Intuitively,
can we say that this code has a "perfect secrecy"?   *Solution on page 282.*

Having revised the basic theory of random events, now let us present what randomness means for computers.

1.2.3   Entropy

1.2.3.1   Source of Information   Let S be the alphabet of the source message. Thus,
a message is an element of S^+. For each message, we can compute the frequencies
of appearance of each element of the alphabet and build a probability distribution
over S.

A *source of information* is constituted by a couple $S = (S, \mathcal{P})$ where $S = (s_1, \ldots, s_n)$ is the source alphabet and $\mathcal{P} = (p_1, \ldots, p_n)$ is a probability distribution over S,
namely p_i is the probability of occurrence of s_i in an emission. We can create a source
of information with any message by building the probability distribution from the
frequencies of the characters in the message.

The source of information $S = (S, \mathcal{P})$ is said *without memory* when the events
(occurrences of a symbol in an emission) are independent and when their probabilities
remain stable during the emission (the source is *stable*).

The source is said to follow a *Markov model* if the probabilities of the occurrence
of the characters depend on the one issued previously. In the case of dependence on
one predecessor, we have the probability set $\mathcal{P} = \{p_{ij}\}$, where p_{ij} is the probability of
appearance of s_i knowing that s_j has just been issued. Hence, we have $p_i = \sum_j p_{ij}$.

For instance, a text in English is a source whose alphabet is the set of Latin letters.
The probabilities of occurrence are the frequencies of appearance of each character. As the probabilities strongly depend on the characters that have just been issued
(a U is much more probable after a Q than after another U), the Markov model will
be more adapted.

An image also induces a source. The characters of the alphabet are the color levels. A sound is a source whose alphabet is a set of frequencies and intensities.

A source S is *without redundancy* if its probability distribution is uniform. This is obviously not the case for common messages, in which some letters and words are much more frequent than others. This will be the angle of attack of compression methods and also pirates trying to read a message without being authorized.

1.2.3.2 *Entropy of a Source*

Entropy is a fundamental notion for the manipulation of a code. Indeed, it is a measure of both the amount of information we can allocate to a source (this will be useful for the compression of messages) and the level of order and redundancy of a message, the crucial information in cryptography.

The *entropy* of a source $S = (S, P)$, $S = (s_1, \ldots, s_n)$, $P = (p_1, \ldots, p_n)$ is

$$H(S) = H(p_1, \ldots, p_n) = - \sum_{i=1}^{n} p_i \log_2(p_i) = \sum_{i=1}^{n} p_i \log_2\left(\frac{1}{p_i}\right).$$

By extension, one calls entropy of a message the entropy of the source induced by this message, the probability distribution being computed from the frequencies of appearance of the characters in the message.

Property 1 *Let $S = (S, P)$ be a source:*

$$0 \le H(S) \le \log_2 n.$$

Proof. We apply Gibbs' lemma to the distribution $(q_1, \ldots, q_n) = (\frac{1}{n}, \ldots, \frac{1}{n})$, we have $H(S) \le \log_2 n \sum_{i=1}^{n} p_i \le \log_2 n$ for any source S. Finally, positivity is obvious noticing that the probabilities p_i are less than 1. □

We can notice that for a uniform distribution, entropy reaches its maximum. It decreases when the distribution differs from the uniform distribution. This is why it is called a "measure of disorder," assuming that the greatest disorder is reached by a uniform distribution.

Exercise 1.8 *What is the entropy of a source where the character 1 has probability 0.1 and the character 0 has probability 0.9? Why will a small entropy be good for compression?* Solution on page 282.

1.2.3.3 *Joint Entropies, Conditional Entropies*

The definition of entropy can be easily extended to several sources. Let $S_1 = (S_1, P_1)$ and $S_2 = (S_2, P_2)$ be two sources without memory, whose events are not necessarily independent. Let $S_1 = (s_{11}, \ldots, s_{1n})$, $P_1 = (p_i)_{i=1\ldots n}$, $S_2 = (s_{21}, \ldots, s_{2m})$ and $P_2 = (p_j)_{j=1\ldots m}$; then $p_{i,j} = P(S_1 = s_{1i} \cap S_2 = s_{2j})$ is the probability of joint occurrence of s_{1i} and s_{2j} and $p_{i|j} = P(S_1 = s_{1i} | S_2 = s_{2j})$ is the probability of the conditional occurrence of s_{1i} and s_{2j}.

We call *joint entropy* of S_1 and S_2 the quantity

$$H(S_1, S_2) = -\sum_{i=1}^{n}\sum_{j=1}^{m} p_{i,j} \log_2(p_{i,j}).$$

For example, if the sources S_1 and S_2 are independent, then $p_{i,j} = p_i p_j$ for all i,j. In this case, we can easily show that $H(S_1, S_2) = H(S_1) + H(S_2)$.

On the contrary, if the events of S_1 and S_2 are not independent, we might want to know the amount of information in one source, knowing one event of the other source. Thus, we compute the *conditional entropy* of S_1 relative to the value of S_2, given by

$$H(S_1 | S_2 = s_{2j}) = -\sum_{i=1}^{n} p_{i|j} \log_2(p_{i|j}).$$

Finally, we extend this notion to a conditional entropy of S_1 knowing S_2, which is the amount of information remaining in S_1 if the law of S_2 is known:

$$H(S_1 | S_2) = \sum_{j=1}^{m} p_j H(S_1 | S_2 = s_{2j}) = \sum_{i,j} p_{i,j} \log_2\left(\frac{p_j}{p_{i,j}}\right).$$

This notion is crucial in cryptography. Indeed, it is very important for all ciphertexts to have a strong entropy in order to prevent the signs of organization in a message from giving some information on the way it was encrypted. Moreover, it is also important for entropy to remain strong even if a third party manages to obtain some important information concerning the plaintext. For instance, if some mails are transmitted, then they share common patterns in Headers; yet this knowledge should typically not provide information on the secret key used to encrypt the mails.

Then, we have the simple – but important – following relations:

$$H(S_1) \geq H(S_1 | S_2)$$

with equality if and only if S_1 and S_2 are independent; and also

$$H(S_1, S_2) = H(S_2) + H(S_1 | S_2).$$

However, the entropy of a source without memory does not capture all the order or the disorder included in a message on its own. For example, the messages "1 2 3 4 5 6 1 2 3 4 5 6" and "3 1 4 6 4 6 2 1 3 5 2 5" have the same entropy; yet the first one is sufficiently ordered to be described by a formula, such as "1...6 1...6," which is probably not the case for the second one. To consider this kind of organization, we make use of the extensions of a source.

1.2.3.4 *Extension of a Source* Let S be a Source without memory. The *kth extension* S^k of S is the couple $(S^k, \mathcal{P}^k)$, where S^k is the set of all words of length k over S

and $\mathcal{P}^k$ the probability distribution defined as follows: for a word $s = s_{i_1} \ldots s_{i_k} \in S^k$, then $P^k(s) = P(s_{i_1} \ldots s_{i_k}) = p_{i_1} \ldots p_{i_k}$.

Example 1.1 If $S = (s_1, s_2)$, $\mathcal{P} = (\frac{1}{4}, \frac{3}{4})$, then $S^2 = (s_1 s_1, s_1 s_2, s_2 s_1, s_2 s_2)$ and $P^2 = (\frac{1}{16}, \frac{3}{16}, \frac{3}{16}, \frac{9}{16})$.

If $\mathcal{S}$ is a Markov source, we define S^k in the same way, and for a word $s = s_{i_1} \ldots s_{i_k} \in S^k$, then $P^k(s) = p_{i_1} p_{i_2 i_1} \ldots p_{i_k i_{k-1}}$.

Property 2 *Let S be a source, and S^k its kth extension, then*

$$H(S^k) = kH(S).$$

In other words this property stresses the fact that the amount of information of a source extended to k characters is exactly k times the amount of information of the original source. This seems completely natural.

However, this does not apply to the amount of information of a *message* (a file for instance) "extended" to blocks of k characters. More precisely, it is possible to enumerate the occurrences of the characters in a message to compute their distribution and then the entropy of a source that would have the same probabilistic characteristics. Indeed, this is used to compress files as it will be seen in Chapter 2. Now if the message is "extended" in the sense that groups of k characters are formed and the occurrences of each group is computed to get their distribution, then the entropy of this "message extension" is necessarily lower than k times the entropy corresponding to the original message as shown in the following.

Property 3 *Let $\mathcal{M}$ be a message of size n, $S_{\mathcal{M}^k}$ be the source whose probabilities correspond to the occurrences of the successive k-tuples of $\mathcal{M}$ and $S_{\mathcal{M}}^k$ be the kth extension of the induced source $S_{\mathcal{M}}$. Then*

$$H(S_{\mathcal{M}^k}) \leq H(S_{\mathcal{M}}^k).$$

Proof. We give some details for $k = 2$. Let (q_i) be the probabilities of the induced source $S_{\mathcal{M}}$, $(q_{i,j} = q_i \cdot q_j)$ those of the second extension $S_{\mathcal{M}}^2$ and $(p_{i,j})$ those of an source induced by the successive pairs of elements of M, $S_{\mathcal{M}^2}$. Gibbs lemma, page 17, applied to $p_{i,j}$ and $q_{i,j}$ shows that $\sum_{i,j} p_{i,j} \log_2 \left(\frac{q_i q_j}{p_{i,j}} \right) \leq 0$. This is also

$$H(S_{\mathcal{M}^2}) \leq - \sum_{i,j} p_{i,j} \log_2(q_i q_j). \tag{1.1}$$

Now, denote by n_i the number of occurrences of the i symbol in $\mathcal{M}$. With $n = |\mathcal{M}|$, we have $q_i = n_i/n$. Also denote by $n_{i,j}$ the number of occurrences of the pair (i,j) in $\mathcal{M}^2$. Then $|\mathcal{M}^2| = n/2$ and $p_{i,j} = 2n_{i,j}/n$. We also have $n_i = \sum_j n_{i,j} + \sum_k n_{k,i}$ so that $2q_i = \sum_j p_{i,j} + \sum_k p_{k,i}$.

Therefore, the right-hand side of Inequation (1.1) can be rewritten as follows:

$$\sum_{i,j} p_{i,j} \log_2(q_i q_j) = \sum_{i,j} p_{i,j} \log_2(q_i) + \sum_{i,j} p_{i,j} \log_2(q_j)$$

$$= \sum_i \log_2(q_i) \left(\sum_j p_{i,j} \right) + \sum_j \log_2(q_j) \left(\sum_i p_{i,j} \right)$$

$$= \sum_i \log_2(q_i) \left(\sum_j p_{i,j} + \sum_k p_{k,i} \right) \tag{1.2}$$

$$= \sum_i \log_2(q_i) \left(2q_i \right)$$

$$= -2H(S_{\mathcal{M}})$$

$$= -H(S_{\mathcal{M}}^2).$$

This proves that Inequation (1.1) is actually

$$H(S_{\mathcal{M}^2}) \leq H(S_{\mathcal{M}}^2).$$

This construction generalizes to any k, in the same manner, by enumeration of all the k-tuples.   □

The following example illustrates both situations.

Example 1.2   The messages "1 2 3 4 5 6 1 2 3 4 5 6" and "3 1 4 6 4 6 2 1 3 5 2 5" have the same entropy taking the first extension of the source: six characters of probability one $\frac{1}{6}$ each, giving an entropy of $\sum_{i=1}^6 \frac{1}{6} \log_2(6) = \log_2(6) \approx 2.585$. With the second extension of the source $(\frac{1}{6}, \frac{1}{6}, \frac{1}{6}, \frac{1}{6}, \frac{1}{6}, \frac{1}{6})$, we obtain 36 possible groups of probability $\frac{1}{36}$ each and the entropy conforms to Property 2: $\log_2(36) = \log_2(6^2) = 2\log_2(6)$. However, for example, when regrouping the messages in blocks of two characters, we have

- (12)(34)(56)(12)(34)(56): three different couples of probability $\frac{1}{3}$ each corresponding to an entropy of $\log_2(3) \approx 1.585$.
- All the same, the sequence (31)(46)(46)(21)(35)(25) gives five different couples and is of entropy $\frac{1}{6} \log_2(6) + \frac{2}{6} \log_2 \left(\frac{6}{2} \right) + \frac{1}{6} \log_2(6) + \frac{1}{6} \log_2(6) + \frac{1}{6} \log_2(6) \approx 2.252$.

In both cases, the entropy obtained is definitely lower than twice the entropy of the original message. We will make this statement precise in Property 4.

Property 4   *Let $\mathcal{M}$ be a message of size n and let $S_{\mathcal{M}^k}$ be the source whose probabilities correspond to the occurrences of the successive k-tuples of $\mathcal{M}$. Then*

$$H(S_{\mathcal{M}^k}) \leq \log_2 \left(\left\lceil \frac{n}{k} \right\rceil \right).$$

Proof. There are $\left\lceil \frac{n}{k} \right\rceil$ k-tuples in the message $\mathcal{M}$. Besides, entropy is maximal for the greatest number of distinct possible k-tuples with the same number of occurrences. In this case, the corresponding source would contain at most $\left\lceil \frac{n}{k} \right\rceil$ distinct characters of probability of occurrence $\frac{1}{\left\lceil \frac{n}{k} \right\rceil}$. Thus, the entropy is $log_2 \left(\left\lceil \frac{n}{k} \right\rceil \right)$. □

This leads us to the problem of randomness and its generation. A sequence of numbers randomly generated should meet harsh criteria – in particular, it should have a strong entropy. The sequence "1 2 3 4 5 6 1 2 3 4 5 6" would not be acceptable as one can easily notice some kind of organization. The sequence "3 1 4 6 4 6 2 1 3 5 2 5" would be more satisfying – having a higher entropy when considering successive pairs of characters. We detail the random number generators in Section 1.3.7.

1.2.4 Steganography and Watermarking

Entropy is a powerful tool to model the information in a code. For instance, it can be used to detect steganography by a study of the quantity of information contained in a device.

Steganography is the art of covering information. The knowledge of the mere existence of some covert information could then be sufficient to discover this information.

Steganographic devices include invisible ink, microdot in images, Digital Right Management (DRM), information encoding in white spaces of a plaintext, and so on.

Nowadays, steganography is quite often combined with cryptography in order to not only conceal the existence of information but also keep its secrecy even if its existence is revealed. It is also combined with error-correcting codes. Indeed, even if the resulting *stegotext* is modified and some parts of the information are altered, the information remains accessible if sufficiently many bits remain unchanged by the media modification.

Digital watermarking is a variant of steganography, which is used to conceal some information into digital media such as images, audio, or video.

We distinguish two major kinds of watermarking:

- Fragile watermarking is very close to classical steganography, it is usually invisible and used to detect any modification of the stream. For instance, secure paper money often encloses fragile watermarks that disappear after photocopy.
- Robust watermarking might be visible and should at least partially resist to simple modifications of the source as lossy compression. This is what is required for instance for Digital Right Management.

It is difficult to hide a large quantity of information into a media without begin detectable. Indeed, consider a covering media M, some information X and a stegotext S where the information is embedded into the covertext. As the stegotext should not be very different from the covertext to be undetected, the quantity of information in the stegotext should be very close to that of the covertext added to that of the embedded information: $H(S) \approx H(M) + H(X)$. Therefore, a classical steganalysis is to compute the entropy of a suspected media and compare it to classical values of unmarked ones. If the obtained entropy is significantly higher than the average, then it can mean that some additional information if carried by this media. In other words, to remain undetected steganography must use a small quantity of information into a large media.

Exercise 1.9 We have hidden a number in the spacing of this text. Can you find it?   *Solution on page 283.*

We will see an example of watermarking of digital images using the JPEG format in Section 2.5.3.

1.2.5 Perfect Secrecy

Using the concept of entropy, it is also now possible to make precise the concept of unconditional security (also called perfect secrecy).

An encryption scheme is said unconditionally secure or perfect if the ciphertext C does not give any information on the initial plaintext M; hence, the entropy of M knowing C is equal to the entropy of M:

$$H(M|C) = H(M)$$

In other words, unconditional security means that M and C are statistically independent.

Exercise 1.10 (Perfect Secrecy of the One-Time-Pad Encryption Scheme)

1. *We consider a secret code wherein the key K is generated randomly for each message M. Prove that $H(M|K) = H(M)$.*

2. *Using conditional entropies and the definition of a Vernam code, prove that in a Vernam code $(C = M \oplus K)$, we always have $H(M,K,C) = H(M,C) = H(M,K) = H(C,K)$; deduce the relations between the conditional entropies of M, C, and K.*

3. *Prove that the OTP system is a perfect encryption scheme.*
                                                        Solution on page 283.

1.2.6 Perfect Secrecy in Practice and Kerckhoffs' Principles

Now, we have an encryption method (the one-time-pad) and the proof of its security. It is the only known method to be proved unconditionally secure. Yet in order to use this method in practice, we should be able to generate random keys of the same size of the message, which is far from being trivial. One solution is to rely on PRNG (Section 1.3.7) to create the successive bits of the key that are combined with the bit stream of the plaintext. It leads to a bitwise encryption (stream cipher) as illustrated in Figure 1.2.

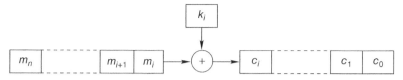

Figure 1.2   Bitwise encryption (Stream cipher)

However, key exchange protocols between the sender and the recipient remain problematic as the keys cannot be used twice and are generally big (as big as the message).

Exercise 1.11 (Imperfection Mesure and Unicity Distance)   *We consider messages M written in English, randomly chosen keys K and ciphertexts C, produced by an imperfect code over the 26 letters alphabet. A length l string is denoted by $X_1 \ldots X_l$ and we suppose that any key is chosen uniformly from the space K. The unicity distance of a code is the average minimal length d (number of letters) of a ciphertext required to find the key. In other words d satisfies $H(K|C_1 \ldots C_d) = 0$: if you know d letters of a ciphertext, you have, at least theoretically, enough information to recover the used key.*

1. *For a given symmetric cipher, knowing the key and the cleartext is equivalent to knowing the key and the ciphertext: $H(K, M) = H(K, C)$. From this and the choice of the key, deduce a relation between $H(K)$, $H(M_1 \ldots M_d)$, $H(C_1 \ldots C_d)$ with the unicity distance d.*

2. *Using Table 1.1, the entropy of this book is roughly 4.19 per character. What is therefore the entropy of a similar plaintext of d letters?*

3. *What is the entropy of a randomly chosen string over the alphabet with 26 letters ? Use these entropies to bound $H(C_1 \ldots C_d)$ for a good cipher.*

4. *Overall, deduce a lower bound for the unicity distance depending on the information contained in the key.*

5. *If the cipher consists in choosing a single permutation of the alphabet, deduce the average minimal number of letters required to decipher a message encoded with this permutation.*   *Solution on page 283.*

In general, coding schemes are not perfect, and theoretical proofs of security are rare. Empirical principles often state the informal properties we can expect from a cryptosystem. Auguste Kerckhoffs formalized the first and most famous ones in 1883 in his article "La cryptographie militaire," which was published in the "Journal des Sciences Militaires." Actually, his article contains six principles, which are now known as "*Kerckhoffs' principles.*" We will summarize three of them, the most useful nowadays:

1. Security depends more on the secrecy of the key than on the secrecy of the algorithm.

For a long time, the security of a cryptosystem concerned the algorithms that were used in this system. For instance, this was the case of Caesar encryption (Section 1.1) or of the ADFVGX code, used by German forces during World War I. Security is illusory because, sooner or later, details of the algorithm are going to be known and its potential weaknesses will be exploited. In addition, it is easier to change a key if it is compromised than to change the whole cryptosystem. Moreover, you can believe in the resistance of public cryptosystems as they are continuously attacked: selection is rough, therefore if a cryptosystem, whose internal mechanisms are freely available, still resists the continuous attacks performed by many cryptanalysts, then there are more chances that the system is really secure.

2. Decryption without the key must be impossible (in reasonable time);
3. Finding the key from a plaintext and its ciphertext must be impossible (in reasonable time).

Therefore, **one must always assume that the attacker knows all the details of the cryptosystem**. Although these principles have been known for a long time, many companies continue to ignore them (voluntarily or not). Among the most media-related recent examples, one may notice the A5/0 and A5/1 encryption algorithms that are used in Global System for Mobile Communications (GSM) and most of all Content Scrambling System (CSS) software for the protection against DVD copying. The latter algorithms were introduced in 1996 and hacked within weeks, despite the secrecy surrounding the encryption algorithm.

Following the Kerckhoffs principles, it is possible to devise codes that are not perfect but tend toward this property. In Section 1.3, we, for instance, see how to build codes which use a single (short) key and make the exchange protocol less time consuming than the OTP. The idea is to split the message into blocks such that each of them is encrypted separately.

1.3 BLOCK CIPHERS, ALGEBRA, AND ARITHMETIC

In this section, we introduce most of the mathematical background used in coding theory and applications. It contains the bases of algebra, and efficient ways to compute in algebraic structures. Some arithmetics is also useful to construct large finite structures. All these notions are widely used in the book and become necessary as soon as block coding methods are envisaged.

Today, the Vernam cipher is the only symmetric cryptographic algorithm that has been proved unconditionally secure. Thus, all other known systems are theoretically breakable.

For these systems, we use *almost secure* encryption schemes: the knowledge of the ciphertext (or the knowledge of some couples plaintext/ciphertext) does not enable to recover the secret key or the plaintext *in humanly reasonable time* (see the orders of magnitude and computing limits in Section 1.1.7).

For instance, we can decide to choose a unique key and to reuse it in order to avoid too frequent key exchange protocols. This implies that we have to split the source messages into blocks of some size, depending on the size of the key. Block cipher is also a standard, which is widely used in error detection and correction.

This is also the principle of one of the most famous codes – the ASCII code (*"American Standard Code for Information Interchange"*) – which is a numerical representation of the letters and signs of the Latin alphabet. In ASCII code, the source alphabet is the Latin alphabet, and the code alphabet is $V = \{0, 1\}$. The set of *codewords* is the set of all the words of size 8 over V:

$$C = \{00000000, 00000001, \ldots, 11111111\}.$$

Each one of the $2^8 = 256$ characters (uppercases, lowercases, special characters, and control characters) is represented with a word of size 8 over V according to an encoding function. The following Table 1.3 gives an extract of this function.

For example, the ASCII code of the message: *A KEY*, is the string: 0100000100100000010010110100010101011001.

1.3.1   Blocks and Chaining Modes from CBC to CTR

It is possible to encode independently each block of a message with the same algorithm. This is called Electronic Code Book (ECB) cipher mode. More generally, the independence of encryption between the blocks is not required and the several ways of combining the blocks are called *encryption modes*.

ECB mode: Electronic Code Book. In this mode, the message M is split into blocks m_i of constant size. Each block is encrypted separately with a function E_k (the key k being a parameter of the function) as illustrated in Figure 1.3.

$$c_i = E_k(m_i) \tag{1.3}$$

Thus, a given block of the message m_i will always be encrypted in the same way. This encryption mode is the easiest one but does not provide any security and is normally never used in cryptography.

TABLE 1.3   Extract of the ASCII Code

A	01000001	J	01001010	S	01010011
B	01000010	K	01001011	T	01010100
C	01000011	L	01001100	U	01010101
D	01000100	M	01001101	V	01010110
E	01000101	N	01001110	W	01010111
F	01000110	O	01001111	X	01011000
G	01000111	P	01010000	Y	01011001
H	01001000	Q	01010001	Z	01011010
I	01001001	R	01010010	Space	00100000

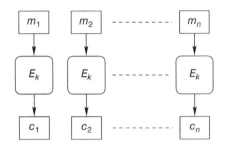

Figure 1.3   Block ciphers: ECB mode

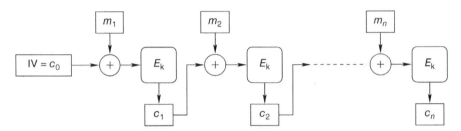

Figure 1.4   Block ciphers: CBC mode

CBC mode: Cipher Block Chaining. The CBC mode was introduced to avoid encrypting a block in the same way in two different messages. We add some initial value $IV = c_0$, possibly generated randomly. Each block m_i is encoded by an *XOR* operation with the previous cipherblock c_{i-1} before being encrypted. Figure 1.4 illustrates this mode.

$$c_i = E_k(m_i \oplus c_{i-1}) \tag{1.4}$$

This is the most widely used encryption mode. Decryption uses the inverse of the encoding function $D_k = E_k^{-1}$: $m_i = c_{i-1} \oplus D_k(c_i)$.

CFB mode: Cipher FeedBack. To avoid using the inverse function for decryption, it is possible to perform an *XOR* after the encryption. This is the principle of the CFB mode, which is illustrated in Figure 1.5.

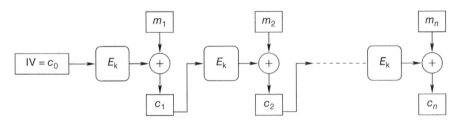

Figure 1.5   Block ciphers: CFB mode

$$c_i = m_i \oplus E_k(c_{i-1}) \qquad (1.5)$$

The benefit of this mode is to avoid implementing the function D_k for decryption: $m_i = c_i \oplus E_k(c_{i-1})$. Thus, this mode is less secure than the CBC mode and is used in network encryption for example.

OFB mode: Output FeedBack. OFB is a variant of the previous mode and it provides symmetric encryption and decryption. Figure 1.6 illustrates this scheme.

$$z_0 = c_0 \; ; \; z_i = E_k(z_{i-1}) \; ; \; c_i = m_i \oplus z_i \qquad (1.6)$$

Decryption is performed by $z_i = E_k(z_{i-1}) \; ; \; m_i = c_i \oplus z_i$. This mode is useful when one needs to minimize the number of embedded circuits, especially for communications in spacecrafts.

CTR mode: Counter Mode Encryption. The CTR mode is also completely symmetric, but encryption can be perfomed in parallel. It uses the encryption of a counter of initial value T (Figure 1.7):

$$c_i = m_i \oplus E_k(T + i) \qquad (1.7)$$

Decryption is performed in the same way: $m_i = c_i \oplus E_k(T + i)$. The advantage of such a mode is that the several computations are independent, as in the ECB mode, but a block is also never encrypted twice in the same way *a priori*.

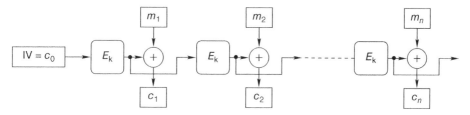

Figure 1.6   Block ciphers: OFB mode

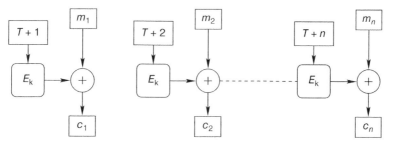

Figure 1.7   Block ciphers: CTR mode

Exercise 1.12 *A message M is split into n blocks $M_1, \ldots, M_n$ that are encrypted into $C = C_1, \ldots C_n$ using an encryption mode. Bob receives the blocks C_i, but unfortunately, he does not know that one (and only one) of the blocks was incorrectly transmitted (for example, some 0s became 1s and some 1s became 0s during the transmission of block C_1). Show that the number of miss-decrypted blocks is equal to 1 if ECB, OFB or CTR modes were used and equal to 2 if CBC, or CFB modes were used.*

Solution on page 283.

1.3.2 Algebraic Structure of Codewords

Developing block ciphers implies that we have to be able to perform operations and computations over blocks. For example, the $\oplus$ operation over a block of bits is a bitwise addition modulo 2 of two vectors. Furthermore, as encoding functions have to be reversible, we need structures for which we can easily compute the inverse of a block. In order to perform these computations using solid algebraic bases, let us recall some fundamental structures. All along the book, $\mathbb{Z}$ denotes the set of integers, and $\mathbb{N}$ denotes the set of nonnegative integers.

1.3.2.1 Groups A *group* $(G, *)$ is a set equipped with an internal binary operator satisfying the following properties:

1. $*$ is associative: for all $a, b, c \in G$, $a * (b * c) = (a * b) * c$.
2. There exists a neutral element $e \in G$, such that for all $a \in G$, one has $a * e = e * a = a$.
3. Each element has an inverse: for all $a \in G$, there exists $a^{-1} \in G$ such that $a * a^{-1} = a^{-1} * a = e$.

Moreover, if the law is commutative ($a * b = b * a$ for all $a, b \in G$), G is called *abelian*.

A subset H of G is called a *subgroup* of G if the operations of G restricted to H give a group structure to H. For an element a of a group G, we denote by a^n the repetition of the law $*$, $a * \cdots * a$, performed on n terms equal to a for all $n \in \mathbb{N}^*$. Moreover, one has $a^0 = e$ and $a^{-n} = (a^{-1})^n$ for all $n \in \mathbb{N}^*$.

If an element $g \in G$ is such that for all $a \in G$, there exists $i \in \mathbb{Z}$, such that $a = g^i$, then g is a *generator* of the group $(G, *)$ or a *primitive root*. A group is called *cyclic* if it has generator.

For example, for a given n fixed, the set of integers $\mathbb{Z}/n\mathbb{Z} = \{0, 1, \ldots, n-1\}$, equipped with the law of addition modulo n is a cyclic group generated by 1; if $n = 7$ and if we choose the multiplication modulo 7 as a law of composition, the set $\{1, \ldots, 6\}$ is a cyclic group generated by 3. Indeed $1 = 3^0$, $2 = 3^2 = 9$, $3 = 3^1$, $4 = 3^4$, $5 = 3^5$, $6 = 3^3$.

Let $(G, *)$ be a group and $a \in G$. The set $\{a^i, i \in \mathbb{Z}\}$ is a subgroup of G, denoted by $< a >$ or G_a. If this subgroup is finite, its cardinal number is the *order* of a.

Property 5 (Lagrange) *If G is a finite group, the cardinal number of any subgroup of G divides the cardinal number of G. In particular, the order of any elements divides the cardinal number of G.*

Proof. Let H be a subgroup of a finite group G. $|H|$ is the cardinal number of H and consider the sets $aH = \{ah, h \in H\}$ for any $a \in G$. First of all, all the sets aH have the same cardinal number: if $ah_1 = ah_2$, then since a is invertible $h_1 = h_2$, so that $|aH| = |H|$. Then these sets form a partition of G: indeed take aH and bH with $a \neq b$ and suppose that there exist an element x in their intersection, that is, $x = ah_1 = bh_2$. Then for any element $u \in aH$, $u = ah_u = b(h_2 h_1^{-1} h_u)$. But as H is a subgroup, $h_2 h_1^{-1} h_u \in H$ and thus $u \in bH$. This proves that aH is included in bH. With the reverse argument, one can prove also that bH is included in aH. Therefore, two sets aH and bH are either equal or disjoint. Finally, any element x in G is in xH. Now, as the sets aH form a partition of G and they are all of cardinal number $|H|$, the cardinal order of G is a multiple of $|H|$. □

Theorem 1 (Lagrange) *In a finite abelian group $(G, *)$ of cardinal number n, for all $a \in G : a^n = e$.*

Proof. Let a be any element in G. The set of the multiples of a, $G_a = \{y = ax$ for $x \in G\}$ is equal to G. Indeed, as a is invertible, for all $y \in G$, we can define $x = a^{-1}y$. Reciprocally, if a and x are elements of G a group, then so is their product $((ax)^{-1} = x^{-1}a^{-1})$. Hence, the two sets being equal, the products of all their respective elements are also equal:

$$\prod_{x \in G} x = \prod_{y \in G_a} y = \prod_{x \in G} ax.$$

Yet, as multiplication is commutative in an abelian group, we can then extract a from the product. Moreover, there are n elements in G and we thus obtain the following formula:

$$\prod_{x \in G} x = a^n \prod_{x \in G} x.$$

In order to conclude, we use the fact that – all elements in G being invertible – so is their product and we can simplify the previous formula: $e = a^n$. □

1.3.2.2 Rings A *ring* $(A, +, \times)$ is a set equipped with two internal binary operators satisfying the following properties:

1. $(A, +)$ is an abelian group.
2. $\times$ is associative: for all $a, b, c \in A$, $a \times (b \times c) = (a \times b) \times c$.
3. $\times$ is distributive over $+$: for all $a, b, c \in A$, $a \times (b + c) = (a \times b) + (a \times c)$ and $(b + c) \times a = (b \times a) + (c \times a)$.

Moreover, if there exists a neutral element for $\times$ in A, A is called *unitary*. This neutral element is noted 1_A, or simply 1 if it is not ambiguous from the context. If $\times$

is commutative, A is called *commutative*. All elements in A have an *opposite*, namely their inverse for the law $+$. However, they do not necessarily have an inverse for the law $\times$. The *set of invertible elements* for the law $\times$ is denoted by A^*.

For an element a in a ring A, one denotes by $n \cdot a$ (or more simply na) the sum $a + \cdots + a$ of n terms equal to a for all $n \in \mathbb{N}^*$.

If the set $\{k \in \mathbb{N}^* : k \cdot 1 = 0\}$ is not empty, the smallest element of this set is called the *characteristic* of the ring. Otherwise, the ring is said to be of characteristic 0. For example, $(\mathbb{Z}, +, \times)$ is a unitary, commutative ring of characteristic 0.

Two rings $(A, +_A, \times_A)$ and $(B, +_B, \times_B)$ are *isomorphic* if there exists a bijection $f : A \longrightarrow B$ satisfying for all x and y in A:

$$f(x +_A y) = f(x) +_B f(y) \quad \text{and} \quad f(x \times_A y) = f(x) \times_B f(y). \tag{1.8}$$

If E is any set and $(A, +, \times)$ is a ring such that there exists a bijection f from E to A, then E can be equipped with a ring structure:

$$x +_E y = f^{-1}(f(x) + f(y)) \quad \text{et} \quad x \times_E y = f^{-1}(f(x) \times f(y)). \tag{1.9}$$

The ring $(E, +_E, \times_E)$ defined as such is obviously isomorphic to A. If two rings are isomorphic, one ring can be identified with the other.

An *ideal* I is a subgroup of a ring A for the law $+$ and "absorbing" for the law $\times$: for $g \in I$, the product $a \times g$ remains in I for any element a of the ring A. For all $x \in A$, the set $Ax = \{ax; a \in A\}$ is an ideal of A, which is *generated* by x. An ideal I of A is called *principal* if there exists a generator x (such that $I = Ax$). A ring A is *principal* if an only if any ideal of A is principal.

A *Euclidean function* v is a mapping of all nonzero elements of a unitary ring to $\mathbb{N}$. A unitary ring with a Euclidean function is *Euclidean* if it has the property that for every couple of elements a and b of the ring, there exist q and r such that $a = bq + r$ and $v(r) < v(b)$. This operation is the *Euclidean division*, and the numbers q and r are, respectively, called the Euclidean quotient and the remainder and are denoted by $q = a$ div b and $r = a \mod b$ (for a modulo b). Any Euclidean ring is principal. This implies that there exists a Greatest Common Divisor (GCD) for all couples of elements (a, b). Any generator of the ideal $Aa + Ab$ is a *gcd*.

For example, the ring $\mathbb{Z}$ with the absolute value as Euclidean function, it is a Euclidean ring. The following famous theorem of Bézout extends the properties of Euclidean rings. It is true for any Euclidean ring, and its proof in $\mathbb{Z}$ will follow from the Euclidean algorithm page 37.

Theorem 2 (Bézout) *Let a and b be two nonzero elements of a Euclidean ring A, and let d be their GCD. There exist two elements x and y, called the Bézout's numbers, such that $v(x) \leq v(b)$ and $v(y) \leq v(a)$ satisfying*

$$ax + by = d.$$

The modulo operation allows to define a ring on $\mathbb{Z}/n\mathbb{Z}$, the set of nonnegative integers strictly inferior to n, for $n \in \mathbb{N} \setminus \{0, 1\}$. The set $\mathbb{Z}/n\mathbb{Z}$ equipped with the addition and the multiplication modulo n [that is, $a +_{\mathbb{Z}/n\mathbb{Z}} b = (a +_{\mathbb{Z}} b) \mod n$ and $a \times_{\mathbb{Z}/n\mathbb{Z}} b = (a \times_{\mathbb{Z}} b) \mod n$] is a (finite) ring. It is widely used in coding.

Exercise 1.13 *Bézout's theorem is very useful to prove properties in number theory. In particular, use it to prove the famous Gauss's lemma stated as follows:*

Lemma 2 (Gauss) *If an integer number a divides the product of two integers b and c, and if a and b are coprime, then a divides c.*

Solution on page 284.

1.3.2.3 Fields A *field* $(A, +, \times)$ is a set equipped with two internal binary operators satisfying the following properties:

1. $(A, +, \times)$ is an unitary ring.
2. $(A \setminus \{0\}, \times)$ is a group.

If $(A, +, \times)$ is commutative, the field is *commutative*; the inverse (or opposite) of x with regard to the law $+$ is denoted by $-x$; the inverse of x with regard to the law $\times$ is denoted by x^{-1}. The *characteristic* of a field is its characteristic when considered as a ring.

For instance, $(\mathbb{Q}, +, \times)$ is a commutative field of characteristic 0.

As all the rings and fields we are dealing with are commutative, thereafter the word ring (respectively field) will refer to a unitary commutative ring (respectively a commutative field).

Two fields are *isomorphic* if they are isomorphic when considered as rings.

A subset W of a field V is called a *subfield* of V if the operations of V restricted to W give a field structure to W.

The standard notation is used for classical fields in this book: $\mathbb{Q}$ denotes the field of rational numbers, and $\mathbb{R}$ denotes the field of real numbers.

If p is a prime number, the ring $\mathbb{Z}/p\mathbb{Z}$ is a field of characteristic p.

Indeed, with Bézout's theorem (see page 32), we have for all couples of integers a and b, there exists two integers x and y such that

$$ax + by = \gcd(a, b).$$

If p is prime and a is a nonzero element of $\mathbb{Z}/p\mathbb{Z}$, this identity applied to a and p gives $ax + bp = 1$, hence $ax = 1 \mod p$. Thus, a is invertible and x is its inverse. This field is denoted by $\mathbb{F}_p$.

The field of rational numbers $\mathbb{Q}$ and the fields $\mathbb{F}_p$ are called *prime fields*.

1.3.2.4 Vector Spaces and Linear Algebra Rudiments of linear algebra are necessary for the reading of the major part of this book. Without any explicative pretention, here we define useful concepts and we introduce the main notation. A set $\mathbb{E}$ is a *vector space* over a field V if it has one internal law of composition $+$ and an external law of composition "." such that

1. $(\mathbb{E}, +)$ is a commutative group.
2. For all $u \in \mathbb{E}$, $1_V.u = u$.
3. For all $\lambda, \mu \in V$, and $u \in \mathbb{E}$, $\lambda.(\mu.u) = (\lambda \times \mu).u$.
4. For all $\lambda, \mu \in V$, and $u \in \mathbb{E}$, $\lambda.u + \mu.u = (\lambda + \mu).u$.
5. For all $\lambda \in V$ and $u, v \in \mathbb{E}$, $\lambda.(u + v) = \lambda.u + \lambda.v$.

An element of a vector space is called a *vector*, and the elements of the field V are called *scalars*. The set $\{0, 1\}$ equipped with the addition $\oplus$ and the multiplication $\wedge$ is a commutative field denoted by $\mathbb{F}_2$. Thus, the set of bit tables of size n can be equipped with a vector space structure. The set of codewords is then $\mathbb{F}_2^n$.

A set of vectors $x_1, \ldots, x_n$ is an *independent* set if for all scalars $\lambda_1, \ldots, \lambda_n$, $\sum_{i=1}^n \lambda_i x_i = 0$ implies $\lambda_1 = \cdots = \lambda_n = 0$.

The *dimension* of a vector space V, denoted by $\dim(V)$, is the cardinal number of the greatest set of independent vectors of V.

For example, if V is a field, V^n is a space of dimension n because the vectors $(1, 0, \ldots, 0), (0, 1, 0, \ldots, 0), \ldots, (0, \ldots, 0, 1)$ are independent.

A *linear mapping* is an application from one vector space to another, which preserves the laws of composition. Namely, if A and B are two vectors spaces, an application f is said to be linear if for all x, y in A, $f(x +_A y) = f(x) \times_B f(y)$ and for all $\lambda \in V$ and $x \in A$, $f(\lambda ._A x) = \lambda ._B f(x)$.

The *image* of a linear mapping f from a vector space $\mathbb{E}$ to a vector space $\mathbb{F}$, denoted by $\operatorname{Im}(f)$, is the set of vectors $y \in \mathbb{F}$ such that there exists $x \in \mathbb{E}$ with $f(x) = y$.

The *kernel* of a linear application f from a vector space $\mathbb{E}$ to a vector space $\mathbb{F}$, denoted by $\operatorname{Ker}(f)$, is the set of vectors $x \in \mathbb{E}$ such that $f(x) = 0$.

It is easy to verify that $\operatorname{Ker}(f)$ and $\operatorname{Im}(f)$ are vector spaces.

If the dimension of $\operatorname{Im}(f)$ is finite, this quantity is called the *rank* of the linear mapping and is denoted by $\operatorname{Rk}(f) = \dim(\operatorname{Im}(f))$. Moreover, if the dimension of $\mathbb{E}$ is also finite, then we have the following result: $\dim(\operatorname{Ker}(f)) + \dim(\operatorname{Im}(f)) = \dim(\mathbb{E})$.

A *matrix* M of size (m, n) is an element of the vector space $V^{m \times n}$, represented by a table of m horizontal lines (rows) of size n or n vertical lines (columns) of size m. The element that lies in the ith row and the jth column of the matrix is written as $M_{i,j}$. Multiplication of a vector x of size n with such as matrix gives a vector y of size m satisfying $y_i = \sum_{k=1}^n M_{i,k} x_k$ for all i from 1 to m; multiplication is written as $y = Mx$.

Each matrix M is associated to a linear application f from V^m to V^n, defined by $f(x) = Mx$. Reciprocally, any linear application can be written using a matrix. The coding processes studied throughout this book – mainly in Chapter 4 – often use linear applications, which enable us to illustrate the properties of these functions.

Depending on the chosen structure, codewords can be manipulated with additions and multiplications over integers or vectors. All these structures are very general and common in algebra. Codes are particular as they are finite sets. Finite groups and finite fields have some additional properties, which will be widely used throughout this work.

1.3.3 Bijective Encoding of a Block

Now that we have some structures, we are able to perform additions, multiplications, and Euclidean divisions on blocks. We can also compute their inverses. Here, we give some fundamental examples of computations that can be performed on sets with good algebraic structure. As blocks are of finite size, we will manipulate finite sets in this section.

1.3.3.1 Modular Inverse: Euclidean Algorithm Bézout's theorem (see page 32) guarantees the existence of Bézout numbers and thus the existence of the inverse of a number modulo a prime number in $\mathbb{Z}$. The Euclidean algorithm makes it possible to compute these coefficients efficiently.

In its fundamental version, the Euclidean algorithm computes the Greatest Common Divisor (GCD) of two integers according to the following principle: assuming that $a \geq b$,

$$\gcd(a, b) = \gcd(a - b, b) = \gcd(a - 2b, b) = \cdots = \gcd(a \bmod b, b),$$

where $a \bmod b$ are the remainder of the Euclidean division of a by b. Indeed, if a and b have a common divisor d, then $a - b, a - 2b, \ldots$ are also divisible by d.

The recursive principle appears:

Algorithm 1.3 GCD: Euclidean Algorithm

Input Two integers a and b, $a \geq b$.
Output $\gcd(a, b)$
1: **If** $b = 0$ **then**
2:   **return** a;
3: **else**
4:   Compute recursively $\gcd(b, a \bmod b)$ and return the result
5: **End If**

Example 1.3 (The gcd of 522 and 453)
We compute

$$
\begin{aligned}
\gcd(522, 453) \quad &= \gcd(453, 522 \bmod 453 = 69) \quad &= \gcd(69, 453 \bmod 69 = 39) \\
&= \gcd(39, 69 \bmod 39 = 30) \quad &= \gcd(30, 39 \bmod 30 = 9) \\
&= \gcd(9, 30 \bmod 9 = 3) \quad &= \gcd(3, 9 \bmod 3 = 0) \\
&= 3.
\end{aligned}
$$

The gcd of 522 and 453 is equal to 3.

Extended Euclidean algorithm. The "extended" version of the Euclidean algorithm – the one we will use most of the time in this book – enables us to compute the gcd of two numbers and a pair of Bézout numbers.

This algorithm is also extended because it is meant to be more general: It can be not only applied to number sets but also applied to any Euclidean ring. This is the case for polynomials, as we see in the following sections.

The principle of the algorithm is to iterate with the following function G:

$$G : \begin{bmatrix} a \\ b \end{bmatrix} \longmapsto \begin{bmatrix} 0 & 1 \\ 1 & -(a \text{ div } b) \end{bmatrix} \begin{bmatrix} a \\ b \end{bmatrix}.$$

Example 1.4 We wish to find x and y such that $x \times 522 + y \times 453 = \gcd(522, 453)$. We write the matrices corresponding to the iterations with the function G starting from

$$\begin{bmatrix} 522 \\ 453 \end{bmatrix}$$

One first computes $-(a \text{ div } b)$ with $a = 522$ and $b = 453$ and one gets the matrix

$$\begin{bmatrix} 0 & 1 \\ 1 & -1 \end{bmatrix}.$$

Then, one iterates the algorithm with $\begin{bmatrix} 0 & 1 \\ 1 & -1 \end{bmatrix} \begin{bmatrix} 522 \\ 453 \end{bmatrix}$. Thus, at the end, one gets

$$\begin{bmatrix} 3 \\ 0 \end{bmatrix} = \begin{bmatrix} 0 & 1 \\ 1 & -3 \end{bmatrix} \begin{bmatrix} 0 & 1 \\ 1 & -3 \end{bmatrix} \begin{bmatrix} 0 & 1 \\ 1 & -1 \end{bmatrix} \begin{bmatrix} 0 & 1 \\ 1 & -1 \end{bmatrix} \begin{bmatrix} 0 & 1 \\ 1 & -6 \end{bmatrix}$$
$$\begin{bmatrix} 0 & 1 \\ 1 & -1 \end{bmatrix} \begin{bmatrix} 522 \\ 453 \end{bmatrix}$$
$$= \begin{bmatrix} 46 & -53 \\ -151 & 174 \end{bmatrix} \begin{bmatrix} 522 \\ 453 \end{bmatrix}$$

Hence, we have $46 \times 522 - 53 \times 453 = 3$. Thus, $d = 3$, and the Bézout's numbers are $x = 46$ and $y = -53$.

Here is a version of the extended Euclidean algorithm that performs this computation while storing only the first line of G. It modifies the variables x, y, and d in order to verify at the end of each iteration that $d = \gcd(a, b)$ and $ax + by = d$.

In order to resolve it "by hand," we can calculate recursively the following equations (E_i) (we stop when $r_{i+1} = 0$):

$$
\begin{array}{lllllll}
(E_0): & & 1 \times a & + & 0 \times b & = & a \\
(E_1): & & 0 \times a & + & 1 \times b & = & b \\
(E_{i+1}) = (E_{i-1}) - q_i(E_i) & & u_i \times a & + & v_i \times b & = & r_i
\end{array}.
$$

The following exercise gives examples of resolution using this method.

Exercise 1.14 (Extended Euclidean Algorithm)   *Find pairs of Bézout numbers for the following integers:*

- $(a, b) = (50, 17)$
- $(a, b) = (280, 11)$
- $(a, b) = (50, 35)$

Solution on page 284.

Now let us prove that this algorithm is correct if the Euclidean ring is the set $\mathbb{Z}$ of integers. This will also provide a constructive proof of Bézout's theorem (see page 32) in $\mathbb{Z}$.

Theorem 3   *The extended Euclidean algorithm is correct in $\mathbb{Z}$.*

Proof. First of all, let us show that the sequence of remainders is always divisible by $d = \gcd(a, b)$: recursively, if $r_{j-2} = kd$ and $r_{j-1} = hd$, then $r_j = r_{j-2} - q_j r_{j-1} = d(k - q_j h)$ and thus $\gcd(a, b) = \gcd(r_{j-1}, r_j)$. Moreover, the sequence of positive remainders r_j is monotonically decreasing and is bounded below by 0. Hence, the algorithm ends.

Besides, after a finite number of steps, one has $r_j = 0$. Thus, there exists an index i such that $r_{i-1} = q_{i+1} r_i + 0$. In that case, $\gcd(r_{i-1}, r_i) = r_i$ and the previous remark indicates that r_i is the gcd we are looking for.

Finally, we need to prove that the Bézout numbers are correct. Let us do it recursively. Obviously, the initial case $a \mod b = 0$ is correct and so is the algorithm. Then, let us denote $r = a \mod b$ and $q = a$ div b. Hence $a = bq + r$. Recursively, and using the notation introduced in Algorithm 1.4, we have $d = xb + yr$ with $|x| \leq b$ and $|y| \leq r$. This relation implies that $d = ya + (x - qy)b$ with $|y| \leq r \leq b$ and $|x - qy| \leq |x| + q|y| \leq b + qr = a$. Thus, the algorithm is correct.   □

Algorithm 1.4 GCD: Extended Euclidean Algorithm

Input Two elements a and b of an Euclidean ring.
Output $d = \gcd(a, b)$ and x, y such that $ax + by = d$, and $v(x) \leq v(b)$, $v(y) \leq v(a)$.
  1: **If** $b = 0$ **then**
  2:     Return $d \leftarrow a, x \leftarrow 1, y \leftarrow 1$
  3: **else**
  4:     Recursive call of extended Euclidean algorithm on b, $a \mod b$
  5:     Let d, u, v be the elements of the result.
  6:     Compute $y \leftarrow u - (a$ div $b) * v$
  7:     **return** $d, x \leftarrow v, y$
  8: **End If**

Exercise 1.15 (Modular Computation)   *The extended Euclidean algorithm also enables one to solve linear modular equations in $\mathbb{Z}$.*

Give a method to solve the following equations:

1. $17x = 10 \mod 50$

2. $35x = 10 \mod 50$
3. $35y = 11 \mod 50$

Solution on page 284.

Complexity of the Euclidean algorithm. At each step, the greatest number is, at least, divided by two, hence its size decreases by 1 bit, at least. Thus, the number of steps is bounded by $O(\log_2(a) + \log_2(b))$. At each step, we also compute the remainder of the Euclidean division. The algorithms for Euclidean division we learned in elementary school have a cost $O(\log_2^2(a))$. Finally, the overall cost is bounded by $O(\log_2^3(a)) = O(n^3)$ if n is the size of the data. However, a closer study of the algorithm can make this complexity more precise. Indeed, the cost of the Euclidean algorithm is rather of the order $O(\log_2^2(a))$!

The proof is technical, but the idea is rather simple: either there are actually about $O(\log_2(a))$ steps, thus each quotient is very small and then each division and multiplication can be performed with $O(\log_2(a))$ operations, or the quotients are large and thus each division and multiplication has to be performed with $O(\log_2^2(a))$ operations (but then the number of steps is small).

Exercise 1.16 *Implement the extended Euclidean algorithm on the set of integer numbers with your favorite programming language (solution coded in C++).*

Solution on page 285.

1.3.3.2 Euler's Totient Function and Fermat's theorem

Let $n \geq 2$ be an integer. We denote by $\mathbb{Z}/n\mathbb{Z}^*$ the set of positive integers lower than n and coprime with n:

$$\mathbb{Z}/n\mathbb{Z}^* = \{x \in \mathbb{N} : 1 \leq x < n \text{ and } \gcd(x, n) = 1\}.$$

The cardinal number of $\mathbb{Z}/n\mathbb{Z}^*$ is denoted by $\varphi(n)$. The function φ is called *Euler's totient function*. For example, $\varphi(8) = 4$. Moreover, if p is prime, $\varphi(p) = p - 1$. Exercise 1.19 focuses on a more general formula.

Each element in $\mathbb{Z}/n\mathbb{Z}^*$ has an inverse: indeed, as x is coprime with n, Bézout's identity guarantees the existence of two integers u and v of opposite sign ($|u| \leq n$ and $|v| \leq x$), such that

$$u.x + v.n = 1.$$

Thus, $u.x = 1 \mod n$, that is, $u = x^{-1} \mod n$. The integer u is nonzero and not equal to n because of the relation $u.x = 1 \mod n$ and $n > 1$. So it is an element of $\mathbb{Z}/n\mathbb{Z}^*$ and is called the inverse of x modulo n. Computation of u is performed with the extended Euclidean algorithm.

Theorem 4 (Euler) *Let a be any element in $\mathbb{Z}/n\mathbb{Z}^*$. One has $a^{\varphi(n)} = 1 \mod n$.*

Proof. $\mathbb{Z}/n\mathbb{Z}^*$ is a finite multiplicative and abelian group, with neutral element 1 and of cardinal number $\varphi(n)$. Therefore, Lagrange Theorem 1, page 31, applies directly to give $a^{\varphi(n)} = 1 \mod n$. $\qquad \square$

Fermat's theorem can be immediately deduced from Euler's theorem when n is prime.

Theorem 5 (Fermat)   *If p is prime, then any $a \in \mathbb{Z}/p\mathbb{Z}$ satisfies the following result: $a^p = a$ mod p.*

Proof. If a is invertible, then Euler's theorem gives $a^{p-1} = 1$ mod p. We multiply the equation by a in order to obtain the relation. The only noninvertible element in $\mathbb{Z}/p\mathbb{Z}$ (if p is prime) is 0. In that case, we have obviously $0^p = 0$ mod p.   □

The Chinese Remainder Theorem – which was first formulated by Chinese mathematician Qin Jiu-Shao during the *XIII*th century – enables one to combine several congruences modulo pairwise coprime numbers in order to obtain a congruence modulo the product of these numbers.

Theorem 6 (Chinese Remainder Theorem)   *Let $n_1, \dots, n_k$ be positive pairwise coprime numbers and $N = \prod n_i$. Then, for all set of integers $a_1, \dots, a_k$, there exists a unique solution $0 \leq x < N$ to the modular equation system $\{x = a_i$ mod n_i, for $i = 1 \dots k\}$. If we call $N_i = \frac{N}{n_i}$, this unique solution is given by*

$$x = \sum_{i=1}^{k} a_i N_i N_i^{-1 \text{ mod } n_i} \quad \text{mod } N,$$

where $N_i^{-1 \text{ mod } n_i}$ is the inverse of N_i modulo n_i.

Proof. Let us proceed in two steps: first, we prove the existence of x, and then we prove the uniqueness of x. As n_i are pairwise coprime, N_i and n_i are coprime. Bézout's theorem gives us the existence of the inverse of N_i modulo n_i, which is written $y_i = N_i^{-1 \text{ mod } n_i}$. Let $x = \sum_{i=1}^{n} a_i y_i N_i$ mod N. It is easy to check that x is a solution of the system of congruences ! Indeed, for all i, as n_i divides all N_j (with $j \neq i$), $x = a_i y_i N_i$ mod n_i. According to the definition of y_i, we have $x = a_i.1 = a_i$ mod n_i.

Now let us prove the uniqueness of x. Let us suppose that there exist two solutions x_1 and x_2. Then $x_2 - x_1 = 0$ mod n_1 and $x_2 - x_1 = 0$ mod n_2. Thus, $x_2 - x_1 = k_1 n_1 = k_2 n_2$ for some k_1 and k_2. Hence, n_1 divides $k_2 n_2$. Yet, n_1 and n_2 are coprime, thus n_1 also divides k_2; hence $x_2 - x_1 = 0$ mod $n_1 n_2$. Processing recursively, as n_{i+1} is coprime with the product $n_1 n_2 \dots n_i$, we can deduce that $x_2 - x_1 = 0$ mod N, or $x_2 = x_1$ mod N, which gives us the uniqueness of the solution.   □

Exercise 1.17   *Find all integers x such that $x = 4$ mod 5 and $x = 5$ mod 11. Deduce the inverse of 49 modulo 55.*   *Solution on page 285.*

Exercise 1.18   *Find all integers x whose remainders after division by 2, 3, 4, 5, 6 are, Respectively, 1, 2, 3, 4, 5.*   *Solution on page 285.*

Exercise 1.19 (A formula for Euler's Totient Function)

1. *Let p be a prime number, $\varphi(p) = p - 1$. Compute $\varphi(n)$ with $n = p^k$ and $k \in \mathbb{N}^*$.*
2. *Show that φ is* multiplicative, *that is, if m and n are coprime, then $\varphi(mn) = \varphi(m)\varphi(n)$.*
3. *Deduce a general formula for Euler's previous theorem, using the prime factor decomposition.*

Solution on page 286.

Exercise 1.20 (The Chinese Remainder Theorem) *Let $(n_1, \dots, n_k)$ be pairwise coprime integers and $N = \prod_{i=1}^{k} n_i$. We consider the following application:*

$$\Psi : \quad \mathbb{Z}/N\mathbb{Z} \quad \longrightarrow \quad \mathbb{Z}/n_1\mathbb{Z} \times \dots \times \mathbb{Z}/n_k\mathbb{Z}$$
$$a \quad \longrightarrow \quad (a_1, \dots, a_k) \qquad \forall i \in [1, k], \ a = a_i \mod n_i$$

1. *Prove that Ψ is a ring isomorphism.*
2. *Characterize the function Ψ^{-1}*
   Hint: Use $N_i = \dfrac{N}{n_i}$ and notice that $\gcd(N_i, n_i) = 1$.
3. *Give the unique solution modulo N of the system:*

$$\begin{cases} x = a_1 \mod n_1 \\ \vdots \\ x = a_k \mod n_k \end{cases}$$

Solution on page 286.

Exercise 1.21 (Application: The Chinese Remainder Problem) *This exercise is a typical application of the Chinese Remainder Theorem. A group of 17 pirates has laid hands on a booty composed of golden coins of equal value. They decide to share it equally and to give the rest to the Chinese cook. The latter would receive three coins. However, the pirates quarrel and six of them are killed. The cook would receive four coins. Unfortunately, the boat sinks and only six pirates, the treasure and the cook are saved. The sharing would give five golden coins to the cook. What is the minimal fortune the latter can expect if he decides to poison the rest of the pirates ?*

Note*: one may use the following equalities:*

- $17 \times 11 \times 6 = 1122$ *and* $66 = 3 \times 17 + 15$
- $8 \times 66 \times 3 = 1584$ *and* $16 \times 102 = 1632$
- $4151 = 3 \times 1122 + 785$

Solution on page 287.

1.3.3.3 Modular Exponentiation and Discrete Logarithm   Modular exponentiation is a form of coding widely used in modern encryption methods. Let a be a generator of $\mathbb{Z}/n\mathbb{Z}$. Consider the function

$$E_a : \quad \mathbb{Z}/n\mathbb{Z} \quad \longrightarrow \quad \mathbb{Z}/n\mathbb{Z}$$
$$b \quad \longrightarrow \quad a^b \mod n.$$

It is associated with a decoding function. As a is a generator, every element c in $\mathbb{Z}/n\mathbb{Z}$ may be written as a power of a. The lowest positive integer b such that $a^b = c$ mod n is called the *discrete logarithm* (or the *index*) in base a of b modulo n. We denote $b = \log_a c \mod n$.

$$D_a : \quad \mathbb{Z}/n\mathbb{Z} \quad \longrightarrow \quad \mathbb{Z}/n\mathbb{Z}$$
$$c \quad \longrightarrow \quad \log_a c \mod n.$$

The coding function is easy to compute. The method is called the *exponentiation by squaring* (or *binary exponentiation*, or even *square-and-multiply*). It consists in writing b as successive squares.

For example,

$$a^{11} = a \times a^{10} = a \times (a^5)^2 = a \times (a \times a^4)^2 = a \times (a \times (a^2)^2)^2.$$

With this principle, the computation of a^{11} only requires five multiplications: three exponentiations by squaring and two multiplications.

More generally, the complexity bound of Algorithm 1.5 is $O(\log_2 n)$ multiplications modulo n.

Algorithm 1.5 Modular Exponentiation

Input Three integers $a \neq 0$, b and $n \geq 2$.
Output $a^b \mod n$
  1: **If** $b = 0$ **then**
  2:      **return** 1
  3: **else**
  4:      Compute recursively the modular exponentiation $a^{\lfloor b/2 \rfloor} \mod n$
  5:      Let d be the result
  6:      Compute $d \leftarrow d * d \mod n$
  7:      **If** b is odd **then**
  8:          Compute $d \leftarrow d * a \mod n$
  9:      **End If**
 10:      **return** d
 11: **End If**

Indeed, at each call, the exponent b is divided by 2. Hence, there are at most $\log_2 b$ recursive calls. At each call, we perform at most two multiplications: a squaring and possibly a multiplication by a. These operations are performed modulo n, that is to say on numbers of $\log_2 n$ bits. Even using the naive multiplication algorithms (those we have seen in elementary school), the cost of such multiplication is $O(\log_2^2 n)$.

Thus, the overall cost of the algorithm is $O(\log_2 b \log_2^2 n)$. This cost is reasonable with regard to $O(\log_2 n)$, which is the time required to read a or write the result.

Exercise 1.22 (Computations of the Inverse)

1. *Propose an algorithm for the computation of the inverse in $\mathbb{Z}/n\mathbb{Z}$ whenever it exists, based on Euler's theorem.*
   Application: compute (quickly) 22^{-1} mod 63 and 5^{2001} mod 24. One can use the following results: 22^2 mod $63 = 43$; 22^4 mod $63 = 22$.
2. *Give three different algorithms for the computation of the inverse of y modulo $N = p_1^{\delta_1} \cdot p_2^{\delta_2} \cdot \ldots \cdot p_k^{\delta_k}$, with p_i distinct prime integers.*

Solution on page 287.

The Discrete Logarithm Problem (DLP) deals with the computation of the inverse of the modular power. We have seen that modular exponentiation can be computed in reasonable time. However, this is not the case for discrete logarithms. This skewness is a fundamental principle in cryptography.

The following result is called the discrete logarithm theorem. Recall that a *generator* of the set $\mathbb{Z}/n\mathbb{Z}^*$ is a number g such that $\{g^i, i \in \mathbb{N}\} = \mathbb{Z}/n\mathbb{Z}^*$.

Theorem 7 (Discrete Logarithm) *If g is a generator of $\mathbb{Z}/n\mathbb{Z}^*$, then for all $x, y \in \mathbb{N}$: $g^x = g^y$ mod n if and only if $x = y$ mod $\varphi(n)$.*

Proof. ($\Leftarrow$) If $x = y$ mod $\varphi(n)$, one has $x = y + k * \varphi(n)$. Yet, $g^{\varphi(n)} = 1$ mod n, hence $g^x = g^y$ mod n.

($\Rightarrow$) As the sequence of powers of g is periodic of period $\varphi(n)$, then $g^x = g^y$ mod $n \Longrightarrow x = y$ mod $\varphi(n)$. □

However, this does not enable one to compute the discrete logarithm with reasonable complexity. Given y, it is difficult to compute x such that $g^x = y$. The only simple method consists in enumerating exhaustively all possible x and it takes a time $O(n)$. No polynomial time algorithm in $\log_2 n$ (size of the input) is known for this problem.

Thereby, if $n = 10^{100}$, modular exponentiation requires less than 10^8 operations, and it takes less than a second for a PC. On the contrary, exhaustive enumeration for computing the discrete logarithm requires 10^{100} operations, which is unimaginable in reasonable time according to what we have seen before !!!

In practice, one can apply principles similar to those used in factorization algorithms in order to attempt to solve the discrete logarithm problem.

This kind of function – for which one way can be easily computed but not the other one – is crucial in coding, especially for public key cryptography.

1.3.3.4 One-Way Functions In cryptosystems called *public key cryptosystems*, the "encoding system" has to be known while the decoding has to remain unknown. In this example of encoding with modular exponentiation and decoding with the discrete logarithm, the point of having the encoding function E known and the decoding function D unknown seems contradictory: if one knows E, one inevitably knows D as $D = E^{-1}$.

Actually, replacing "unknown" by "extremely difficult to compute on a computer" (i.e., several years for instance), the functions E and D of a public key cryptosystem must satisfy:

- $D = E^{-1}$ in order to insure $D(E(M)) = M$;
- it is easy (i.e., it can be done quickly) to compute $\widetilde{M} = E(M)$ from M; and
- it is difficult (i.e., it takes a very long time) to recover M from $\widetilde{M}$.

In other words, the problem is to find an encryption function E, which is fast to compute but is long to invert. Such a function is called a *one-way function* (also known as OWF). This notion is absolutely crucial in cryptography and all modern codes are based on it. The principle is illustrated in Figure 1.8.

Adding a key to the functions will make decoding easier if one has the key and will make it more difficult if one does not have the key.

Good OWFs are functions such that the research of x given $f(x)$ is a mathematical problem that is putatively difficult.

There are two interests in calculating in modular arithmetic. First of all, computations "modulo n" are quite fast: their cost is $O(log^2 n)$ using the most naive algorithms. Moreover, iterations of a function F – even a simple one – computed using arithmetic modulo n tend to have some random behavior. We see in Section 1.3.7 that this kind of computation is used in the major part of pseudo-random generators. Knowing F and n large, it seems difficult to solve the equation: find x such that $F(x) = a \mod n$, hence to invert the function F.

1.3.4 Construction of Prime Fields and Finite Fields

We have mentioned that we try to give field structures to our codes when possible in order to make operations easier. Now we have a first method of generating good codes: prime fields. It is sufficient to choose a prime number p, and to equip the set

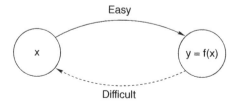

Figure 1.8 Principle of a one-way function

$\{0, \dots, p-1\}$ with the addition and the multiplication modulo p. However, "finding a prime number" is not easy. It is a full-fledged field of research of which we will give a survey in order to leave no algorithmic void in our coding methods.

1.3.4.1 *Primality Tests and Prime Number Generation*
Even if one does not know a polynomial time algorithm for the factoring of an integer n (polynomial with respect to the size $\log_2 n$ of n), it is still possible to quickly generate a prime number p. In coding, it is very useful to be able to generate prime numbers, both for building structured codes such as fields – which can easily be manipulated for error correction – and for setting up secured cryptosystems. For this, one uses primality tests, namely algorithms that determine whether a given number is prime or not. Taking a large odd number n, and applying the test on it, if n is "composite" one can restart the algorithm with $n+2$ until one finds a prime number. The number of prime numbers less than n is asymptotically $n/\ln(n)$. One deduces that – starting from n odd – on average $O(\ln(n))$ iterations are sufficient to find a prime number by adding 2 to n at each step.

The most used primality test was proposed by Miller and was made efficient in practice by Rabin. The Miller–Rabin test is an algorithm that determines whether a given number is probably prime or not. Therefore, the response given by the computation is only a probabilistic one, and it might be erroneous. Nevertheless, if one repeats the test a sufficient number of times and if the latter constantly gives the same response, the error probability will become smaller and smaller and eventually negligible.

Miller-Rabin test. Let n be odd and let s and t such that $n-1 = t2^s$ with t odd. For any integer $a < n$, one has

$$a^{(n-1)} - 1 = a^{t2^s} - 1 = (a^t - 1)(a^t + 1)(a^{2t} + 1) \dots (a^{(2^{s-1})t} + 1).$$

If n is prime, according to Fermat's theorem, $a^{n-1} - 1 = 0 \mod n$; therefore

- Either $a^t - 1 = 0 \mod n$;
- Or $a^{t2^i} + 1 = 0 \mod n$ for some i, $0 \le i < s$.

The Miller–Rabin composition test is based on this property.

One says that a has succeeded in the Miller–Rabin composition test for n if $a^t - 1 \ne 0 \mod n$ and $a^{t2^i} + 1 \ne 0 \mod n$ for all $i = 0, \dots, s-1$.

If n is odd and composite, there are less than $(n-1)/4$ integers a, which fail in the Miller–Rabin composition test. Therefore, by choosing a randomly in $\{1, \dots, n-1\}$, the error probability is lower than $\frac{1}{4}$.

This test can be efficiently used in order to build a probable prime number with an error probability lower than 4^{-k}. One proceeds as follows:

1. Choose randomly an odd integer n.

Algorithm 1.6 Miller–Rabin Primality Test

Input An odd integer $n \geq 5$.
Output n is either *composite* or *probably prime*.
1: Let s and t be such that $n - 1 = t2^s$
2: Let a be a randomly chosen integer between 2 and $n - 1$.
3: Let $q \leftarrow a^t \mod n$
4: **If** $q = 1$ or $q = n - 1$ **then**
5:   **return** "n is probably prime"
6: **End If**
7: **For** i from 1 to $s - 1$ **do**
8:   $q \leftarrow q * q \mod n$
9:   **If** $q = n - 1$ **then**
10:     **return** "n is probably prime"
11:   **End If**
12: **End For**
13: **return** "n is composite".

---

2. Choose randomly k distinct numbers a_i, $1 < a_i < n$. Apply the Miller–Rabin composition test for each integer a_i.

3. If no a_i succeeds in the composition test, we deduce that n is prime; the error probability is lower than 4^{-k};

4. Otherwise, repeat the loop using $n + 2$ instead of n.

The complexity bound of the Miller–Rabin test is similar to that of modular exponentiation, namely $O(\log_2^3 n)$; and $O(k \log_2^3 n)$ if one wants an error probability of around 4^{-k}.

Thus, the average arithmetic cost of the generation of prime numbers is bounded by $O(k \log^4 n)$. Indeed, as there are about $\frac{n}{\ln(n)}$ prime numbers less than n, it would take an average of $\ln(n)$ tries to find a prime number less than n.

In practice, using this test, it is easy to generate a 1000 digit prime number with an error probability arbitrarily low.

Besides, it is possible to make the Miller–Rabin algorithm deterministic by testing a sufficient number of integers a. For example, Burgess proved that testing all integers a lower than $n^{0.134}$ was enough to obtain a prime number with certainty. However, the test would then become exponential in the size of n.

Finally, in 1990, a theorem proved that, assuming the generalized Riemann hypothesis, one of the most famous conjectures in mathematics, it is enough to test the $2 \log_2 n$ first integers. Thus, theoretical studies show that this test is efficient and reliable.

Agrawal–Kayal–Saxena (AKS) primality test. In order to have an overall survey of this topic, let us mention a new primality test – the AKS test – which was built by Agrawal, Kayal, and Saxena. In 2002, they proved the existence of a polynomial time deterministic algorithm that determines whether a number is prime or not without using the Riemann hypothesis. So far, despite this important theoretical result, in practice, one prefers probabilistic algorithms because of their efficiency.

The idea is close to Mille-r-Rabin's and uses the formalism of polynomials: if n is prime, then for all a

$$(X - a)^n = (X^n - a) \quad \text{mod } n. \tag{1.10}$$

The AKS algorithm checks this equality for some values of a, by developing explicitly $(X - a)^n$. For this test to have a polynomial algorithmic complexity bound, one needs to reduce the size of the polynomials (this is done by performing the test modulo $(X^r - 1)$ with r satisfying some properties[3]) and to use a sufficient number of witnesses a, but only of the order of $log^{O(1)}(n)$, that is, a polynomial of the size of n.

We only give a rough idea of the justification of the AKS test, all the more as we have not introduced polynomials yet. This is what we are going to do now, because they constitute a necessary formalism to construct finite fields and codes.

We know how to build large prime fields by just computing large prime numbers. However, these are not the only existing finite fields. In order to build finite fields of any size (even if this size is not a prime number) – and provided that there exist such fields – we now have to introduce the ring of polynomials over any field.

1.3.4.2 Arithmetic of Polynomials Let V be a field. We call a *sequence* a mapping of $\mathbb{N}$ onto V. The image of $i \in \mathbb{N}$ in a sequence a is denoted by a_i. The *support* of a sequence a is the number of nonzero elements in the image of a. A *polynomial P* on V is a sequence with a finite support. The numbers a_i are called the *coefficients* of P. The *degree* of a polynomial P is the highest i, such that a_i is nonzero and is denoted by $\deg(P)$. The coefficient $a_{\deg(P)}$ is then called the *leading coefficient*. A polynomial is *monic* if its leading coefficient is equal to the neutral element for the multiplication in V.

The addition of two polynomials P and Q with coefficients a_i and b_i results in the polynomial $R = P + Q$ with coefficients $c_i = a_i + b_i$ for all $i \in \mathbb{N}$. The multiplication of the two polynomials P and Q results in the polynomial $R = P.Q$, with coefficients $c_i = \sum_{k=0}^{i} a_k b_{i-k}$ for all $i \in \mathbb{N}$.

Let X be the polynomial such that $X_0 = 0$, $X_1 = 1$, and $X_i = 0$ for all $i > 1$. Any polynomial P of degree d may be written as

$$P(X) = \sum_{i=0}^{d} a_i X^i , \text{ where } d \in \mathbb{N}, (a_0, \dots a_d) \in V^{d+1}.$$

The utility of such a notation is among others to define a function P for any polynomial P: to each element x of V, $P(x) = \sum_{i=0}^{d} a_i x^i$. Now to efficiently evaluate the latter expression for an element x, one would use the *Horner scheme* of Algorithm 1.7.

---

[3]r must be coprime with n, the greatest prime factor q of r must satisfy $q \geq 4\sqrt{r} \log n$, and n must also satisfy $n^{\frac{r-1}{q}} \neq 1 \mod r$.

Algorithm 1.7 Horner Polynomial Evaluation

Input $(a_0, \ldots a_d) \in V^{d+1}$, and $x \in V$.
Output $\sum_{i=0}^{d} a_i x^i$.
  1: Let $s = a_d$;
  2: **For** i from $d - 1$ to 0 **do**
  3:     $s = s * x + a_i$;
  4: **End For**
  5: **return** s.

The set of all polynomials with these operations is a ring, denoted by $V[X]$. The null element is the all-zero sequence and the neutral element is the polynomial with coefficients $e_0 = 1$ and $e_i = 0$ for all $i > 0$. It is a principal and Euclidean ring, with the degree as an Euclidean function. Indeed, one can define a Euclidean division: for all nonnull polynomials A and B, there exist two unique polynomials Q and R with $\deg(R) < \deg(B)$ such that

$$A = B \cdot Q + R.$$

The polynomial $Q = A$ div B is the *quotient* in the Euclidean division of A by B; also the *remainder R* is denoted $A \mod B$.

The notion of Greatest Common Divisor (GCD) is then defined; the extended Euclidean algorithm can be applied to two nonzero polynomials A and B and provides a polynomial of maximum degree (it is unique if monic) that divides both A and B. Besides, Bézout's identity is valid. In other words, if A and B are two polynomials in $V[X]$ and $D \in V[X]$ is their gcd, there exist two polynomials S and T in $V[X]$ such that $\deg(S) \leq \deg(B)$ and $\deg(T) \leq \deg(A)$ and

$$A.S + B.T = D.$$

If A and B are different from the polynomial 1 (the neutral element), the *extended Euclidean algorithm* enables one to compute two polynomials S and T whose respective degrees are strictly lower than those of A div D and B div D.

Two polynomials A and B are said to be *coprime* if their GCD is equal to the polynomial 1; in other words, A and B have no common factor of nonzero degree. One says that the nonconstant polynomial P of $V[X]$ is an *irreducible polynomial* over V if P is coprime with all nonconstant polynomials of degree lower than $\deg(P)$.

As for the prime factor decomposition of any integer, any monic polynomial of nonzero degree has a unique factorization in powers of monic irreducible factors over V (up to a constant); one says that $V[X]$ is a *unique factorization domain*. In other words, it is possible to decompose any polynomial of nonzero degree A of $V[X]$ in the form

$$A = P_1^{d_1} \ldots P_k^{d_k},$$

where the d_i are nonzero integers and the polynomials P_i irreducible over V. If A is monic, the P_i factors can be chosen monic: the decomposition is then unique, up to a permutation of the indices.

An element α of V is a *root* of $A \in V[X]$ if $A(\alpha) = 0$, where $A(\alpha)$ is the value of the function associated to the polynomial A evaluated in α.

If α is a root of A, then $(X - \alpha)$ divides A. Let B be the polynomial such that $A = (X - \alpha).B$. One says that α is a *simple root* of A if α is not a root of B, that is, $B(\alpha) \neq 0$. Otherwise, if $B(\alpha) = 0$, one says that α is a *multiple* root of A.

Example 1.5 In $\mathbb{F}_2[X]$, the polynomial $X^3 - 1$ can be factorized into $X^3 - 1 = (X - 1) \cdot (X^2 + X + 1)$. One can easily check that $X^2 + X + 1$ is irreducible (the only irreducible polynomials in $\mathbb{F}_2[X]$ of nonzero degree lower than 2 are X and $X - 1$; and neither 0 nor 1 are roots of $X^2 + X + 1$).

1.3.4.3 The Ring $V[X]/P$ and Finite Fields Let $(V, +, \times)$ be a field and let P be a polynomial of degree $d \geq 1$. One denotes by $V[X]/P$ the set of polynomials of degree strictly lower than d equipped with the addition and multiplication modulo P. Namely, for all polynomials A, B in $V[X]$, with $\deg(A) < d$ and $\deg(B) < d$:

$$A +_{V[X]/P} B = (A +_{V[X]} B) \mod P$$

$$A \times_{V[X]/P} B = (A \times_{V[X]} B) \mod P.$$

This is a commutative monic ring of neutral elements 0 and 1 with regard to the laws $+$ and $\times$. This ring is called the *quotient ring* of $V[X]$ modulo P.

If P is an irreducible polynomial, then $V[X]/P$ is a field. Indeed, if Q is a nonzero polynomial of degree lower than $\deg P$, then Q and P are coprime and with Bézout's identity $AQ + BP = 1$, one obtains $AQ = 1 \mod P$. In other words, Q is invertible in the quotient ring $V[X]/P$.

Example 1.6 (Over the Field $V = \mathbb{F}_2$) If $P = (X + 1)(X^2 + X + 1)$ (a nonirreducible polynomial), the ring $V[X]/P$ is such that:

$$V[X]/P = \left\{ 0, 1, X, 1 + X, X^2, 1 + X^2, X + X^2, 1 + X + X^2 \right\}.$$

This ring is not a field because $(1 + X)(1 + X + X^2) = 0$ proves that $1 + X$ is not invertible. On the other hand, if one considers $P = X^2 + X + 1$ (an irreducible polynomial), the ring $V[X]/P$ is such that $V[X]/P = \{0, 1, X, 1 + X\}$. This ring is a field as $X(X + 1) = 1$.

Therefore, we now have finite fields that are more general than prime fields. Indeed, our last example provided us with a field of four elements, which is not a prime field.

Finite fields are called *Galois fields*. They are denoted by $\mathbb{F}_q$, where q is the cardinal number of the field. The next property enables us to handle all finite fields by this construction principle and to explain the notation $\mathbb{F}_q$ for "the" finite field of cardinal number q.

Property 6 *Two finite fields of same cardinal number are isomorphic.*

One can use an irreducible polynomial in order to build a finite field. As for prime number generation, looking for irreducible polynomials is a fully fledged domain of which we will give a survey.

1.3.4.4 Irreducible Polynomials

In order to build finite fields, we need some irreducible polynomials, as we needed prime numbers in order to build prime fields.

In the same way as we have seen primality tests for numbers in Section 1.3.4.1, we begin by giving a test that enables to recognize irreducible polynomials.

The first test which is easy to perform is to make sure that the polynomial is *square-free*, namely that it does not have for divisor the square of another polynomial. This can be done over a finite field as for any other field by considering the derivative P' of P. For $P(X) = \sum_{i=0}^{d} a_i X^i$, we note $P'(X) \sum_{i=1}^{d} a_i \times i X^{i-1}$ its *derivative* polynomial.

Property 7 *A polynomial P is square free if and only if $\gcd(P, P') = 1$.*

Proof. If P is divisible by a square, then $P = g^2 h$ for some polynomials h and g. It follows that $P' = 2g'gh + g^2h' = g(2g'h + gh')$ and thus g divides the GCD of P and P'. Reciprocally, if $g = \gcd(P, P')$, let us consider an irreducible factor γ of g of degree at least 1. Then $P' = \gamma f$ and $P = \gamma \lambda$ with f and λ polynomials. By differentiating P, one obtains $\gamma f = \gamma' \lambda + \gamma \lambda'$, or $\gamma(f - \lambda') = \gamma' \lambda$. The polynomial γ being irreducible and γ' being of degree strictly lower than the degree of γ, γ, and γ' are coprime. By Gauss's lemma (see page 33), γ necessarily divides λ and γ^2 divides P. $\square$

The principle of the irreducibility test is given by the following property.

Proposition 1 *For p prime and $d \geq 1$, in $\mathbb{F}_p[X]$, the polynomial $X^{p^d} - X$ is the product of all irreducible, monic polynomials whose degree divides d.*

In order to prove this proposition, we will need the following lemma:

Lemma 3 *$r > 0$ divides $d > 0$ if and only if $p^r - 1$ divides $p^d - 1$.*

Proof. If r divides d, then $p^d = (p^r)^k = (1)^k = 1 \mod p^r - 1$. Reciprocally, one has $p^d - 1 = 0 \mod p^r - 1$. Let us suppose that $d = qr + s$, with $s < r$. Then, one has $p^d - 1 = p^{qr}p^s - 1 = p^s - 1 \mod p^r - 1$. Yet, $0 \leq s < r$, thus one obtains $p^s - 1 = 0$ over the integers, which implies that $s = 0$. Thus, r divides d. $\square$

Proof. [of Proposition 1] Let P be irreducible of degree r, such that r divides d. Then $V = \mathbb{F}_p[X]/P$ is a field. In V, the order of any nonzero element divides the cardinal number of the group of its invertible elements, namely $p^r - 1$ (Section 1.3.2.1). One applies this property to $X \in V$, so that $X^{p^r-1} = 1$. According to the lemma, $p^r - 1$ divides $p^d - 1$, hence $X^{p^d-1} = 1 \mod P$, and thus P divides $X^{p^d-1} - 1$.

Reciprocally, let P be an irreducible divisor of $X^{p^d} - X$ of degree r. Then, one has $X^{p^d} = X \mod P$. Now, set $G(X) = \sum a_i X^i$ of maximum order $p^r - 1$ in the group of invertible elements of the field $\mathbb{F}_p[X]/P$ (there always exists at least one such element, see page 56). One then applies Equation (1.10) d times in order to obtain $G^{p^d} = \sum a_i(X^{p^d})^i \mod p$. Now, $X^{p^d} = X \mod P$ and thus $G^{p^d} = G \mod P$ or $G^{p^d-1} = 1 \mod P$. Hence, $p^d - 1$ is necessarily a multiple of $p^r - 1$, the order of G. The lemma enables to conclude that r actually divides d.

One then just needs show that no square divides $X^{p^d} - X$. Indeed, its derivative polynomial is $p^d X^{p^d-1} - 1 = -1 \mod p$ and the polynomial -1 is coprime with any other polynomial. □

Thus, the factors of $X^{p^d} - X$ are all the irreducible, monic polynomials whose degree divides d. If a polynomial of degree d has no common factor with $X^{p^i} - X$ for $1 \leq i \leq d/2$, it is irreducible. From this property, we can build a test called Ben-Or's irreducibility test (Algorithm 1.8).

Algorithm 1.8 Ben-Or's Irreducibility Test

Input A polynomial, $P \in \mathbb{F}_p[X]$.
Output "P is reducible" or "P is irreducible".
1: Let P' be the derivative polynomial of P.
2: **If** gcd $(P, P') \neq 1$ **then**
3:     **return** "P is reducible".
4: **End If**
5: Let $Q \leftarrow X$
6: **For** i from 1 to $\frac{\deg(P)}{2}$ **do**
7:     $Q \leftarrow Q^p \mod P$
8:     **If** gcd$(Q - X, P) \neq 1$ **then**
9:         **return** "P is reducible" (end of the algorithm).
10:     **End If**
11: **End For**
12: **return** "P is irreducible".

Therefore, we may generate random polynomials and, using this test, see if they are irreducible. One denotes by $m_r(p)$ the number of irreducible, monic polynomials of degree r in $\mathbb{F}_p[X]$. As $X^{p^r} - X$ is the product of all irreducible, monic polynomials whose degree divides r, one obtains

$$\frac{1}{r}(p^r - p^{\lfloor \frac{r}{2} \rfloor + 1}) \leq m_r(p) \leq \frac{1}{r}p^r. \tag{1.11}$$

Indeed, p^r is the degree of $X^{p^r} - X$, thus $p^r = \sum_{d|r} dm_d(p) \geq rm_r(p)$. Hence $m_r(p) \leq p^r/r$. On the other hand, $xm_x(p) \leq p^x$ implies that $p^r - rm_r = \sum_{d|r, d\neq r} dm_d(p) \leq \sum_{d|r, d\neq r} p^d \leq \sum_{d \leq \lfloor r/2 \rfloor} p^d$. The latter is a geometric series whose value is $\frac{p^{\lfloor r/2 \rfloor + 1} - 1}{p-1} < p^{\lfloor r/2 \rfloor + 1}$. Finally, $\frac{1}{r}(p^r - p^{\lfloor \frac{r}{2} \rfloor + 1}) \leq m_r(p)$.

This statement shows that among all polynomials of degree r, about one over r is irreducible. One wishes to build an irreducible polynomial. At first sight, it is possible to choose a polynomial randomly, test its irreducibility, and restart the process until one chances on an irreducible polynomial. On average, one needs r draws to find an appropriate polynomial. However, in order to make computations with polynomials easier, it is interesting to obtain sparse polynomials, namely polynomials with very few nonzero coefficients. In this case, exhaustive research might turn out to be more efficient in practice.

We propose the following hybrid Algorithm 1.9 that produces an irreducible polynomial – preferably a sparse one. It is based on the idea of taking polynomials in the form $X^r + g(X)$ with $g(X)$ chosen randomly of degree significantly lower than r.

Algorithm 1.9 Generation of a sparse irreducible polynomial

Input A finite field $\mathbb{F}_p$, an integer $r > 0$.
Output An irreducible polynomial in $\mathbb{F}_p[X]$, of degree r.
 1: **For** d from 2 to $r - 1$ **do**
 2:    **For all** $a, b \in \mathbb{F}_q, a \neq 0$ **do**
 3:      **If** $X^r + bX^d + a$ is irreducible **then**
 4:         Return $X^r + bX^d + a$
 5:      **End If**
 6:    **End For**
 7: **End For**
 8: **Repeat**
 9:    Select P, monic of degree r, chosen randomly in $\mathbb{F}_q[X]$.
10: **Until** P is irreducible
11: **return** P.

1.3.4.5 Construction of Finite Fields Now, we have all the elements necessary to build a finite field of size p^n with p a prime number. The method of building finite fields is contained in the proof of the following result:

Theorem 8 *For all prime number p and all integers $d > 0$, there exists a field K of p^d elements. This field is unique up to isomorphism.*

Proof. Let p be a prime number and let $\mathbb{F}_p[X]$ be the field of polynomials with coefficients in $\mathbb{F}_p$. For $d = 1$, $\mathbb{F}_p$ is a field with p elements. For $d = 2$, Proposition 1 guarantees the existence of at least one irreducible polynomial as there are p irreducible polynomials of degree strictly less than 2 and p^2, the degree of $X^{p^2} - X$, satisfies $p^2 > p$. For larger d, Equation (1.11) shows that $1 \leq m_d(p)$ and thus there exists at least one irreducible polynomial P of degree d in $\mathbb{F}_p[X]$. Then, the quotient ring $V = \mathbb{F}_p[X]/P$ is a field.

As P is of degree d and $|\mathbb{F}_p| = p$, there are p^d possible remainders. Thus $|V| = p^d$.

According to Property 6 on page 48, any field of cardinal number p^d is isomorphic to V. $\qquad\qquad\square$

Remark 1   *The isomorphism between $V[X]/P$ and $V^{\deg(P)}$ equips $V^{\deg(P)}$ with a field structure.*

Indeed, to any vector $u = [u_0, \ldots, u_{d-1}]$ in the vector space V^d, one can associate in a bijective way the polynomial $\psi(u) = \sum_{i=0}^{d-1} u_i X^i$. Moreover, one has the following property:

$$\text{For all } u, v \in V^d, \ \lambda \in V, \ \psi(u + \lambda \cdot v) = \psi(u) + \lambda \cdot \psi(v).$$

Hence, ψ is an isomorphism between V^d and $\psi(V^d) = V[X]/P$. This equips V^d with a field structure in which multiplication is defined by

$$\text{For all } u, v \in V^d, \quad u \cdot v = \psi^{-1}(\psi(u) \cdot \psi(v)).$$

Hence, one can use a field structure with the vectors in $V^{\deg(P)}$.

Exercise 1.23   *Let K be a finite field of cardinal number $q > 0$. Using the map Ψ : $\mathbb{Z} \to K$, defined by*

$$\text{For all } n \in \mathbb{Z}, \ \Psi(n) = \underbrace{1_K + 1_K + \ldots + 1_K}_{n \text{ times}} = n.1_K,$$

prove that there exists a unique prime number p (called the characteristic *of K), such that for all $x \in K$, $px = 0$.*   Solution on page 288.

Exercise 1.24   *Sequel of the previous exercise*
Deduce from the previous exercise that the cardinal number of K is a power of p using the fact that K is a vector space over its subfields. Hint: One may obtain a subfield of K isomorphic to $\mathbb{F}_p$.   Solution on page 289.

Exercise 1.25 (Construction of the Field $\mathbb{F}_4$)

1. *Give a necessary and sufficient condition for a polynomial in $\mathbb{F}_2[X]$ of degree $2 \leq n \leq 3$ to be irreducible. From this condition, deduce all irreducible polynomials of degrees 2 and 3.*
2. *Deduce all irreducible polynomials of degree 4.*
3. *Set $\mathbb{F}_4 = \{e_0, e_1, e_2, e_3\}$ with e_0 the neutral element for the addition and e_1 the neutral element for the multiplication. Using the first question, write the operation tables $(+, \times, \text{inverse})$ in $\mathbb{F}_4$.*

Solution on page 289.

1.3.5   Implementation of Finite Fields

1.3.5.1   Operations on Polynomials   A typical construction of arithmetic in a finite field $\mathbb{F}_p$ is – for a given prime number p – to look for some irreducible polynomial P

in $\mathbb{F}_p[X]$ of degree d, then to write the elements of $\mathbb{F}_q = \mathbb{F}_p[X]/P$ as polynomials, or as vectors, and finally to implement the arithmetic operations in $\mathbb{F}_q$.

Example 1.7 (Construction of the Field $\mathbb{F}_{16}$)   There exists a field with 16 elements as $16 = 2^4$. In order to build the field $\mathbb{F}_{16}$, one first looks for some monic irreducible polynomial P of degree 4 in $\mathbb{F}_2[X]$. Then one establishes the rules of calculation in $\mathbb{F}_2[X]/P$.

- *Finding P.*
  The irreducible polynomial P is written as $P = X^4 + aX^3 + bX^2 + cX + 1$ with a, b, and c in $\mathbb{F}_2$. In order to determine P, let us examine all possible values for the triplet (a, b, c). One cannot have $(a, b, c) \in \{(0, 1, 1), (1, 0, 1), (1, 1, 0), (0, 0, 0)\}$ as for all these cases, 1 is a root of P. Thus, the triplet (a, b, c) is to be searched for in the set $\{(0, 0, 1), (0, 1, 0), (1, 0, 0), (1, 1, 1)\}$. The only irreducible polynomials over $\mathbb{F}_2$ of degree at most 2 are X, $1 + X$, and $X^2 + X + 1$. To see whether P is irreducible, it is sufficient to compute the GCD of P and $(1 + X)(X^2 + X + 1)$. The calculation (with the Euclidean algorithm for example) of these **GCDs!** (GCDs!) shows that the only values of (a, b, c) for which P is irreducible are $(0, 0, 1)$, $(1, 0, 0)$, and $(1, 1, 1)$. Thus, $P = X^4 + X^3 + 1$ is a possible choice for P. Let us make this choice.

- *Operations on polynomials.*

Thus, the elements of the field are $0, X, X^2, X^3, 1 + X^3, 1 + X + X^3, 1 + X + X^2 + X^3, 1 + X + X^2, X + X^2 + X^3, 1 + X^2,\quad X + X^3, 1 + X^2 + X^3, 1 + X, X + X^2, X^2 + X^3, 1$. Therefore, the operations are performed modulo P. For example, $(X^2)(X + X^3) = 1 + X$.

1.3.5.2   Use of Generators   There exist other ways to implement finite fields in which the multiplication will be performed much more quickly.

The idea is to use the property of finite fields according to which the multiplicative group of invertible elements of a finite field is cyclic. Namely, there exists at least one generator and the nonzero elements of the field are generated by this element. Hence, if g is a generator of the multiplicative group of a finite field $\mathbb{F}_q$, all invertible elements can be written as g^i.

One can choose to represent each invertible element g^i simply by using its index i and represent zero by a special index. This construction – in which one represents the elements using their logarithm – is called *exponential representation* or *cyclic representation*, or *Zech's construction*. Then, typical arithmetic operations are greatly simplified using the following proposition:

Proposition 2   *Let $\mathbb{F}_q$ be a finite field and let g be a generator of $\mathbb{F}_q^*$. Then $g^{q-1} = 1_{\mathbb{F}_q}$. In addition, if the characteristic of $\mathbb{F}_q$ is odd, then $g^{\frac{q-1}{2}} = -1_{\mathbb{F}_q}$. Otherwise, $1_{\mathbb{F}_{2^n}} = -1_{\mathbb{F}_{2^n}}$.*

Proof.   Clearly, one has $g^{q-1} = 1_{\mathbb{F}_q}$. If the field is of characteristic 2, then, as in $\mathbb{F}_2[X]$, one has $1 = -1$. Otherwise $\frac{q-1}{2} \in \mathbb{Z}$ thus $g^{\frac{q-1}{2}} \in \mathbb{F}_q$. Yet, as we consider a field, the equation $X^2 = 1$ has at most two roots, 1 and -1. g is a generator, thus the order of g is $q - 1$ rather than $\frac{q-1}{2}$. The only remaining possibility is $g^{\frac{q-1}{2}} = -1$.   □

This statement gives the following encoding for an element $x \in \mathbb{F}_q$, if $\mathbb{F}_q$ is generated by g:

$$\begin{cases} 0 & \text{if } x = 0 \\ q - 1 & \text{if } x = 1 \\ i & \text{if } x = g^i, x \neq 1. \end{cases}$$

In particular, in our encoding scheme, let us denote by $\bar{q} = q - 1$ the codeword associated with $1_{\mathbb{F}_q}$. We will also denote by i_{-1} the index of $-1_{\mathbb{F}_q}$; it is equal to $\frac{q-1}{2}$ if the characteristic of $\mathbb{F}_q$ is odd and equal to $q - 1$ otherwise. This enables one to write in a simple way all arithmetic operations.

- Multiplication and division of invertible elements are, respectively, implemented as an addition and a subtraction of indexes modulo $q - 1$.
- Therefore, negation (taking the opposite) is simply the identity in characteristic 2 or an addition with $\frac{q-1}{2}$ modulo $q - 1$ if the characteristic is odd.
- Addition is the most complex operation. One must implement it using other operations. For example, it is possible to do so the following way: if g^i and g^j (with $j > i$) are two nonzero elements in a finite field, $g^i + g^j = g^i(1 + g^{j-i})$. This requires to store the index of $1 + g^k$ for all k. This is done by precomputing a table, t_plus1, of size q, containing the index of the successor of each element in the field. Eventually, addition is implemented with one subtraction of indexes $(j - i)$, one access to a table $(t\_plus1[g^{j-i}])$ and one addition of indices $(i + t\_plus1[g^{j-i}])$.

In Table 1.4, we study the calculation of these operations over the indices, assuming the existence of a single "table of successors" of size q. Here, we focus on the

TABLE 1.4   Zech's Construction on Invertible Elements in Odd Characteristic

			Average Cost		
Operation	Elements	Indexes	$+/-$	Tests	Access
Multiplication	$g^i * g^j$	$i + j \, (-\bar{q})$	1.5	1	0
Division	g^i / g^j	$i - j \, (+\bar{q})$	1.5	1	0
Negation	$-g^i$	$i - i_{-1} \, (+\bar{q})$	1.5	1	0
Addition	$g^i + g^j$	$k = j - i \, (+\bar{q})$			
		$i + t\_plus1[k] \, (-\bar{q})$	3	2	1
Subtraction	$g^i - g^j$	$k = j - i + i_{-1} \, (\pm\bar{q})$			
		$i + t\_plus1[k] \, (-\bar{q})$	3.75	2.75	1

complexity of the calculation using the least amount of memory possible, considering random elements. We indicate the cost of the computations taking the mean number of additions and subtraction (+/−), the number of tests, and the number of times we use the table.

Exercise 1.26 *Check that the polynomial X is a generator of the field* $\mathbb{F}_{16}$, *constructed with the irreducible polynomial* $P = X^4 + X^3 + 1$. *Then for the two polynomials* $P_1 = X + 1$ *and* $P_2 = X^2 + X$, *perform* $P_1 + P_2$ *and* $P_1 \times P_2$ *using the operations described in Table 1.4.* *Solution on page 289.*

1.3.5.3 Primitive Roots In order to put this implementation into practice, we need to find a way of producing generators of finite fields in the same way as we needed a way of producing prime numbers in order to build prime fields or irreducible polynomials to build nonprime fields.

Generators of prime fields. A generator of the group of invertible elements in $\mathbb{Z}/n\mathbb{Z}$ is called a *primitive root* of n. The least primitive root of m is denoted by $\chi(m)$.

If p is a prime number, then $\mathbb{Z}/p\mathbb{Z}$ always has exactly $\varphi(p-1)$ primitive roots. Indeed, by Lagrange's theorem (Proposition 5 page 5), the order of an element of a group divides the number of elements in the group. This means that the order of any nonzero element of $\mathbb{Z}/p\mathbb{Z}$ divides $p-1$. Now suppose that there exists one primitive root g, that is, g generates the group of invertible elements of $\mathbb{Z}/n\mathbb{Z}$. Then for any nonzero element x, there exists an index j such that $x = g^j$. Then, the order of x is $p-1$, that is, x is also a generator primitive root, if and only if its index is coprime with $p-1$. Now, one has to compute at least one of these $\varphi(p-1)$ primitive roots. For this, one uses the following test, which checks whether the order of an element taken at random is $p-1$ or not. The main difficulty is to factorize $p-1$, at least partially, and we see how to do this in Section 1.4.3.5.

Algorithm 1.10 Test Primitive Root

Input A prime number $p > 0$.
Input An integer $a > 0$.
Output Yes, if a is a primitive root of p; No, otherwise.
  1: **For all** q prime and dividing $p-1$, **do** {Factoring of $p-1$}
  2:   **If** $a^{\frac{p-1}{q}} = 1 \mod p$ **then**
  3:     Return "No".
  4:   **End If**
  5: **End For**
  6: **return** "Yes".

Theorem 9 *Algorithm Test Primitive Root is correct.*

Proof. One uses the result of Section 1.3.2.1: if a is an integer, of order k modulo p, then $a^h = 1 \mod p$ if and only if $k|h$.

One deduces that if the order of a is lower than $p - 1$, as it divides $p - 1$, then necessarily one of the values $\frac{p-1}{q}$ will be a multiple of the order of a. Otherwise, the only possible value for the order of a is $p - 1$.   □

Therefore, a first method of finding a primitive root is to test all integers lower than p one after the other, which are not equal to 1, nor to -1, nor any power of an integer; in this way, one is able to find the least primitive root of p. Numerous theoretical results exist, proving that it does not take a great number of attempts to find this first primitive root. It is generally of the order of

$$\chi(p) = O\left(r^4 (\log(r) + 1)^4 \log^2(p)\right)$$

with r the number of distinct prime factors of $p - 1$. Another method is to draw random integers lower than p and to test whether they are primitive roots or not. As that there are $\varphi(p - 1)$ primitive roots, the probability of success is $\frac{\varphi(p-1)}{p-1}$; thus, the expected value for the number of draws before finding a primitive root is $\frac{p-1}{\varphi(p-1)}$. This gives us a better chance than the brute-force method (trying all possibilities).

Generators of finite fields. Now we know how to find a generator for a prime field. Let us consider the finite fields $\mathbb{F}_{p^k}$. In order to build them, let us recall that, one has first to build $\mathbb{F}_p$ and then to find an irreducible polynomial over this field whose degree is k. The question is how to find a *generator polynomial* of this field in order to encode elements with their index rather than using polynomials. Encoding and arithmetic operations are then the *same* as those of prime fields.

Once again, we use a probabilistic approach. First of all, let us consider an algorithm testing whether a polynomial is a generator in $\mathbb{F}_p[X]$. This algorithm is similar to the one we have seen for primitive roots in $\mathbb{F}_p$.

Algorithm 1.11 Test Generator Polynomial

Input A polynomial $A \in \mathbb{F}_p[X]$.
Input An irreducible polynomial F of degree d in $\mathbb{F}_p[X]$.
Output Yes, if A is a generator of the field $\mathbb{F}_p[X]/F$; No, otherwise.
1: **For all** q, prime and dividing $p^d - 1$ **do** {Factoring of $p^d - 1$}
2:   **If** $A^{\frac{p^d-1}{q}} = 1 \mod F$ **then** {Recursive computation using square exponentiation}
3:     Return "No".
4:   **End If**
5: **End For**
6: **return** "Yes".

Therefore, once the field is built, an algorithm looking randomly for a generator is easy to implement. Besides, one can start the search into the set of polynomials of small degree ($O(\log(n))$). However, in order to manipulate sparse polynomials, it is useful to find an irreducible polynomial for which X is a primitive root. Such a polynomial is called X-*irreducible*, or *primitive* and in general can be quickly found. In practice, for finite fields of size between 4 and 2^{32}, it is possible to show that more than one irreducible polynomial in 12 is X-irreducible! Therefore, an algorithm looking randomly for an X-irreducible polynomial requires less than 12 attempts on average. Thus, an algorithm for finding an irreducible polynomial having X as generator is a simple modification of Algorithm 1.9. If Algorithm 1.11 returns that X is not a generator. one does not select the irreducible polynomial found in Algorithm 1.9.

Example 1.8 Let us return to the example of the field $\mathbb{F}_{16}$, which we built with the irreducible polynomial $P = X^4 + X^3 + 1$.

Algorithm 1.11 performed on X returns that X is a generator. Therefore, one can perform computations using the powers of X (Exercise 1.26).

Recall the identification of the elements in $\mathbb{F}_{16}$ and operation rules:
$X^1 = X \mod P$; $X^2 = X^2 \mod P$; $X^3 = X^3 \mod P$; $X^4 = 1 + X^3 \mod P$; $X^5 = 1 + X + X^3 \mod P$; $X^6 = 1 + X + X^2 + X^3 \mod P$; $X^7 = 1 + X + X^2 \mod P$; $X^8 = X + X^2 + X^3 \mod P$; $X^9 = 1 + X^2 \mod P$; $X^{10} = X + X^3 \mod P$; $X^{11} = 1 + X^2 + X^3 \mod P$; $X^{12} = 1 + X \mod P$; $X^{13} = X + X^2 \mod P$; $X^{14} = X^2 + X^3 \mod P$; and $X^{15} = 1 \mod P$.

With $\mathbb{F}_{16}$ written in form $\mathbb{F}_{16} = \{0, 1, X, X^2, X^3, X^4, X^5, X^6, X^7, X^8, X^9, X^{10}, X^{11}, X^{12}, X^{13}, X^{14}\}$, multiplication and inverse calculation in $\mathbb{F}_{16}$ are performed more easily. Addition is also much easier considering that $X^k + X^t = X^t(1 + X^{k-t})$ for all k and t in $\{1, \ldots, 14\}$ such that $k > t$.

1.3.6 Curves Over Finite Fields

The exponentiation over finite fields is a good example of a one-way function, and we now have almost all tools to construct and efficiently compute in those fields. On one hand, the field structure provides many tools for the construction of codes. On the other hand, this structure itself allows more possibilities for code breakers in cryptography. It is possible to define this type of one-way function in a more general structure, a group, so that cryptanalysis is even more difficult. An example of such a group structure is the set of points of a curve defined over a finite field.

In a generic group, we denote by $+$ the group law (which is the multiplication in the group of invertible elements of a finite field $\mathbb{F}_q^*$ for example). Then, the multiplication by an integer (i.e., that integer number of calls to the group law, which is the exponentiation by an integer in $\mathbb{F}_q^*$) can be used as a one-way function. The discrete logarithm problem, in this general formulation, is to find the number of times one has to add a given generator of the group in order to obtain a given element of the group. We denote this as $[n]P = P + P + P + \cdots + P$ for some scalar (integer) n and an element P of a group (Table 1.5).

TABLE 1.5   Discrete Logarithm and Exponentiation in Finite Fields and Generic Groups

Group	Exponentiation	DLP
$\mathbb{F}_q^*$	a^e with $a \in \mathbb{F}_q^*$ and $e \in \mathbb{N}$	Find $x \in \mathbb{N}$ s.t. $g^x = b \in \mathbb{F}_q^*$
G	$a + \ldots + a$, $e \in \mathbb{N}$ times, that is, $[e]a$	Find $x \in \mathbb{N}$ s.t. $[x]g = b \in G$

1.3.6.1   Weierstrass Model Let $p \geq 5$ be a prime number, $q = p^k$, and let $a, b \in \mathbb{F}_{p^k}$ such that the polynomial $x^3 + ax + b$ does not have multiple roots and consider the equation

$$y^2 z = x^3 + axz^2 + bz^3. \tag{1.12}$$

If $(x, y, z) \in \mathbb{F}_q^3$ is a solution of (1.12), then any multiple $c(x, y, z)$ is also a solution. Two solutions are called *equivalent* if they are equal up to a constant multiplicative factor. This defines an equivalence relation. The *elliptic curve* $\mathbb{E}(q; a, b)$ is the set of equivalence classes of solutions of (1.12), which are called *points* of the curve. For one equivalence class, noted $(x : y : z)$, if $z \neq 0 \in \mathbb{F}_q$, there exists a representative of the class of the form $(x' : y' : 1)$. Indeed, just set $x' = xz^{-1}$ and $y' = yz^{-1}$. On the other hand, If $z = 0$ then x must also be zero, and there is exactly one equivalence class of solutions with this form. It is denoted by $\mathcal{O}$ and its chosen representative is usually $(0 : 1 : 0)$. In summary the set of points is entirely defined by the cases $z = 1$ and $z = 0$; therefore, the definition of an elliptic curve can be simplified to

$$\mathbb{E}(q; a, b) = \{(x, y) \in \mathbb{F}_q^2, y^2 = x^3 + ax + b\} \cup \{\mathcal{O}\}. \tag{1.13}$$

In fact, the general form of the equation of an ellipse is $y^2 + a_1 xy + a_3 y = x^3 + a_2 x^2 + a_4 x + a_6$. Now if the characteristic of the field is neither 2 nor 3, then the change of variable $(x, y) \hookrightarrow (x, y - a_1 x/2 - a_3/2)$ yields an isomorphic curve $y^2 = x^3 + b_2 x^2 + b_4 x + b_6$ and then a second change of variable $(x, y) \hookrightarrow (x - b_2/3, y)$ enables to simplify the equation to (1.13). This can be generalized for fields of characteristics 2 and 3:

1. If $a_1 \neq 0 \in \mathbb{F}_{2^k}$, use $(x, y) \hookrightarrow (a_1^2 x + a_3/a_1, y)$ to get $y^2 + b_1 xy = x^3 + b_2 x^2 + b_4 x + b_6$, followed by $(x, y) \hookrightarrow (x, a_1^3 y - b_4/a_1)$, to obtain $\mathbb{E}(2^k; a, b) = \{(x, y) \in \mathbb{F}_{2^k}^2, y^2 + xy = x^3 + ax^2 + b\} \cup \{\mathcal{O}\}$.

2. Else, $a_1 = 0 \in \mathbb{F}_{2^k}$ and $(x, y) \hookrightarrow (x + a_2, y)$ gives $\mathbb{E}(2^k; a, b, c) = \{(x, y) \in \mathbb{F}_{2^k}^2, y^2 + cy = x^3 + ax + b\} \cup \{\mathcal{O}\}$.

3. If $a_1^2 \neq -a_2 \in \mathbb{F}_{3^k}$, use $(x, y) \hookrightarrow (x, y + a_1 x - a_3/2)$ to get $y^2 = x^3 + b_2 x^2 + b_4 x + b_6$, followed by $(x, y) \hookrightarrow (x - b_4/(2b_2), y)$ to obtain $\mathbb{E}(3^k; a, b) = \{(x, y) \in \mathbb{F}_{3^k}^2, y^2 = x^3 + ax^2 + b\} \cup \{\mathcal{O}\}$.

4. Else, $a_1^2 + a_2 = 0 \in \mathbb{F}_{3^k}$ and $(x, y) \hookrightarrow (x, y + a_1 x + a_3)$ gives $\mathbb{E}(3^k; a, b) = \{(x, y) \in \mathbb{F}_{3^k}^2, y^2 = x^3 + ax + b\} \cup \{\mathcal{O}\}$.

Exercise 1.27 *Verify that the given variable changes are correct.*

Solution on page 289.

To make an exhaustive search for a discrete logarithm impossible in practice, the group of points in an elliptic curve has to be large enough. The following theorem states that the number of points is of the order of the size of the involved finite field.

Theorem 10 (Hasse) *For any prime power* $q = p^k$, *let* $N_{q;a,b}$ *be the number of points of* $\mathbb{E}(q; a, b)$, *then*

$$|N_{q;a,b} - (q + 1)| \leq 2\sqrt{q}.$$

1.3.6.2 The Group of Points of an Elliptic Curve Now that we have defined the points in an elliptic curve, we need to provide a group law. We first give the abstract definition.

Theorem 11 *Let* $\mathbb{F}_q$ *be a field of characteristic greater than 5 and* $\mathbb{E}(q; a, b)$ *an elliptic curve. Then* $(\mathbb{E}(q; a, b), \oplus)$ *with the following rules for addition is an abelian group:*

- $\mathcal{O}$ *is the neutral element for* $\oplus$.
- *For* $P = (x, y)$, $-P = (x, -y)$ *is the opposite of* P *for* $\oplus$.
- *For* $P = (x_1, y_1)$ *and* $Q(x_2, y_2)$ *then:*
  - *if* $x_1 \neq x_2$, *then* $\lambda = \frac{y_2 - y_1}{x_2 - x_1}$ *and*

  $$P \oplus Q = (x_3, y_3) = \left(\lambda^2 - x_1 - x_2, \lambda(x_1 - x_3) - y_1\right)$$

  - *else,* $x_1 = x_2$ *and:*
    * *if also* $y_1 = y_2$, *then* $Q = P$, $P \oplus Q = P \oplus P = [2]P$,

    $$\lambda = \frac{3x_1^2 + a}{2y_1} \text{ and } [2]P = \left(x_3 = \lambda^2 - 2x_1, y_3 = \lambda(x_1 - x_3) - y_1\right)$$

    * *else* $Q = -P$ *and* $P \oplus -P = \mathcal{O}$.

The rules of addition derives from the representation of elliptic curves over the real field: if P and Q are two different points on the curve, then $P \oplus Q$ is the symmetric (with respect to the x-axis) of the third intersection of the curve with the line PQ. In the same manner, $[2]P$ is the symmetric (with respect to the x-axis) intersection of the tangent in P with the curve, as shown on Figure 1.9. In both cases, λ is the slope of the line and the y-intercept can naturally be recovered as, for example, $y_1 - \lambda x_1$.

Exercise 1.28 *Let* $\mathbb{F}_{5^2} = \mathbb{F}_5[T]/(T^2 + 2)$, $\mathbb{E}(5^2; -1, 1)$, $P = (1, 1)$ *and* $Q = (3 + T, 2 + T)$.

1. *Check that* $P, Q \in \mathbb{E}(5^2; -1, 1)$.
2. *Check that* $2 + T = (2 - T)^{-1} \in \mathbb{F}_{5^2}$.

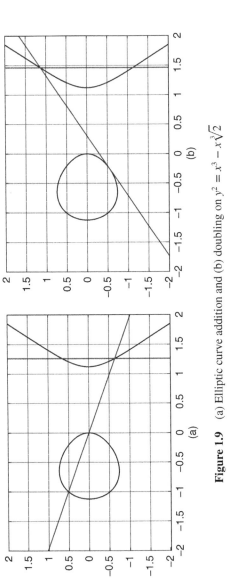

Figure 1.9 (a) Elliptic curve addition and (b) doubling on $y^2 = x^3 - x\sqrt[3]{2}$

3. *Compute $P \oplus Q$ and check that it belongs to the curve.*
4. *Compute $[2]P$, the doubling of P, and check that it belongs to the curve.*
5. *Compute $[2]Q$, the doubling of Q, and check that it belongs to the curve.*

Solution on page 290.

Once again, this law of addition can be generalized in characteristics 2 and 3 as given in Table 1.6.

Moreover, note that using any of these addition laws, the algorithm for multiplication by an integer remains almost exactly Algorithm 1.5, page 41, where multiplications are replaced by $\oplus$ and squarings are replaced by doublings. In this setting, exponentiation by squaring (or square-and-multiply) is often called *double-and-add*.

Exercise 1.29 *Let $\mathbb{E}(7; -1, 1)$ and $P = (1, 1)$, compute $[6]P$ with only three operations.*
Solution on page 290.

Note that there exists many other coordinate systems, such as projective and Jacobian, which differ in the number of multiplications, squarings, additions, or inversions in the base field, for the same group law. The choice of system depends on the respective speed of these operations and the target architecture. Note also that for certain subset of curves, such as Edwards curves, the coordinate system can be simplified, often leading to practical enhancements.

The US National Institute of Standards and Technology (NIST) recommends some elliptic curves[4], which contains a large number of points, with sizes ranging

TABLE 1.6 **Group Laws in Characteristics 2 and 3 with $P = (x_1, y_1) \neq -P$ and $Q = (x_2, y_2) \neq \pm P$**

p	Curve	Addition	Doubling
2	$y^2 + xy = x^3 + ax^2 + b$	$\lambda = \dfrac{y_2 + y_1}{x_2 + x_1}$	$\lambda = \dfrac{y_1}{x_1} + x_1$
		$(\lambda^2 + \lambda + x_1 + x_2 + a,$	$(\lambda^2 + \lambda + a,$
	opposite: $(x_1, y_1 + x_1)$	$\lambda(x_1 + x_3) + y_1 + x_3)$	$\lambda(x_1 + x_3) + y_1 + x_3)$
	$y^2 + cy = x^3 + ax + b$	$\lambda = \dfrac{y_2 + y_1}{x_2 + x_1}$	$\lambda = \dfrac{x_1^2 + a}{c}$
		$(\lambda^2 + x_1 + x_2,$	$(\lambda^2,$
	opposite: $(x_1, y_1 + c)$	$\lambda(x_1 + x_3) + y_1 + c)$	$\lambda(x_1 + x_3) + y_1 + c)$
3	$y^2 = x^3 + ax^2 + b$	$\lambda = \dfrac{y_2 - y_1}{x_2 - x_1}$	$\lambda = a\dfrac{x_1}{y_1}$
		$(\lambda^2 - x_1 - x_2 - a,$	$(\lambda^2 + x_1 - a,$
	opposite: $(x_1, -y_1)$	$\lambda(x_1 - x_3) - y_1)$	$\lambda(x_1 - x_3) - y_1)$
	$y^2 = x^3 + ax + b$	$\lambda = \dfrac{y_2 - y_1}{x_2 - x_1}$	$\lambda = -\dfrac{a}{y_1}$
		$(\lambda^2 - x_1 - x_2,$	$(\lambda^2 + x_1,$
	opposite: $(x_1, -y_1)$	$\lambda(x_1 - x_3) - y_1)$	$\lambda(x_1 - x_3) - y_1)$

[4] http://csrc.nist.gov/publications/fips/fips186-3/fips_186-3.pdf

from 2^{160} to 2^{570}. Many other databases exist, let us mention Bernstein and Lange's Explicit-Formula database[5] and the Acrypta database[6], which contains some Edwards curves.

1.3.7   Pseudo-Random Number Generators (PRNG)

Generation of random numbers is widely used in all the methods we have just seen and will be often used in the sequel. In particular, generating numbers randomly is a condition for the perfection of Vernam's OTP scheme (see page 15). Now, it is time to look more deeply at this problem which needs some development.

The definition of randomness is crucial in coding. Indeed, any message presenting some kind of organization (organization is supposed to be the opposite of randomness) is an angle of attack for compression and code breaking. Therefore, one should rely on a solid theory concerning randomness in order to build secure and efficient codes.

Producing a truly random event is unsolvable by computers – which by definition only respond to determined and predictable processes. In order to obtain values produced by "true" randomness (even if this notion is not completely absolute and refers to what one can observe and predict), one has to call upon assumed unpredictable physical phenomena, such as thermal noise or the description of the Brownian motion of electrons in a resistor.

However, this production of numbers may be called randomness only because we are not able – given our current knowledge in these areas – to explain their mechanisms and because only probabilistic theories enable us to grasp them. With computers, we wish to proceed in the same way in order to generate random numbers. We apply some procedures that make the result unpredictable in practice. This is what we call pseudo-random generation.

Production of random numbers is a very complicated task that has attracted the attention of both machine designers ("hardware" components, such as thermal noise) and software designers ("software" products, see examples in the next section) for some time. One must pay attention to this main issue because there exist some efficient methods (we will study some of them) that enable one to detect nonrandom features in a sequence, which is supposed to be random, to recover the method that produced it, and then to break a randomly generated key. If the machine that generates the winning lotto combination were not based on some good random generation process, one would be able to predict the next winning combination.

One often generates a sequence of pseudo-random numbers by computing each number from the previous one (which obviously makes the process completely deterministic and eliminates all randomness), in such a significantly complicated way that – examining the sequence without knowing the method – one could believe that it was truly generated randomly.

---

[5]http://hyperelliptic.org/EFD/index.html
[6]http://galg.acrypta.com/telechargements/ARCANA_ECDB.tgz

A generator must satisfy certain properties to be called a pseudo-random generator. All generated numbers have to be independent from each other. Moreover, they must have a great entropy, and hopefully no rule can be recovered from the sequence of generated numbers. There are several ways to determine whether a generator is acceptable. First of all, one has to make it pass some statistical tests in order to check that the distribution it produces does not significantly differ from the one expected from a theoretical model of randomness. Besides, one can also use algorithmic complexity principles: that is show that in reasonable time no algorithm will be able to predict the mechanisms of the generator.

For example, one can build a generator based on the model of Fibonacci's sequence, by producing the numbers $x_n = x_{n-1} + x_{n-2} \mod m$, m being the maximum integer that can be produced. The main advantages of this method are the following: it is very easy to implement, very fast in execution, and "modulo" operation enables one to obtain some hard-to-predict behavior for the generator. However, this generator – like most typical and simple generators – has drawbacks, and it is possible to recover its behavior based on statistical analysis.

The requirements for a pseudo-random generator are very similar to the properties one expects from a ciphertext. Indeed, it must be impossible, when receiving a message or a number, to find out the way it was produced without knowing the key. That is why some methods for random number generation look like cryptographic methods or use them.

1.3.7.1 Congruential Generators

One says that a generator is a Linear Congruential Generator (LCG) if it satisfies the following principle: if x_i, $i \in \mathbb{N}$ is the sequence of generated random numbers, one calculates x_i from its predecessor: $x_i = ax_{i-1} + b \mod m$, with m a large number, and $a, b \in \mathbb{Z}/m\mathbb{Z}$. The generator is called multiplicative if $b = 0$. Such a sequence is always periodic; thus, one will have to choose a, b, m such that the period is significantly high. For example, for $m = 10, x_0 = a = b = 7$, the period is 4. Hence, this generator is not satisfactory at all.

The maximum period is obviously m. There exists a result providing a description of all generators of period m with $b = 0$:

Theorem 12 *The Linear Congruential Generator defined by $a, b = 0, m, x_0$ is of period m if and only if x_0 is coprime with m and a is a primitive root of m.*

One usually chooses m as the greatest prime number which can be given by a machine (we have seen how to generate such a number on page 44). Obviously, a large period is not a sufficient criterion for the production of random generators (consider the choice $a = 1, b = 1$). Exercise 1.42, on page 85, is an approach to methods of attacking LCGs.

1.3.7.2 Linear Feedback Shift Register (LFSR)

One can generalize Linear Congruential Generators using not only the previous value to build the next element in the sequence but also several previous values, namely x_n is computed from linear combinations of $x_{n-1}, \ldots, x_{n-k}$. In other words:

$$x_n = (a_1 x_{n-1} + \ldots + a_k x_{n-k}) \quad \text{mod } m.$$

These generators are particularly interesting if m is a prime number because their maximum period is then $m^k - 1$, and this maximum is reached, see Theorem 13. Hence, it is possible, even with a small modulo, to have very large periods.

For example, in order to generate random sequences of bits, one chooses $m = 2$. In this case, the operations can be performed very quickly on a machine with "eXclusive ORs" (xor) for the addition modulo 2 and with shifts on the bits x_i to generate the next bits. There even exist specialized chips performing the necessary operations. Then, one talks about Linear Feedback Shift Register (LFSR). Figure 1.10 summarizes their mechanisms.

For some computations, it is interesting to write an LFSR in a polynomial form: set $\Pi(X) = X^k - a_1 X^{k-1} - \ldots - a_k$.

Hence, $LFSR_\Pi(x_0, \ldots, x_{k-1})$ refers to the infinite sequence of bits x_i linearly generated by the polynomial Π, having the first k initial values set to $x_0, \ldots, x_{k-1}$.

Exercise 1.30 *Write the first eight values generated by the following shift register:*

$$LFSR_{X^4+X^3+X^2+1}(0, 1, 1, 0)$$

Solution on page 290.

Finally, we have the equivalent of Theorem 12 for LCG with the primitive root replaced by a primitive polynomial.

Theorem 13 *For some polynomial Π of degree k, the $LFSR_\Pi$ modulo a prime number p is of maximum period $p^k - 1$ if and only if Π is a primitive polynomial in $\mathbb{F}_p[X]$.*

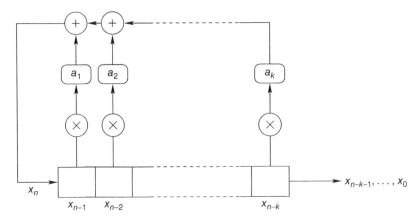

Figure 1.10 Functional diagram of an LFSR

These generators are quite fast. Besides, they have also a very large period. However, we will see in Section 1.4.3.2 that the Berlekamp–Massey algorithm enables one to predict the following bits without knowing the generator polynomial, provided that $2k$ successive values have been intercepted.

These generators are used in practice to generate quickly some bits with good statistical properties but they have to be combined with other generators to be cryptographically secure.

Example 1.9 (Securing the *Bluetooth* Protocol) *Bluetooth* is a short-range wireless technology whose aim is to simplify the connections between electronic equipment. It was designed to replace the wires between computers and their devices such as printers, scanners, mice, cell-phones, pocket-PCs, or even numerical cameras.

In order to make this protocol safe, one uses some kind of Vernam encryption scheme (Section 1.2.1) but with a pseudo-random generator based on LFSR: the encryption algorithm uses four LFSRs of respective length 25, 31, 33, and 39 for an overall $25 + 31 + 33 + 39 = 128$ bits. The 128 bits of the initial value represent the secret key of *Bluetooth* encryption. Figure 1.11 shows the functional diagram of this encryption scheme.

We notice that the four polynomials that are used are as follows:

- $X^{39} + X^{36} + X^{28} + X^4 + 1$;
- $X^{33} + X^{28} + X^{24} + X^4 + 1$;
- $X^{31} + X^{24} + X^{16} + X^{12} + 1$;
- $X^{25} + X^{20} + X^{12} + X^8 + 1$.

These four polynomials are primitive polynomials in $\mathbb{F}_2[X]$ for an overall period of $\operatorname{lcm}(2^{39} - 1, 2^{33} - 1, 2^{31} - 1, 2^{25} - 1) = 7 \cdot 23 \cdot 31 \cdot 79 \cdot 89 \cdot 601 \cdot 1801 \cdot 8191 \cdot 121369 \cdot 599479 \cdot 2147483647 \approx 2^{125}$.

The 4 bits $\{a; b; c; d\}$ produced by these four successive LFSRs are then combined using a nonlinear discrete function f which produces the next bit z_t on the output, from its initial state $(\{cl_{-1}; ch_{-1}; cl_0; ch_0\} = IV \in \{0,1\}^4)$ and the successive values

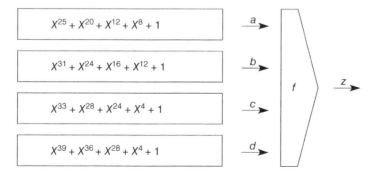

Figure 1.11 *Bluetooth* encryption

of the LFSR, according to the following algorithm:

1. $z_t = a_t \oplus b_t \oplus c_t \oplus d_t \oplus cl_t$ (operations over $\mathbb{F}_2$);
2. $s_{t+1} = \lfloor \frac{a_t + b_t + c_t + d_t + 2ch_t + cl_t}{2} \rfloor \in [0, 3]$ (operations over $\mathbb{Z}$);
3. sl_{t+1} and sh_{t+1}) are the 2 bits encoding $s_{t+1} \in [0, 3]$;
4. $cl_{t+1} = sl_{t+1} \oplus cl_t \oplus cl_{t-1} \oplus ch_{t-1}$ (operations over $\mathbb{F}_2$); and
5. $ch_{t+1} = sh_{t+1} \oplus ch_t \oplus cl_{t-1}$ (operations over $\mathbb{F}_2$).

1.3.7.3 Cryptographically Secure Generators One can use the principle of
a one-way function, namely a function easy to compute but difficult to invert
(computation in unreasonable time), to determine the quality of a generator.

The formal definition of a good quality generator is as follows. Given a generator
and a finite sequence of bits it has generated, if it is possible, without knowing the
method, to predict with good probability and in reasonable time the next bit of the
sequence, then the generator cannot be considered as a random generator. Here, a
good probability means significantly greater than a random guess, that is, $\frac{1}{2}$ for a
sequence of bits.

If one is able to prove that there exists no efficient algorithm performing this pre-
diction, then the generator is called *cryptographic* or *cryptographically secure*.

For example, the Blum–Micali generator proceeds in the following way:

- Generate a large prime number p.
- Let α be a primitive root of p (a generator of the group of invertible elements
  in $\mathbb{F}_p$).
- Let f be the modular exponentiation function $f(x) = \alpha^x \mod p$.
- Let B be the function with values in $\{0, 1\}$ defined by:
  - $B(x) = 1$ if $0 \leq log_\alpha x \leq (p-1)/2$;
  - $B(x) = 0$ if $log_\alpha x > (p-1)/2$.

The pseudo-random sequence of bits $b_1 \ldots b_k$ is then computed from the sequence
$x_0, x_1, \ldots, x_k$, with x_0 any nonzero element in $\mathbb{F}_p$ and $x_i \leftarrow f(x_{i-1})$ for $i > 0$. One sets
$b_i = B(x_i)$.

The function B is easy to compute: we have seen in the previous subsections how
to generate a prime number, how to find a primitive root, and how to carry out modular
exponentiation. Finally, when computing B, one has the value of $log_\alpha x$ using $f(x) = \alpha^x$
mod p that has just been calculated. However, without the sequence $x_0, x_1, \ldots, x_k$, one
can prove that finding $B(x_i)$ is as difficult as computing the discrete logarithm. As we
do not know any efficient algorithm solving the discrete logarithm problem, it is a
difficult problem. Therefore, the generator is cryptographically secure.

1.3.7.4 Several Statistical Tests The previous methods are based on the
well-known algorithmic difficulty of some problems, which makes it impossible to
predict the behavior of generators. In order to measure the quality of a generator,

one can also examine the sequences generated, and test whether they diverge from what we expect from a truly random generator. This is a difficult task as the criteria are numerous and are not necessarily trivial.

Statistics provide us with an adequate tool for these tests. For example, the χ^2 test enables one to measure the deviance with respect to an expected uniform discrete law.

For all characters v_i in the alphabet V, one has the expected probability p_i and the number e_i of occurrences in the generated sequence of size n. The expected frequencies are never exactly equal to the empiric frequencies. Therefore, one has to set the threshold of divergence from which the generator is no longer considered as random.

One has to keep in mind that, when considering a random generator, all sequences are possible *a priori*, even those whose distribution is completely different from the expected one because the generator is actually random. These sequences are only very unlikely to appear. If one observes such sequences in the output of a generator, then the generator is probably not so good (even if these sequences can theoretically appear in the output of a good generator). Here is how the χ^2 test works.

One measures the gap between the expected distribution and the observed distribution using the parameter:

$$K = \sum_{i=1}^{n} \frac{(e_i - np_i)^2}{np_i}.$$

Now, it remains to determine the acceptable values for the parameter K. They are given by the tables of the χ^2, of which we give an extract in Table 1.7.

In this table, the first column gives the number of "degrees of liberty." One sets this number to the value $|V| - 1$. Namely, for an alphabet of size 21, the line number 20. The first line gives the probability of having the value K lower than the value of the table. For example, the probability of having K greater than 24.72 for an alphabet of size 12 is 0.01.

Exercise 1.31 (χ^2 test)   *A pseudo-random generator which is supposed to generate numbers between 0 and 10 according to a uniform law gives the sequence: 0 0 5 2 3 6 4 2 0 2 3 8 9 5 1 2 2 3 4 1 2.*

TABLE 1.7 χ^2 Table (Extract)

Degrees of liberty	$p = 0.75$	$p = 0.95$	$p = 0.99$
9	11.39	16.92	21.67
10	12.55	18.31	23.21
11	13.70	19.68	24.72
12	14.85	21.03	26.22
15	18.25	25.00	30.58
20	23.83	31.41	37.57
30	34.80	43.77	50.89

Perform the χ^2 test on this sequence. What do you think of this generator? What do you think of the test?   *Solution on page 290.*

Obviously, such a test – although it can be useful and sufficient to reject a generator – is not sufficient to accept a generator. For example, it will not be able to reject the sequence 123456123456123456, whereas a not-so-drilled eye will notice the regularity in it (although one should distrust the impression of regularity one can have looking at a sequence, as it can be biased by false intuitions on what is actually true randomness).

One can, for example, strengthen this test by applying it to the extensions of the source induced by the message (Section 1.2.3.4). There exist numerous statistical tests reinforcing the trust one could have concerning a generator. It is important to notice that each test enables one to reject a generator, but only the set of all tests will enable one to accept it (besides, without mathematical rigor). There is no guarantee that – after succeeding in x tests – the generator will not reveal itself to be weak under the $(x + 1)$th test.

1.4   DECODING, DECRYPTION, ATTACKS

To conclude this introductory chapter, we develop encoding methods adopting the point of view of the inverse operation, decoding. We have already seen that, for many reasons, decoding – which consists in inverting the encoding functions – is not a trivial task:

- as in the fax code we detailed at the beginning of this chapter, if the ciphertext is a sequence of bits, recovering the source message without ambiguity by parsing the sequence into blocks requires a particular form of the code;

- an exact decoding is sometimes not even completely attainable, if the encoding method does not include all the initial information, when performing a compression for example; we have seen that the fax image loses in quality; there exist many encoding methods "with loss," which makes encoding and decoding asymmetrics;

- we have seen that the principle of one-way functions makes the computation of the encoding function and the decoding function completely different; it may happen that there is an efficient algorithm for one of them but not for the other.

We are going to develop all these aspects, using the word *decoding* as a general term allowing one to recover the source from a codeword, the word *decryption* for cryptographic decoding, and the words *breaking* or *attack* for an unauthorized decryption, namely when the recipient is the only one possessing the information.

1.4.1   Decoding without Ambiguity

The first virtue of a code is its ability to be decoded. This is obvious, but not necessarily a trivial issue.

Let us suppose that the code is a bijective function, which transforms the message written by the sender into a message transmitted through the channel. For a source message $a_1...a_n$, a string over any source alphabet, and for a code alphabet V, let us denote by f the encoding function. Then, one has the codeword $c_1...c_n = f(a_1)...f(a_n)$, with $c_i \in V^+$ for all i. The *code*, seen as the set of all codewords, is then the image of the encoding function f. However, f being bijective is not enough for the message to be decoded without ambiguity by the recipient.

As an example, let us consider the encoding of the 26 alphabet letters $S = \{A, ..., Z\}$ using integers $C = \{0, ..., 25\}$ written in base 10:

$$f(A) = 0, \; f(B) = 1, ..., f(J) = 9, \; f(K) = 10, \; f(L) = 11, ..., f(Z) = 25.$$

Then, the codeword 1209 may correspond to several messages: for example, BUJ, MAJ, or BCAJ.

Thus, in order to avoid such a problem, one has to add some constraints on the code for any message to be decoded without ambiguity. That is to say, when receiving a codeword, the recipient has to be able to recover a *unique* message from it. A code C over an alphabet V is called *nonambiguous* (one sometimes says *uniquely decodable*) if, for all $x = x_1 ... x_n \in V^+$, there exists at most one sequence $c = c_1 ... c_m \in C^+$ such that

$$c_1 ... c_m = x_1 ... x_n.$$

The following property is just a simple reformulation:

Property 8 *A code C over an alphabet V is nonambiguous if and only if for all sequences $c = c_1 ... c_n$ and $d = d_1 ... d_m$ in C^+:*

$$c = d \implies (n = m \text{ and } c_i = d_i \text{ for all } i = 1, ..., n).$$

Example 1.10 (Over the Alphabet $V = \{0, 1\}$)

- the code $C = \{0, 01, 001\}$ is not uniquely decodable.
- the code $C = \{01, 10\}$ is uniquely decodable.
- the code $C = \{0, 10, 110\}$ is uniquely decodable.

The decoding constraint implies that all codewords should have a minimum length. Kraft's theorem gives a necessary and sufficient condition on the length of codewords to insure the existence of a uniquely decodable code.

Theorem 14 (Kraft) *There exists a uniquely decodable code over some alphabet V with n codewords of length $l_1, ..., l_n$ if and only if*

$$\sum_{i=1}^{n} \frac{1}{|V|^{l_i}} \leq 1.$$

Proof. ($\Rightarrow$) Let C be a uniquely decodable code, of arity q (the vocabulary of the code contains q characters). Let m be the length of the longest word in C. For $1 \leq k \leq m$, let r_k be the number of words of length k. One develops the following expression, for any integer u, with $u \geq 1$:

$$\left(\sum_{i=1}^{n} \frac{1}{q^{l_i}} \right)^u = \left(\sum_{k=1}^{m} \frac{r_k}{q^k} \right)^u.$$

Once developed, each term of this sum is of the form $\frac{r_{i_1} \dots r_{i_u}}{q^{i_1 + \dots + i_u}}$. Then, by regrouping for each value $s = i_1 + \dots + i_u$, one obtains the terms $\sum_{i_1 + \dots + i_u = s} \frac{r_{i_1} \dots r_{i_u}}{q^s}$. Set $N(s) = \sum_{i_1 + \dots + i_u = s} r_{i_1} \dots r_{i_u}$. The initial expression can be written as follows:

$$\left(\sum_{i=1}^{n} \frac{1}{q^{l_i}} \right)^u = \sum_{s=u}^{mu} \frac{N(s)}{q^s}.$$

Notice that $N(s)$ is the number of combinations of words in C whose overall length is equal to s. As C is uniquely decodable, two combinations of words in C cannot be equal to the same word over the alphabet of C. As C is of arity q, and $N(s)$ is lower than the overall number of messages of length s on this alphabet, one has $N(s) \leq q^s$. This implies that

$$\left(\sum_{i=1}^{n} \frac{1}{q^{l_i}} \right)^u \leq mu - u + 1 \leq mu.$$

Thus, $\sum_{i=1}^{n} \frac{1}{q^{l_i}} \leq (mu)^{1/u}$, and $\sum_{i=1}^{n} \frac{1}{q^{l_i}} \leq 1$ when u tends toward infinity. ($\Leftarrow$) The reciprocal proposition is a consequence of McMillan's theorem, which is studied later on in this chapter.

$\square$

1.4.1.1 Prefix Property One says that a code C over an alphabet V has the *prefix property* (one sometimes says that it is *instantaneous*, or *irreducible*) if and only if for all pairs of distinct codewords (c_1, c_2), c_2 is not a prefix of c_1.

Example 1.11 $a = 101000, b = 01, c = 1010$: b is not a prefix of a. However, c is a prefix of a.

If the prefix property applies, one is able to decode the words of such a code as soon as one has received the whole word (instantaneousness), which is not always the case with uniquely decodable codes: for instance, if $V = 0, 01, 11$, and one receives message $m = 001111111111 \dots$. Then one will have to wait for the next occurrence of a 0 to be able to decode the second word (0 or 01?).

Property 9 *Any code having the prefix property is uniquely decodable.*

Proof. Let C be a code over V that is not uniquely decodable and has the prefix property. Then there exists a string $a \in V^n$ such that $a = c_1 \ldots c_l = d_1 \ldots d_k$, with c_i and d_i codewords of C and $c_i \neq d_i$ for at least one index i. Let us choose the minimum index i such that $c_i \neq d_i$ (for all $j < i$, $c_j = d_j$). Then $length(c_i) \neq length(d_i)$, otherwise, given the choice of i, one would have $c_i = d_i$, which contradicts the definition of i. If $length(c_i) < length(d_i)$, then c_i is a prefix of d_i. Otherwise, d_i is a prefix of c_i. Thus, C does not have the prefix property. $\qquad\qquad\qquad\qquad\qquad\qquad\qquad$ □

The reciprocal proposition is false: indeed, the code $C = \{0, 01\}$ is uniquely decodable but it does not have the prefix property. The following property is obvious, but it insures the decoding ability for some widely used kinds of codes.

Property 10 *If all the words of some code are of the same length, then it has the prefix property.*

Exercise 1.32 *Let S be the source of alphabet $\{a, b, c, d\}$ with probabilities:*

S	a	b	c	d
$P(S)$	0.5	0.25	0.125	0.125

One encodes S using the following codes:

a	b	c	d
0	10	110	111

1. *Encode adbccab. Decode 1001101010.*
2. *Is it an instantaneous code?*
3. *Compute the entropy of the source.*

Solution on page 291.

Exercise 1.33 *We wish to build a binary compression code over a source $S = (S, P)$ (supposed to be infinite) where $S = (0, 1)$ is the source alphabet and $P = (P(0) = p, P(1) = 1 - p)$ is the probability law of S.*

One proposes the following code: one enumerates the number of occurrences of "0" before the appearance of "1." The two encoding rules are as follows:

- *A string of four consecutive "0"s (without "1") is encoded with 0.*
- *If less than four "0s" appear before a symbol "1," one encodes the string with the codeword "$1e_1e_2$," e_1e_2 being the binary representation of the number of "0s" before the symbol "1."*

For instance, the appearance of four consecutive zeros "0000" is encoded with "0," whereas the string "001" is encoded with "110" because two "0"s appear before the symbol "1" (and "10" is the binary representation of 2).

1. *Write explicitly the five codewords of this compression code. Does this code have the prefix property?*

2. *Knowing that the probability of appearance of two successive symbols s_1 and s_2 is – when supposing that the source is without memory – $p(s_1) * p(s_2)$, compute the probability of occurrence in S of a string composed of k "0"s followed by a "1."*

3. *For each codeword, compute the number of bits of code required per bit of the source. Deduce the* compression rate *of this code, namely the* mean length per bit of the source.

Solution on page 291.

1.4.1.2 Huffman Trees A Huffman tree is an object that enables one to easily represent all codes having the prefix property, and this representation makes their manipulation a lot easier. Here, we give the definitions in the binary case. However, these can be extended to codes of any arity.

One calls a *Huffman tree* a binary tree such that any subtree has either 0 or 2 sons (the tree is locally complete). One assigns the symbol "1" to the edge connecting the local root to the left subtree and "0" to the edge connecting the local root to the right subtree.

To each leaf of a Huffman tree, one can associate a word in $\{0, 1\}^+$: it is a string composed of the symbols marking the edges of the path from the root to the leaf.

The maximum length of the words in a Huffman tree is called the *depth* of the tree. One calls a *Huffman code* the set of words corresponding to the paths in a Huffman tree; the depth of this tree is also called *depth* of the code C.

Example 1.12 (Code corresponding to the tree of Figure 1.12)

$$\{111, 110, 10, 0111, 0110, 010, 001, 0001, 0000\}.$$

1.4.1.3 Representation of Instantaneous Codes The introduction of Huffman trees is justified by the two following properties, which enable one to manipulate instantaneous codes with such trees.

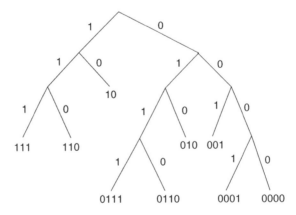

Figure 1.12 Example of a Huffman tree

Property 11 *A Huffman code has the prefix property.*

Proof. If a codeword c_1 is a prefix of c_2, then the path representing c_1 in the Huffman tree is included in the path representing c_2. As c_1 and c_2 are, by definition, associated with the leaves of the tree, $c_1 = c_2$. Thus, there do not exist two different codewords such that one of them is a prefix of the other. Hence, the Huffman code has the prefix property. □

Property 12 *Any code having the prefix property is included in a Huffman code.*

Proof. Let us consider a complete Huffman tree (all leaves are at the same distance from the root) of depth l (the length of the longest word in C). Each codeword c_i in C is associated to a path from the root to a node. Then, one can prune the subtree having this node as a root (all the words that could be represented in the nodes of this subtree would have c_i as a prefix). All other codewords in C remain in the nodes of the resulting tree. It is possible to perform the same operation for all the other words. One eventually obtain a Huffman tree containing all codewords in C. □

1.4.1.4 McMillan's Theorem We have seen that Huffman trees enable one to represent all instantaneous codes. However, they do not enable one to represent all uniquely decodable codes. McMillan's theorem insures that one can avoid the use of uniquely decodable codes (nonambiguous) not having the prefix property. Indeed, there always exists another code that has the prefix property with the same lengths of codewords. Therefore, nothing can be gained by using ambiguous codes.

Theorem 15 (McMillan) *Over an alphabet V, there exists a code having the prefix property whose codewords $\{c_1, \ldots, c_n\}$ are of length $l_1, \ldots, l_n$ if and only if*

$$\sum_{i=1}^{n} \frac{1}{|V|^{l_i}} \leq 1.$$

Exercise 1.34 *Using the representation of instantaneous codes with Huffman trees, give a proof of McMillan's theorem.* Solution on page 291.

Corollary 1 *If there exists a uniquely decodable code whose words are of length $l_1, \ldots, l_n$, then there exists an instantaneous code whose words are of the same length.*

This is a consequence of Kraft's and McMillan's theorems. All decodable codes not having the prefix property do not produce codes with shorter words than instantaneous codes; therefore, one can limit oneself to the latter codes for information compression (their properties make them easier to use).

1.4.2 Noninjective Codes

All codes do not insure a nonambiguous decoding and are not even bijective. It might happen, for several reasons, that encoding functions only process a *digest* (or a *fingerprint*) of a message, or only the information which is considered to be sufficient for the needs of transmission. For instance, fingerprints are used for error detection: when receiving a message and its fingerprint, the recipient is able to check that the overall message has not been modified during the transmission by recomputing the fingerprint from the message he has received and comparing it to the fingerprint that was transmitted.

Lossy compression is used, for example, in processing images or sounds. The information is encoded in a way that will enable one to retrieve maybe only a variation of the original data. The differences should be slight enough so that they are not perceptible (for human ear or eye) or so that the new data is still useful.

1.4.2.1 Fingerprint Integrity Check

1.4.2.1 Fingerprint Integrity Check   The most simple principle of error detection is an example of fingerprint computation. We have seen an example of this kind of encoding with the fax code, even if the code we added to each line did not depend on the content of the line. Besides, this only had a limited detection capacity.

The first principle of fingerprints for error detection is the addition of a simple *parity bit* to the cipherblocks. For a word $m = s_1 \ldots s_k$, the parity bit is equal to $b(m) = (\sum_{i=1}^{k} s_i) \mod 2$. Obviously, this equality is false when an odd number of bits change their value in the set "message+fingerprint." Hence, the addition of a parity bit enables one to detect errors on a odd number of bits. We will see this mechanism in more detail in Chapter 4, in particular in Figure 4.2 on page 212.

1.4.2.2 Hash Functions

1.4.2.2 Hash Functions   The hash function follows the same principle, but it encodes a more evolved fingerprint, as it is meant to identify the message. This is the definition of a summary of the message, which will enable one not to recover it, but to identify it using a correspondence table. This works as a human fingerprint, which does not enable one to reconstitute the other characteristics of an individual but which enables one to identify him.

Hash functions are particularly useful in cryptography. They notably enable one to decrease the amount of information to be encrypted. If the image of x by the hash function is called the *fingerprint* of x, one can – for example – encrypt only the fingerprint. Moreover, they enable one to set up electronic signature and message authentication protocols (see Section 3.5.3) and also to check the integrity of a document, in the same way as the parity bit (which is a particular hash function). Formally, a *hash function* $H : \{0,1\}^* \longrightarrow \{0,1\}^n$ is an application that transforms a string of any size into a string of fixed size n, as illustrated in Figure 1.13.

One talks about a *collision* between x and x' when

$$\begin{cases} x \neq x' \\ H(x) = H(x'). \end{cases}$$

Considering that the input of a hash function can be of any size (in particular $> n$), collisions are inevitable. If y is such that $y = H(x)$, then x is called the *preimage* of y (one recalls that y is the *fingerprint* of x).

One of the basic constraints in setting up a hash function is efficiency: a fingerprint must be easy to compute. Besides, hash functions have a natural compression property.

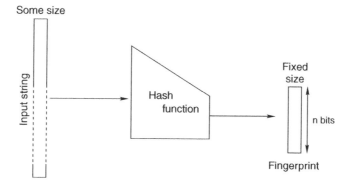

Figure 1.13   Principle of a hash function

Other properties can be expected:

- **Preimage resistant**: given y, one cannot find – in reasonable time – some x such that $y = H(x)$.
- **Second preimage resistant**: given x, one cannot find – in reasonable time – $x' \neq x$ such that $H(x) = H(x')$;
- **Collision resistant**: one can not find in reasonable time – x and x' such that $H(x) = H(x')$;

A *one-way* hash function is a hash function satisfying the properties of preimage resistance and second preimage resistance.

Exercise 1.35 (Security of Hash Functions)   *Prove, using the contrapositive proposition, that collision resistance implies second preimage resistance, which implies preimage resistance.*   *Solution on page 292.*

Exercise 1.36 (A Bad Hash Functionxs)   *Let $f : \mathbb{F}_2^m \to \mathbb{F}_2^m$ be any function. One proposes an iterative hash function $g : \mathbb{F}_2^{2m} \to \mathbb{F}_2^m$, such that, for some x of size $2m$ bits, divided into two blocks x_h and x_l, one has $g(x) = g(x_h||x_l) = f(x_h \oplus x_l)$ where $x_h||x_l$ is the concatenation of x_h and x_l. Prove that g is not second preimage resistant.*
                                                                              Solution on page 292.

Hash functions can be used for

- Manipulation Detection Code (MDC) that enable one to check the integrity of a message (in the manner of parity bits);
- MAC that manage both the integrity and the authentication of the source of data.

We will see several examples of such applications in Chapter 3.

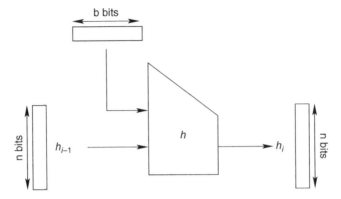

Figure 1.14   Compression function of a hash function

Construction of a Merkle–Damgård hash function. One of the most famous construc-tions of hash functions relies on a compression function

$$h : \{0,1\}^b \times \{0,1\}^n \longrightarrow \{0,1\}^n.$$

Such a function is illustrated in Figure 1.14.

Message M is split into blocks of b bits $M_1, \ldots, M_k$ (one will possibly have to add some padding bits for the size of M to be divisible by b).

One iterates the compression function h according to the scheme presented in Figure 1.15.

IV (Initial Value) is a string (of size n) fixed by the algorithm or the implemen-tation. A theorem – which was proved independently by Ralph Merkle and Ivan Damgård – enables one to describe the theoretical properties of such a construction:

Theorem 16 (Merkle–Damgård)   *If h is collision resistant, then so is H (Figure 1.15).*

It is this result that actually makes Merkle–Damgård construction the most used construction in fingerprint computation.

Exercise 1.37   *Prove Merkle–Damgård's theorem using the contrapositive propo-sition.*   *Solution on page 292.*

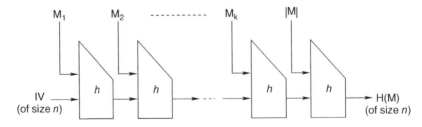

Figure 1.15   Merkle–Damgård construction

Exercise 1.38 (Construction by Composition) *Let* $f : \mathbb{F}_2^{2m} \rightarrow \mathbb{F}_2^{m}$ *be a hash function and let* $h : \mathbb{F}_2^{4m} \rightarrow \mathbb{F}_2^{m}$ *another hash function such that, if* $x_1, x_2 \in \mathbb{F}_2^{2m}$, *then* $h(x_1 || x_2) = f(f(x_1) || f(x_2))$, *|| standing for the concatenation operation.*

1. *Prove that if* f *is collision resistant, then so is h.*
2. *What is the drawback of this construction ?*

Solution on page 293.

Hence, one only needs to make explicit the construction of compression functions h, which are collision resistant. For instance, the Davies–Meyer construction (Figure 1.16) defines $h_i = E_{M_i}(h_{i-1}) \oplus h_{i-1}$, where E_{M_i} is a symmetric block encryption function.

But an attack on preimage resistance was set up by Drew Dean in 1999, who exploited the existence of fixed points in this construction. Therefore, compression functions using this construction are less robust.

The Miyaguchi–Preneel construction (Figure 1.17) is an improvement on the previous construction and is particularly robust from a cryptographic point of view.

Function g adapts the construction to the size of the key of the encryption function E. Hence, one has $h_i = E_{g(h_{i-1})}(M_i) \oplus h_{i-1} \oplus M_i$.

Galois hashing. Another popular hash function is GHASH, for Galois hashing, which uses multiplication in the field with 2^{128} elements and Horner scheme. The idea is to choose an element h of $\mathbb{F}_{2^{128}}$ where the field is usually build as polynomials modulo 2 and modulo the primitive polynomial $X^{128} + X^7 + X^2 + X + 1$. Then, a message m is cut into $d + 1$ blocks m_i of 128 bits and each block is considered as a coefficient of the reverse polynomial $\sum m_{d-i} Y^i$. The hash value is obtained as the evaluation of this polynomial in h via Algorithm 1.7, where each block $m_i = b_0 \ldots b_{127}$ is considered

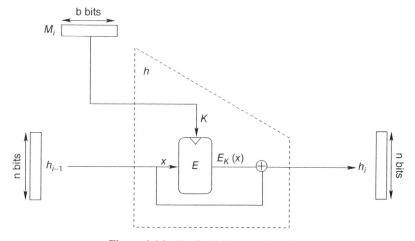

Figure 1.16 Davies–Meyer construction

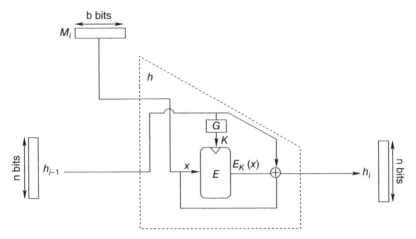

Figure 1.17   Miyaguchi–Preneel construction

as the element $m_i(X) = \sum_{j=0}^{127} b_j X^j \in \mathbb{F}_{2^{128}} = \mathbb{F}_2[X]/\left(X^{128} + X^7 + X^2 + X + 1\right)$:

$$GHASH_h \; : \; (m_0, \dots, m_d) \hookrightarrow \sum_{i=0}^{d} m_{d-i} h^i \in \mathbb{F}_{2^{128}}.$$

Exercise 1.39 (Security of GHASH)

1. *Suppose that there exist i and j with $i < j$ such that for the chosen element of the $GHASH_h$ multiplication, we have $h^i \equiv h^j \in \mathbb{F}_{2^{128}}$. Deduce a way to build a collision in the hash function.*

2. *We know that $2^{128} - 1 = 3 \cdot 5 \cdot 17 \cdot 257 \cdot 641 \cdot 65537 \cdot 274177 \cdot 6700417 \cdot c_{14}$, with $c_{14} = 67280421310721$. How many possible distinct orders are there for elements of $\mathbb{F}_{2^{128}}$?*

3. *For a given h, with a given order o, what size of message would be required to obtain a collision using the first question?*

4. *If you were to choose an element h for the hashing, which elements would be best?*

5. *For a randomly chosen non zero element h, what is the probability that c_{14} does not divide its order?*

6. *If this is not the case what size of message would be required to obtain a collision using the first question?*

Solution on page 293.

1.4.2.3   Lossy Transformations   Other transformation processes end with a message encoded with loss and make full decoding impossible. For example, a fax is just a bad copy of the original image, but one sees that it fulfills its duty of transmitting the information contained in the document. One can also encode an image (respectively a sound) without keeping all the information, provided that the loss is not noticeable to the naked-eye (respectively to the ear).

Numerical information is, in essence, discrete information. We have seen that continuous or analogical data, like sounds and images, can be easily digitized. As for sounds, one can encode at each instant a frequency and an amplitude. For images, one decomposes them into pixels and encodes a color for each pixel.

Yet, this natural digitization might not be the best model for many codes. In images, for example, the colors of two contiguous pixels are often not independent, and it will be more judicious to encode a set of pixels as a function rather than a single pixel as a value. Therefore, one encodes blocks of pixels with a periodic (or almost periodic) function.

Hence, encoding happens to be performed on functions rather than on discrete or numerical entities, and this is the principle of the following section. Therefore, encoding will be a particular function, which will be applied to functions, and that we will call rather a *transform*, or a *transformation*.

1.4.2.4 Fourier Transform and Discrete Fourier Transform (DFT) Let us suppose that a message, or part of a message, can be formulated as a periodic and integrable function h (more precisely h should be in $\mathcal{L}^1(\mathbb{R})$), varying with respect to time t, and of period 2π. This happens with sounds. As we assume that h is periodic, the same message can be formulated as an amplitude H, varying with respect to a frequency f. The Fourier transform is an encoding process that enables one to switch from one representation another. Like any encoding process, it is associated to its inverse, decoding, and is formulated with the following formulas (Figure 1.18).

For a sound, even if the natural and immediate encoding is rather $h(t)$, one often uses $H(f)$ that encodes exactly the same information – as encoding is reversible – and is a lot cheaper, because it makes good use of the periodicity of h. Therefore, the Fourier transform is very efficient for compression.

The DFT follows the same principle but with discrete functions. This will obviously be very useful as – by essence – our numerical messages have to be encoded with discrete information. Now let us suppose that our functions $h(t)$ and $H(f)$ are discrete functions, that is to say some vectors $h_0, \ldots, h_{n-1}$ and $H_0, \ldots, H_{n-1}$ with discrete variables. One formulates the transformation by denoting $\omega = e^{-\frac{2i\pi}{n}}$ an nth root of unity. ω satisfies the equalities: $\sum_{k=0}^{n-1} \omega^k = \sum_{k=0}^{n-1} \left(e^{-\frac{2i\pi}{n}} \right)^k = \frac{e^{-\frac{2in\pi}{n}} - 1}{e^{-\frac{2i\pi}{n}} - 1} = 0$.

$$\text{Encoding: } H(f) = \int_{-\infty}^{+\infty} h(t)e^{-2i\pi ft}dt$$

$$\text{Decoding: } h(t) = \int_{-\infty}^{+\infty} H(f)e^{2i\pi ft}df$$

Figure 1.18 Fourier transform

$$\text{Encoding: } H_k = \frac{1}{\sqrt{n}} \sum_{j=0}^{n-1} h_j \omega^{kj} \qquad \text{Decoding: } h_j = \frac{1}{\sqrt{n}} \sum_{k=0}^{n-1} H_k \omega^{-kj}$$

Figure 1.19 Discrete Fourier Transform (DFT)

In other words following Figure 1.19, if $h(X) = \sum_{j=0}^{n-1} h_j X^j$, then

$$DFT(h) = [H_0, \ldots, H_{n-1}] = \frac{1}{\sqrt{n}} [h(\omega^0), \ldots, h(\omega^{n-1}).] \qquad (1.14)$$

Decoding is correct as

$$h_j = \frac{1}{\sqrt{n}} \sum_{k=0}^{n-1} \frac{1}{\sqrt{n}} \sum_{i=0}^{n-1} h_i \omega^{ki} \omega^{-kj} = \frac{1}{n} \sum_{i=0}^{n-1} h_i \sum_{k=0}^{n-1} (\omega^{i-j})^k = \frac{1}{n} \sum_{i=0}^{n-1} h_i \times \begin{cases} 0 & \text{if } i \neq j \\ n & \text{otherwise.} \end{cases}$$

The Discrete Cosine Transform (DCT) is a direct consequence of the DFT for some discrete function h. But instead of being time-varying (which is a good model for a sound), it is space varying (which enables one to encode an image); hence, h is a two-variable discrete function $h(x, y)$. For instance, it is the color of a pixel whose coordinates are x and y. In the same way, it is possible to represent differently the same information with a two-variable discrete function $H(i, j)$ standing for a *spectral* analysis of the image. The DCT and its inverse are shown in Figure 1.20, where $c(u) = 1$ whenever $u \neq 0$ and $c(0) = \frac{1}{\sqrt{2}}$.

DCT is also a good compression principle for images, as for any periodic (or almost periodic, i.e., periodic up to a small error) message.

These transformations are reversible. Moreover, not only do they prove themselves to be good compression processes but their interest also lies in the easiness of choosing and keeping only important information. Indeed, during such encoding, it is possible to keep only some coefficients of the DFT or the DCT – to reduce the size of information one has to encode – while not necessarily changing the audio/visual result. We will handle these principles in more detail in Chapter 2.

$$\text{Encoding: } H(i, j) = \frac{2}{n} c(i)c(j) \sum_{x=0}^{n-1} \sum_{y=0}^{n-1} h(x, y) \cos\left(\frac{(2x+1)i\pi}{2n}\right) \cos\left(\frac{(2y+1)j\pi}{2n}\right)$$

$$\text{Decoding: } h(x, y) = \frac{2}{n} \sum_{i=0}^{n-1} \sum_{j=0}^{n-1} c(i)c(j) H(i, j) \cos\left(\frac{(2x+1)i\pi}{2n}\right) \cos\left(\frac{(2y+1)j\pi}{2n}\right)$$

Figure 1.20 Discrete Cosine Transform (DCT)

1.4.2.5 *DFT Algorithm* One can write the DFT transformation as a matrix $H = \Omega h$ with $\Omega_{k,j} = \frac{1}{\sqrt{n}}\omega^{kj}$. Thus, the inverse transformation can be written as $(\Omega^{-1})_{k,j} = \frac{1}{\sqrt{n}}\omega^{-kj}$.

Remark 2 *In some fields, $\sqrt{n}$ simply does not exist. It is therefore sometimes useful to define the transform with another constant factor: $\Omega = [\lambda\omega^{kj}]$ and $\Omega^{-1} = [\frac{\lambda}{n}\omega^{-kj}]$. For the sake of simplicity, in the following, we will avoid $\sqrt{n}$ and use $\lambda = 1$ so that $\Omega = [\omega^{kj}]$ and $\Omega^{-1} = [\frac{1}{n}\omega^{-kj}]$.*

An immediate algorithm for the calculation of this transform uses a matrix vector product and thus has a complexity of $O(n^2)$.

A "divide and conquer" algorithm decreases this complexity, which is extremely important for encoding. The "divide and conquer" principle is to split the problem into equivalent subproblems of lower size. Here, one divides the expression of the transform into two parts. Assuming that n is even, and setting $m = \frac{n}{2}$, one has

$$H_k = \text{DFT}_{k;\omega}(h) = \sum_{j=0}^{m-1} h_j \omega^{kj} + \sum_{j=m}^{n-1} h_j \omega^{kj}$$

$$= \sum_{j=0}^{m-1} h_j \omega^{kj} + \sum_{j=0}^{n-m+1} h_{j+m} \omega^{k(j+m)}$$

$$= \sum_{j=0}^{m-1} h_j \omega^{kj} + \sum_{j=0}^{m-1} h_{j+m} \omega^{kj} \omega^{km}$$

$$= \sum_{j=0}^{m-1} (h_j + \omega^{km} h_{j+m}) \omega^{kj}$$

However, as ω is an nth root of unity, $\omega^{km} = (\omega^m)^k = (\omega^{n/2})^k = (-1)^k$ is equal to 1 or -1 according to the parity of k.

If k is even, then one defines the vector

$$\tilde{h}^p = (h_0 + h_m, \ldots, h_{m-1} + h_{n-1})$$

and the even coefficients of H (the transform of h) are the coefficients of the transform $\widetilde{H^p}$ of $\tilde{h}^p$, which is half the size of h:

$$H_{2t} = \text{DFT}_{2t;\omega}(h) = \sum_{j=0}^{m-1} (h_j + h_{j+m}) \omega^{2tj}$$

$$= \text{DFT}_{t;\omega^2}(\tilde{h}^{(p)}).$$

Now, if k is odd, one defines the vector

$$\tilde{h}^{(i)} = (h_0 - h_m, (h_1 - h_{m+1})\omega, \ldots, (h_{m-1} - h_{n-1})\omega^{m-1})$$

and the odd coefficients of H (the transform of h) are the coefficients of the transform $\tilde{H}^i$ of $\tilde{h}^i$, which is half the size of h:

$$H_{2t+1} = \text{DFT}_{2t+1;\omega}(h) = \sum_{j=0}^{m-1} (h_j - h_{j+m})\omega^{(2t+1)j}$$

$$= \sum_{j=0}^{m-1} (h_j - h_{j+m})\omega^j \left(\omega^2\right)^j$$

$$= \text{DFT}_{t;\omega^2}(\tilde{h}^{(i)}).$$

One obtains Algorithm 1.12.

Algorithm 1.12 Discrete Fast Fourier Transform

Input Vector h whose size is a power of 2
Output Vector H: the transform of h
1: **If** the size of h is equal to 1 **then**
2:     **return** h
3: **else**
4:     Compute $\tilde{h}^{(p)} = (h_0 + h_m, \ldots, h_{m-1} + h_{n-1})$;
5:     Compute $\tilde{h}^{(i)} = (h_0 - h_m, (h_1 - h_{m+1})\omega, \ldots, (h_{m-1} - h_{n-1})\omega^{m-1})$;
6:     Compute recursively $\tilde{H}^{(p)} = DFT_{\omega^2}(\tilde{h}^{(p)})$ of size $n/2$;
7:     Compute recursively $\tilde{H}^{(i)} = DFT_{\omega^2}(\tilde{h}^{(i)})$ of size $n/2$;
8:     The even coefficients of H are the coefficients of $\tilde{H}^{(p)}$ and the odd coefficients of H are the coefficients of $\tilde{H}^{(i)}$.
9: **End If**

The complexity of this algorithm is $C(n) = 2C(n/2) + 3n/2$, in consequence $C(n) = \frac{3}{2}n\log_2 n$. It is almost a linear complexity, thus an important improvement with respect to the initial algorithm. Moreover, the algorithm for the inverse Fourier transform is then straightforward, as

$$\text{DFT}_\omega^{-1} = \frac{1}{n}\text{DFT}_{\omega^{-1}}.$$

1.4.2.6 DFT and nth Roots of Unity in a Finite Field One considers the polynomial $X^n - 1$ in a field $\mathbb{F}_q$ with $n < q$. An *nth root of unity* in $\mathbb{F}_q$ is a simple root, if there exists such root, of the polynomial $X^n - 1$. The *order* of a root of unity γ is the least integer o such that $\gamma^o = 1$. As γ is a root of $X^n - 1$, one has obviously $o \leq n$. Besides, o divides n. Indeed, if one sets $n = ob + r$, then one has $\gamma^r = 1$. Thus $r = 0$.

A *nth primitive root of unity* is an *n*th root of unity of order *n*.

This notion is crucial for the application of the DFT: in order to compute the DFT in the field $\mathbb{C}$, we used a particular *n*th root $-e^{-\frac{2i\pi}{n}}$ – which is primitive in $\mathbb{C}$.

Now, *n*th primitive roots are available for any *n* in $\mathbb{C}$, whereas one is not even sure of their existence in a given finite field. Indeed, in $\mathbb{F}_q$, a $(q-1)$th primitive root of unity is what we simply called a primitive root in Section 1.3.5.3. In the same way as we did for these roots, the following theorem enables one to determine the fields in which it is possible to make fast calculations on vectors of a given size *n*:

Theorem 17 *Let q be a power of some prime number and let n be coprime with q. The finite field $\mathbb{F}_q$ contains an nth primitive root of unity if and only if n divides $q-1$.*

Proof. If *a* is an *n*th primitive root, then $a^n = 1$ and *n* is the order of *a*. As *a* is also an element of the field with *q* elements, its order necessarily divides $q-1$. Reciprocally, one uses a generator *g* of the field (a $(q-1)$th primitive root) whose existence is ensured by the algorithm in Section 1.3.5.3. Hence, if $q - 1 = kn$ then g^k is an *n*th primitive root of unity. □

One says that a field *supports the DFT at order n* if there exist *n*th primitive roots of unity in this field. All fields supporting DFT for *n* equal to a power of 2 are obviously very interesting for applying the fast divide and conquer algorithm above. For instance, as we will see in Algorithm 1.13, the field with 786433 elements enables one to multiply polynomials of degree up to 2^{18} with the fast algorithm as $786433 - 1 = 2^{18} \cdot 3$.

Therefore, one has to compute such an *n*th root of unity. It is possible to use a generator, but one would rather use a variant of the algorithm presented in Section 1.3.5.3: draw randomly an *n*th root (a root of the polynomial $X^n - 1$ in $\mathbb{F}_q$) and test whether its order is actually *n*. The following corollary gives us the probability of success: $\varphi(n)$ chances over *n*.

Corollary 2 *If a finite field has at least one nth primitive root of unity, then it has exactly $\varphi(n)$ primitive roots.*

Proof. Let $q - 1 = kn$. Let *g* be a generator of the field. Thus, g^k is an *n*th primitive root, as well as all g^{tk} for *t* between 1 and $n - 1$ coprime with *n*. All these g^{tk} are distinct; otherwise *g* would not be a generator; and these are the only ones as g^{tk} with *t* not coprime to *n* is of order strictly lower than *n*. The *n*th primitive roots are necessarily written as g^{tk}: if g^u is an *n*th primitive root, then $g^{un} = 1$. As *g* is a generator, one has $un = t(q - 1) = tkn$. This proves that *u* is in the form *tk*. □

Exercise 1.40 *Find a 6th primitive root of unity modulo 31.*

Solution on page 293.

However, if the field $\mathbb{F}_q$ does not contain an *n*th primitive root of unity, one may extend the field. In the same way as $\mathbb{C}$ with respect to $\mathbb{R}$, one can consider a field containing $\mathbb{F}_q$ in which the polynomial $X^n - 1$ can be completely factorized into polynomials of degree 1. This field is an *extension* of the field $\mathbb{F}_q$ and it is called a *splitting field* of $X^n - 1$.

Exercise 1.41   *Find a 4th primitive root of unity in a field of characteristic 31.*
Solution on page 293.

1.4.2.7   Fast Product of Polynomials Using DFT   As for the discrete Fourier transform (DFT), the product of two polynomials – which is often used in coding theory (see all constructions based on polynomials in this chapter) – has a naive algorithm of complexity bound $O(n^2)$.

The DFT and the calculation algorithm we have just seen enables one to perform this computation in time $O(n \log(n))$.

Given two polynomials $P = a_0 + a_1 X + \cdots + a_m X^m$ and $Q = b_0 + b_1 X + \cdots + b_n X^n$, one denotes by $A = DFT(P)$ and $B = DFT(Q)$ the respective discrete Fourier transform of vectors $a = a_0 \ldots a_m 0 \ldots 0$ and $b = b_0 \ldots b_n 0 \ldots 0$, where the coefficients of the polynomials are extended with zeros up to the degree $n + m$ (degree of the product). Then, from the definition of the transform, one can immediately write the coefficients as $A_k = \sum_{i=0}^{n+m} a_i \omega^{ki} = P(\omega^k)$ and $B_k = Q(\omega^k)$. By simply multiplying these two scalars and using the arithmetic of polynomials, one obtains the value of the product PQ evaluated at ω^k: $C_k = A_k B_k = P(\omega^k)Q(\omega^k) = (PQ)(\omega^k)$; in other words $C = DFT(PQ)$.

This property enables one to build Algorithm 1.13 that computes the product of two polynomials in time $O(n \log(n))$.

Algorithm 1.13 Fast product of two polynomials

Input Two polynomials $P = a_0 + a_1 X + \cdots + a_m X^m$ and $Q = b_0 + b_1 X + \cdots + b_n X^n$.

Output The product polynomial PQ.

  1: Extend the polynomials with zeros up to the degree $m + n$ (degree of the product).
  2: Compute the discrete Fourier transforms $DFT(P)$ and $DFT(Q)$ of the vectors of coefficients of P and Q, with Algorithm 1.12.
  3: Using termwise multiplication, Compute vector $DFT(P).DFT(Q)$.
  4: Compute the inverse transform in order to obtain $PQ = DFT^{-1}(DFT(P).DFT(Q))$.

The complexity is truly $O(n \log n)$, as termwise multiplication is linear and the Fourier transform – as well as its inverse - has a complexity $O(n \log n)$.

1.4.3   Cryptanalysis

We have studied some skewness properties between encoding and decoding. One of them, probably the most important one in cryptography, is that which differentiates decryption (by the recipient) from breaking (by a third party). We dedicate a small part of this book to attack techniques based on the weaknesses of codes, which are developed too quickly.

Cryptographic codes use pseudo-random generators for secret key generation, hash functions for authentication, and one-way functions for public key techniques. We will present separately known attacks for each of these steps. Knowing these attack techniques is essential to generate codes that can resist them.

1.4.3.1 Attacks on Linear Congruential Generator

Linear congruential generators have been looked at in Section 1.3.7 A random number x_i is generated as a function of the previously generated number x_{i-1}, using the formula $x_i = ax_{i-1} + b$ mod m.

Exercise 1.42 (Attack on LCGs)

- *If m is prime, what is the maximum period of an LCG? In particular, Fishman and Moore studied generators modulo $2^{31} - 1 = 2147483647$ in 1986. They determined that if $a = 950706376$ then the period is maximum and the generator has good statistical properties. What can you say about 950706376?*
- *For $m = p^e$ with p an odd prime, what is the maximum period of an LCG? One can prove that if $\lambda(m)$ is the maximum period, then $\lambda(2^e) = 2^{e-2}$ for $e > 2$ and that $\lambda(m) = lcm(\lambda(p_1^{e_1}) \dots \lambda(p_k^{e_k}))$ if $m = p_1^{e_1} \dots p_k^{e_k}$ with $p_1, \dots, p_k$ distinct primes.*
- *Assuming that m is known, how can one recover a and b?*
- *Now, suppose that m is unknown. How can one find the generator if $b = 0$? Hint: one may study $x_{n+1} - x_n$. What happens if $b \neq 0$?*
- *What is the next integer in this list: 577,114,910,666,107?*

Solution on page 294.

1.4.3.2 Berlekamp–Massey Algorithm for the Synthesis of LFSRs

The Berlekamp–Massey algorithm enables one to detect, for an infinite sequence (S_i), $i \in \mathbb{N}$, of elements in a field $\mathbb{F}$, whether – beyond some rank – its elements are linear combinations of the previous elements. This is what we have called *linear recurrent sequences*.

This algorithm is very useful in coding theory, notably in order to perform the cryptanalysis of random generators and cryptographic keys and even to correct the errors of cyclic codes (Section 4.4.6.1). In particular, it enables one to recover the generator polynomial of an LFSR (Section 1.3.7.2) only knowing the first terms of the sequence generated by this LFSR.

The question is, for the sequence $(S_i)_{i \in \mathbb{N}}$, how to find coefficients $\Pi_0 \dots \Pi_d \in \mathbb{F}$, if they exist, such that

$$\Pi_0 S_t = S_{t-1}\Pi_1 + S_{t-2}\Pi_2 + \dots + S_{t-d}\Pi_d \text{ for all } t \geq d.$$

If one uses these constants in order to define the polynomial $\Pi(X) = \Pi_d X^d + \Pi_{d-1}X^{d-1} + \Pi_{d-2}X^{d-2} + ... + \Pi_0$, this polynomial is called an annihilator of the sequence.

The set of annihilators is an ideal in the ring $\mathbb{F}[X]$ of polynomials over $\mathbb{F}$. As $\mathbb{F}[X]$ is a principal ideal ring, there exists a unitary annihilator polynomial of minimum degree, called the minimal polynomial of the sequence.

How does one find this polynomial only from the coefficients of the sequence? If one knows the degree d of this polynomial, one has to write d linear equations corresponding to the property of linear recurrence for $2d$ coefficients. Then one has to solve the following linear system:

$$
\begin{bmatrix}
S_0 & S_1 & \cdots & S_{d-1} \\
S_1 & S_2 & \cdots & S_d \\
\vdots & & & \vdots \\
S_{d-1} & S_d & \cdots & S_{2d-1}
\end{bmatrix}
\cdot
\begin{bmatrix}
\Pi_d \\
\Pi_{d-1} \\
\vdots \\
\Pi_1
\end{bmatrix}
=
\begin{bmatrix}
S_d \\
S_{d+1} \\
\vdots \\
S_{2d}
\end{bmatrix}.
\tag{1.15}
$$

The only thing that remains to do is to determine the degree of the minimal polynomial. At first sight, one may try iteratively all possible degrees (starting from a constant polynomial of degree 0) and match each polynomial produced with the sequence in order to see whether it is an annihilator or not. If the sequence is truly infinite, this might never stop.

Otherwise, if the sequence is finite, one notices, when considering the system, that the maximum degree of the minimal polynomial is half the number of elements in the sequence. This algorithm implies that one should solve successively several linear systems. In practice, it is possible to take advantage of the symmetric structure of the system in order to solve it on-the-fly, while adding the elements of the sequence progressively. This gives the following Berlekamp–Massey algorithm that has a complexity bound of only $O(d^2)$.

The main idea of this algorithm is to explicitly compute the coefficients of the polynomial. Thus, the update of Π is performed in two steps. The trick of the test $2L > k$ is to enable one to perform each of these two steps alternately. Let us explain the algorithm by looking at the three first terms of the sequence. The degree of the minimal polynomial increases by one (at most) every time one adds two elements of the sequence. The δ are called discrepancies.

The first discrepancy is the first term of the sequence, $\delta_0 = S_0$ and $\Pi(X)$, becomes $1 - S_0 X$. Discrepancies correspond to the values taken by the polynomial in the sequel of the sequence. If the discrepancy is null, then the polynomial one considers is an annihilator of an additional part of the sequence. Hence, the second discrepancy is $1 - S_0 X$ applied to the sequence S_0, S_1, namely $\delta_1 = S_1 - S_0^2$. Therefore, the update of Π is $\Pi - \frac{\delta_1}{\delta_0}X\psi = (1 - S_0 X) - \frac{S_1 - S_0^2}{S_0}X$, namely $\Pi = 1 - \frac{S_1}{S_0}X$, which is an annihilator of the sequence S_0, S_1. Then, the third discrepancy is equal to $\delta_2 = S_2 - \frac{S_1^2}{S_0}$ and the two polynomials Π and ψ are, respectively, equal to $1 - \frac{S_1}{S_0}X - \frac{\delta_2}{S_0}X^2$ and $1 - \frac{S_1}{S_0}X$. Hence, Π annihilates S_0, S_1, S_2 and ψ annihilates S_0, S_1.

Algorithm 1.14 Berlekamp–Massey Algorithm

Input $S_0, \ldots, S_n$ a sequence of elements in a field K.
Output The minimal polynomial of the sequence.
1: $b \leftarrow 1; e \leftarrow 1; L \leftarrow 0; \Pi \leftarrow 1 \in \mathbb{F}[X]; \psi \leftarrow 1 \in \mathbb{F}[X]$
2: **For** k from 0 to n **do**
3:     $\delta \leftarrow S_k + \sum_{i=1}^{L} \Pi_i S_{k-i}$
4:     **If** $(\delta = 0)$ **then**
5:       $e \leftarrow e + 1$
6:     **elsif** $2L > k$ **then**
7:       $\Pi \leftarrow \Pi - \frac{\delta}{b} X^e \psi$
8:       $e \leftarrow e + 1$
9:     **else**
10:      $temp \leftarrow \Pi - \frac{\delta}{b} X^e \psi$
11:      $\psi \leftarrow \Pi$
12:      $\Pi \leftarrow temp$
13:      $L \leftarrow k + 1 - L; b \leftarrow \delta; e \leftarrow 1$
14:     **End If**
15:     **If** $e > EarlyTermination$ **then**
16:      Stop the algorithm
17:     **End If**
18: **End For**
19: **return** $\Pi(X)$

Hence, as multiplication by X of these annihilator polynomials comes to shifting by one position their application in the initial sequence, one obtains $\delta_3 = \Pi[S_1, S_2, S_3]$ and $\delta_2 = \psi[S_1, S_2] = (X\psi)[S_1, S_2, S_3]$. Then, it is possible to combine these two polynomials in order to also annihilate the sequence S_1, S_2, S_3, by $\Pi - \frac{\delta_3}{\delta_2} X \psi$, which is exactly what the algorithm does. In the sequel, if all next discrepancies are null, this means that the polynomial we have obtained is an annihilator of the sequel of the sequence. One can still continue until one is sure of having the minimal polynomial of the $n + 1$ terms of the sequence or one can stop the algorithm earlier without checking the last discrepancies (using the control variable $EarlyTermination$).

As for complexity, the loop ends after $2d + EarlyTermination$ and at most $n + 1$ iterations. In each iteration, computing the discrepancy operations and updating the polynomial require both $2\frac{k}{2}$ operations, for an overall number of operation of $(2d + EarlyTermination)(2d + EarlyTermination + 1)$.

It is even possible to use a fast algorithm to reduce this complexity, at least asymptotically. The idea is to see the sequence as a polynomial too. Then, the minimal polynomial of the sequence is such that the product of $\Pi(X)$ and $(S_0 + S_1 X + S_2 X^2 + \ldots)$ has only a finite number of nonzero terms, the terms of degree at most d. It is possible to rewrite this statement in the following way:

$$\Pi(X) \cdot (S_0 + S_1 X + \ldots + S_{2n-1} X^{2n-1}) - Q(X) \cdot X^{2n} = R(X). \tag{1.16}$$

Hence, one notices that computing Π, Q, and R can be performed by the Euclidean algorithm interrupted in the middle of the computation, as the degree of R is lower than n. Thus, the complexity bound of the computation is the same as for Euclidean algorithm, namely $O(d log^2(d))$. However, in practice, the Berlekamp–Massey algorithm remains more efficient for values of d up to dozens of thousands.

1.4.3.3 The Birthday Paradox   The Birthday Paradox is a probability result, and it is called a paradox because it seems to go against the first intuition one could have. It is used in several attack methods in cryptanalysis. It also shows that one should distrust intuitions when talking about probabilities.

There are 365 days in a year and still, in a group of more than 23 people, there is more than one chance in two of having at least two of them with the same birth date !

Indeed, let us take a population of k people. Knowing that the number of days in a year is n, the number of combinations of k distinct birth dates is $A_n^k = \frac{n!}{(n-k)!}$. Therefore, the probability of having all people with distinct birth dates is $\frac{A_n^k}{n^k}$. Thus, the probability of having at least two people with the same birthday is

$$1 - \frac{A_n^k}{n^k}.$$

Hence, when considering 365 days, this probability is around one chance in 10 in a group of 9 people, more than one chance in 2 in a group of 23 people, and 99.4% in a group of 60 people. More generally, one has the following theorem:

Theorem 18   *In a set of* $\lceil 1.18\sqrt{n}\rceil$ *elements chosen randomly among n possibilities, the probability of collision is higher than 50%.*

Proof. We have seen that the number of collisions, in a space of size $n = 2^m$ with k draws, is $1 - \frac{A_n^k}{n^k}$. One has to give an estimation of this probability: $1 - \frac{A_n^k}{n^k} = 1 - (1 - \frac{1}{n})(1 - \frac{2}{n})\dots(1 - \frac{k-1}{n})$. Yet, $1 - x < e^{-x}$, for x positive, thus

$$1 - \frac{A_n^k}{n^k} > 1 - \prod_{i=1}^{k-1} e^{-\frac{i}{n}} = 1 - e^{-\frac{k(k-1)}{2n}}.$$

Then, for this probability to be greater than α, it is sufficient to have $k(k-1) = -2n\ln(1-\alpha)$, namely, as k is positive, $k = \frac{1}{2} + \sqrt{n}\sqrt{\frac{1}{4n} - 2\ln(1-\alpha)}$. Hence, for $\alpha = 0.5$, $k \approx 1.18\sqrt{n}$ (again one has, for $n = 365$, $k \approx 22.5$).   □

This kind of collision probability – that one's intuition would tend to weaken – enables one to build attacks against systems for which intuition would give a limited chance of success.

1.4.3.4 Yuval's Attack on Hash Functions   Resistance to collision of hash functions can be measured: one has to determine the probability of finding collisions, which is close to the probability of collision in birth dates (birth dates play the role of fingerprints for individuals).

That is why Yuval's attack on hash functions is also called a birthday attack. It is a question of transmitting some corrupted message $\widetilde{M}$ instead of a legitimate message M, in such way that the corruption is unnoticeable for a hash function h. Then, one looks for M' and $\widetilde{M}'$, such that $h(M') = h(\widetilde{M}')$. After that, one can, for example, fraudulently change M into $\widetilde{M}$, or send M and pretend to have sent $\widetilde{M}$, which is precisely what h should prevent!

Algorithm 1.15 Yuval's birthday attack

Input $h : \{0,1\}^* \longrightarrow \{0,1\}^m$ a hash function.

M legitimate, $\widetilde{M}$ fraudulent.

Output $M' \approx M$ (*i.e.* M' close to M) and $\widetilde{M}' \approx \widetilde{M}$ such that $h(M') = h(\widetilde{M}')$.

1: Generate $t = 2^{\frac{m}{2}} = \sqrt{2^m}$ slight modifications of M, denoted by M'.

2: For all t, compute $h(M')$.

3: Generate several $\widetilde{M}'$, slight modifications of $\widetilde{M}$, until finding a collision, with some M' (*i.e.* $h(\widetilde{M}') = h(M')$).

As a consequence of Theorem 18, the expected number of draws of $\widetilde{M}'$ in Yuval's attack is $O(t) = O(\sqrt{2^m})$.

If one uses Yuval's attack to send M' and then to repudiate it later arguing that $\widetilde{M}'$ was actually sent, one has more than one chance in two of succeeding in $\sqrt{2^m}$ attempts. This shows that brute force can be efficient if a hash function is not collision resistant.

But is this attack really feasible? A simple calculation is enough to be convinced: for a numerical fingerprint on 128 bits, one should perform around $O(2^{64})$ attempts, which is feasible on general public machines of today: a computer running at 3 GHz performs $3 * 10^9 * 24 * 3600 \approx 2^{48}$ operations per day, thus it would take a little more than two months on the 1000 PCs of a company to find a collision.

But if one uses hash functions on 160 bits, the cost is multiplied by a factor $2^{16} = 65536$, which is unreachable so far.

1.4.3.5 Factoring Composite Numbers   It is quite easy to distinguish a composite number from a prime number. But knowing the numbers composing it seems to be a much more difficult problem. It is the factorization problem. Although it can be formulated in a quite simple way, so far there does not exist an efficient solution to it (for instance, the famous Sieve of Eratosthenes is useless for numbers of more than *10* digits).

The difficulty of this problem and the efficiency of attack methods are very important, as a lot of one-way functions rely on the difficulty of factorization or on the difficulty of equivalent problems, such as the discrete logarithm problem. Thus, looking for good factorization algorithms is almost a cryptanalysis method.

Many different algorithms do exist. The goal of this section is not to enumerate them all but rather to give an idea of the most efficient ones for numbers of different sizes.

Pollard's Rho algorithm (Numbers of few digits). The first class of target numbers is composed of "everyday composite numbers," namely numbers of less than *20* digits. Pollard's algorithm is very efficient for such numbers.

The algorithm only requires a few lines of code (around forty) and is very easy to implement. Let m be the composite number one wishes to factorize. First of all, one has to compute a sequence of the form $u_{k+1} = f(u_k) \mod m$ of large period (the longer the u_k are distinct the better).

Then, the idea is to notice that, if p is a factor of m, the distinct u_k modulo m are less often distinct modulo p (Table 1.8). In this case, if $u_i = u_j \mod p$ then the GCD of m and $u_i - u_j$ is equal to kp and it is a nontrivial factor of m. If the u_i are actually pairwise distinct, the computation ends in at most p steps. A first version of the algorithm consists in producing some u_i and, when adding a new element, computing the GCD with all previous u_k's. This version has two major drawbacks: first of all, one has to store around p elements; also, it takes j^2 GCD computations if i and $j > i$ are the smallest indexes such that $u_i = u_j \mod p$. The second trick of Pollard is to use Floyd's cycle detection. It consists in storing only the u_k such that k is a power of 2. Indeed, as the u_k are generated by a function, if $u_i = u_j$, then for all $h \geq 0, u_{i+h} = u_{j+h}$ and a cycle is created modulo p, even if it is not directly noticeable.

When only storing powers of 2, the cycle will only be detected for $u_{2^a} = u_{2^a + j - i}$ with $2^{a-1} < i \leq 2^a$, as illustrated in Figure 1.21.

Yet, $2^a + j - i < 2i + j - i = i + j < 2j$. Hence, one performs at most twice the number of requested operations. One single GCD is computed at each step and one single additional element is stored throughout the algorithm. This gives the very fast algorithm presented in Algorithm 1.16.

If one takes $f(u) = u^2 + 1$, so that the u_i is actually pairwise distinct modulo m, for example, it will take at worst $2p$ iterations if p is the smallest factor of m, and even less in general:

Theorem 19   *Pollard's Rho algorithm has more than one chance in two of succeeding in $O(\sqrt{p})$ steps.*

Proof. Once again, the proof is similar to that of the birthday paradox. If k distinct values u_i are drawn randomly, then there are A_p^k combinations without collisions between

TABLE 1.8   Distribution of the Multiples of p Modulo m

0	1	2	...	p	p+1	p+2	...	kp	kp+1	kp+2	...	m-1
		u_i						u_h				
			u_l							u_j		
					u_k							

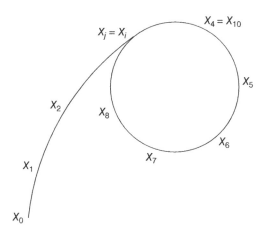

Figure 1.21 Floyd's cycle detection, in the form of a rho

Algorithm 1.16 Pollard's Factoring

Input An integer m, composite.
Output p, non trivial factor of m.
1: $p \leftarrow 1$;
2: Generate y randomly;
3: $k \leftarrow 0$;
4: **While** $(p = 1)$ **do**
5:     **If** k is a power of 2 **then**
6:       $x \leftarrow y$;
7:     **End If**
8:     $y \leftarrow f(y) \mod m$;
9:     $p \leftarrow \gcd(y - x, m)$;
10:    Increase k;
11: **End While**
12: **return** p.

---

the u_i for an overall p^k. For the probability of finding a nontrivial factor to be greater than $1/2$, one must have – according to Theorem 18 - $k > 0.5 + 1.18\sqrt{p}$.   ☐

In practice, this algorithm factorizes numbers of 1 up to around 25 digits within seconds (with factors of 12 or 13 digits, this gives approximately 10 million operations!) but very quickly, it becomes useless when considering factors of more than 15 digits.

Elliptic curves (Numbers with a few dozen of digits). To go further, one can use a method based on elliptic curves, designed by Pollard and Lenstra.

This method uses elliptic curves of the form $y^2 = x^3 + ax + b$, defined in Section 1.3.6. The idea is to consider the set of solutions of the latter equation modulo the number m to be factorized and to try to add them as if this set was a group. As the addition of points (see Theorem 11) requires to invert coordinates modulo m, if the inversion of say y_1 fails then it means that y_1 is not invertible. In other words y_1 contains a proper factor of m, which can be revealed by computing $gcd(y_1, m)$. To simplify, suppose $m = pq$ is the product of only two distinct primes. Then, the curve equation defines two proper elliptic curves, one modulo p and one modulo q. In consequence for any point P, Lagrange's theorem (Theorem 1, page 31), ensures that $[k]P = \mathcal{O}$, say modulo q, only if k divides N_q, the number of points of the curve modulo q. If the curve is chosen randomly, then N_q and N_p are close to p and q, and not necessarily primes. Hence, some of their prime factors will differ with high probability. Therefore, if we compute $[e]P$, for a small e, it is likely that e will divide one of N_p or N_q, but less likely that it divides both numbers at the same time. When this is the case, it means that $[e]P$ is *not* on the curve modulo m and therefore that its computation will crash. The overall procedure is thus to try many small prime factors e. A way to perform this efficiently is to compute $[B!]P$ with a not too large B. The algorithm is detailed as Algorithm 1.17.

Algorithm 1.17 Lenstra's elliptic curve factoring

Input An integer m, composite.
Input A small bound B on the prime factors to be used.
Output p, non trivial factor of m, or Failure.
 1: Pick a random point $P = (x, y)$ with random non-zero coordinates;
 2: Pick a random non zero $a \mod m$ and compute $b \equiv y^2 - x^3 - ax \mod m$;
 3: **For** i=2 **to** B **do**
 4:    $P \leftarrow [i]P$; {Via recursive double-and-add in the pseudo-group of the $\mathbb{E}(m; a, b)$ curve}
 5:    **If** Inversion of P_y fails **then**
 6:       **return** $gcd(P_y, m)$;
 7:    **End If**
 8:    **If** $P = \mathcal{O}$ **then**
 9:       **return** Failure;
10:    **End If**
11: **End For**
12: **return** Failure;

The computational procedure remains simple (around 150 lines of code) and we can give a few ideas concerning the properties of this algorithm: it is conjectured that, in order to factorize an integer m of smallest factor p, this algorithm requires an average number of operations of the order of

$$O\left((\ln m)^2 e^{\sqrt{2 \ln p \ln(\ln p)}}\right).$$

In practice, this algorithm factorizes numbers of 25 to 40 digits (with two factors of similar sizes) within seconds. Besides, if one is lucky and chooses some particular elliptic curve, the latter might enable one to factorize very quickly: the project ECMNET (Elliptic Curve Method on the Net) provides an implementation of this algorithm, available on the Internet. This project has allowed the factorization of numbers with factors up to 73 digits.

The main issue is that good elliptic curves vary for each number one wishes to factorize and so far there does not exist a method of finding the appropriate curve for a given number. Notwithstanding, the rapidity of computation when one has found a "good" elliptic curve is at the origin of the factorization program on the Internet: indeed, many Internet users can retrieve the ECM program and launch it in order to try several elliptic curves. Hence, numerous elliptic curves can be studied at the same time and possibly speed up the search of prime factors.

Number Field Sieve (World champion). Finally, the current champion of RSA key factorization (product of two large prime numbers, see Section 3.4.2) is the *Number Field Sieve* algorithm, which seems to require – in order to factorize some number m, product of two factors of similar sizes – an average number of operations of the order of

$$O\left(e^{\sqrt[3]{(7.11112)\ln(m)\ln(\ln(m))^2}}\right).$$

A number field is an extension of the field of rational numbers (one considers the infinite field $\mathbb{Q}[X]/P$).

The number field sieve is a generalization of the quadratic sieve when considering the field of all integers modulo m. For the sake of simplicity, we only present the main idea of the latter.

The aim is to find couples of numbers whose squares are congruent modulo $m : x^2 = y^2 \mod m$. Then $x^2 - y^2 = (x - y)(x + y)$ is a multiple of m. Now, let $d = gcd(x - y, m)$, if one is lucky, $x \neq \pm y \mod m$ so that $1 < d < m$ and thus d is a nontrivial factor of m.

Example 1.13 Let us try to factorize 7429. We compute randomly some squares: $87^2 = 7429 + 140$ and $88^2 = 7429 + 315$. Yet, 140 and 315 are small with respect to 7429 and thus easier to factorize, for example using Pollard's method. One obtains $140 = 2^2 \cdot 5 \cdot 7$ and $315 = 3^2 \cdot 5 \cdot 7$. Therefore, one can write $(227)^2 = (87 \cdot 88)^2 = (2 \cdot 3 \cdot 5 \cdot 7)^2 = (210)^2 \mod 7429$. We have found a relation of the form $x^2 = y^2 \mod 7429$, which gives us a factor of 7429: $(227 - 210) = 17$, and $7429 = 17 \cdot 437$.

The whole difficulty of the algorithm is to find such integers x and y. For this, one has to compute several squares and store those whose remainders modulo m are small enough to be factorized using another method. Then, one has to find a linear combination of these squares that would give another square: in a matrix, let us store the exponents in the columns and the squares in the lines (Table 1.9).

TABLE 1.9   Quadratic Sieve for 7429

	Exponent of 2	Exponent of 3	of 5	of 7	of …
83^2	2	3	1	0	…
87^2	2	0	1	1	…
88^2	0	2	1	1	…
⋮					

According to this table, $(87 * 88)^2$ is a square if and only if the line of 87^2 added to the line of 88^2 only gives even exponents. In other words, if M is the matrix of exponents (rows and columns of Table 1.9), one has to find some binary vector x such that xM is even or to find a solution modulo 2 to the associated linear system: x such that $xM = 0 \mod 2$.

Although the basic idea is quite simple, the calculation is a little more delicate than for the previous algorithms. Still, this algorithm holds the current records. In particular, it enabled one to factorize a 200 digit (665 bits) RSA key in 2005. The computing time for this last factorization was gigantic: more than a year and a half of computation on more than 80 machines !

1.4.3.6   Strong Prime Numbers   RSA cryptography (see Chapter 3) is based on the use of two prime numbers p and q and on the difficulty of factorizing their product m. In order to resist various factorization methods (some of them are presented in the form of exercises in Chapter 3, on page 173), the prime numbers one uses must satisfy several properties:

- In order to resist factorization based on elliptic curves, p and q must have similar sizes and must be large enough. For instance, in order to work with numbers on 1024 bits, they should both have a size of around 512 bits.
- $p - q$ must be large enough: otherwise, it is sufficient to try as a value for p or q all integers close to $\sqrt{m}$ (Fermat's square root attack).
- In order to resist Pollard's algorithms $p - 1$ and $p + 1$ (which take advantage of the factorization of $p - 1$ and $p + 1$ when possible), p and q have to be *strong* prime numbers, that is, each of them must satisfy the conditions:
  - $p - 1$ has a large factor, denoted by r.
  - $p + 1$ has a large factor.
  - $r - 1$ has a large factor.

Gordon's Algorithm 1.18 enables one to generate strong prime numbers:

Exercise 1.43   *Prove that the output of Gordon's algorithm is a strong prime number.*   *Solution on page 294.*

Algorithm 1.18 Gordon's algorithm

Input A number of bits b.
Output A strong prime number on at least $2b + 1$ bits.
  1: Generate two prime numbers s and t on b bits.
  2: Look for r prime in the form $2kt + 1$.
  3: Compute $l \leftarrow 2(s^{r-2} \mod r)s - 1$.
  4: **return** p, the smallest prime number of the form $l + 2hrs$.

1.4.3.7 Solving the Discrete Logarithm Problem
Alongside modular exponentiation, the other major class of one-way functions relies on the discrete logarithm problem.

Let G be a group of size n admitting a generator (i.e., G is cyclic). For instance, one could consider the group of invertible elements modulo some prime number p, $\mathbb{Z}/p\mathbb{Z}^*$.

Given a primitive root g and an element b in G, the problem is to find the discrete logarithm of b in base g, namely to find x such that $b = g^x$.

The naive algorithm for solving this problem is to try all possible x until one finds the right one. The worst and the average complexity bounds are $O(n)$, thus an exponential complexity with respect to $\log(n)$, the size of n.

So far, the best known algorithms for solving this problem have a complexity bound $O(\sqrt{n})$ in the general case. Most of the time, these algorithms are based on factorization algorithms: we will see that variants of Pollard's Rho $- O(\sqrt{n}) -$ and index calculus $- O(n^{1/3}) -$ algorithms can be applied to groups. However, complexities are raised to the square with respect to factorization. Indeed, if one considers numbers modulo some composite number – a product of two prime numbers – $n = pq$, factorization algorithms have a complexity bound that depends on the smallest prime factor, roughly: $O(p^{1/3}) = O(n^{1/6})$. That is why the discrete logarithm method enables one to consider numbers half the size as those used for factorization-based methods with the same level of security. These sizes are even further reduced if one considers more generic groups, such as the group of points of an elliptic curve, for which the best discrete logarithm methods do not apply.

Baby step, Giant step. This method was developed by Shanks, and it is divided into two phases: the baby step, tests from g^x to g^{x+1} for all x in some interval, and the giant step, jumps from $g^{x\lfloor \sqrt{n} \rfloor}$ to $g^{(x+1)\lfloor \sqrt{n} \rfloor}$.

The idea is to decompose x into two pieces $x = i\lfloor \sqrt{n} \rfloor + j$, with i and j between 1 and $\lceil \sqrt{n} \rceil$. Hence, one can write $b = g^x = (g^{\lfloor \sqrt{n} \rfloor})^i g^j$, or $b(g^{-\lfloor \sqrt{n} \rfloor})^i = g^j$. Thus, one has to compute all possible g^j (baby step), and all possible $b(g^{-\lfloor \sqrt{n} \rfloor})^i$ in order to checks if one of these values has been computed in the baby step (giant step).

Although computing all these values only takes $2\sqrt{n}$ multiplications, looking for the correspondences with a naive method implies that one has to try $\sqrt{n}\sqrt{n} = n$ possibilities in the worst case.

The trick that decreases this complexity is to sort the g^j in increasing order (complexity $O(\sqrt{n}\log(\sqrt{n}))$) in order to be able to perform comparisons with a dichotomous research with only $\sqrt{n}\log_2(\sqrt{n})$ tests!

Therefore, the time complexity is improved; unfortunately, the space complexity is such that this algorithm is not practical: one has to store all $\sqrt{n}$ integers. Even for a reasonable number of operations (around $n = 2^{128}$ nowadays), the required memory space is then of the order of several billion gigabytes.

Pollard's Rho returns. Pollard's Rho algorithm enables one to modify the baby step, giant step method and to introduce Floyd's cycle detection. Hence, one can preserve the time complexity bound $O(\sqrt{n}\log(n))$, while reducing significantly the memory complexity bound down to only $O(\log(n))$ bytes. In comparison with the factorization algorithm, one has to modify the generator function of the sequence in the following way:

Build three subsets S_1, S_2, and S_3 of G of similar sizes forming a partition of G (for example, in $\mathbb{F}_p^*$, with $p \geq 3$ one can always take $S_1 = \{u = 1 \mod 3\}$, $S_2 = \{u = 2 \mod 3\}$, and $S_3 = \{u = 0 \mod 3\}$).

Then, one defines the generator function f such that

$$u_{k+1} = f(u_k) = \begin{cases} bu_k & \text{if } u_k \in S_1 \\ u_k^2 & \text{if } u_k \in S_2 \\ gu_k & \text{if } u_k \in S_3 \end{cases}.$$

Hence, each element of the sequence can be written in the form $u_k = g^{i_k} b^{j_k}$ for some i_k and some j_k. Yet, in the same way as the Rho algorithm for factorization, the u_k are more or less equally spread modulo p. Therefore, a collision $u_k = u_l$ occurs on the average after $\sqrt{p}$ draws, even if $j_k \neq j_l$ and $i_k \neq i_l$. The function f insures, as for factorization, that this collision will be constantly reproduced after k steps; thus, it is possible to find y such that $u_y = u_{2y}$ thanks to Floyd's algorithm with only a memory complexity bound of several integers of size $O(\log(n))$.

Then, one has $u_k = g^{i_k} b^{j_k} = g^{i_l} b^{j_l} = u_l$ and – at the same time $-j_k \neq j_l$. In this case, one obtains $b^{j_k - j_l} = g^{i_l - i_k}$, which means that, in the space of indexes, one directly finds x (one recalls that $b = g^x$):

$$x = (i_l - i_k) \cdot (j_k - j_l)^{-1} \mod n.$$

Be careful: we are solving logarithms in $\mathbb{Z}/p\mathbb{Z}^*$ but the latter equation lies in $\mathbb{Z}/n\mathbb{Z}$ where $n = p - 1$; thus although $j_k - j_l$ is nonzero, it is not necessarily invertible modulo n. If this is not the case, then restart the algorithm.

Coppersmith's Index Calculus. The same way as we have just modified Pollard's algorithm and adapted it to the computation of discrete logarithms, it is possible to modify sieve algorithms. Then, the obtained method works for the discrete logarithm over the group of invertible of a finite field, but not for any group. In particular, cryptology over curves are still resisting this kind of attack. Let us show anyway how this attack works over finite fields with an example.

Example 1.14 How to find x, such that $17 = 11^x \mod 1009$? One recalls that 1009 is prime and that 11 is a primitive root of $\mathbb{Z}/1009\mathbb{Z}$: $Z/1009Z^* = \{11^i,$ for $i = 1 \ldots \varphi(1009) = 1008\}$. The idea is to draw randomly some values of i such that $v_i = 11^i \mod 1009$ can be easily factorized (i.e., it only has small prime factors, or *smooth*). In practice, one is given a basis of prime factors, for example $B = \{2, 3, 5, 7, 11\}$.

Then, for each prime number $p_j \in B$, one divides v_i with the greatest possible power of p_j. At the end of the process, if one obtains the value 1, then v_i can be factorized in the basis B.

After several random draws, we keep the values 104, 308, 553, and 708:

$$11^{104} = 363 = 3 \cdot 11^2 \qquad\qquad \mod 1009$$

$$11^{308} = 240 = 2^4 \cdot 3 \cdot 5 \qquad\qquad \mod 1009$$

$$11^{553} = 660 = 2^2 \cdot 3 \cdot 5 \cdot 11 \qquad\qquad \mod 1009$$

$$11^{708} = 1000 = 2^3 \cdot 5^3 \qquad\qquad \mod 1009$$

When considering the logarithms, Theorem 7 guaranties that one obtains a linear system in the space of exponents whose unknown values are the discrete logarithms of 2, 3, and 5, now modulo 1008:

$$104 = \log_{11}(3) + 2 \qquad\qquad \mod 1008$$

$$308 = 4\log_{11}(2) + \log_{11}(3) + \log_{11}(5) \qquad\qquad \mod 1008$$

$$553 = 2\log_{11}(2) + \log_{11}(3) + \log_{11}(5) + 1 \qquad\qquad \mod 1008$$

$$708 = 3\log_{11}(2) + 3\log_{11}(5) \qquad\qquad \mod 1008.$$

This gives $\log_{11}(3) = 102 \mod 1008$ (or in other words $11^{102} = 3 \mod 1008$), then $\log_{11}(2) = (308 - 553 + 1)/2 = 886 \mod 1008$ and

$$\log_{11}(5) = 308 - 4 \cdot 886 - 102 = 694 \quad \mod 1008.$$

One has to find a number in the form $17 \cdot 11^y$ whose remainder can be factorized in the basis $B = \{2, 3, 5, 7, 11\}$. Still with the same method, one finds – for example – after several random attempts: $17 \cdot 11^{218} = 2 \cdot 3 \cdot 5 \cdot 11 \mod 1009$. Thus, $x = 886 + 102 + 694 + 1 - 218 = 457 \mod 1008$ satisfies $17 = 11^{457} \mod 1009$.

Such index calculus algorithms are more efficient in some particular fields. The record is held by a French team which managed – in November 2005 – to compute a discrete logarithm in the field $\mathbb{F}_{2^{613}}$ in only 17 days on the 64 processors of the Bull supercalculator Teranova.

Now we have at our disposal enough tools to start specializing. We are able to build the objects we will use throughout this book, and we have described the common algorithms that are the foundations of coding. Each of the following chapters will refer to the work in this chapter, depending on needs of the specific objectives: compression, encryption, or correction.

2

INFORMATION THEORY AND COMPRESSION

The previous chapter already contains several coding principles for compression: fax coding, instantaneous coding, the principle of entropy, and so on. We now carry out a deeper and more exhaustive survey of these principles, from the understanding of why compression is theoretically possible to examples of compression codes which are commonly used in computer science and in everyday life for storing and exchanging music and videos.

The objective is to improve the transmission time of each message as well as the storage space. For this purpose, one has to build codes that optimize the size of messages.

Here we assume that the channel is not subject to perturbations (one says that encoding is without noise); error handling will be studied in the last chapter. We are going to build encoding techniques, which enable one to choose efficient codes, as well as an important theory in order to quantify the information included in a message, to compute the minimum size of an encoding scheme and thus to determine the "value" of a given code.

We first focus on lossless data compression, that is, compression followed by decompression does not modify the original file. The first section describes the theoretical limits of lossless compression, and the second algorithms to approach those limits. Then the third section shows how changes of representations can expand these presupposed boundaries, with applications to usual codes.

Foundations of Coding: Compression, Encryption, Error Correction, First Edition.
Jean-Guillaume Dumas, Jean-Louis Roch, Éric Tannier and Sébastien Varrette.
© 2015 John Wiley & Sons, Inc. Published 2015 by John Wiley & Sons, Inc.
http://foundationsofcoding.imag.fr

Then, at the end of this chapter, we introduce several techniques for the compression of images or sounds that allow some loss on the visual or the audio quality by modeling human perception.

Exercise 2.1 (It is Impossible to Compress ALL Files Without Loss)

1. *How many distinct files of size exactly N bits are there?*
2. *How many distinct files of size strictly lower than N bits are there?*
3. *Conclude on the existence of a method that will reduce the size of any file.*

Solution on page 295.

Exercise 2.2 (On The Scarcity of Files Compressible Without Loss)
Show that less than one N-bits file over a million, with N > 20 is compressible by more than 20 bits, without loss of information. *Solution on page 295.*

2.1   INFORMATION THEORY

Information theory gives the mathematical framework for compression codes. Recall that an *alphabet* is a finite set on which messages are composed, containing the information to encode or the information already encoded. The set of letters of the source message (data compression is often called *source coding*) is the *source alphabet*, and the set of code letters is the *code alphabet*. For example, the Latin alphabet is the set of letters we are using to write this text, and $\{0, 1\}$ is the alphabet used to write the messages that are transmitted through most of the numerical channels.

The set of finite strings over some alphabet V is denoted by V^+, and the image of the source alphabet through the encoding function is a subset of V^+ called the set of *codewords*, or sometimes also simply called the *code*, especially in information theory.

Therefore, a *code C* over some alphabet V is a finite subset of V^+. The code is composed of the basic elements from which messages are built. An element m in C is called a *codeword*. Its length is denoted by $l(m)$. The *arity* of the code is the cardinal number of V. A code of arity 2 is said to be *binary*.

For example, $C = \{0, 10, 110\}$ is a binary code of arity 2, over the alphabet $V = \{0, 1\}$.

2.1.1   Average Length of a Code

In all this section, for the sake of simplicity and because of their practical importance in telecommunications, we mainly focus on binary codes. Nevertheless, most of the following results can be applied to any code.

As all codewords are not always of the same size, one uses a measure dependent on the frequencies of appearance in order to evaluate the length of the messages that will encode the source. One recalls that a *source of information* is composed of an alphabet

S and a probability distribution P over S. For a symbol s_i in a source $S = (S, P)$, $P(s_i)$ is the probability of occurrence of s_i.

Let $S = (S, P)$ with $S = \{s_1, \ldots, s_n\}$, and let C be a code in S, whose encoding function is f (C is the image of S through f). The *average length* of the code C is

$$l(C) = \sum_{i=1}^{n} l(f(s_i))P(s_i).$$

Example 2.1 $S = \{a, b, c, d\}$, $P = (\frac{1}{2}, \frac{1}{4}, \frac{1}{8}, \frac{1}{8})$, $V = \{0, 1\}$.

If $C = \{f(a) = 00, f(b) = 01, f(c) = 10, f(d) = 11\}$, the average length of the scheme is 2.

If $C = \{f(a) = 0, f(b) = 10, f(c) = 110, f(d) = 1110\}$, then the average length of the scheme is $1 * \frac{1}{2} + 2 * \frac{1}{4} + 3 * \frac{1}{8} + 4 * \frac{1}{8} = 1.875$.

One uses the average length of an encoding scheme in order to measure its efficiency.

2.1.2 Entropy as a Measure of the Amount of Information

We are reaching the fundamental notions of information theory. Let us consider a source $S = (S, P)$. One only knows the probability distribution of this source, and one wishes to measure quantitatively his/her ignorance concerning the behavior of S. For instance, this *uncertainty* is higher if the number of symbols in S is large. It is low if the probability of occurrence of a symbol is close to 1, and it reaches its highest value if the distribution is uniform.

One uses the entropy of a source in order to measure the average amount of information issued by this source.

For example, let us imagine a fair die whose value is only given by comparison with a number we are able to choose: how many questions are required in order to determine the value of the die? If one proceeds by dichotomy, it only takes $3 = \lceil \log_2(6) \rceil$ questions. Now let us suppose that the die is unfair: one has a probability 1 over 2 and each of the five other values has a probability 1 over 10. If the first question is "is it 1?" then in half of the cases, this question is enough to determine the value of the die. For the other half, it will require three additional questions. Hence, the average number of questions required is $\frac{1}{2} * 1 + \frac{1}{2} * 4 = -\frac{1}{2} \log_2(\frac{1}{2}) - 5 * \frac{1}{10} \lceil \log_2(\frac{1}{10}) \rceil = 2.5$.

Actually, it is still possible to refine this result by noticing that three questions are not always required in order to determine the right value among $2, 3, 4, 5, 6$: if dichotomy splits these five possibilities into two groups $2, 3$ and $4, 5, 6$, then only two additional questions will be required in order to find 2 or 3. Only 5 and 6 will require three questions to be separated. For a large number of draws, it is still possible to improve this method if the questions do not always split the set the same way, for example, in $2, 3, 5$ and $4, 6$, so that two questions are alternatively required and so on. By extending this reasoning, one shows that the average number of questions required for the five possibilities is equal to $\log_2(10)$.

Hence, the amount of information included in this throw of die (which can be easily applied generally to any source) is defined intuitively by the average number of questions.

Formally, entropy is defined, for a source $(S, \mathcal{P})$, $\mathcal{P} = (p_1, \ldots, p_n)$, as

$$H(S) = \sum_{i=1}^{n} p_i \log_2(\frac{1}{p_i}) \,.$$

This is a measure of the *uncertainty* relying on a probability law, which is always illustrated using the example of the die: one considers the random variable (source) generated by the throw of an n-face die. We have seen that there is more uncertainty in the result of this experiment if the die is fair than if the die is unfair. This can be written in the following way: for all $p_1, \ldots, p_n$, $H(p_1, \ldots, p_n) \leq H(\frac{1}{n}, \ldots, \frac{1}{n}) = \log_2 n$, according to Property 1 in Chapter 1.

2.1.3   Shannon's Theorem

This fundamental theorem of information theory is known as *Shannon's theorem* or the *theorem of noiseless encoding*.

First of all, we formulate the theorem when considering a source without memory.

Theorem 20   *Let S be a source without memory of entropy $H(S)$. Any code uniquely decodable of S over an alphabet V of size q (i.e., $q = |V|$), and an average length l, satisfies*

$$l \geq \frac{H(S)}{\log_2 q} \,.$$

Moreover, there exists a code uniquely decodable of S over an alphabet of size q, and an average length l, that satisfies

$$l < \frac{H(S)}{\log_2 q} + 1 \,.$$

Proof.   *First part*: Let $C = (c_1, \ldots, c_n)$ be a code of S, uniquely decodable, over some alphabet of size q, and let $(l_1, \ldots, l_n)$ be the lengths of the words in C. If $K = \sum_{i=1}^{n} \frac{1}{q^{l_i}}$, then $K \leq 1$ from Kraft's theorem (see page 69). Let $(q_1, \ldots, q_n)$ be such that $q_i = \frac{q^{-l_i}}{K}$ for all $i = 1, \ldots, n$. One has $q_i \in [0, 1]$ for all i, and $\sum_{i=1}^{n} q_i = 1$, thus $(q_1, \ldots, q_n)$ is a probability distribution. Gibbs' lemma (see page 17) can be applied, and one obtains

$$\sum_{i=1}^{n} p_i \log_2 \frac{q^{-l_i}}{K p_i} \leq 0;$$

in other words,

$$\sum_{i=1}^{n} p_i \log_2 \frac{1}{p_i} \leq \sum_{i=1}^{n} p_i l_i \log_2 q + \log_2 K.$$

Yet, because $\log_2 K \leq 0$, one has $H(S) \leq l * \log_2 q$; Hence, the result.

Second part: Let $l_i = \lceil \log_q \frac{1}{p_i} \rceil$. As $\sum_{i=1}^n \frac{1}{q^{l_i}} \leq 1$ (indeed, $q^{l_i} \geq \frac{1}{p_i}$), there exists a code of S over an alphabet of size q, uniquely decodable, with lengths of codewords equal to $(l_1, \ldots, l_n)$. Its average length is $l = \sum_{i=1}^n p_i l_i$. Then, the property of the ceiling function gives us $\log_q \frac{1}{p_i} + 1 > l_i$ and, as a consequence,

$$\sum_{i=1}^n p_i \log_2 \frac{1}{p_i} > \sum_{i=1}^n p_i l_i \log_2 q - \log_2 q.$$

This can be written as $H(S) > \log_2 q \left(\left(\sum_{i=1}^n p_i l_i \right) - 1 \right) = \log_2 q(l - 1)$. This proves the theorem.   □

One deduces the theorem for the kth extension of S:

Theorem 21   *Let S be a source without memory of entropy $H(S)$. Any uniquely decodable code in S^k over some alphabet of size q, and an average length l_k, satisfies*

$$\frac{l_k}{k} \geq \frac{H(S)}{\log_2 q}.$$

Moreover, there exists a uniquely decodable code in S^k over some alphabet of size q, and an average length l_k, that satisfies

$$\frac{l_k}{k} < \frac{H(S)}{\log_2 q} + \frac{1}{k}.$$

Proof. The proof of the theorem is immediate: according to Property 2 on page 21, one has $H(S^k) = k * H(S)$.   □

For any stationary source, the theorem can be formulated as follows:

Theorem 22   *For any stationary source S of entropy $H(S)$, there exists some uniquely decodable encoding process over an alphabet of size q, and an average length l, as close as one wants to its lower bound:*

$$\frac{H(S)}{\log_2(q)}.$$

In theory, it is then possible to find a code endlessly approaching this bound (which depends on the entropy of the source). However, in practice, if the process consists of encoding the words of an extension of the source, one is obviously limited by the number of these words ($|S^k| = |S|^k$, which might represent a large number of words). In the sequel, we see several encoding processes as well as their relation with this theoretical bound.

2.2 STATISTICAL ENCODING

Statistical encoding schemes use the frequency of each character of the source for compression and, by encoding the most frequent characters with the shortest code-words, put themselves close to the entropy.

2.2.1 Huffman's Algorithm

These schemes enable one to find the best encoding for a source without memory $S = (S, P)$. The code alphabet is V of size q. For the optimal nature of the result, one must check that $q - 1$ divides $|S| - 1$ (in order to obtain a locally complete tree). Otherwise, one can easily add some symbols in S, with probability of occurrence equal to zero, until $q - 1$ divides $|S| - 1$. The related codewords (the longest ones) will not be used.

Algorithm 2.1 Description of Huffman's Algorithm

Using the source alphabet S, one builds a set of isolated nodes associated to the probabilities of P (Figure 2.1).

Figure 2.1 Huffman encoding: beginning of the algorithm

Let $p_{i_1}, \cdots, p_{i_q}$ be the q symbols of lowest probabilities. One builds a tree (on the same model as Huffman tree), whose root is a new node associated with the probability $p_{i_1} + \cdots + p_{i_q}$. The edges of this tree are incident to the nodes $p_{i_1}, \ldots, p_{i_q}$. Figure 2.2 shows an example of this operation for $q = 2$.

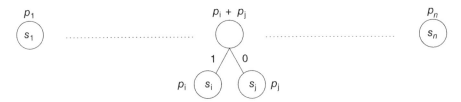

Figure 2.2 Huffman's encoding: first step ($q = 2$)

One then restarts with the q lowest values among the nodes of highest level (the roots), until one obtains a single tree (at each step, the number of nodes of highest level is decreased by $q - 1$ elements), whose leaves are the elements in S. The associated codewords in this scheme are the words corresponding to the paths from the root to the leaves.

The idea of the method is given in Algorithm 2.1.

Example 2.2 (Source Coding)   One wishes to encode the following source over $V = \{0, 1\}$:

Symbol	Probability
a	0.35
b	0.10
c	0.19
d	0.25
e	0.06
f	0.05

The successive steps of the algorithm are given in Figure 2.3.
Then, one builds the following Huffman code:

Symbol	Codeword
a	11
b	010
c	00
d	10
e	0111
f	0110

Exercise 2.3   *This exercise introduces some theoretical elements concerning the efficiency of the code generated by the Huffman algorithm. Let $S = (S, P)$ be the source with $S = (0, 1)$, $P(0) = 0.99$, and $P(1) = 0.01$.*

1. *Compute the entropy of S.*
2. *Give the code generated by the Huffman algorithm over the third extension S^3. What is its compression rate?*
3. *What can you say about the efficiency of the Huffman algorithm when comparing the compression rates obtained here with those of Exercise 1.33 ? Does it comply with Shannon's theorem?*

Solution on page 295.

Exercise 2.4 (Heads or Tails to Play 421 Game)   *One wishes to play with a die, while having only a coin. Therefore, the exercise concerns encoding a six-face fair die with a two-face fair coin.*

1. *What is the entropy of a die?*

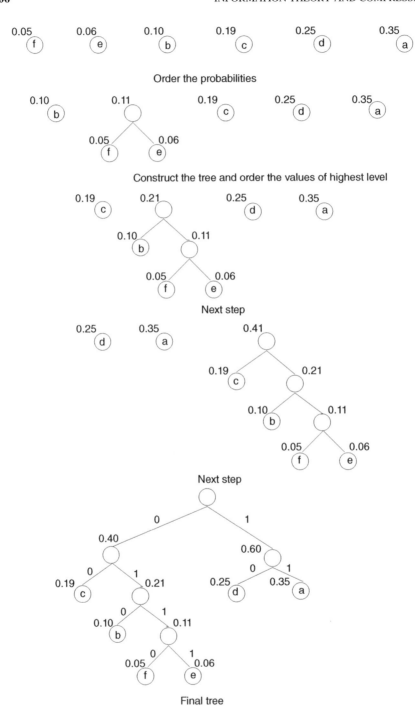

Figure 2.3   Example of a construction of the Huffman code

2. *Propose an encoding algorithm.*

3. *Compute the average length of this code.*

4. *Is this encoding optimal?*

Solution on page 296.

2.2.1.1 Huffman's Algorithm is Optimal

Theorem 23   *A code generated by the Huffman algorithm is optimal among all instantaneous codes in S over V.*

Proof. In order to simplify the notation in this proof, we suppose that $q = 2$. However, the results can be generalized at each step.

One knows that an instantaneous code can be represented with the Huffman tree. Let A be the tree representing an optimal code, and let H be the tree representing a code generated by the Huffman algorithm.

One notices that in A, there does not exists a node with a single child whose leaves contain codewords (indeed, such a node can be replaced with its child in order to obtain a better code).

Moreover, if the respective probabilities of occurrence p_1, p_2 for two codewords c_1, c_2 in A satisfy $p_1 < p_2$, then the respective depth of the leaves representing c_1, c_2 – l_1, l_2 – satisfy $l_1 \geq l_2$ (indeed, otherwise one replaces c_1 with c_2 in the tree to get a better code).

Thus, one can assume that A represents an optimal code for which the two words of lowest probabilities are two "sister" leaves (they have the same father node).

Then, one thinks inductively on the number n of leaves in A. For $n = 1$, the result is obvious. For any $n \geq 2$, one considers the two "sister" leaves corresponding to the words c_1, c_2 of lowest probability of occurrence p_1, p_2 in A. According to the Huffman construction principle, c_1 and c_2 are "sister" leaves in H. Then, one defines $H' = H \backslash \{c_1, c_2\}$. This is the Huffman encoding scheme for the code $C' = C \backslash \{c_1, c_2\} \cup \{c\}$, c being a word of probability of occurrence $p_1 + p_2$. According to the recursive principle, H' represents the best instantaneous code over C'; thus its average length is lower than that of $A' = A \backslash \{c_1, c_2\}$. Therefore, and according to the preliminary remarks, the average length H is lower than the average length of A.   □

One must understand the true meaning of this theorem: it does not say that the Huffman algorithm is the best one for encoding information in all cases, but rather that when fixing the model of a source S without memory over some alphabet V, there is no code more efficient than this one having the prefix property.

In practice (see the end of this chapter), one chooses a model for the source that is adapted to the code. In particular, one can obtain more efficient codes from the extensions of the source, as we can notice in the following example.

Let $S = (S, P), S = (s_1, s_2), P = (1/4, 3/4)$. The Huffman code for S gives immediately $s_1 \to 0$ and $s_2 \to 1$, and its average length is 1. The Huffman code for $S^2 =$

$(S^2, \mathcal{P}^2)$ gives

$$
\begin{aligned}
s_1 s_1 &\rightarrow 010 \\
s_1 s_2 &\rightarrow 011 \\
s_2 s_1 &\rightarrow 00 \\
s_2 s_2 &\rightarrow 1
\end{aligned}
$$

and its average length is $3 * \frac{1}{16} + 3 * \frac{3}{16} + 2 * \frac{3}{16} + \frac{9}{16} = \frac{27}{16} = 1.6875$. Therefore, the average length of this code is $l = 1.6875$ and, when compared to the code over S (codewords in S^2 have length 2), $l = 1.6875/2 = 0.84375$, which is better than the code over the original source.

One can still improve this encoding scheme considering the source S^3. It is also possible to refine the encoding with a better model for the source: often the occurrence of some symbol is not independent of the previous symbols issued by the source (e.g., as for a text). In that case, the probabilities of occurrence are conditional and there exist some models (in particular the Markov model) that enable a better encoding. Nevertheless, such processes do not lead to infinite improvements. Entropy remains a threshold for the average length, under which there is no code.

Exercise 2.5 *One wishes to encode successive throws (one assumes these are infinite) of an unfair die. The symbols of the source are denoted by (1,2,3,4,5,6), and they follow the probability law of occurrence (0.12, 0.15, 0.16, 0.17, 0.18, 0.22).*

1. *What is the entropy of this source?*
2. *Propose a ternary code (over some alphabet with three digits) generated by the Huffman algorithm for this source. What is its average length? What minimum average length can we expect for such a ternary code?*
3. *Same question for a binary code.*

Solution on page 296.

Exercise 2.6 *(Sequel of the previous exercise) The Huffman algorithm builds a code in which source words of fixed length are encoded with codewords of varying lengths. The organization of the memory in which the code is stored sometimes imposes a fixed length for codewords. Thus, one encodes sequences of digits of varying length from the source to meet this constraint.*

Tunstall codes are optimal codes following this principle. Here is the construction method for the case of a binary alphabet. If the chosen length for codewords is k, one has to find the 2^k sequences of digits from the source one wishes to encode. At the beginning, the set of candidates is the set of words of length 1 (here, {1,2,3,4,5,6}). Let us consider – in this set – the most probable word (here, 6). One builds all possible sequences when adding a digit to this word, and this word is replaced by these sequences in the set of candidates (here, one gets {1,2,3,4,5,61,62,63,64,65,66}). Then, one restarts this operation while having the size of the set strictly lower than 2^k (one stops before rising above this value).

1. *Over some binary alphabet, build the Tunstall code for the die, for codewords of length $k = 4$.*

2. *What is the codeword associated to the sequence "6664" with the Tunstall? with the Huffman?*

3. *For each codeword, compute the number of necessary bits of code per character of the source. Deduce the average length* per bit of the source *of the Tunstall code.*

Solution on page 297.

2.2.2 Arithmetic Encoding

Arithmetic encoding is a statistical method that is often better than the Huffman encoding! Yet, we have seen that the Huffman code is optimal, so what kind of optimization is possible? In arithmetic encoding, each character can be encoded on a noninteger number of bits: entire strings of characters of various sizes are encoded on a single integer or a computer real number. For instance, if some character appears with a probability 0.9, the optimal size of the encoding of this character should be

$$\frac{H}{\log_2 Q} = \frac{9/10 \log_2(10/9) + 1/10 * \log_2(10/1)}{\log_2 10}.$$

Thus the optimal encoding is around 0.14 bits per character, whereas an algorithm such as Huffman's would certainly use an entire bit. Thus, we are going to see how arithmetic encoding enables one to do better.

2.2.2.1 Floating Point Arithmetics The idea of arithmetic encoding is to encode the characters using intervals. The output of an arithmetic code is a simple real number between 0 and 1 that is built the in following way: to each symbol is associated a subdivision of the interval [0, 1] whose size is equal to its probability of occurrence. The order of the association does not matter, provided that it is the same for encoding and decoding. For example, a source and the associated intervals are given in the following table.

Symbol	a	b	c	d	e	f
Probability	0,1	0,1	0,1	0,2	0,4	0,1
Interval	[0,0.1)	[0.1,0.2)	[0.2,0.3)	[0.3,0.5)	[0.5,0.9)	[0.9,1)

A message will be encoded with a number chosen in the interval whose bounds contain the information of the message. For each character of the message, one refines the interval by allocating the subdivision corresponding to this character. For instance, if the current interval is $[0.15, 0.19)$ and one encodes the character b, then one allocates the subdivision $[0.1, 0.2)$ related to $[0.15, 0.19)$; hence, $[0.15 + (0.19 - 0.15) * 0.1 = 0.154, 0.15 + (0.19 - 0.15) * 0.2 = 0, 158)$.

If the message one wishes to encode is "bebecafdead," then one obtains the real interval $[0.15633504384, 01563354640)$. The steps in the calculation are presented in Table 2.1. Let us choose, for example, "0.15633504500." The encoding process is

TABLE 2.1   Arithmetic Encoding of "bebecafdead"

Symbol	Lower bound	Upper bound
b	0.1	0.2
e	0.15	0.19
b	0.154	0.158
e	0.1560	0.1576
c	0.15632	0.15648
a	0.156320	0.156336
f	0.1563344	0.1563360
d	0.15633488	0.15633520
e	0.156335040	0.156335168
a	0.156335040	0.1563350528
d	0.15633504384	0.15633504640

Algorithm 2.2 Arithmetic Encoding

1: Set lowerBound ← 0.0
2: Set upperBound ← 1.0
3: **While** there are symbols to encode **do**
4:    C ← symbol to encode
5:    Let x, y be the bounds of the interval corresponding to C in Table 2.1
6:    size ← upperBound − lowerBound;
7:    upperBound ← lowerBound + size $* y$
8:    lowerBound ← lowerBound + size $* x$
9: **End While**
10: **return** upperBound

---

very simple, and it can be explained in broad outline in Algorithm 2.2.

For decoding, it is sufficient to locate the interval in which lies "0.15633504500": namely, $[0.1, 0.2)$. Thus, the first letter is a "b."

Then, one has to consider the next interval by subtracting the lowest value and dividing by the size of the interval containing "b," namely, $(0.15633504500 − 0.1)/0.1 = 0.5633504500$. This new number indicates that the next value is a "e." The sequel of the decoding process is presented in Table 2.2, and the program is described in Algorithm 2.3.

Remark 3 *Note that the stopping criterion $r \neq 0.0$ of Algorithm 2.3 is valid only if the input number is the lower bound of the interval obtained during encoding. Otherwise, any element of the interval is returned, as in the previous example, another stopping criterion must be provided to the decoding process. This could be, for instance,*

- *the exact number of symbols to be decoded (this could typically be given as a header in the compressed file).*

TABLE 2.2   Arithmetic Decoding of "0.15633504500"

Real number	Interval	Symbol	Size
0.15633504500	[0.1,0.2[	b	0.1
0.5633504500	[0.5,0.9[	e	0.4
0.158376125	[0.1,0.2[	b	0.1
0.58376125	[0.5,0.9[	e	0.4
0.209403125	[0.2,0.3[	c	0.1
0.09403125	[0.0,0.1[	a	0.1
0.9403125	[0.9,1.0[	f	0.1
0.403125	[0.3,0.5[	d	0.2
0.515625	[0.5,0.9[	e	0.4
0.0390625	[0.0,0.1[	a	0.1
0.390625	[0.3,0.5[	d	0.2

Algorithm 2.3 Arithmetic Decoding

1: Let r be the number one wishes to decode
2: **While** $r \neq 0.0$ **do**
3:    Let C be the symbol whose associated interval in Table 2.1 contains r
4:    Print C
5:    Let a, b be the bounds of the interval corresponding to C in Table 2.1
6:    $size \leftarrow b - a$
7:    $r \leftarrow r - a$
8:    $r \leftarrow r/size$
9: **End While**

- *another possibility is to use a special character (such as EOF) added to the end of the message to be encoded. This special character could be assigned to the lowest probability.*

In summary, encoding progressively reduces the interval proportionately to the probabilities of the characters. Decoding performs the inverse operation, increasing the size of this interval.

2.2.2.2   *Integer Arithmetics*

The previous encoding depends on the size of the mantissa in the computer representation of real numbers; thus it might not be completely portable. Therefore, it is not used, as it is with floating point arithmetics. Decimal numbers are rather issued one by one in a way that fits the number of bits of the computer word. Integer arithmetics is then more natural than floating point arithmetics: instead of a floating point interval [0,1), an integer interval of the type [00000,99999] is used. Then, encoding is the same. For example, a first occurrence of "b" (using the frequencies in Table 2.1) gives [10000,19999], then "e" would give [15000,18999].

Then one can notice that as soon as the most significant number is identical in the two bounds of the interval, it does not change anymore. Thus it can be printed on the output and subtracted in the integer numbers representing the bounds. This enables one to manipulate only quite small numbers for the bounds. For the message "bebe-cafdead," the first occurrence of "b" gives [10000, 19999], one prints "1" and subtracts it; hence, the interval becomes [00000, 99999]. Then, the "e" gives [50000, 89999]; the sequel is given in Table 2.3. The result is 156335043840.

Decoding almost follows the same procedure by only reading a fixed number of digits at the same time: at each step, one finds the interval (and thus the character) containing the current integer. Then if the most significant digit is identical for both the current integer and the bounds, one shifts the whole set of values as presented in Table 2.4.

2.2.2.3 In Practice This encoding scheme encounters problems if the two most significant digits do not become equal throughout the encoding. The size of the integers bounding the interval increases, but it can not increase endlessly because of the limitations in any machine. One confronts this issue if he/she gets an interval such as [59992, 60007]. After a few additonal iterations, the interval converges toward [59999, 60000] and nothing else is printed!

To overcome this problem, one has to compare the most significant digits and also the next ones if the latters differ only by 1. Then, if the next ones are 9 and 0, one has to shift them and remember that the shift occurred at the second most significant digit.

TABLE 2.3 Integer Arithmetic Encoding of "bebecafdead"

Symbol	Lower bound	Upper bound	Output
b	10000	19999	
Shift 1	00000	99999	1
e	50000	89999	
b	54000	57999	
Shift 5	40000	79999	5
e	60000	75999	
c	63200	64799	
Shift 6	32000	47999	6
a	32000	33599	
Shift 3	20000	35999	3
f	34400	35999	
Shift 3	44000	59999	3
d	48800	51999	
e	50400	51679	
Shift 5	04000	16799	5
a	04000	05279	
Shift 0	40000	52799	0
d	43840	46399	
			43840

TABLE 2.4   Integer Arithmetic Decoding of "156335043840"

Shift	Integer	Lower bound	Upper bound	Output
	15633	>10000	<19999	b
1	56335	00000	99999	
	56335	>50000	<89999	e
	56335	>54000	<57999	b
5	63350	40000	79999	
	63350	>60000	<75999	e
	63350	>63200	<64799	c
6	33504	32000	47999	
	33504	>32000	<33599	a
3	35043	20000	35999	
	35043	>34400	<35999	f
3	50438	44000	59999	
	50438	>48800	<51999	d
	50438	>50400	<51679	e
5	04384	04000	16799	
	04384	>04000	<05279	a
0	43840	40000	52799	
	43840	>43840	<46399	d

For example, $[59123, 60456]$ is shifted into $[51230, 64569]_1$; index 1 meaning that the shift occured at the second digit. Then, when the most significant digits become equal (after k shifts of 0 and 9), one will have to print this number, followed by k 0's or k 9's. In decimal or hexadecimal format, one has to store an additional bit indicating whether the convergence is upwards or downwards; in binary format, this information can be immediately deduced.

Exercise 2.7   *With the probabilities ("a": 4/10; "b": 2/10; "c": 4/10), the encoding of the string "bbbbba" is given as follows:*

Symbol	Interval	Shift	Output
b	[40000; 59999]		
b	[48000; 51999]		
b	[49600; 50399]	*Shift 0 and 9:* $[46000; 53999]_1$	
b	$[49200; 50799]_1$	*Shift 0 and 9:* $[42000; 57999]_2$	
b	$[48400; 51599]_2$		
a	$[48400; 49679]_2$	*Shift 4:* [84000; 96799]	*499, then 84000*

Using the same probabilities, decode the string 49991680.

Solution on page 297.

2.2.3 Adaptive Codes

The encoding scheme represented by the Huffman tree (when considering source extensions) or arithmetic encoding are statistical encodings working on the source model introduced in Chapter 1. Namely, these are based on the knowledge a priori of the frequency of the characters in the file. Moreover, these encoding schemes require a lookup table (or a tree) correlating the source words and the codewords to be able to decompress. This table might become very large when considering source extensions.

Exercise 2.8   *Let us consider an alphabet of four characters ("a","b","c","d") of probability law (1/2,1/6,1/6,1/6).*

1. *Give the lookup table of the static Huffman algorithm for this source.*
2. *Assuming that characters a, b, c, and d are written in ASCII (8 bits), what is the minimum memory space required to store this table?*
3. *What would be the memory space required in order to store the lookup table of the extension of the source on three characters?*
4. *What is the size of the ASCII file containing the plaintext sequence "aaa aaa aaa bcd bcd bcd"?*
5. *Compress this sequence with the static Huffman code. Give the overall size of the compressed file. Is it interesting to use an extension of the source?*

Solution on page 297.

In practice, there exists dynamic variants (on-the-fly) enabling one to avoid the pre-computation of both frequencies and lookup tables. These variants are often used in compression. They use character frequencies, and they calculate them as the symbols occur.

2.2.3.1 *Dynamic Huffman's Algorithm* – pack   The dynamic Huffman algorithm enables one to compress a stream on-the-fly performing a single reading of the input; contrary to the static Huffman algorithm, this method avoids performing two scans of an input file (one for the computation of the frequencies and the other for the encoding). The frequency table is built as the reading of the file goes on; hence, the Huffman tree is modified each time one reads a character.

The Unix "pack" command implements this dynamic algorithm.

2.2.3.2 *Dynamic Compression*   Compression is described in Algorithm 2.4. One assumes that the file to be encoded contains binary symbols, which are read on-the-fly on the form of blocks of k bits (k is often a parameter); therefore, such a block is called a *character*". At the initialization phase, one defines a symbolic character (denoted by @ in the sequel) initially encoded with a predefined symbol (e.g., the symbolic 257th character in the ASCII code). During the encoding, each time one meets a new unknown character, one encodes it on the output with the code of @ followed by the k bits of the new character. The new character is then introduced in the Huffman tree.

Algorithm 2.4 Dynamic Huffman Algorithm: Compression

1: Let $nb(c)$ be the number of occurrences of character c
2: Initialize the Huffman tree (AH) with character @, $nb(@) \leftarrow 1$
3: **While** NOT end of the source **do**
4:   Read a character c from the source
5:   **If** it is the first occurrence of c **then**
6:     $nb(c) \leftarrow 0$
7:     $nb(@) \leftarrow nb(@) + 1$
8:     Print on the output the code of @ in AH followed by c.
9:   **else**
10:    Print the code of c in AH
11: **End If**
12: $nb(c) \leftarrow nb(c) + 1$
13: Update AH with the new frequencies
14: **End While**

In order to build the Huffman tree and update it, one enumerates the number of occurrences of each character as well as the number of characters already read in the file; therefore, one knows, at each reading of a character, the frequency of each character from the beginning of the file to the current character; thus the frequencies are dynamically computed.

After having written a code (either the code of @, or the code of an already known character, or the k uncompressed bits of a new character), one increases by 1 the number of occurrences of the character that has just been written. Taking the frequency modifications into account, one updates the Huffman tree at each step.

Therefore, the tree exists for compression (and decompression), but there is no need to send it to the decoder.

Possibly there are several choices for the number of occurrences of @: in Algorithm 2.4, it is the number of distinct characters (this enables one to have few bits for @ at the beginning), but it is also possible to provide it, for example, with a constant value close to zero (in that case, the number of bits for @ evolves according to the depth of the Huffman tree that lets the most frequent characters have the shortest codes).

2.2.3.3 Dynamic Decompression Dynamic decompression is described in Algorithm 2.5. At the initialization, the decoder knows one single code, that of @ (e.g., 0). First it reads 0 which we suppose to be the code associated to @. It deduces that the next k bits contain a new character. It prints these k bits on its output and updates the Huffman tree, which already contains @, with this new character.

Notice that the coder and the decoder maintain their own Huffman's trees, but they both use the same algorithm in order to update it from the occurrences (frequencies) of the characters that have already been read. Hence, the Huffman trees computed separately by the coder and the decoder are exactly the same.

Algorithm 2.5 Dynamic Huffman's Algorithm Decompression

1: Let $nb(c)$ be the number of occurrences of character c
2: Initialize the Huffman tree (AH) with character @, $nb(@) \leftarrow 1$
3: **While** NOT end of coded message **do**
4:    Read a codeword c in the message (until reaching a leaf in AH)
5:    **If** $c = @$ **then**
6:       $nb(@) \leftarrow nb(@) + 1$
7:       Read in c the k bits of the message and print them on the output.
8:       $nb(c) \leftarrow 0$
9:    **else**
10:      Print the character corresponding to c in AH
11:   **End If**
12:   $nb(c) \leftarrow nb(c) + 1$
13:   Update AH with the new frequencies
14: **End While**

Then, the decoder reads the next codeword and decodes it using its Huffman's tree. If the codeword represents symbol @, it reads the k bits corresponding to a new character, writes them on its output, and introduces the new character in its Huffman's tree (from now on, the new character is associated with some code). Otherwise, the codeword represents an already known character; using its Huffman's tree, it recovers the k bits of the character associated with the codeword and writes them on its output. Then it increases by 1 the number of occurrences of the character it has just written (and of @ in case of a new character) and updates the Huffman tree.

This dynamic method is a little bit less efficient than the static method for estimating the frequencies. The encoded message is likely to be a little bit longer. However, it avoids the storage of both the tree and the frequency table, which often make the final result shorter. This explains why it is used in practice in common compression utilities.

Exercise 2.9 *Once again, one considers the sequence "aaa aaa aaa bcd bcd bcd"*

1. *What would be the dynamic Huffman code of this sequence?*
2. *What would be the dynamic Huffman code of the extension on three characters of this sequence?*

Solution on page 298.

2.2.3.4 *Adaptive Arithmetic Encoding*   The general idea of the adaptive encoding that has just been developed for the Huffman algorithm is the following:

- At each step, the current code corresponds to the static code one would have obtained using the occurrences already known to compute the frequencies.
- After each step, the encoder updates its occurrence table with the new character it has just received and builds a new static code corresponding to this table. This

must always be done in the same way, so that the decoder is able to do the same when its turn comes.

This idea can also be easily implemented dealing with arithmetic encoding: the code is mainly built on the same model as arithmetic encoding, except that the probability distribution is computed on-the-fly by the encoder on the symbols that have already been handled. The decoder is able to perform the same computations, hence, to remain synchronized. An adaptive arithmetic encoder works on floating point arithmetic: at the first iteration, the interval [0, 1] is divided into segments of same size.

Each time a symbol is received, the algorithm computes the new probability distribution and the segment of the symbol is divided into new segments. But the lengths of these new segments now correspond to the updated probabilities of the symbols. The more the symbols are received, the closer the computed probability is to the real probability. As in the case of the dynamic Huffman encoding, there is no overhead because of the preliminary sending of the frequency table and, for variable sources, the encoder is able to dynamically adapt to the variations in the probabilities.

Possibly not only does arithmetic encoding often offer a better compression, but one should also notice that although the static Huffman implementations are faster than the static arithmetic encoding implementations, in general, it is the contrary in the adaptive arithmetic case.

2.3 HEURISTICS OF ENTROPY REDUCTION

In practice, the Huffman algorithm (or its variants) is used coupled with other encoding processes. These processes are not always optimal in theory, but they make some reasonable assumptions on the form of the target files (i.e., the source model) in order to reduce the entropy or allow the elimination of some information one considers to be inconsequential for the use of the data.

Here, we give three examples of entropy reduction. The principle is to turn a message into another one, using some reversible transformation, so that the new message will have a lower entropy and thus will be more efficiently compressible. Therefore, the whole technique is about using a preliminary code in charge of reducing the entropy before applying the compression.

2.3.1 Run-Length Encoding (RLE)

Although statistical encoding makes good use of the most frequent characters, it does not take their position in the message into account. If the same character often appears several times in a row, it might be useful to simply encode the number of times it appears. For instance, in order to transmit a fax page, statistical encoding will encode a 0 with a short codeword, but each 0 will be written, and this will make this code less efficient than the fax code presented in Chapter 1, especially for pages containing large white areas.

Run-length encoding (RLE) is an extension of the fax code. It reads each character one by one but, when at least three identical characters are met successively, it will rather print some special repetition code followed by the recurrent character and the number of repetitions. For example, using @ as the repetition character, the string "aabbbcddddd@ee" is encoded with "@a2@b3c@d5@@1@e2" (a little trick is necessary to make the code instantaneous if the special character is met).

Exercise 2.10

1. What would be the RLE code of the following image?

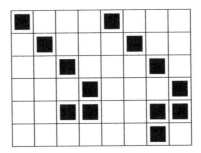

2. Is there a benefit compared to the fax code?

3. What would be the encoding on 5-bit blocks with 16 gray-levels? And the benefit of such a code? Are we able to compress more than this with this system?

4. Same question with 255 gray-levels (with at most 16 consecutive identical pixels).

5. Same questions when scanning the image in columns?

Solution on page 298.

In order to avoid problems related to the special repetition character – which is necessarily encoded as a repetition of length 1 – modems use a variant of RLE called *MNP5*. If the same character is consecutively encountered three times, or more, the idea is to display the three characters followed by some counter indicating the number of additional occurrences of this character. One must obviously specify a fixed number of bits allocated for this counter. If the counter reaches its maximum, the sequel is encoded with several blocks composed of the same three characters followed by a counter. For instance, the string "aabbbcddddd" is encoded as "aabbb0cddd2." In this case, if a string on n bytes contains m repetitions of average length L, the benefit of compression is $\frac{n-m(L-4)}{n}$ if the counter is encoded on 1 byte. Therefore, this kind of encoding scheme is very useful, for example, in black and white images where pixels having the same color are often side by side. A statistical compression can obviously be performed later on the result of an RLE scheme.

2.3.1.1 The Fax Code (end) Let us go back to the fax code – the one we used at the beginning of our presentation of the foundations of coding (Chapter 1) – and let us complete it and give its whole compression principle.

Let us recall that the scanned information is a set of black and white pixels on which one performs an RLE on lines of 1728 characters. Black and white pixels are alternated; thus the message one wishes to encode is a sequence of numbers between 1 and 1728. These numbers will be encoded with their translations in bits, according to the following principle. Suppose that we have a uniquely decodable code that contains the encoded value of all numbers between 0 and 63, as well as the encoded value of several numbers greater than 63, in such a way that for any number greater than n, there exists some large number m in the table, such that $0 \leq n - m < 64$. Therefore, n repetitions are represented with two successive codes: m repetitions and then $n - m$ repetitions.

Figure 2.4 presents some extracts of tables showing the numbers encoding white pixels. Numbers between 0 and 63 are called *terminating white codes* and numbers greater than 64 are called *make up white codes*.

The same tables exist for black pixels, with different encoded values, the whole composing a code uniquely decodable.

2.3.2 Move-to-Front

Another precomputation is possible if one turns an ASCII character into its value between 0 and 255 while modifying the order of the table on-the-fly. For instance, as soon as a character appears in the source, it is first encoded with its value, then it is moved to the front of the list: from now on, it will be encoded with 0, all other characters being shifted by one unit. This "move-to-front" enables one to have more codes close to 0 than codes close to 255. Hence, entropy is modified.

For example, the string "aaaaffff" can be conceptualized as a source of entropy 1, if the table is (a,b,c,d,e,f). It is then encoded with "00005555." The entropy of the code (considered as a source) is 1. It is also the entropy of the source. However, the code of a move-to-front will be "00005000" of entropy $H = 7/8 \log_2(8/7) + 1/8 \log_2(8) \approx 0.55$. The code in itself is then compressible; this is what we call entropy reduction.

Terminating White Codes		Make Up White Codes	
Code	Run	Code	Run
00110101	0	11011	64
000111	1	10010	128
0111	2	010111	192
1000	3	0110111	256
1011	4	00110110	320
...	..	...	...
00110010	61	010011010	1600
00110011	62	011000	1664
00110100	63	010011011	1728

Figure 2.4 Fax code

Under these conditions, one is able to encode the result message – and thus the initial message – a lot more efficiently.

A variant of this method could be for one to move the character to the front in the list by a fixed number of characters, instead of pushing it in the first position. Hence, the most frequent characters will be located around the head of the list. This idea prefigures adaptive codes and dictionary-based codes that are presented in the next sections.

Exercise 2.11   *Let A be an alphabet composed by the eight following symbols: A =* ("a", "b", "c", "d", "m", "n", "o", "p").

1. *One associates a number between 0 and 7 to each symbol, according to its position in the alphabet. What are the numbers representing "abcddcbamnop-ponm" and "abcdmnopabcdmnop"?*

2. *Encode the two previous strings using the "move-to-front" technique. What do you notice?*

3. *How many bits are necessary in order to encode the two first numbers using the Huffman algorithm for example?*

4. *How many bits are necessary to encode the two numbers obtained after "move-to-front"? Compare the entropies.*

5. *What does the Huffman algorithm extended to two characters give for the last number? Then what is the size of the frequency table?*

6. *What are the characteristics of an algorithm performing "move-to-front" followed by some statistical code?*

7. *"Move-ahead-k" is a variant of "move-to-front" in which the character is pushed forward by only k positions instead of being pushed to the front of the stack. Encode the two previous strings with k = 1, then with k = 2 and compare the entropies.*

Solution on page 299.

2.3.3   Burrows–Wheeler Transform (BWT)

The idea behind the heuristic of Michael Burrows and David Wheeler is to sort the characters of a string to make move-to-front and RLE the most efficient possible. Obviously, the problem is that it is impossible in general to recover the initial string from its sorted version! Therefore, the trick is to sort the string and send some intermediate string – with a better entropy than the initial string – that will also enable one to recover the initial string. For example, let us consider the string "COMPRESSED." It is a question of creating all possible shifts as presented in Figure 2.5 and then sorting the lines according to the alphabetic and lexicographic order. Therefore, the first column **F** of the new matrix is the sorted string of all letters in the source word. The last column is called **L**. Only the first and the last columns are written, because they are the only important ones for the code. In the figure and in the text, we put the indices for the characters that are repeated; these indices simplify the visual understanding

													F	L
D_0	C	O	M	P	R	E_1	S_1	S_2	E_2	D		D_0	C	D
D_1	O	M	P	R	E	S	S	E	D	C		D_9	D	E_2
D_2	M	P	R	E	S	S	E	D	C	O		D_8	E_2	S_2
D_3	P	R	E	S	S	E	D	C	O	M		D_5	E_1	R
D_4	R	E	S	S	E	D	C	O	M	P	sort	D_2	M	O
D_5	E_1	S	S	E	D	C	O	M	P	R	$\longrightarrow$	D_1	O	... C
D_6	S_1	S	E	D	C	O	M	P	R	E_1		D_3	P	M
D_7	S_2	E	D	C	C	M	P	R	E	S_1		D_4	R	P
D_8	E_2	D	C	O	M	P	R	E	S	S_2		D_7	S_2	S_1
D_9	D	C	O	M	P	R	E	S	S_2	E_2		D_6	S_1	E_1

Figure 2.5 BWT on COMPRESSED

of the transform. However, they are not taken into account in the decoding algorithm: indeed, the order of the characters is necessarily preserved between **L** and **F**.

Obviously, in order to compute **F** (the first column) and **L** (the last column), it is not necessary to store the whole shift matrix: a simple pointer running along the string is enough. Thus this first phase is quite obvious. Nevertheless, if only **F** is sent, how do we compute the reverse transform?

Here the solution is to send the string **L** instead of **F**: even if **L** is not sorted, it is still taken from the sorted version of an almost identical string, only shifted by one letter. Therefore, one can hope that this method preserves the properties of the sorting and that entropy will be reduced. The magic of decoding comes from the knowledge of this string, coupled with the knowledge of the *primary index* (the number of the line containing the first character of the initial string; in Figure 2.5, it is 4 – considering numbers between 0 and 8) enables one to recover the initial string. It is enough to sort *L* in order to recover **F**. Then, one computes a transform vector **H** containing the correspondence of the indexes between **L** and **F**, namely, the index in **L** of each character taken in the sorted order in **F**. For Figure 2.5, this gives $H = \{4, 0, 8, 5, 3, 6, 2, 1, 7\}$, because C is in position 4 – the primary index in **L** – then E_2 is in position 0 in **L**, and E_1 is in position 8, and so on. Then, one must notice that putting **L** before **F** in column, in each line, two consecutive letters must necessarily be consecutive in the initial string: indeed, because of the shift, the last letter becomes the first one and the first one becomes the second one. This can also be explained by the fact that for all j, $L[H[j]] = F[j]$. Then, it is enough to follow this sequence of couples of letters to recover the initial string, as explained in Algorithm 2.6.

Exercise 2.12 (BWT Code Analysis)

1. The last column **L** *of the sorted matrix of the Burrows–Wheeler Transform (BWT) contains packets of identical characters, that is why* **L** *can be efficiently compressible. However, the first column* **F** *would even be more efficiently compressible if it was totally sorted. Why does one select* **L** *rather than* **F** *as the encoded message?*

Algorithm 2.6 Inverse of BWT

1: One has at one's disposal **L** and the primary index *index*.
2: **F** ← Sort **L**;
3: Compute the transform vector **H** such that $L[H[j]] = F[j]$ for all j.
4: **For** i from 0 to Size Of(**L**) **do**
5:    Print **L**[*index*]
6:    *index* ← **H**[*index*]
7: **End For**

Figure 2.6   bzip2

2. *Let us consider the string S = "sssssssssh." Compute **L** and its move-to-front compression.*

3. *Practical implementation: BWT is efficient on long strings S of length n. In practice, it is, therefore, inconceivable to store the whole n × n permutation matrix. In fact, it is enough to order these permutations. For this, one needs to be able to compare two permutations.*

   (a) Give an index that enables one to designate and differentiate permutations on the initial string.

   (b) Give an algorithm, compare_permutations, *which, given as input a string S and two integers i and j, computes a Boolean function. This algorithm must decide whether the string shifted i times is before the string shifted j times, according to the order obtained by sorting all the permutations with the alphabetic order.*

   (c) Determine the memory space required in order to compute BWT.

   *(d) How does one compute **L** and the primary index from the permutation table?*

Solution on page 299.

Therefore, in the output of the BWT, one obtains – in general – a string of lower entropy, well suited for a move-to-front followed by a RLE. The compression tool bzip2 detailed in Figure 2.6 uses this sequence of entropy reductions before performing the Huffman encoding. In Section 2.4.2, we see that this technique is among the most efficient ones nowadays.

2.4   COMMON COMPRESSION CODES

As for the compression tool bzip2, current implementations combine several compression algorithms. This enables one to take advantage of all these algorithms and minimize the number of cases of bad compression. Among the most widely used techniques, the dictionary-based techniques of Lempel and Ziv enable one to enumerate full blocks of characters.

2.4.1 Lempel–Ziv's Algorithm and `gzip` Variants

The algorithm invented by Lempel and Ziv is a dictionary-based compression algorithm (also called *by factor substitution*); it consists of replacing a sequence of characters (called a *factor*) by a shorter code that is the index of this factor in some dictionary. The idea is to perform entropy reduction, not on a single character, but rather on full words. For example, in the sentence "a good guy is a good guy,"one can dynamically associate numbers to the words already met; therefore, the code becomes "a,good,guy,is,1,2,3." One must notice that, as for dynamic algorithms, Dictionary-based methods only require a single reading of the file. There exist several variants of this algorithm: among the latter, Lempel-Ziv 1977 (LZ77) and Lempel-Ziv 1978 (LZ78) are freely available.

2.4.1.1 Lempel-Ziv 1977 (LZ77) This (published by Lempel and Ziv in 1977) is the first dictionary-based algorithm. Being an efficient alternative to the Huffman algorithms, it relaunched research in compression. LZ77 is based on a window sliding along the text from left to right. This window is divided into two parts: the first part stands for the dictionary and the second part (the reading buffer) meets the text first. At the beginning, the window is placed so that the reading buffer is located on the text, and the dictionary is not. At each step, the algorithm looks for the longest factor that repeats itself in the beginning of the reading buffer in the dictionary; this factor is encoded with the triplet (i, j, c) where

- i is the distance between the beginning of the buffer and the position of the repetition in the dictionary;
- j is the length of the repetition;
- c is the first character of the buffer different from the corresponding character in the dictionary.

After the encoding of the repetition, the window slides by $j + 1$ characters to the right. In the case when no repetition is found in the dictionary, the character c that caused the difference is then encoded with $(0, 0, c)$.

Exercise 2.13 (Encoding a Repetition Using LZ77)

1. *Encode the sequence "abcdefabcdefabcdefabcdef" using LZ77.*
2. *Encode this sequence using LZ77 and a research window whose length is 3 bits.*

Solution on page 300.

One of the most well-known implementations of LZ77 is the Lempel–Ziv–Markov-chain Algorithm (LZMA) library that combines – as expected – an LZ77 compression using a variable size dictionary (adaptive) followed by an integer arithmetic encoding.

2.4.1.2   LZ78   This is an improvement of the latter that consists of replacing the sliding window with a pointer following the text and an independent dictionary in which one looks for the factors read by the pointer. Now let us suppose that during the encoding, one reads the strings sc where s is a string at index n in the dictionary and c is a character such that the string sc is not in the dictionary. Therefore, one writes the couple (n, c) on the output. Then character c appended with factor number n gives us a new factor that is added to the dictionary to be used as a reference in the sequel of the text. Only two pieces of information are encoded instead of three with LZ77.

2.4.1.3   Lempel-Ziv-Welch (LZW)   This is another variant of Lempel–Ziv proposed by Terry Welch. LZW was patented by Unisys. It consists of encoding only the index n in the dictionary; moreover, the file is read bit by bit. Possibly, it is necessary to have an initial dictionary (e.g., an ASCII table). Compression, described by Algorithm 2.7, is then immediate: one replaces each group of characters already known with its code and one adds a new group composed of this group and the next character in the dictionary.

Algorithm 2.7 LZW: compression

 1: Let *string* ← Ø be the current string
 2: **While** Not End Of Source **do**
 3:     Read character c from the source
 4:     **If** *string*|c is in the dictionary **then**
 5:         *string* ← *string*|c
 6:     **else**
 7:         Print the code of the string
 8:         Add *string*|c in the dictionary
 9:         *string* ← c
10:     **End If**
11: **End While**

Decompression is a little bit more tricky, because one has to treat a special case when the same string is reproduced two times consecutively. Algorithm 2.8 describes this mechanism: as for compression, one starts by using the same initial dictionary that is filled in progressively, but with a delay because one has to consider the next character. This delay becomes a problem if the same string is reproduced consecutively. Indeed, in this case, the new code is not known during decompression. Nevertheless, because it is the only case where one meets this kind of problem, one notices that it has the same string at the beginning and one is able to guess the value of the group.

The following exercise illustrates this principle.

Exercise 2.14   *Using the given hexadecimal ASCII table (7bits) as the initial dictionary, compress and uncompress the string "BLEBLBLBA" with LZW.*

Algorithm 2.8 LZW: decompression
1: Read 1 byte *prec* of the encoded message
2: **While** Not End Of Encoded Message **do**
3:   Read 1 byte *curr* of the encoded message
4:   **If** *curr* is in the dictionary **then**
5:     *string* ← translation of *curr* in the dictionary
6:   **else**
7:     *string* ← translation of *prec* in the dictionary
8:     *string* ← *string*|*c*
9:   **End If**
10:   Print *string*
11:   Let *c* be the first character of *string*
12:   Let *word* be the translation of *prec* in the dictionary
13:   Add *word*|*c* in the dictionary
14:   *prec* ← *curr*
15: **End While**

	0	1	2	3	4	5	6	7	8	9	A	B	C	D	E	F
0	NUL	SOH	STX	ETX	EOT	ENQ	ACK	BEL	BS	HT	LF	VT	FF	CR	SO	SI
1	DLE	DC1	DC2	DC3	DC4	NAK	SYN	ETB	CAN	EM	SUB	ESC	FS	GS	RS	US
2	SP	!	"	#	\$	%	&	'	(	)	*	+	,	-	.	/
3	0	1	2	3	4	5	6	7	8	9	:	;	<	=	>	?
4	@	A	B	C	D	E	F	G	H	I	J	K	L	M	N	O
5	P	Q	R	S	T	U	V	W	X	Y	Z	[	\	]	^	_
6	`	a	b	c	d	e	f	g	h	i	j	k	l	m	n	o
7	p	q	r	s	t	u	v	w	x	y	z	{	|	}	~	DEL

Uncompress the result without considering the particular case described above. What do you notice?   *Solution on page 300.*

Several possible variants have been proposed: for example, Lempel-Ziv-Miller-Wegman (LZMW) in which "string + next word" is added to the dictionary instead of only "string + next character" or even Lempel-Ziv All Prefixes (LZAP) in which all prefixes of "string + next word" are added to the dictionary.

The Unix command compress implements LZ77. As for as the gzip tool, it is based on a variant of the latter; it uses two dynamic Huffman's trees: one for the strings and the other for the distances between the occurrences. Distances between two occurrences of some string are bounded: when the distance becomes too high, one restarts the compression from the current character, independently of the compression that has already been performed before this character.

This singularity implies that there is no structural difference between a single file compressed with gzip and a sequence of compressed files. Hence, let f1.gz and f2.gz be the results associated with the compression of two source files f1 and f2: one appends these two files to a third one called f3.gz. Then, when uncompressing the file with gunzip f3.gz, one gets a result file whose content is identical to f1 appended with f2.

Exercise 2.15 (Gzip)

1. *Encode the string "abbarbarbbabbarbaa" with LZ77.*

2. *Cut the previous encoding into three strings (distances, Lengths, and characters), and apply* gzip, *the dynamic Huffman encoding of @ being forced onto
   one single bit,* 1. *Besides, in* gzip, *the first* @ *is not forgotten.*

3. *Let us suppose that the previous string is divided into two pieces, "abbarbarb"
   and "babbarbaa," in two separated files "f1" and "f2." Give the content of
   "f1.gz" and "f2.gz," the compressions of "f1" and "f2" with* gzip.

4. *One appends the two files "f1.gz" and "f2.gz" in a file "f3.gz" (e.g., using the
   Unix command* cat f1.gz f2.gz > f3.gz), *then one uncompresses
   the file "f3.gz" with* gunzip. *What is the result? Deduce the interest of not
   forgetting the first* @.

5. *How does one add compression levels in* gzip *(ex.*
   gzip -1 xxx.txt' *or* gzip -9 xxx.txt')?*

   Solution on page 301.

2.4.2 Comparisons of Compression Algorithms

In Table 2.5, we compare the compression rates and the encoding/decoding speeds of
the common tools on unix/linux using the example of an email file (i.e., containing
texts, images, and binary files).

The gzip and compress programs – which use variants of Lempel–Ziv – are
described in the next section. bzip2 – which uses an entropy reduction like BWT
before performing an entropic encoding – is described in Section 2.3.3. 7-Zip uses

**TABLE 2.5 Comparison of the Compression of an Email File (15.92 Mo: Text, Images,
Programs, etc.) with Several Algorithms, on a PIV 1.5 GHz**

Algorithm	Compressed file, Mo	Rate, %	Encoding speed, s	Decoding speed, s
7-Zip-4.42 (LZMA+?)	5.96	62.57	23.93	6.27
RAR-3.51 (?)	6.20	61.07	14.51	0.46
rzip-2.1 -9 (LZ77+Go)	6.20	61.09	9.26	2.94
ppmd-9.1 (Predictive)	6.26	60.71	11.26	12.57
bzip2-1.0.3 (BWT)	6.69	57.96	7.41	3.16
gzip-1.3.5 -9 (LZ77)	7.68	51.77	2.00	0.34
gzip-1.3.5 -2 (LZ77)	8.28	47.99	1.14	0.34
WinZip-9.0 (LZW+?)	7.72	51.55	5	5
compress (LZW)	9.34	41.31	1.11	0.32
lzop-1.01 -9 (LZW+?)	9.35	41.32	6.73	0.09
lzop-1.01 -2 (LZW+?)	10.74	32.54	0.45	0.09
pack (Huffman)	11.11	30.21	0.33	0.27

the variant Lempel–Ziv–Markov-chain Algorithm (LZMA) of LZ77, associated with an arithmetic encoding and several additional heuristics depending on the kind of input file. WinZip also uses several variants depending on the type of the file and finishes with a LZW encoding. rzip is used for large files and, therefore, uses LZ77 with a very large window. ppmd uses a Markov probabilistic model in order to predict the next character with respect to the knowledge of the characters that are immediately before it. Then lzop uses a collection of algorithms called *Lempel-Ziv-Oberhumer (LZO)*, optimized for decompression speed: it takes care of long matches and long literal runs so that it produces good results on highly redundant data and deals acceptably with low compressible data. Finally, pack implements the simple Huffman encoding.

As a conclusion, practical behavior reflects theory: LZ77 provides a better compression than LZW, but slower. Dictionary-based algorithms are more efficient than naive entropic encodings but are less efficient than an entropic encoding with a good heuristic for reducing the entropy. Common software usually tries several methods in order to find out the best compression. Although the compression rate is improved, the compression time usually suffers from this implementation choice.

2.4.3   GIF and PNG Formats for Image Compression

Common compact data formats take the nature of the data to encode into account. They are different depending on whether it is a question of a sound, an image, or a text. Among the image formats, the Graphics Interchange Format (GIF) is a graphic bitmap file format proposed by the Compuserve company. It is a compression format for a pixel image, that is, for an image described as a sequence of points (pixels) stored in an array; each pixel has a value for its color.

The compression principle is divided into two steps. First pixel colors (at the beginning, there are 16.8 million colors encoded on 24 bits Red/Green/Blue (RGB)) are restricted to a pallet of 2–256 colors (2, 4, 8, 16, 32, 64, 128, or the default value 256 colors). Hence, the color of each pixel is rounded up to the closest color appearing in the pallet. While keeping a large number of different colors with a 256-color pallet, this enables one to have a compression factor 3. Then, the sequence of pixel colors is compressed with the dynamic compression algorithm Lempel-Ziv-Welch (LZW). There exist two versions of this file format, which were, respectively, developed in 1987 and 1989:

- GIF 87a enables one to have a progressive display (using interleaving) and animated images (animated GIFs), storing several images within the same file.
- GIF 89a – in addition to these functionalities – enables one to define a transparent color in the pallet and specify the delay for the animations.

As the LZW compression algorithm was patented by Unisys, all software editors manipulating GIF images would have had to pay royalties to Unisys. This is one of the reasons why the Portable Network Graphics (PNG) format is increasingly used, to the disadvantage of GIF format. The PNG format is similar to the GIF format, but it uses the LZ77 compression algorithm.

2.5 LOSSY COMPRESSION

2.5.1 Deterioration of Information

We have seen that lossless compression does enable one to compress above the threshold of entropy and that heuristics of entropy reduction enable one to drop this threshold by changing the model of the source. But none of these methods do take the type of file to compress and its purpose into account. Let us take the example of a numerical picture. Lossless compressors will transmit the file without using the fact that it is actually an image and the file will still be fully recoverable. But there might exist far more efficient formats for which, if part of the information is lost, the difference with the original picture will never be *visible*.

Therefore, one will not be able to recover the complete initial files. However, it will be possible to visualize images with almost the same quality. This means that the quality that was formerly encoded in the initial file is superfluous, because it does not induce any visible difference. Thus lossy compressors are specific to the type of data one wishes to transmit or store (mostly pictures, sounds, and videos), and they use this information in order to encode the visual result of the file rather than the file itself. This type of compression is necessary for video formats, for example, in which the size of the data and the related computations are very large.

Lossy compressors will enable one to overcome the threshold of entropy and to obtain very high compression rates. Not only do they take the pure information into account but they also consider the way it is perceived by human beings by modeling retinal or audio persistence, for example. One is able to measure the efficiency of these compressors with respect to the compression rate, but still the quality of the resulting pictures can only be evaluated by the experience of the users. Therefore, we present here the standard formats that have been well tried. Besides, for audiovisual information, another important criterion will be coupled with compression rate: that is, decompression speed. In particular, for sounds or videos, hearing and visualization require very fast computations to read the compressed files. Thus the complexity of the decompression algorithms is a constraint as important as the size of the compressed messages when dealing with audiovisual information.

2.5.2 Transformation of Audiovisual Information

Compact formats for storing pictures, sounds, or videos always use extended sources. They do not encode the file pixel by pixel but they take the pixel and its neighborhood into account in order to capture global parameters such as contours, regularities, or intensity variation. These data are treated in the form of pseudo-periodic signals. For instance, if one part of an image is a soft gradation, the frequency of the signal is low, whereas the frequency of another part of the picture in which colors and textures often vary is high. This enables one to perform a very efficient encoding on low frequency zones. Besides, brutally deleting very high frequency zones is often unnoticeable and, hence, acceptable.

2.5.3 JPEG Format

The Joint Photographic Experts Group (JPEG) encoding format compresses static images with a loss of information. The encoding algorithm is complex and is performed in several steps. The main idea is that usually the colors of contiguous pixels in an image hardly differ. Moreover, an image is a signal: instead of computing the value of the pixels, one computes the frequencies (Discrete Fourier Transform or Discrete Cosine Transform for JPEG.

2.5.3.1 DCT-JPEG Indeed, one can consider that an image is a matrix containing the color of each pixel; it appears that digital pictures are mostly composed of zones having low DCT frequencies when considering the color luma (or *luminance*, i.e., the brightness in an image in the encoding of an image in Luma/Chroma mode) rather than the Red/Green/Blue (RGB) mode. There exist several formulas to switch from the RGB mode to the Luminance/Chrominance color space (YUV) mode (Y for the luma and U and V for the color information) depending on the physical model of light.

A classic formula for finding the luma sums weighted values of R, G, and B: $Y = w_r * R + w_g * G + w_b * B$ where $w_r = 0.299$, $w_b = 0.114$, and $w_g = 1 - w_r - w_b$. Then U and V are computed as scaled differences between Y and the blue and red values, using the scales $u_m = 0.436$ and $v_m = 0.615$, and following the linear transformation:

$$
\begin{bmatrix} Y \\ U \\ V \end{bmatrix} = \begin{bmatrix} w_r & 1 - w_r - w_b & w_b \\ -\frac{u_m}{1-w_b}w_r & -\frac{u_m}{1-w_b}(1 - w_r - w_b) & u_m \\ v_m & -\frac{v_m}{1-w_r}(1 - w_r - w_b) & -\frac{v_m}{1-w_r}w_b \end{bmatrix} \cdot \begin{bmatrix} R \\ G \\ B \end{bmatrix}.
$$

Therefore, the idea is to apply the DCT (see Section 1.4.2.4) to the luma matrix.

However, the DCT will transform this matrix into another matrix containing the high frequencies in the bottom right corner and the low frequencies in the top left corner. Hence, the luma of Figure 2.7 is transformed by the DCT such that $L \to D$:

$$
L = \begin{bmatrix}
76 & 76 & 76 & 255 & 255 & 255 & 255 & 255 \\
76 & 255 & 255 & 255 & 255 & 255 & 255 & 255 \\
76 & 76 & 149 & 149 & 149 & 255 & 255 & 255 \\
76 & 255 & 149 & 255 & 149 & 29 & 29 & 29 \\
76 & 255 & 149 & 255 & 149 & 29 & 255 & 255 \\
255 & 255 & 149 & 149 & 149 & 29 & 255 & 255 \\
255 & 255 & 255 & 255 & 255 & 29 & 255 & 255 \\
255 & 255 & 255 & 255 & 255 & 29 & 29 & 29
\end{bmatrix}
$$

Figure 2.7   The 8 × 8 RGB image with white background (here in gray-levels)

$$D = \begin{bmatrix} 1474 & -3 & -38 & -128 & 49 & -8 & -141 & 11 \\ 1 & -171 & -51 & 35 & -45 & -4 & 40 & -58 \\ 93 & -2 & -43 & 45 & 26 & 0 & 38 & 24 \\ 61 & -66 & 70 & -11 & 23 & 15 & -48 & 6 \\ -113 & 62 & -71 & -3 & 27 & -10 & -25 & -33 \\ -47 & 1 & -5 & 18 & 28 & 14 & 4 & 2 \\ -72 & -37 & 37 & 51 & 7 & 18 & 33 & -1 \\ 41 & -100 & 21 & -9 & 2 & 27 & 7 & 7 \end{bmatrix}.$$

Possibly, the human eye gives more importance to brightness than to colors. When only keeping the first terms of the luma DCT decomposition (the most important ones), one looses some information but the picture remains distinguishable.

This operation is called *quantization*, and it is the only step with the loss of information in the whole JPEG encoding scheme. The operation consists of rounding the value $C_{i,j} = \left\lceil \dfrac{DCT_{i,j}}{Q_{i,j}} \right\rceil$, where Q is the following quantization matrix:

$$Q = \begin{bmatrix} 16 & 11 & 10 & 16 & 24 & 40 & 51 & 61 \\ 12 & 12 & 14 & 19 & 26 & 58 & 60 & 55 \\ 14 & 13 & 16 & 24 & 40 & 57 & 69 & 56 \\ 14 & 17 & 22 & 29 & 51 & 87 & 80 & 62 \\ 18 & 22 & 37 & 56 & 68 & 109 & 103 & 77 \\ 24 & 35 & 55 & 64 & 81 & 104 & 113 & 92 \\ 49 & 64 & 78 & 87 & 103 & 121 & 120 & 101 \\ 72 & 92 & 95 & 98 & 112 & 100 & 103 & 99 \end{bmatrix}$$

$$C = \begin{bmatrix} 92 & -1 & -4 & -8 & 2 & -1 & -3 & 0 \\ 0 & -15 & -4 & 1 & -2 & -1 & 0 & -2 \\ 6 & -1 & -3 & 1 & 0 & 0 & 0 & 0 \\ 4 & -4 & 3 & -1 & 0 & 0 & -1 & 0 \\ -7 & 2 & -2 & -1 & 0 & -1 & -1 & -1 \\ -2 & 0 & -1 & 0 & 0 & 0 & 0 & 0 \\ -2 & -1 & 0 & 0 & 0 & 0 & 0 & -1 \\ 0 & -2 & 0 & -1 & 0 & 0 & 0 & 0 \end{bmatrix}.$$

We then obtain the above matrix C. In the example, one can notice that after quantization, many values are identical and close to zero. The choice of a quantization matrix with values close to 1 (respectively far from 1) enables one to increase (respectively to decrease) the detail level.

Eventually, the picture is encoded as a sequence of numbers (a DCT quantization value followed by the number of consecutive pixels having the same value according to the zigzag scan presented in Figure 2.8). Thanks to the small values one has already noticed, one can hope that entropy after this RLE has been considerably reduced.

Then, the JPEG algorithm ends with a statistical encoding, such as the Huffman or the arithmetic codings (Figure 2.9).

Exercise 2.16 (JPEG 3×3) *Suppose that we apply the JPEG algorithm on smaller 3×3 blocks and that the luma value* $\begin{bmatrix} 27 & 45 & 18 \\ 36 & 27 & 36 \\ 36 & 54 & 27 \end{bmatrix}$ *is computed on a given block.*

  1. Compute the DCT matrix of this block.
  2. Apply the quantification $Q_{i,j} = 4 - \max\{i, j\}$, for $i = 0, ..., 2, j = 0, ..., 2$.

Solution on page 301.

This is for the luma. For the chrominance, one can also use subsampling, as the human eye is less sensitive to the position and motion of color than to its luminance. The idea is use the same U and V values for several consecutive pixels. A $(J : a : b)$ subsampling represents a block of $2 \times J$ pixels where the $2J$ luma values are stored,

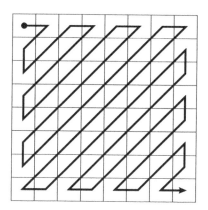

Figure 2.8   JPEG zigzag scan

Figure 2.9   JPEG compression

but only a chroma values for the first J pixels and b chroma values for the second row of J pixels. For instance, (4 : 4 : 4) represents the full resolution without any subsampling.

Exercise 2.17 (Subsampling Formats)   *For the following subsampling formats, give the compression gain with respect to the full resolution and their horizontal and vertical resolutions:* (4 : 2 : 2), (4 : 2 : 0), (4 : 1 : 1).   *Solution on page 301.*

Notice that in the JPEG-2000 standard[1], which replaced the DCT-JPEG standard, the cosine transform and quantization are replaced by a wavelet transform where only some levels are preserved. The number of levels or bands one chooses to keep directly affects the compression rate one wishes to reach.

2.5.3.2 *Watermarking JPEG Images*   A classical way of embedding some information into JPEG images is to use the lower bits of the quantized coefficients. Indeed, by construction, JPEG quantization uses a modifications of the luma that induces little visual distortion. Therefore, a modification of the lower bits of the large coefficients in the C matrices should remain invisible.

For instance, suppose that r is an acceptable distortion rate for the luma coefficient (i.e., that coefficients modified with at most that rate will remain visually close to the original). Then any coefficient $C_{i,j}$ larger than $\frac{1}{r}$ can embed up to $\lfloor \log_2 \left(r \cdot |C_{i,j}| \right) \rfloor$ bits of additional information.

The watermarking algorithm can be introduced within the JPEG compression:

1. Transform the original image into its quantized 8×8 matrices. Use the rate r to identify the coefficients capable of storing some additional information.
2. The lower bits of the large enough coefficients of every C matrix are set to zero. Then $\sum \lfloor \log_2 \left(r \cdot |C_{i,j}| \right) \rfloor$ bits can be added to the image in the latter identified positions (where i and j are taken over all the 8×8 C matrices comprising the image). These bits can be the result of a compression, then potentially followed by an encryption and an error-correction coding depending of the required property.
3. Terminate the JPEG compression with the lossless compressions (the RLE zigzag and the statistical encoding).

Then the extraction of the watermark is performed also during JPEG decompression: after the lossless decoding, the watermark is recovered also by identifying the large enough coefficients with respect to r and extracting their lower bits.

The classical steganalysis consists of comparing the entropy of the suspected image to that of the average entropy of similar images. Another approach uses the statistical tests of Section 1.3.7.4.

---

[1]http://www.jpeg.org/jpeg2000.

Exercise 2.18 (Steganalysis of Watermarked JPEG Images)

1. *An image without any hidden data should have a similar luma for adjacent DCT coefficients. Design a way to build an expected distribution of luma using this fact.*

2. *Which statistical test would you then use to discriminate an image with an embedded content?*

Solution on page 302.

2.5.3.3   *Secure JPEG-2000 (JPSEC)*   Part 8 of the JPEG-2000 standard provides tools to generate, consume, and exchange secure JPEG-2000 codestreams. This is referred to as *JPSEC* and defines a framework that includes confidentiality, integrity, authentication, access control, or Digital Right Management (DRM).

This is achieved using the various techniques presented in this book such as encryption, electronic signature, or watermarking.

Now a first approach could be to treat the JPEG-2000 bitstream as an input for any of the security algorithms. The idea of JPSEC is instead that these security techniques could be performed during the JPEG compression as was shown, for example, for the watermarking example of Section 2.5.3.2. For instance, the JPSEC bitstream still retains the rich structures of the JPEG-2000 standard such as tile, layer, and resolution.

The JPSEC syntax uses three types of security tools: template tools, registration authority tools, and user-defined tools that define which protection methods are used. It defines a Zone of Influence (ZOI) to describe on which part of the image the security tool is applied. The standard already proposed the following tools:

- A flexible access control scheme;
- A unified authentication framework;
- A simple packet-based encryption method;
- Wavelet and bitstream domain scrambling for conditional access control;
- Progressive access;
- Scalable authenticity;
- Secure scalable streaming.

For instance, multilevel access control could uses several keys to decipher selected levels of details in the JPEG image using the JPEG layers; partial encryption could reveal only parts of the image; and so on.

2.5.4   Motion Picture Experts Group (MPEG) Format

The MPEG format defines the compression for animated images. The encoding algorithm uses JPEG in order to encode an image, and it also takes into account the fact that two consecutive images in a video stream are very close. One of the singularities of the MPEG norms is motion compensation (the movement can be a zoom, for instance) from an image to the next one. A MPEG-1 output contains four types of images: images in format I (JPEG), images P encoded using differential encoding (one only encodes the differences between the image and the previous one: motion compensation enables one to have very close consecutive images), bidirectional images B encoded using differential encoding with respect to the previous image and the next one (in case the next image is closer than the previous one), and eventually low resolution images used for fast forward in videotape recorders. In practice, with P and B images, a new full I image every 10–15 images is enough.

As video streams consist of images and sounds, one must also be able to compress sounds. The MPEG group defined three formats: MPEG-1 Audio Layer I, II, and III, the latter being the well-known MP3 format. MPEG-1 is the combination of image and sound compressions, coupled with a time-stamp synchronization and a system reference clock as presented in Figure 2.10.

Since 1992, the MPEG format has evolved from MPEG-1 (320×240 pixels and a throughput of 1.5 Mbits/s) to MPEG-2 in 1996 (with four different resolutions from 352×288 up to 1920×1152 pixels plus an additional subtitle and language multiplexed stream: this format is currently used in DVDs) and to MPEG-4 (format for videoconferences and DivXs: video becomes an object-oriented scene), started in 1999.

Exercise 2.19 (PAL Video Format) *PAL, Phase Alternating Line, is an analogical color television coding system using images of 576 pixels per line and 720 lines. Its frame rate (number of images per second) is usually of 25 images per second.*

1. *If each pixel uses a color encoding of 1 byte per color with a (4 : 2 : 0) subsampling (see Exercise 2.17), what would be the size of an uncompressed, 90-min long, movie?*

2. *Suppose the same movie is compressed in a DivX format and fits onto a 800 MB CD-ROM. What is the compression gain?*

Solution on page 302.

Sound is decomposed into three layers: MP1, MP2, and MP3, depending on the desired compression rate (i.e., the loss of information). In practice, compression is performed with factor 4 for MP1, 6–8 for MP2 (this format is used in Video CDs for instance), and 10–12 for MP3 with respect to the analogical signal.

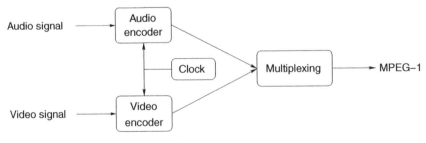

Figure 2.10   MPEG-1 compression

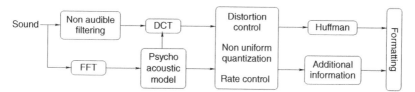

Figure 2.11   MP3 sound compression

In Figure 2.11, we give an idea of the MP3 transform: first of all, analogical sound is filtered and modified by the Fourier transform (with loss) and simultaneously by a Discrete Cosine Transform.

Then, the combination of these two transforms enables one to perform a quantization and control the result in order to preserve only the main audible part. At the end of the algorithm, statistical compression is obviously performed in order to reduce the file size and reach its final entropy.

3

CRYPTOLOGY

Now, let us focus on extending the encoding scheme to cases in which the transmitted information contains a secret. We must assume that roads are not controlled and that the transmitted message can be read by anyone. However, only the recipient must be able to recover the information it contains, that is, the original message. The applications are obviously numerous for both military and commercial uses.

Cryptology – literally "science of secret" - consists of two main components, namely *cryptography*, which deals with studying and building processes for information encryption, and *cryptanalysis*, which deals with analyzing (or attacking) ciphertexts in order to recover the hidden information. In this chapter, we present how to build secure systems, and this requires the knowledge of defense as well as attack techniques, in order to develop a global strategy of security.

First, we model the possible threats and derive general cryptography principles. Then, two types of ciphers are developped: secret key cryptography that mimics perfect secrecy in realistic settings and public key cryptography that eases key exchanges. Authentication of a sender and electronic signature are developed in Section 3.5, and we end this chapter with the study of several usual protocols for secure information exchanges.

Foundations of Coding: Compression, Encryption, Error Correction, First Edition.
Jean-Guillaume Dumas, Jean-Louis Roch, Éric Tannier and Sébastien Varrette.
© 2015 John Wiley & Sons, Inc. Published 2015 by John Wiley & Sons, Inc.
http://foundationsofcoding.imag.fr

3.1 GENERAL PRINCIPLES

3.1.1 Terminology

The fundamental objective of cryptography is to enable two people, traditionally called *Alice* and *Bob*, to communicate through an insecure channel in such way that any opponent, *Oscar*, having access to the information circulating on the communication channel is not able to understand what is exchanged. For instance, the channel can be a phone line or any other communication network.

The information Alice wishes to transmit to Bob is called *plaintext* (or *clear text*). It can be a text in English, numerical data or any other arbitrary information. Encoding, that is to say the transformation processing of a message M in order to make it incomprehensible, is called encryption or ciphering. Hence, one generates a *ciphertext C* from an *encryption function E* by $C = E(M)$. The process of recovering the plaintext from the ciphertext is called *decryption* or *deciphering* and it uses a *decryption function D*. Therefore, one must have $D(C) = D(E(M)) = M$. Thus, E is injective (a ciphertext is associated with at most one source message) and D is surjective or onto.

A *cryptographic algorithm* is an algorithm that computes the value of the mathematical functions related to encryption and decryption. In practice, security of messages is always provided by what we call the *keys*. These are parameters for functions E and D, which are denoted K_e and K_d, whose value belongs to a set called *key space*. Hence, one reaches the fundamental relation of cryptography (illustrated in Figure 3.1):

$$\begin{cases} E_{K_e}(M) = C \\ D_{K_d}(C) = M \end{cases} \tag{3.1}$$

This kind of relation between the keys K_e and K_d – which are used in encryption and decryption – enables one to highlight two main classes of cryptographic systems:

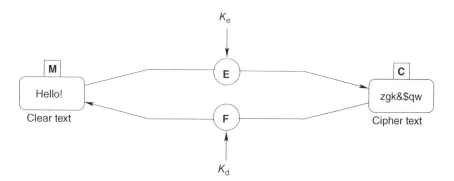

Figure 3.1 Fundamental relation of cryptography

- On the one hand, symmetric cryptosystems: the key is a shared secret between the sender and the recipient; such systems are described in Section 3.2.
- On the other hand, public key (or asymmetric) cryptosystems: no secret information is shared *a priori* among several protagonists; such systems are described in Section 3.4.

3.1.2   What is the Use of Cryptography?

Communications exchanged between Alice and Bob suffer from several threats (these threats are described a little further on, see Section 3.1.3). Cryptography provides several functionalities or services to overcome these threats, which are summarized in the acronym Confidentiality, Authentication, Integrity, Nonrepudiation (CAIN):

1. **Confidentiality** of the information stored or manipulated: this is done using encryption algorithms. Confidentiality consists of *preventing unauthorized access* to information for nonrecipients. They are able to read ciphertexts transmitted on the channel, but they are not able to decrypt them.

2. **Authentication** of the protagonists in a communication (or more generally in a resource) exchange. One must be able to detect identity theft. For instance, Alice may identify herself by proving to Bob that she knows a secret S, and that she is the only one who knows it.

3. **Integrity** of information stored or manipulated. The question here is to check that the message was not *falsified* during transmission (Figure 3.2). This integrity checking is not put on the same level as what we will see in Chapter 4. It rather deals with a voluntary and malicious modification of the information performed by a third party during the transfer on the channel. Generally, these modifications are hidden by the third party so that they are hardly noticeable. In Figure 3.2, for example, integrity checking of a message M is performed using a function f such that it is very difficult to find two messages M_1 and M_2 having the same image A through f.

4. **Nonrepudiation** of information. This is not a protection against a third party, but rather a protection for protagonists against each other. If Alice sends a message M, she must not be able afterward to pretend to Bob that she did not or that

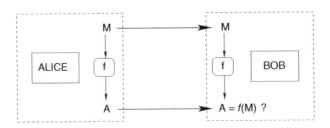

Figure 3.2   Principle of an integrity checking algorithm

she has sent a message M' and that it was actually misunderstood. For this, one associates signature-based algorithms. This aspect is discussed in more detail in Section 3.5.

Up to a recent period, encryption only took confidentiality into account, and only symmetric methods were developed. During recent 40 years, new trends have emerged:

- authentication has become at least as important as secrecy. It is especially true in e-business: one must be able to prove that the order actually came from the person to whom the shipment is sent, in order to avoid disputes.
- some part of the key have to be public, so that the number of keys needed to communicate with a large number of interlocutors does not explode.

Possibly, another criterion is fundamental: one has to consider the computation speed for encryption and decryption and the size of the ciphertexts. As operations are performed on a large amount of data, the efficiency criterion is very important when encrypting – for example – audio or video streams "on-the-fly" while using a minimum part of the bandwidth.

An ideal cryptosystem would solve all these issues simultaneously: it would use public keys, ensure secrecy, authentication, and integrity, and it would be fast enough. Unfortunately, up to now, there does not exist a single technique satisfying all these criteria. Common systems such as AES (Section 3.2.4) are efficient but they use only private keys; public key cryptosystems are able to ensure authentication but their computation is often costlier. They are thus usually inefficient for ciphering a large amount of data. This trade-off has induced the development of hybrid cryptographic protocols, such as Pretty Good Privacy (PGP) (Section 3.6.3), which are based on both symmetric and asymmetric cryptosystems.

In order to build good cryptosystems, one has to study the several types of attacks that Oscar might perform in order to recover the meaning of the exchanged messages. A good knowledge of all types of threats bearing upon the secret enables one to actually ensure secrecy.

3.1.3   Main Types of Threats

3.1.3.1   Passive/Active Attacks   First of all, one distinguishes *passive attacks*, in which Oscar only listens to messages exchanged between Alice and Bob, and *active attacks*, in which Oscar is able to modify the message during transmission. The first type of attack threatens confidentiality of information, whereas the second one might induce modifications of information and identity thefts.

3.1.3.2   Cryptanalysis and Attacks on Encryption Schemes   Generally, one assumes that Oscar knows which cryptosystem is used (according to Kerckhoffs' principles). One distinguishes the possible attack levels:

Ciphertext only attack (COA). Oscar only knows a ciphertext C.

Known plaintext attack (KPA). Oscar disposes of both a plaintext M and its ciphertext C.

Chosen plaintext attack (CPA). Oscar is able to choose the plaintext M and to get its ciphertext C.

Chosen ciphertext attack (CCA). Oscar is able to choose a ciphertext C and to get its plaintext M.

In all cases, ensuring confidentiality of the communications between Alice and Bob means that Oscar is not able to

- find M from $E(M)$; the encryption scheme must resist attacks on ciphertexts.
- find the decryption method D from a sequence $\{E(M_i)\}$ derived from a plaintext sequence $\{M_1, M_2, M_3, \ldots\}$; the system must be resistant against attacks using plaintexts.

Encryption functions use keys as parameters. In order to "break" an encryption algorithm, most of the time one tries to find the value of these keys. For instance, one may consider that a key is good if its entropy (see the definition in Chapter 1) is high because it means that it does not contain recurring patterns providing information on its form.

In addition to the attack levels we have just defined, Oscar may also use several general algorithms:

Brute force attack. This consists in trying all possible values for the key, that is, the exploration of the whole key space. The complexity bound of this method appears immediately: for a key on 64 bits, one has to try $2^{64} = 1.844 * 10^{19}$ distinct combinations.

On a computer trying one billion keys per second, it would take 584 years to be sure to find the key[1].

Known sequence attack. This kind of attack consists in assuming that part of the plaintext is known (for instance, it can be standard headers in the case of e-mails) and in starting from this knowledge in order to guess the key.

This attack may be successful if the encryption algorithm preserves the regularities of the initial message.

Forced sequence attack. This method, which is based on the previous one, consists in leading the victim to ciphering a block of data whose content is known by the attacker.

Differential analysis attack. This attack uses the slight differences between successive messages (server ID (*logs*) for instance) to guess the key.

---

[1] or one year with 584 computers working in parallel.

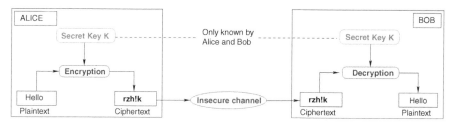

Figure 3.3   Principle of symmetric cryptography

3.2   SECRET KEY CRYPTOGRAPHY

3.2.1   Principle of Symmetric Cryptography

Let us take the notation of the Equation (3.1); symmetric encryption rests upon the following principle: $K_e = K_d = K$. In other words, Alice and Bob secretly agree upon a shared key K, which is used in both encryption and decryption. They also agree upon a cryptographic algorithm for encryption and decryption. The general principle of symmetric cryptography is illustrated in Figure 3.3. One often uses the **analogy of a safe** to qualify symmetric cryptosystems: only the key holders (a priori, Alice and Bob) may be able to open the safe. Oscar, who does not possess the key, will have to force the safe if he wishes to have access to its content. Obviously, if Oscar is able to get the key by any means, he will be able to decrypt all messages exchanged between Alice and Bob.

Let us notice that the expression "symmetric encryption" is used to differenti-ate this scheme from asymmetric cryptography. The main advantage of such systems is that they are very efficient in terms of computation time for both encryption and decryption. On the other hand, the main weakness of this system comes from the necessity of having an absolute secrecy surrounding the key K. Historically, it was the first kind of encryption to be used. Several examples of this type (Caesar encryp-tion and Vernam perfect encryption) were described in Chapter 1. Let us study other examples of this kind in the form of an exercise.

Exercise 3.1 (Affine Encryption)   *On page 6, we studied the case of Caesar encryption defined over some alphabet $\mathcal{A}$ of n characters. This scheme is a particu-lar case of affine encryption. Given a bijective map between $\mathcal{A}$ and $\mathbb{Z}_n$, and denoting $\mathbb{Z}_n^*$ the set of invertible elements in $\mathbb{Z}_n$, one is able to write the affine encryption function for a message $M \in \mathbb{Z}_n$ from a key $K = (a,b) \in \mathbb{Z}_n^* \times \mathbb{Z}_n$:*

$$E_{(a,b)} : \quad \mathbb{Z}_n \quad \longrightarrow \quad \mathbb{Z}_n$$
$$x \quad \longrightarrow \quad E_{(a,b)}(x) = ax + b \quad \mod n$$

1. *Express $|\mathbb{Z}_{26}^*|$ and $\mathbb{Z}_{26}^*$.*
2. *Still considering $n = 26$ and using the key $K = (15,7)$ (justify the use of such key), give the ciphertexts for $x \in \{0, 1, 2\}$.*
3. *Express the affine decryption function $D_{(a,b)}$.*

4. *Although ciphertexts produced by affine encryption seem incomprehensible, this scheme does not modify the frequency of occurrence of the various letters composing the text. Statistical repartition of the letters in a text written in French, as well as the bijective map letter by letter which will used in the sequel, are provided in Table 3.1.*

Alice sends a text to Bob. Tacitely, characters not belonging to $\mathcal{A}$ are not encrypted. One intercepts the following message:

```
        mcahbo isbfock, ekb kp cbfbo vobixo,
            hopcah op esp foi kp rbsmcuo.
        mcahbo bopcbl, vcb j'slokb cjjoixo
            jka haph c vok vboe io jcpucuo:
        "xo! fspdskb, mspeaokb lk isbfock,
    yko nske ohoe dsja! yko nske mo eomfjoz fock!
            ecpe mophab, ea nshbo bcmcuo
            eo bcvvsbho à nshbo vjkmcuo,
    nske ohoe jo vxopat loe xshoe lo ioe fsae."
```

One counts the occurrences of each letter of the alphabet in the ciphertext. Hence, one gets Table 3.2.

(a) From this result, deduce the key used by Alice.

(b) Deduce the decryption key and the plaintext.

Solution on page 303.

TABLE 3.1 Frequency of the Letters in French

A → 0	8.11%	J → 9	0.18%	S → 18	8.87%		
B → 1	0.81%	K → 10	0.02%	T → 19	7.44%		
C → 2	3.38%	L → 11	5.99%	U → 20	5.23%		
D → 3	4.28%	M → 12	2.29%	V → 21	1.28%		
E → 4	17.69%	N → 13	7.68%	W → 22	0.06%		
F → 5	1.13%	O → 14	5.20%	X → 23	0.53%		
G → 6	1.19%	P → 15	2.92%	Y → 24	0.26%		
H → 7	0.74%	Q → 16	0.83%	Z → 25	0.12%		
I → 8	7.24%	R → 17	6.43%				

TABLE 3.2 Frequency Analysis of the Ciphertext

In the Ciphertext		Reference (text in French)	
o → 14	18.11%	e → 4	17.69%
b → 1	9.05%	s → 18	8.87%
c → 2	7.82%	a → 0	8.11%
e → 4	7.41%	⋮	⋮
⋮	⋮		

3.2.2 Classes of Symmetric Encryption Schemes

As we have seen in Chapter 1, Sections 1.2 and 1.3, one distinguishes two kinds of codes. Similarly, there are two kinds of encryption schemes.

3.2.2.1 Symmetric Stream Ciphers In order to get close to Vernam's model (described in Section 1.2.1), such ciphers process the data on-the-fly. Their use is based on a Pseudo-Random Number Generators (PRNG) (1.3.7) and on a fast bitwise substitution mechanism such as "eXclusive OR" (XOR $\oplus$), which is used in the Vernam code. This principle is illustrated in Figure 3.4.

As a consequence of Kerckhoffs' principles, one immediately notices that security of a stream cipher depends on the quality of the key generator.

Among the most famous examples (not necessarily the most secure ones), one may notice LFSR (see the mechanism of the generator on page 63), RC4 (which is used, for example, in the Secure Sockets Layer (SSL) protocol in order to protect Internet communications or in the WEP protocol in order to secure WiFi connections), Py, E0 (used in Bluetooth communications), and A5/3 (used in GSM communications).

As RC4-WEP and A5-GSM were broken, the eSTREAM project has identified a portfolio of seven promising new stream ciphers. Four of them are software oriented (HC-128, Rabbit, Salsa20/12, and Sosemanuk), whereas the three remaining ones are hardware oriented (Grain, Trivium, and Mickey).

A common property of stream ciphers is to generate an internal state from which pseudo-random bits are produced in a stream. The sender and the receiver must synchronize their internal state in order to be able to produce the same sequence of pseudo-random bits.

For instance, the Rabbit stream cipher uses a 128-bits key k_i that, with a 64-bits initial value, generates 512-bits of internal state (8×32-bits $x_{i,j}$) and 512-bits of internal counters (8×32-bits $c_{i,j}$) with:

$$x_{j,0} = k_{j+1 \mod 8} \| k_j \qquad \text{for j even}$$
$$= k_{j+5 \mod 8} \| k_{j+4 \mod 8} \quad \text{for j odd}$$
$$c_{j,0} = k_{j+4 \mod 8} \| k_{j+5 \mod 8} \quad \text{for j even}$$
$$= k_j \| k_{j+1 \mod 8} \qquad \text{for j odd.}$$

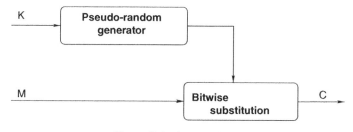

Figure 3.4   Stream cipher

If we set $g_{j,i} = (x_{j,i} + c_{j,i})^2 \oplus ((x_{j,i} + c_{j,i})^2 >> 32) \bmod 2^{32}$, some 32-bits constants ($a_0 = 4D34D34D$, $a_1 = D34D34D3$, $a_2 = 34D34D34$, $a_3 = 4D34D34D$, $a_4 = D34D34D3$, $a_5 = 34D34D34$, $a_6 = 4D34D34D$, $a_7 = D34D34D3$), and

$$\phi_{j,i+1} = \begin{cases} 1 & \text{if } c_{0,i} + a_0 + \phi_{7,i} \geq 2^{32} \text{ and } j = 0 \\ 1 & \text{if } c_{j,i} + a_j + \phi_{j-1,i+1} \geq 2^{32} \text{ and } j > 0 \text{, then the internal state evolution} \\ 0 & \text{otherwise} \end{cases}$$

($x_{i,j}$ and $c_{i,j}$ are computed modulo 2^{32}) and the random bits $s_i^{127..0}$ are given in Table 3.3.

Overall, the major interest of such a stream cipher is its speed as it requires 3.7 cycles per produced bit on a single 1 GHz machine. Now, the generation is intrinsically sequential as the internal state is required to produce new bits. Block ciphers can overcome this latter issue by using the same key to encrypt different parts of a message.

3.2.2.2 Symmetric Block Ciphers

Such ciphers split a message M on n bits into s blocks on $r = \frac{n}{s}$ bits (one may initially add meaningless characters to the message so that its size is a multiple of r). A block cipher algorithm processes blocks on r bits and produces in general blocks on r bits to ensure that the code is bijective. The combination with an encryption mode (ECB, CBC, CFB, OFB, or CTR – see Section 1.3.1) fully describes the encryption of a message M, as illustrated in Figure 3.5.

Common systems such as DES and AES, which use block ciphers, are presented in the sequel.

3.2.2.3 Unconditionally Secure Encryption

One recalls that an encryption scheme is said *unconditionally secure* or *perfect* if the knowledge of the ciphertext provides absolutely no information on the plaintext. Hence, the only possible attack is the exhaustive search for the secret key. Up to now, only Vernam encryption – which uses a secret key as long as the plaintext (Section 1.2.1) – has been proved

TABLE 3.3 Rabbit Stream Internal State Evolution and Bit Extraction

$x_{0,i+1} = g_{0,i} + g_{7,i}^{\lll 16} + g_{6,i}^{\lll 16}$	$c_{0,i+1} = c_{0,i} + a_0 + \phi_{7,i}$	$s_i^{\{15..0\}} = x_{0,i}^{\{15..0\}} \oplus x_{5,i}^{\{31..16\}}$
$x_{1,i+1} = g_{1,i} + g_{0,i}^{\lll 8} + g_{7,i}$	$c_{1,i+1} = c_{1,i} + a_1 + \phi_{0,i+1}$	$s_i^{\{31..16\}} = x_{0,i}^{\{31..16\}} \oplus x_{3,i}^{\{15..0\}}$
$x_{2,i+1} = g_{2,i} + g_{1,i}^{\lll 16} + g_{0,i}^{\lll 16}$	$c_{2,i+1} = c_{2,i} + a_2 + \phi_{1,i+1}$	$s_i^{\{47..32\}} = x_{2,i}^{\{15..0\}} \oplus x_{7,i}^{\{31..16\}}$
$x_{3,i+1} = g_{3,i} + g_{2,i}^{\lll 8} + g_{1,i}$	$c_{3,i+1} = c_{3,i} + a_3 + \phi_{2,i+1}$	$s_i^{\{63..48\}} = x_{2,i}^{\{31..16\}} \oplus x_{5,i}^{\{15..0\}}$
$x_{4,i+1} = g_{4,i} + g_{3,i}^{\lll 16} + g_{2,i}^{\lll 16}$	$c_{4,i+1} = c_{4,i} + a_4 + \phi_{3,i+1}$	$s_i^{\{79..64\}} = x_{4,i}^{\{15..0\}} \oplus x_{1,i}^{\{31..16\}}$
$x_{5,i+1} = g_{5,i} + g_{4,i}^{\lll 8} + g_{3,i}$	$c_{5,i+1} = c_{5,i} + a_5 + \phi_{4,i+1}$	$s_i^{\{95..80\}} = x_{4,i}^{\{31..16\}} \oplus x_{7,i}^{\{15..0\}}$
$x_{6,i+1} = g_{6,i} + g_{5,i}^{\lll 16} + g_{4,i}^{\lll 16}$	$c_{6,i+1} = c_{6,i} + a_6 + \phi_{5,i+1}$	$s_i^{\{111..96\}} = x_{6,i}^{\{15..0\}} \oplus x_{3,i}^{\{31..16\}}$
$x_{7,i+1} = g_{7,i} + g_{6,i}^{\lll 8} + g_{5,i}$	$c_{7,i+1} = c_{7,i} + a_7 + \phi_{6,i+1}$	$s_i^{\{127..112\}} = x_{6,i}^{\{31..16\}} \oplus x_{1,i}^{\{15..0\}}$

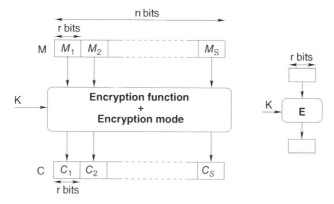

Figure 3.5   Block cipher

unconditionally secure, **assuming that** the secret key is chosen randomly and used only once. In particular, all other systems are theoretically breakable.

Therefore, nowadays one considers *almost* secure encryption algorithms. For such systems, the ciphertext does not enable one to recover the plaintext nor the key in *humanly reasonable time*. This enables one to choose keys of smaller length with respect to Vernam coding. We will now present the two most important standards for block ciphers.

3.2.3   Data Encryption Standard (DES) System

3.2.3.1   Exhaustive Description of DES   This is the most well-known symmetric cryptosystem. It was first presented as an encryption standard by the NIST in 1977.

It processes plaintext blocks of 64 bits using a key K of 56 bits[2] and outputs 64-bit ciphertext blocks. The algorithm is divided into three steps:

1. Let x be a plaintext block of 64 bits. One applies some determined initial permutation IP in order to obtain a string x_0. Thus, one has: $x_0 = IP(x) = L_0 R_0$ where L_0 contains the first 32 (most significant) bits of x_0 and R_0 the remaining (least significant) 32 bits.

2. One performs 16 iterations (called *rounds*) with some function f using the key K as a parameter. The function f will be described in detail in the sequel. One computes $L_i R_i$, $1 \leq i \leq 16$ according to the rule:

$$\begin{cases} L_i = R_{i-1} \\ R_i = L_{i-1} \oplus f(R_{i-1}, K_i) \end{cases} \tag{3.2}$$

---

[2]Actually the key has 64 bits but 1 bit per block of 8 bits is used as a parity check (Section 4.1.2).

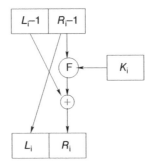

Figure 3.6 One round of DES

Figure 3.6 describes one encryption round. The function f has two parameters: one has 32 bits (it corresponds to R_{i-1} at the ith round) and the other one has 48 bits (K_i). The round keys K_i are obtained from the so-called *key derivation* performed on the bits of the original key K: this process will be described later on.

3. One applies the inverse permutation IP^{-1} on $R_{16}L_{16}$ in order to get a ciphertext block $y = IP^{-1}(R_{16}L_{16})$ (Notice that L_{16} and R_{16} are inverted).

The same algorithm, with the same key, but performing the rounds in the inverse order, is used in order to decrypt the blocks.

The security of DES comes from the application of the function f at each round. This function has two parameters:

- a string A of 32 bits (the right part of the block one wishes to encrypt);
- a string J of 48 bits (the round key).

The computation of $f(A, J)$ is divided into several steps, which are illustrated in Figure 3.7:

1. A is expanded to get a string of 48 bits using an *expansion function E*.
2. $B = E(A) \oplus J$ is computed and split into eight consecutive substrings of 6 bits each: $B = B_1.B_2 \ldots B_8$. Each substring B_i is then passed through a substitution box S_i (the famous SBox), which outputs a block C_i of four bits.
3. The 32-bit string $C = C_1.C_2 \ldots C_8$ is then reorganized using a determined permutation P. The result $P(C)$ defines $f(A, J)$.

Exercise 3.2 (DES Decryption) *Show that it is not necessary to invert f in order to invert a DES round. Deduce the decryption algorithm of the DES system.*
Solution on page 304.

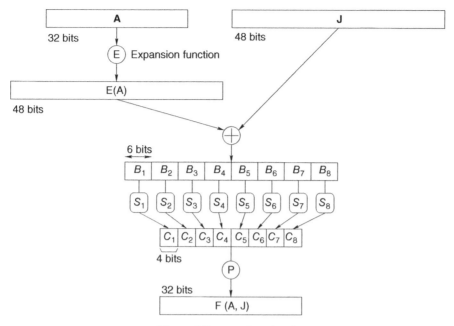

Figure 3.7   DES: Function f

*3.2.3.2   DES **Key Derivation***   We have seen that at round i the second parameter of the function f is a subkey K_i extracted from the initial key K. This paragraph details the algorithm that is used to generate the 16 subkeys $\{K_i\}_{1 \leq i \leq 16}$.

1. The key K of 64 bits is reorganized with an initial permutation PC-1 that removes the parity bits (those located at the positions 8,16,...,64). One denotes PC-1$(K) = C_0.D_0$, where C_0 contains the 28 most significant bits of PC-1(K) and D_0 contains the 28 least significant bits.

2. C_i, D_i, and K_i $(1 \leq i \leq 16)$ are computed recursively in the following way:

$$\begin{cases} C_i = LS_i(C_{i-1}) \\ D_i = LS_i(D_{i-1}) \\ K_i = \text{PC-2}(C_i.D_i) \end{cases} \qquad (3.3)$$

LS_i is a circular shift by one or two positions depending on the value of i and PC-2 is another bit permutation.

All these steps are illustrated in Figure 3.8.

*3.2.3.3   **Advantages and Practical Uses of** DES*   After 16 rounds the output of DES is statistically "flat", namely the general features of the source message (the frequencies of the characters, the number of spaces, etc.) are undetectable. Moreover, DES

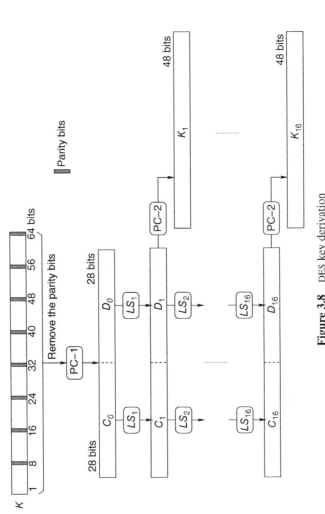

Figure 3.8 DES key derivation

has a very important characteristic for avoiding differential analysis attacks: the least modification of the key or the plaintext induces important changes in the ciphertext.

The main advantage of DES is that – for both encryption and decryption – computation uses operations that are easy to implement at the hardware level. Therefore, it is possible to obtain very high encryption speeds (already of the order of 190 MB/s 10 years ago on certain machines).

The DES system has been used for securing credit card payments (for example, *UEPS, Universal Electronic Payment System*), network authentication protocols such as *Kerberos*, and e-mail clients such as *PEM* (*Privacy-Enhanced Mail*). From its cryptanalysis, see next section, we will however see that nowadays its successor, the AES, should in general be preferred. When the DES is nonetheless in use, it is in general at least used in its triple form, as discussed also in the following section.

Exercise 3.3 (Confidentiality of DES)

1. *Show that a perfect encryption scheme (the ciphertext does not give any information about the plaintext or in terms of entropy, $H(M|C) = H(M)$; see Section 1.2.5) satisfies $|K| \geq |M|$.*
2. *Discuss the perfect confidentiality of DES for a block.*

Solution on page 304.

3.2.3.4 Cryptanalysis of DES After publication, many research efforts have been invested in the cryptanalysis of DES, first on versions with less rounds and then on the full version. Meaningful breakthroughs (including the techniques that were used) appeared at the beginning of the nineties. Nowadays, one distinguishes four cryptanalysis methods for DES:

- Exhaustive research. Obviously, this method can be applied on any cryptosystem.
- Exhaustive precomputation. The objective is to store the result of the encryption of a chosen plaintext using DES for all possible keys K. Hence, if one manages to obtain a ciphertext associated with this particular plaintext from a target cryptosystem, one is able to easily recover the secret key (the cost is constant). This implies that one is able to store 2^{56} blocks of 64 bits, which is possible using current hard disks.
- **Differential cryptanalysis.** This attack aims to study the differences in the encryption of two similar texts in order to extract a subset of probable keys. It represented a significant breakthrough in the cryptanalysis of DES.
- **Linear cryptanalysis.** This was another major breakthrough in the cryptanalysis of block ciphers in general. The objective is to find linear relations between some bits of the ciphertext and some bits of the plaintext in order to interpolate certain bits of the secret key.

Table 3.4 summarizes the complexities of the attacks on DES.

TABLE 3.4   Complexities of Cryptanalysis Methods on DES

Attack method	Known Plaintext	Chosen Plaintext	Memory Space	Computations
Exhaustive research	1			2^{55}
Exhaustive precomputation		1	2^{56}	1 table
Linear cryptanalysis	2^{47} then 2^{36}		Texts	2^{47} then 2^{36}
Differential cryptanalysis	2^{55}	2^{47}	Texts	2^{47}

TABLE 3.5   Cost and Efficiency of Attacks on DES in 1996

Attacker	Budget	Tool	Time to Find a 56-bit Key
Hacker	300 €	Software	38 years
Small company	7500 €	Circuit	18 months
Big company	225 K €	ASIC Circuit	19 d. 3 h
International Co.	7.5 M €	ASIC	6 min
Government	225 M €	ASIC	12 s

With the breakthroughs in the field of cryptanalysis and the growth of computational possibilities, a study was proposed in 1996 to estimate the efficiency of the attacks on DES for a given budget. The result of this study is given in Table 3.5.

Nowadays, DES is no longer considered to be almost secure because of its key of 56 bits. A small calculation is enough to explain the main idea of this statement: there are 2^{56} possible keys, that is, less than $10^{17} = 10^8 10^9$. Let us consider 1000 cores running at 1 GHz$=10^9$ Hz. Thus, it takes 10^5 s (30 h) to perform $1000 * 10^9 * 10^5 = 10^{17}$ operations; therefore, brute force attack is not impossible in reasonable time!

In order to improve the security of DES, a first solution was to combine two keys. One obtained the "double DES" system, for which $C = E_2(E_1(M))$ and $M = D_1(D_2(C))$. However, it quickly appeared that actually breaking this system is in this way only 100 times more difficult than breaking the simple DES (and not 2^{56} times more difficult as one might have expected using two keys). Indeed, the "meet-in-the-middle" attack uses a fast sort to break the double DES with almost no computation overhead with respect to breaking the simple DES:

1. Compute all 2^{56} possible encryptions X_i of a given message M.
2. Sort the X_i with a fast sort in $O(n \log(n))$ steps. There are approximately 56×2^{56} operations.
3. Compute all Y_j possible decryptions of C with a single key j: $Y_j = DES_j^{-1}(C)$; in the same time, compare the Y_j with the X_i (as the latter are sorted, the research requires at most $\log(n)$ steps for each Y_j by dichotomy).
4. When one finds $X_{i_0} = Y_{j_0}$, the target keys are i_0 and j_0.

Therefore, the security of the key of double DES is only around 64 bits.

Later, the use of "triple DES" was proposed with an effective key of 112 bits but with a computational time multiplied by three. This operation can be performed using three keys and the encryption $C = E_3(E_2(E_1(M)))$ (this is called $3DES - EEE$); in this case, the previous attack gives a security of the key rather of around 120 bits. That is why one often prefers to use only two keys and the encryption $C = E_1(D_2(E_1(M)))$ ($3DES - EDE$), which provides a security of 112 bits and is compliant with simple DES encryption taking $K_1 = K_2$.

Finally, a new faster standard has taken its place since 2000: the AES, *Advanced Encryption Standard.*

3.2.4 Rijndael: Advanced Encryption Standard (AES)

Rijndael is a symmetric cipher chosen by the NIST (*National Institute of Standards and Technology*) to be the new American encryption standard (AES: *Advanced Encryption Standard*). This system was chosen after a contest organized by the NIST. Among the five finalists (Rijndael, Serpent, Twofish, RC6, and Mars), Rijndael appeared to be the most resistant and became the new American standard, replacing DES. It is a block cipher processing 128-bit blocks with a key of 128, 192, or 256 bits. It is important to notice that Rijndael was also among the proposals giving the fastest results, as we can see in Table 3.6 (which is taken from the report of the New European Schemes for Signatures, Integrity, and Encryption (NESSIE)-D21).

All the operations of AES are operations performed on bytes that are considered as elements of the finite field of 2^8 elements, $\mathbb{F}_{256}$. One recalls that for p prime, $\mathbb{F}_{p^m}$ is isomorphic to $\mathbb{F}_p[X]/g(X)$, where $g(X)$ is an irreducible polynomial on $\mathbb{F}_p[X]$ of degree m (see Section 1.3.4).

For AES, $p = 2$, $m = 8$, and $g(X) = P_8(X) = X^8 + X^4 + X^3 + X + 1$ (one easily checks that $P_8(X)$ is actually an irreducible polynomial on $\mathbb{F}_2[X]$, see Algorithm 1.8). Hence, the byte $b_7b_6b_5b_4b_3b_2b_1b_0$ is represented by the polynomial $b_7X^7 + b_6X^6 + b_5X^5 + b_4X^4 + b_3X^3 + b_2X^2 + b_1X + b_0$. By extension, the polynomial $P_8(X)$ is written `0x11B`, namely the corresponding byte in hexadecimal notation.

- The addition of two polynomials is the bitwise addition of their coefficients (the addition in $F_2 = \mathbb{Z}/_{2\mathbb{Z}}$), which corresponds to the eXclusive OR (XOR $\oplus$) on the bytes.
- The multiplication is a multiplication of polynomials modulo $P_8(X)$.

Exercise 3.4 (Operations in $\mathbb{F}_{256}$)

1. *One considers the bytes $a = 0x57$ and $b = 0x83$ (in hexadecimal notation; one can also write $a = [57]$ and $b = [83]$ if there is no ambiguity) seen as elements in $\mathbb{F}_{256}$.*

   (a) *Compute $a + b$*

   (b) *Compute $a \times b$*

TABLE 3.6   Performance of Several Block Ciphers

		Clock cycles/Byte	
Algorithm	Key size	Encryption	Decryption
IDEA	128	56	56
Khazad	128	40	41
Misty1	128	47	47
Safer++	128	152	168
CS-Cipher	128	156	140
Hierocrypt-L1	128	34	34
Nush	128	48	42
DES	56	59	59
3-DES	168	154	155
kasumi	128	75	74
RC5	64	19	19
Skipjack	80	114	120
Camellia	256	47	47
RC6	256	18	17
Safer++	256	69	89
Anubis	256	48	48
Grand cru	128	1250	1518
Hierocrypt-3	260	69	86
Nush	256	23	20
Q	256	60	123
SC2000	256	43	46
Rijndael	256	34	35
Serpent	256	68	80
Mars	256	31	30
Twofish	256	29	25

2. *Now, let us use the polynomial notation. Let $a(X) \in \mathbb{F}_{256}$.*

  (a) *Give an algorithm for computing the element in $\mathbb{F}_{256}$ corresponding to $X.a(X)$.*

  (b) *Deduce an algorithm for computing the element $X^i a(X)$ in $\mathbb{F}_{256}$.*

3. *Let $w(X)$ be a generator of $\mathbb{F}_{256}$. In this case, any nonzero element in $\mathbb{F}_{256}$ can be represented uniquely by $w(X)^i \mod g(X)$, $0 \le i < 255$. Deduce an efficient way of performing the multiplication of two elements in $\mathbb{F}_{256}$. Remark: For AES, $w(X) = X + 1 = $ 0x03.*

Solution on page 304.

Blocks of bytes are organized in a matricial form, according to the model illustrated in Figure 3.9. This matrix has necessarily four lines and a number of columns depending on the size of the block. One denotes N_b the number of columns of the matrix representing a block and N_k the number of columns of the matrix representing a key.

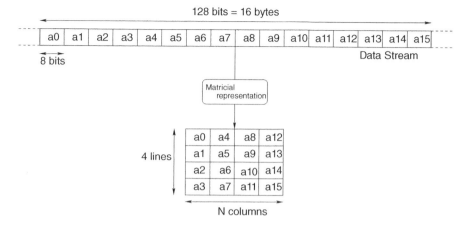

Figure 3.9   Matricial representation of a 16-byte block

For instance, for input/output streams that correspond in the AES to 16-byte sequences, one obtains matrices of 4 lines and $N_b = 4$ columns. In the same way:

- the matrix associated to a key of 128 bits has 4 lines and $N_k = 4$ columns;
- for a key of 192 bits, the matrix has 4 lines and $N_k = 6$ columns; and
- for a key of 256 bits, the matrix has 4 lines and $N_k = 8$ columns.

To be more precise, the AES algorithm is not *stricto sensu* exactly the Rijndael algorithm. The latter may have more block sizes than that of AES. AES **considers only 128-bit data blocks** ($N_b = 4$), whereas the Rijndael algorithm considers **data blocks of 128, 192, or 256 bits**.

3.2.4.1   Principle of the Algorithm   Similar to DES, AES performs a sequence of rounds that are given in detail in the sequel. One denotes N_r the number of rounds that are to be performed. This number depends on the values of N_b and N_k. The different configurations are given in Table 3.7.

We have seen previously that AES operates on blocks that are represented with matrices of $4 \times N_b$ elements in $\mathbb{F}_{256}$. AES encryption consists of a preliminary addition with a key (`AddRoundKey`), followed by $N_r - 1$ rounds. Each round is divided into

TABLE 3.7   Configurations for AES

	N_k	N_b	N_r
AES-128	4	4	10
AES-192	6	4	12
AES-256	8	4	14

four stages:

1. SubBytes is a nonlinear substitution: each byte is replaced by another byte chosen in a particular table (an *SBox*).
2. ShiftRows is a transposition stage. Each element of the matrix is shifted for some number of position to the left.
3. MixColumns performs a matrix multiplication operating on each column (seen as a vector) of the matrix.
4. AddRoundKey performs a bytewise addition with a round key derived from the encryption key.

A FinalRound is applied (it corresponds to a round in which the MixColumns stage is removed). The round key for stage i is denoted RoundKeys[i], and RoundKeys[0] refers to the parameter of the preliminary key addition. The derivation of the encryption key K in the table RoundKeys[] is denoted KeySchedule and explained in detail later on. Algorithm 3.1 describes the AES encryption.

Algorithm 3.1 AES Encryption

Input A matrix State corresponding to the plaintext block, a key K
Output A matrix State corresponding to the cipherblock
  1: KeySchedule(K, RoundKeys)
  2: AddRoundKey(State, RoundKeys[0]); // Preliminary addition
  3: **For** $r = 1$ to $N_r - 1$ **do**
  4:     SubBytes(State);
  5:     ShiftRows(State);
  6:     MixColumns(State);
  7:     AddRoundKey(State, RoundKeys[r]);
  8: **End For**
  9: // Final round
 10: SubBytes(State);
 11: ShiftRows(State);
 12: AddRoundKey(State, RoundKeys[N_r]);

SubBytes (State). This stage corresponds to the only nonlinear transformation of the algorithm. In this stage, each element of the matrix State is permuted according to an invertible substitution table denoted SBox. For instance, Figure 3.10 illustrates the transformation of the element $a_{2,2}$ into the element $b_{2,2} = S[a_{2,2}]$.

Remark: The SBox table is derived from the inverse function $t : a \longrightarrow a^{-1}$ over $\mathbb{F}_{256}$. This function is known for its good properties of nonlinearity (as 0 has no inverse, it is mapped onto 0 in this stage). In order to avoid attacks based on simple algebraic properties, the SSBoxBox is built combining this inverse function and an affine invertible transformation f. Therefore, one has

$$\text{SBox}[a] = f(t(a)), \text{ for all } a \in \mathbb{F}_{256}$$

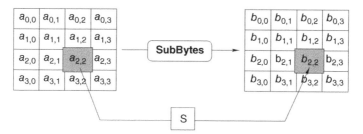

Figure 3.10 SubBytes operation in AES

Moreover, AES was designed to avoid any fixed point and opposite fixed point:

$$SBox[a] + a \neq 0x00, \quad \text{for all } a \in \mathbb{F}_{256}$$

$$SBox[a] + a \neq 0xFF, \quad \text{for all } a \in \mathbb{F}_{256}.$$

Finally, the affine function f is defined as follows:

$$b = f(a) \Longleftrightarrow \begin{bmatrix} b_7 \\ b_6 \\ b_5 \\ b_4 \\ b_3 \\ b_2 \\ b_1 \\ b_0 \end{bmatrix} = \begin{bmatrix} 1 & 0 & 0 & 0 & 1 & 1 & 1 & 1 \\ 1 & 1 & 0 & 0 & 0 & 1 & 1 & 1 \\ 1 & 1 & 1 & 0 & 0 & 0 & 1 & 1 \\ 1 & 1 & 1 & 1 & 0 & 0 & 0 & 1 \\ 1 & 1 & 1 & 1 & 1 & 0 & 0 & 0 \\ 0 & 1 & 1 & 1 & 1 & 1 & 0 & 0 \\ 0 & 0 & 1 & 1 & 1 & 1 & 1 & 0 \\ 0 & 0 & 0 & 1 & 1 & 1 & 1 & 1 \end{bmatrix} \times \begin{bmatrix} a_7 \\ a_6 \\ a_5 \\ a_4 \\ a_3 \\ a_2 \\ a_1 \\ a_0 \end{bmatrix} + \begin{bmatrix} 0 \\ 1 \\ 1 \\ 0 \\ 0 \\ 0 \\ 1 \\ 1 \end{bmatrix}$$

Exercise 3.5 (InvSubBytes) *Give the details of the inverse operation of this stage.* *Solution on page 306.*

Exercise 3.6 (Operations on SubBytes) *One sets $a = 0x11 \in \mathbb{F}_{256}$ (hexadecimal notation) with the same representation convention used in AES. Compute SBox[a].* *Solution on page 306.*

ShiftRows (State). In this stage, one operates on the lines of the matrix State and one performs, for each element of a line, a cyclic shift of n positions to the left. The value of the shift depends on the line one considers. The line i is shifted by C_i elements, such that the element in position j in the line i is moved to the position $(j - C_i) \mod N_b$. The values of the C_i depend on the value of N_b and are given in detail in Table 3.8.

This table is provided only to give an idea of the general Rijndael algorithm as the AES standard sets the size of the blocks to $N_b = 4$.

The overall ShiftRows stage in AES is illustrated in Figure 3.11.

Exercise 3.7 (InvShiftrows) *Give the details of the inverse operation of this stage.* *Solution on page 306.*

TABLE 3.8   Value of the Shift According to the Value of N_b in ShiftRows

N_b	C_0	C_1	C_2	C_3
4	0	1	2	3
5	0	1	2	3
6	0	1	2	3
7	0	1	2	4
8	0	1	3	4

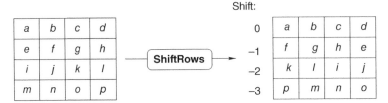

Figure 3.11   ShiftRows stage in AES

MixColumns (State). After rotating the rows, the MixColumns transformation operates on the column a of the matrix State considering each column as a polynomial $a(Y)$ of degree 3 with coefficients in $\mathbb{F}_{256}$. It consists in performing on each column a multiplication with $c(Y) = 03\,Y^3 + 01\,Y^2 + 01\,Y + 02$, or simply $c(Y) = 03\,Y^3 + Y^2 + Y + 02$, modulo the polynomial $Y^4 + 01$ (the coefficients of the polynomials are elements in $\mathbb{F}_{256}$ represented with hexadecimal numbers; for instance with $\mathbb{F}_{256} = \mathbb{F}_2[X]/P_8(X)$, 03 represents $X + 1$, 02 represents X, and 01 represents simply 1). Thus, in MixColumns, one performs the following operation: $(03\,Y^3 + Y^2 + Y + 02) \times a(Y) \mod (Y^4 + 1)$. From a matricial point of view, this operation (illustrated in Figure 3.12) is written as follows:

$$b(Y) = c(Y) \times a(Y) \mod (Y^4 + 1) \Longleftrightarrow \begin{bmatrix} b_0 \\ b_1 \\ b_2 \\ b_3 \end{bmatrix} = \begin{bmatrix} 02 & 03 & 01 & 01 \\ 01 & 02 & 03 & 01 \\ 01 & 01 & 02 & 03 \\ 03 & 01 & 01 & 02 \end{bmatrix} \times \begin{bmatrix} a_0 \\ a_1 \\ a_2 \\ a_3 \end{bmatrix}$$

Besides, as $c(Y)$ and $Y^4 + 1$ are coprime, $c(Y)$ is actually invertible modulo $Y^4 + 1$ and the MixColumn transformation is invertible too, which enables the decryption.

Exercise 3.8 (Flash Back to $\mathbb{F}_{256}$ and InvMixColumns)   *Let us look again at the representation of the elements in $\mathbb{F}_{256}$ which are used in AES. The elements are written in the form of two hexadecimal digits in square brackets. For instance, $X^7 + X^6 + X^2 + 1$ is written 11000101 in binary, 0xC5, [C5] or simply C5 in hexadecimal.*

1. Compute $[0B] + [A2]$, $-[03]$, $[FD] - [F0]$, $[FD] + [F0]$, $[23] + [45]$.

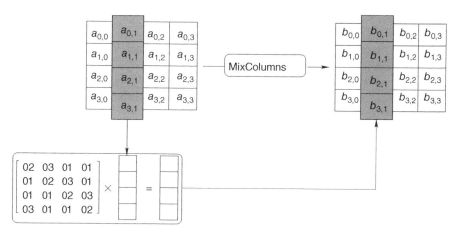

Figure 3.12 `MixColumns` operation in AES

2. What is the result of the Euclidean division of $P_8(X) = X^8 + X^4 + X^3 + X + 1$ by $X + 1$ in $\mathbb{F}_2[X]$?

3. Find the inverse of $[03]$ in $\mathbb{F}_{256}$.

4. Give the algorithm for the multiplication by X in the binary form over $\mathbb{F}_{256}$. Deduce the binary values of $X^8, X^9, X^{10}, X^{11}, X^{12}, X^{13}$, and X^{14}. Give the details of the multiplication with $[02]$?

5. What is the value of $(a + b)^2$ modulo 2? Deduce the expression of $(a_1 + a_2 + \ldots + a_n)^2$ modulo 2.

6. From the two previous questions, deduce the value of $[F6]^2$.

7. In AES, the MixColumns stage is performed by multiplying the column with the polynomial $c(Y) = [03]Y^3 + Y^2 + Y + [02]$ modulo the polynomial $M = Y^4 + [01]$. Compute the polynomial Q such that $M = cQ + R$ with $R(Y) = [A4]Y^2 + [A5]Y + [A5]$.

8. Assuming that one knows the value of two polynomials U and V such that $Uc + VR = 1$, give the Bézout relation between c and M.

9. Practical application: given $U = [A0]Y + [FE]$ and $V = [1D]Y^2 + [1C]Y + [1D]$, make the reciprocal function of twothe AES MixColumns explicit. This function is denoted `InvMixColumns` in the sequel.
   One may use the following multiplications: $[F6][1D] = [0B]$, $[F6][1C] = [FD]$, $[52][1D] = [F0]$, $[52][1C] = [A2]$, $[52][F6] = [C7]$.

Solution on page 307.

`AddRoundKey(State,Ki)`. This operation is a simple addition of the two matrices `State` and `Ki`. As the addition operates on elements in $\mathbb{F}_{256}$, it is actually a bitwise eXclusive OR $\oplus$ performed on the bytes of the matrices.

Exercise 3.9 (`InvAddRoundKey`) *Give the detail of the inverse operation of this stage.* *Solution on page 307.*

3.2.4.2 Key Schedule in AES This stage, denoted KeySchedule, enables one
to expand the encryption key K ($4N_k$ bytes) and to obtain an expanded key W of
$4N_b(N_r + 1)$ bytes. Hence, one gets $N_r + 1$ round keys (each key has $4Nb$ bytes –
see Figure 3.13).

K and W tables can be seen as a sequence of columns of 4 bytes, as illustrated in
Figure 3.14. In the sequel, we will denote c[i] (respectively k[i]) the $(i + 1)$th
column of W (respectively of K).

The algorithm used for the key expansion slightly differs depending on whether
$N_k \le 6$ or $N_k > 6$. In all cases, the N_k first columns of K are copied without modifications to the N_k first columns of W. The next columns are recursively computed
from the previous columns. KeySchedule notably uses the two functions and the
constant table defined as follows:

- SubWord is a function that takes a word of 4 bytes as input and applies an
  SBox to each byte.
- RotWord is a function that takes a word of 4 bytes $a = [a_0, a_1, a_2, a_3]$ as input
  and performs a cyclic permutation and outputs the word $[a_1, a_2, a_3, a_0]$.

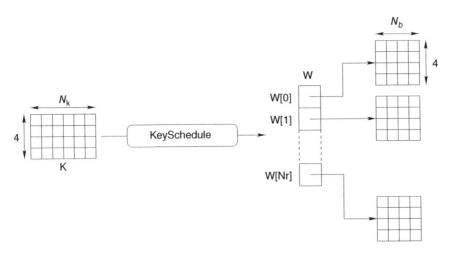

Figure 3.13 KeySchedule operation in AES

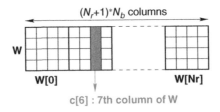

Figure 3.14 Representation of the expanded key W as a sequence of columns

- The table of round constants Rcon[i] is independent of N_k and is defined recursively by

$$\text{Rcon}[i] = [x^{i-1}, 00, 00, 00], \ \forall i \geq 1$$

Algorithm 3.2 summarizes the key schedule in AES.

Algorithm 3.2 Key Schedule in AES

Input A key K on $4N_k$ bytes.
Output An expanded key W on $4N_b(N_r + 1)$ bytes
 1: **For** $i = 0$ to $N_k - 1$ **do**
 2:   W[i] = K[i]
 3: **End For**
 4: **For** $i = N_k$ to $N_b(N_r + 1) - 1$ **do**
 5:   tmp = W[i-1]
 6:   **If** $i \mod N_k = 0$ **then**
 7:     tmp = SubWord(RotWord(tmp)) + Rcon[i/Nk]
 8:   **elsif** $(N_k > 6)$ AND $(i \mod N_k = 4)$ **then**
 9:     tmp = SubWord(tmp);
10:   **End If**
11:   W[i] = W[i-N_k] + tmp
12: **End For**

Exercise 3.10 (AES Decryption)   *Give the details of the decryption of the AES system.*   *Solution on page 307.*

Exercise 3.11 (Block Sizes and Collisions)   *One recalls that several encryption modes were introduced on Section 1.3.1.*

1. *ECB mode: Describe a scenario that illustrates the weakness of this mode.*
2. *CBC mode:*
   (a) *Assuming that one encrypts 35 GB of data on a hard disk using the Triple-DES in CBC mode, what is the number of cipherblocks and what is the probability of having a collision between two cipherblocks Y_i and Y_j ?*
   (b) *How could this flaw be exploited?*
   (c) *What about AES ? Derive a conclusion concerning the importance of the size of the blocks.*

Solution on page 308.

3.2.4.3   Security of the AES The "Sbox" was designed to resist cryptanalysis. In particular, it does not have any fixed point $S(a) = a$, nor any opposite fixed point $S(a) = \bar{a}$, nor any inverse fixed point $S(a) = S^{-1}(a)$. In addition, the operator ShiftRows creates a high diffusion of the data by separating the initially consecutive bytes. Finally, when combined with MixColumn, it allows, after several rounds, each output bit to depend on all input bits. Besides, MixColumn is a linear code of maximum distance (see Section 4.4.1).

So far, there does not exist any significant attack on AES. However, one must temper this statement insomuch as this standard is still quite recent and it has only been submitted to worldwide cryptanalysis for a little more than 10 years. Today, the only known attacks on AES, that is to say anything that gives some information with a complexity less than brute force search, are applicable only to a reduced number of rounds when compared to those of Table 3.7.

Exercise 3.12 (Square Attack on AES-128) *Take* 256 *messages differing only on their first byte (the first byte is called* active, *while the others are called* passive*). Using a selected number of active bytes or bits and trying all their possible values, leads to what is called* saturation attacks. *Such an attack was designed for the Square cipher of which the AES is an evolution and this attack is still applicable. Suppose we apply Algorithm 3.1 of AES-128 with only four rounds, that is, $N_r = 4$. The successive values of the state are denoted by capital letters and coordinate indices: the starting state is $A_{i,j}$, then $B_{i,j}$ after the first* AddRoundKey, *then $C_{i,j}$ after the first* SubBytes, *... and ends by $Q_{i,j}$ after the fifth* AddRoundKey. *Using the saturation we will denote by $X_{i,j}^{(m)}$ the value of the state if the first byte of the initial state was m (i.e., $A_{0,0}^{(m)} = m$).*

1. *Suppose that $\{X^{(m)}\}$ is a permutation of* 0..255.

   (a) *Show that $\bigoplus\limits_{m=0}^{255} X^{(m)} = 0$.*

   (b) *Show that $\{AddRoundKey(X^{(m)}, K)\}$ and $\{SubBytes(X^{(m)})\}$ are also permutations of* 0..255.

2. *Using the polynomial view, show that if two columns differ only on a single byte, then all the bytes of their* MixColumns *must differ.*

3. *Deduce from the preceding two questions that right before the third and last* MixColumns, *we have that $\{L_{i,j}^{(m)}\}$ is a permutation of* 0..255 *for any i,j.*

4. *Deduce that $\bigoplus\limits_{m=0}^{255} M_{i,j}^{(m)} = 0$, for all i,j and $\bigoplus\limits_{m=0}^{255} N_{i,j}^{(m)} = 0$, for all i,j.*

5. *In general, the latter does not imply that $M_{i,j}^{(m)}$ is a permutation of* 0..255 *and $\bigoplus\limits_{m=0}^{255} O_{i,j}^{(m)} \neq 0$, for all i,j.*

   (a) *Show that if* RoundKeys [4] *is known, then $N_{i,j}$ can be deduced from the output ciphertext $Q_{i,j}^{(m)}$.*

   (b) *Deduce a way to test independently for each byte of* RoundKeys [4].

6. *What is the complexity of this attack?*

Solution on page 308.

3.3   KEY EXCHANGE

In order to be able to exchange confidential informations, two entities using symmetric cryptography need to have a common secret. This common secret can be the symmetric key they will be using or something that will enable them to build such a key. Now, the question is how can they share a common secret? With perfect secrecy for instance they should meet in person and find a way to exchange this common secret in shelter. This might not always be very practical. An alternative is to use cryptographic tools to perform this key exchange. In this section, we present the classical Diffie–Hellman scheme for key exchange and the nonetheless classical Man-in-the-middle attack that can break it. Then we present the Kerberos system that uses a third party to authentify both entities when they do not even know each other beforehand. We will see that these systems have limitations that will be overcome via the use of asymmetric cryptography.

3.3.1   Diffie–Hellman Protocol and Man-in-the-Middle Attacks

Using a one-way function like modular exponentiation makes key sharing possible.

Thus, let us suppose that Alice and Bob wish to share a secret key K. They first agree on a prime integer p and on a generator g of $\mathbb{Z}_p^*$. Then, one can define the following two-stage protocol that enables them to construct K in secret:

1. (a) Alone, Alice chooses a secret number $a \in \mathbb{Z}_p^*$ and computes

$$A = g^a \quad \bmod p$$

   She sends A to Bob.

   (b) Symmetrically, Bob chooses a secret number $b \in \mathbb{Z}_p^*$ and computes

$$B = g^b \quad \bmod p$$

   He sends B to Alice.

2. (a) Alone, Alice computes $K = B^a \bmod p$.

   (b) Symmetrically, Bob computes $A^b \bmod p$ at his end.

Finally, Alice and Bob share the same secret key $K = g^{a.b} \bmod p$ without ever having disclosed it to each other directly.

Exercise 3.13   *One supposes that Oscar sees A and B. Explain why Oscar cannot easily deduce K.*   *Solution on page 309.*

Exercise 3.14   *Alice and Bob agree on the following parameters: $p = 541$ and $g = 2$. Alice chooses the secret number $a = 292$. At his end, Bob chooses the number $b = 426$. What is the secret key resulting from the Diffie–Hellman key exchange protocol?*   *Solution on page 309.*

The most classic attack on interchange protocols consists in Oscar cutting the communication line between Alice and Bob before they start the key sharing (transmission of A and B). This is the so-called Man-in-the- middle attack. The general idea is that Oscar passes himself off as Bob as far as Alice is concerned and as Alice as far as Bob is concerned.

In this way, Oscar can read all communications between Alice and Bob with the key that they think they have constructed in secret. In practice, Oscar produces a' and b'. He intercepts A and B and then produces $K_A = A^{b'}$ and $K_B = B^{a'}$. Then, he sends $g^{b'}$ to Alice and $g^{a'}$ to Bob. The progress of the attack is given Table 3.9.

Next, Oscar has to decode the messages sent by Alice or Bob on-the-fly and then re-encode them with the other key in the manner given in Table 3.10.

Thus, Alice and Bob think that they are sending each other secret messages, whereas Oscar is intercepting them and decrypting them in the middle! So not only is Oscar able to obtain all the exchanges between Alice and Bob but he is also able to modify these exchanges. Indeed, nothing prevents him, being in the middle, from replacing the message sent by Alice with whatever information he wants. In the sequel, we describe various secret key and public key protocols developed to prevent such an attack.

TABLE 3.9 Man-in-the-Middle Attack on the Diffie–Hellman Protocol

Alice		Oscar		Bob
G a		Generates b' and a'		Generates b
$A = g^a \mod p$		$B' = g^{b'} \mod p$		$B = g^b \mod p$
		$A' = g^{a'} \mod p$		
	$\xrightarrow{A}$		$\xrightarrow{B}$	
	$\xleftarrow{B'}$		$\xrightarrow{A'}$	
(knows $[a, A, B']$)				(knows $[b, A', B]$)
Secret key:		Secret keys:		Secret key:
$K_A = B'^a \mod p$		K_A and K_B		$K_B = A'^b \mod p$

TABLE 3.10 Sending of a Message Intercepted by the Man-in-the-Middle

Alice		Oscar		Bob
$C = E_{K_A}(M)$				
	$\xrightarrow{C}$			
		$M = E_{K_A}(C)$		
		$\Gamma = E_{K_B}(M)$		
			$\xrightarrow{\Gamma}$	
				$M = E_{K_B}(C)$

3.3.2   Kerberos: a Secret Key Provider

To agree on the enciphering and deciphering functions E and D, the safest solution is for Alice and Bob to meet physically. The Diffie–Hellman protocol allows one to do away with this physical meeting, but its weakness is that an active intruder placed between Alice and Bob may intercept all communications.

One solution for avoiding excessively numerous exchanges while protecting oneself against the *"Man-in-the-middle "* attack is to introduce a third party. Developed by the *Massachusetts Institute of Technology*, Kerberos is a secure authentication system with a trusted third party (or Trusted Authority (TA)), which is designed for TCP/IP networks. However, it is not a system for authorizing access to resources, although there are extensions considering this issue. The MIT distribution of Kerberos is free. This system shares with each entity U of the network a secret key K_U (a password in the case of a user), and knowing this key stands stead of a proof of identity.

The authentication is negotiated by means of a trusted third party : the Key Distribution Center (KDC) Kerberos incorporates a number of features:

- the authentication is secure;
- there is no sending of passwords over the network;
- the authentication is unique: the user only enters his/her password once (for a given period of time, one day for instance) to connect several times with the remote services (this principle is called *"Single Sign On "*);
- the authentication is managed in a centralized way; and
- this standard is compatible with several operating systems (notably unix, linux, Mac®, and Windows®).

Kerberos identifies the users of the system (a physical person, a Server, or a service) via a triplet *<name, role, domain>* (where *domain* identifies the administration domain associated with at least one Kerberos server) – more precisely, in the form of a `name/role@domain` string. Hence, one physical person is identified by the string `login/staff@DOMAIN`. For a service, it is better to refer to the server that provides the service: it would be identified by the string `service/hostname@DOMAIN`.

3.3.2.1   General Description of the Kerberos Protocol   Kerberos is based on the use of *tickets* that are used to convince an entity of the identity of another entity. It also creates *session keys* that are given to two participants and are used to encrypt data between these two participants, following the steps shown in Figure 3.15. There are two types of accreditations:

- the **tickets** that are used to securely give the future recipient (Bob or the Ticket Granting Service (TGS)) the identity of the sender (Alice) to whom the ticket has been supplied. It also contains information items that the recipient can use

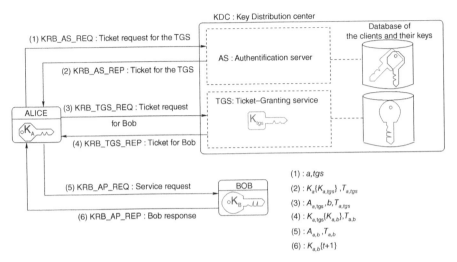

Figure 3.15   Kerberos authentication steps

to make sure that the sender using the ticket is indeed the party to whom the ticket was issued.

- the **authenticators**, which are additional accreditations presented with the ticket.

A ticket takes the following form:

$$T_{a,s} = s, E_{K_s}(id_a, t, t_{end}, K_{a,s}).$$

Thus, it contains the name of the service s that Alice wishes to use (TGS, or Bob) as well as a list of information items enciphered with the service's secret key (that only the service will be able to decrypt); more precisely:

- the identity of Alice, id_a
- the date of the request, t
- the date of expiration of the ticket, t_{end}
- and (above all) a session key $K_{a,s}$, which will be used for the authenticator (see below) and for enciphering future communications between Alice and the service s.

Although Alice is not able to decrypt the ticket (it is enciphered with the secret key K_s), she can nonetheless give it encrypted to s. Thus, in parallel with tickets, Kerberos also uses authenticators taking the following form:

$$A_{a,s} = E_{K_{a,s}}(id_a, t).$$

Alice generates an authenticator each time she wants to use a service s (TGS or Bob). Contrary to the ticket, which Alice can use several times for gaining access to the service, an authenticator is unique and can only be used once. However, as Alice possesses the session key $K_{a,s}$, she will be able to generate one whenever necessary.

3.3.2.2 Details of Kerberos Messages
Figure 3.15 shows the various messages that are exchanged. To sum up:

- Messages 1 and 2 enable Alice to obtain the first ticket, which she then presents to the TGS each time she wants to contact a recipient.
- Messages 3 and 4 let Alice get a service ticket, which she then presents to Bob for a service request.
- Messages 5 and 6 correspond, respectively, to the service request from Alice to Bob and to the response from Bob. As we will see, this step enables Alice and Bob to mutually authenticate themselves and to provide them with a session key that lets them encrypt their future messages. This is the sense in which one should understand the concept of service.

Now let us look at the explicit content of these messages:

1. KRB_AS_REQ = $[a ; tgs]$: this message simply acts as an introduction to Alice. She states her name and the name of the TGS she wants to deal with[3].
2. KRB_AS_REP = $[E_{K_a}(K_{a,tgs}) ; T_{a,tgs}]$: the authentication server (AS in Figure 3.15) looks for the client in its database. If it finds it, it generates a session key $K_{a,tgs}$ thta should be used between Alice and the TGS. First, this key is enciphered with Alice's secret key K_a[4]: this is the first part of the message ($E_{K_a}(K_{a,tgs})$). Then, it creates a ticket $T_{a,tgs}$ for Alice, so that she is able to authenticate herself with the TGS. As we have seen earlier, this ticket is enciphered with the TGS's secret key K_{tgs}. Alice is not able to decrypt it, but she can still present it at each request to the TGS. In this particular case, the ticket is called TGT. One may notice that only the genuine Alice is able to retrieve the session key $K_{a,tgs}$ (she is the only one who possesses the secret key K_a). Therefore, Alice now has the session key $K_{a,tgs}$ and the TGT ticket $T_{a,tgs}$.
3. KRB_TGS_REQ = $[A_{a,tgs} ; b ; T_{a,tgs}]$: Now, Alice has to obtain a new ticket for each Bob she wishes to contact. For this, Alice contacts the TGS providing it firstly with the TGT ticket $T_{a,tgs}$ she already possesses and also with an authenticator $A_{a,tgs}$ (in addition to the name of the server she wishes to contact). The authenticator contains formatted, genuine information items from the ticket via the TGS. As these information items are enciphered with the session key $K_{a,tgs}$, it proves that Alice knows it and thus, authenticates her. (Hence the name "authenticator" given to $A_{a,tgs}$).

---

[3] There can be several TGSs.
[4] In the case of a human user, K_a corresponds to the hashing of his/her password.

4. KRB_TGS_REP = $[E_{K_{a,tgs}}(K_{a,b})\,;\,T_{a,b}]$: Thanks to its secret key K_{tgs}, the TGS decrypts the ticket, retrieves the session key $K_{a,tgs}$, and is then able to decipher the authenticator $A_{a,tgs}$. It compares the content of the authenticator with the information items contained in the ticket. If everything agrees (Alice is authenticated), it can generate a session key $K_{a,b}$ (which will be used between Alice and Bob) enciphered with the session key $K_{a,tgs}$ and a new ticket $T_{a,b}$ that Alice will have to present to Bob. After receiving the message and deciphering it, in addition to $K_{a,tgs}$ and $T_{a,tgs}$ (that she will keep until the ticket expires for interacting with the TGS), Alice will have a new session key $K_{a,b}$ and a new ticket $T_{a,b}$ that she can use with Bob.

5. KRB_AP_REQ = $[A_{a,b}\,;\,T_{a,b}\,]$: Now, Alice is ready to authenticate herself to Bob; this is performed in the same way as between Alice and the TGS[5] (see message KRB_TGS_REQ).

6. KRB_AP_REP = $[E_{K_{a,b}}(t+1)]$: Now, Bob must authenticate himself by proving that he is able to decrypt the ticket $T_{a,b}$, hence that he possesses the session key $K_{a,b}$. He has to send back a piece of information that can be checked by Alice, encrypted with this key. By verifying it, Alice is now sure of the identity of Bob and has a session key $K_{a,b}$ that can be used for enciphering the communications between Alice and Bob.

3.3.2.3 *Weaknesses of Kerberos*

- *Attack by repetition*: although the datings are supposed to prevent it, the messages might be replayed during the lifetime of the tickets (around 8 h by default).
- *Dating services*: the authenticators depend on the fact that all the clocks on the network are more or less synchronized. If one is able to mislead a computer as regards to the true time, then the old authenticators can be replayed. Most of the time maintenance protocols are not secure. Hence, this can be a serious vulnerability.
- *Password gamble*: an intruder has to collect the first halves, $E_{K_a}(K_{a,tgs})$, of the KRB_AS_REP messages in order to predict the value of K_a (in general, $K_a = H(Password)$). By gambling on the password $\tilde{P}$, the intruder is able to compute $\tilde{K}_a$, decode, and obtain $\tilde{K}_{a,tgs}$. He can then check the correctness of his choice by decrypting the authenticator $A_{a,tgs} = E_{K_{a,tgs}}(id_a, t)$ of which he knows the content (at least, he knows id_a).
- *Login name usurping* (commonly referred to as *"spoofing"*): one may imagine an attack in which all the Kerberos client programs are replaced by a version not only implementing the Kerberos protocol but also recording passwords.

The KDC holds the keys of all users and all servers. While this reduces the total number of secret keys (otherwise every user would have to have one key for each server and vice versa), it also means that if the KDC is successfully attacked, all the

---

[5] Actually, Bob is just a particular server.

keys have to be changed. Public key architectures enable one to get rid of this last problem.

Exercise 3.15 (Needham–Schroeder Protocol Attack) *Alice and Bob want to exchange a session key. Ivan shares one secret key I_1 with Alice and one secret key I_2 with Bob. The Needham and Schroeder protocol is as follows:*

    i. Alice sends $(Alice||Bob||Random_1)$ to Ivan.

    ii. Ivan generates a session key K and sends
        $E_{I_1}(Random_1||Bob||K||E_{I_2}(K||Alice))$ *to Alice.*

    iii. Alice sends $E_{I_2}(K||Alice)$ to Bob.

    iv. Bob sends $E_K(Random_2)$ to Alice.

    v. Alice sends $E_K(Random_2 - 1)$ to Bob.

    1. What is the purpose of $Random_1$?

    2. What is the purpose of $Random_2$ and why does Alice have to send it back as $Random_2 - 1$?

    3. One security problem with this protocol is that the old session keys keep their value. If Eve is able to eavesdrop on the messages exchanged and was able to obtain an old session key, explain how she can convince Bob that she is Alice.

    4. What should be added to messages to prevent this vulnerability? What does the resulting protocol look like?

    5. In the resulting system, a user doesn't need to authenticate himself with the KDC each time he wants access to a service. Why? What is the weakness of this method?

    6. In this system, Ivan has a list of keys (or password fingerprints) for all his clients. What could happen if this list was stolen? How can one protect oneself from such a danger?

Solution on page 310.

To overcome the problem of key theft, one solution would be to use a public key system for authentication instead. This system is explained in Section 3.4.

3.4 PUBLIC KEY CRYPTOGRAPHY

3.4.1 Motivations and Main Principles

We have seen that symmetric cryptosystems can be almost secure and efficient in terms of computation time. Nevertheless, from the middle of the seventies, new questions were raised:

- Before using a symmetric cryptosystem, how is a key agreed upon?
- How is a secure communication between two entities with no preliminary key exchange established ?

In order to answer these questions, Diffie and Hellman laid the foundations of public key cryptosystems in 1976, using the **analogy with a mail-box** and assuming that Bob is the only person having the key:

- any person is able to send a message to Bob;
- only Bob is able to read the messages stored in his mail- box.

On the other hand, a symmetric cryptosystem can be seen as a safe whose key is shared between Alice and Bob.

Keeping in mind such a system and in order to keep the notation introduced in Equation (3.1), one has $K_e \neq K_d$. To be more precise, K_e is a public key that is published in some kind of directory (actually in the form of a certificate: see Section 3.6.2) in such way that anyone is able to obtain this key, check its origin, and encrypt a message with it. K_d is a private and secret key that is kept and used by Bob in order to decrypt the ciphertexts. As the two keys are distinct, public key encryption is also called *asymmetric encryption* (Figure 3.16).

Is it possible to give the characteristics of such a cryptosystem using the notions of information theory? In such a context, the measure of the secrecy consists in computing the remaining information in the private key, assuming that the public key is known: $H(K_d|K_e)$. Besides, an asymmetric algorithm must satisfy $D_{K_d} = E_{K_e}^{-1}$ with the functions D and E publicly known. This point implies that the key K_d is completely determined once the public key K_e is known: one only has to invert the function E_{K_e}. In theory, at least, it implies that $H(K_d|K_e) = 0$ and, thus, that an asymmetric system has no secret at all. In practice, the two keys K_e and K_d are linked but they are chosen in such way that it is far too difficult to compute the value of the key K_d from K_e.

For this purpose, one uses the principle of *one-way functions*, which was introduced in Section 1.3.3.4. Therefore, the secret of a public key cryptosystem cannot be characterized by Shannon's information theory; this secret does not come from the uncertainty of the private key K_d but rather from the inner difficulty of computing K_d from the only K_e and the ciphertext C. The mathematical tool that enables one to characterize this difficulty is the theory of *algorithmic complexity*.

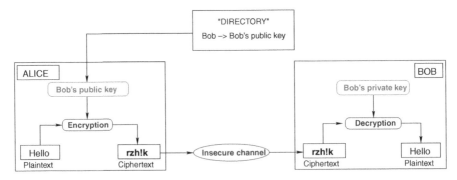

Figure 3.16 Principle of public key encryption

The most well-known and most widely used public key encryption algorithm – mainly because of its ease of use – is the RSA system, whose name comes from its designers, Rivest, Shamir, and Adleman. The difficulty of RSA is based on the difficulty of factoring an integer.

3.4.2 Rivest–Shamir–Adleman (RSA) Encryption

When combining the Euler theorem and the Chinese Remainder theorem (see page 38), one is able to obtain a common congruence relation for all elements in $\mathbb{Z}/_{n\mathbb{Z}}$ when n is the product of two prime numbers. This result, which was presented by Rivest, Shamir, and Adleman in 1978, is at the origin of RSA public key cryptography.

Theorem 24 (RSA Theorem) *Let $n = pq$ be the product of two prime numbers. Let a be any element in $\mathbb{Z}/_{n\mathbb{Z}}$. Then, for any positive integer k, one has $a^{k\varphi(n)+1} = a$ mod n.*

Proof. There are two cases: if a is invertible in $\mathbb{Z}/_{n\mathbb{Z}}$, then one directly applies the Euler theorem and thus $a^{\varphi(n)} = 1 \mod n$. Computing the kth power of this relation and multiplying it by a, one obtains the desired relation.

If a is zero, the relation modulo n is immediate. Otherwise, one uses the Fermat theorem twice modulo p and modulo q.

Indeed, if a is nonzero modulo p prime, then $a^{p-1} = 1 \mod p$. Computing the $k(q-1)^{th}$ power and multiplying by a, one obtains $a^{k\varphi(n)+1} = a \mod p$.

On the other hand, if $a = 0 \mod p$, then one has necessarily $a^{k\varphi(n)+1} = 0 = a$ mod p. In the same way, one obtains a similar relation modulo q: $a^{k\varphi(n)+1} = a \mod q$.

As p and q are coprime, it is enough to apply the uniqueness of the Chinese Remainder theorem to have $a^{k\varphi(n)+1} = a \mod pq$.   □

From this statement, one deduces the RSA cryptosystem. In such system, a user generates a pair (public key and private key) using the following procedure:

1. Choose two large primes p and q. p and q must contain at least 150 digits each.
2. Compute $n = pq$
3. Choose a small integer e coprime with $\varphi(n) = (p-1)(q-1)$
4. Compute d, the inverse of e modulo $\varphi(n)$.
5. Release the pair $K_e = (e, n)$ as the RSA public key.
6. Keep the pair $K_d = (d, n)$ secret: this pair is the RSA private key.

Therefore, one has

RSA encryption: $E(M) = M^e \mod n$
RSA decryption: $D(\widetilde{M}) = \widetilde{M}^d \mod n$

One easily checks that, for $0 \le M < n$, one has $D_{K_d}(E_{K_e}(M)) = M$. Indeed, $D_{K_d}(E_{K_e}(M)) = M^{ed} \mod n = M^{1+\alpha\varphi(n)} \mod n = M$, according to RSA theorem.

Exercise 3.16 (RSA **Encryption**)

1. *Determine the public key and the private key for $p = 47$ and $q = 59$ with $e = 17$ (and justify the validity of this choice).*
2. *Encrypt the letter B in ASCII code (66) using the public key and check that the private key actually enables one to recover the original message.*

Solution on page 310.

Exercise 3.17 (RSA **Encryption/Decryption**) *We now consider the toy* RSA *public key $K_e = (e, n) = (11, 319)$.*

1. *What is the ciphertext associated with the message $M = 100$ using this key?*
2. *Compute the private key K_d corresponding to the public key K_e.*
3. *Decrypt the message $C = 133$. One may use the following result: $133^{25} = 133$ (mod 319).*
4. *Is it possible to obtain a ciphertext equal to 625 using this public key? Same question with the private key.*

Solution on page 311.

Exercise 3.18 (Vigenère Encryption and RSA) *We consider a cryptosystem over the alphabet $\{A, B, C, \ldots, Z, \_\}$ where each symbol in the alphabet is represented with a number between 0 and 26 as follows:*

A	B	C	D	E	F	G	H	I	J	K	L	M	N	O	P	Q	R	S	T	U	V	W	X	Y	Z	–
0	1	2	3	4	5	6	7	8	9	10	11	12	13	14	15	16	17	18	19	20	21	22	23	24	25	26

Given a key $K = K_0 K_1 \ldots K_k$ and a plaintext $M = M_0 M_1 \ldots M_k$, the ciphertext $C = C_0 C_1 \ldots C_k$ is given by

$$\text{For all } i \in [0, k], \quad C_i = M_i + K_i \mod 27.$$

This is what we call Vigenère *encryption. Here is a French ciphertext that Oscar intercepted for you:*

```
HWQIO QVPIF TDIHT Y_WAF NGY_F COMVI CGEVZ CVIAF JDFZK
YLYHG YGEHR SHMMX CVHBF AJYKN ZIXHP ZHEQY YJRHT YWMUK
   YKPBY YGEHA G_DY_ YWDTF MHFZK YZYHX CISVI CHIVZ
```

1. *Propose a method for the cryptanalysis of the Vigenère encryption starting by determining the length of the key.*
2. *Oscar and Eve also work on the cryptanalysis of this text they have intercepted. Oscar sends to Eve the length of the key that he has managed to determine. For this, he uses the* RSA *public key of Eve $(e, n) = (5, 35)$. Ivan intercepts the* RSA

ciphertext containing the length of the key: he obtains 10. *What is the length of the key?*

3. *Eve has managed to decrypt the second and the third encryption key. She sends them to Oscar using the RSA public key of the latter* $(e, n) = (7, 65)$. *In the same way, Ivan intercepts the ciphertexts of* K_1 *(he obtains 48) and* K_2 *(4). What are the values of* K_1 *and* K_2?
Note: *one may use the following results:*
$48^2 = 29 \mod 65$ *and* $48^5 = 3 \mod 65$.

4. *Now that you have the length of the key, decrypt this text. Specify the key used for the encryption **and** the decryption (in the form of a string of characters). The repartition (in %) of the symbols used in a text written in French is summarized in Table 3.11.*

Solution on page 311.

3.4.2.1 *Efficiency and Robustness of RSA.* Thanks to the algorithms that we have seen in the previous sections:

- It is easy to generate large prime numbers, at least when accepting an error margin (see Miller–Rabin test, Section 1.3.4.1, on page 44). In the case of RSA, the error is not very dangerous. Indeed, if one commits an error and believes that p and q are prime numbers, one will soon realize that they are not: either the key d is not invertible or some parts of the decrypted message are incomprehensible. In this case, one is still able to change the RSA keys (by recomputing p and q);
- Computing the pair (e, d) is very easy: it is enough to apply the extended Euclidean algorithm;
- Finally, encryption and decryption are performed using modular exponentiation. We have seen that such exponentiation can be performed quite efficiently.

The security provided by RSA mainly relies on the difficulty of factoring large integers. Indeed, if an attacker is able to factorize the number $n = pq$ of the public key, then he is able to deduce directly $\varphi(n) = (p-1)(q-1)$ and thus to compute the private key K_d from the public key K_e using the extended Euclidean algorithm. Therefore, if there exists a fast algorithm for factoring large numbers, breaking RSA also becomes easy.

TABLE 3.11 Frequential Repartition of Symbols in a Text Written in French

–	18.35%
E	14.86%
S	6.97%
A	6.40%
N	6.23%
...	...

After 20 years of research, no more efficient method than factoring n has been published to break RSA. However, the reciprocal proposition : "if factoring large numbers is hard then breaking an RSA ciphertext is hard" has not been proved. In other words, today, one does not know if breaking RSA is as difficult as factoring n.

However, one is able to demonstrate the equivalence between "determining d from (e, n)" and "factoring n." One way is trivial: knowing p and q, one is able to easily compute d for this is what is done during the key generation. Reciprocally, computing p and q from (n, e, d) can be obtained:

- by a deterministic algorithm if e is small (typically $e \leq \log n$ – see Exercise 3.19);
- by a probabilistic algorithm (a variant of Miller–Rabin algorithm) in general (Exercise 3.20).

Exercise 3.19 (Factoring n from n, e, and d for e Small)
We consider the RSA cryptosystem, with (n, e, d) as keys, where e is "small."

1. *Prove that there exists $k \in \mathbb{Z}$, such that $ed - 1 = k(n - (p + q) + 1)$.*
2. *One assumes that p and q are different from 2 and 3. Prove that $k \leq 2e$.*
3. *Then propose an algorithm for factoring n.*

Solution on page 313.

Exercise 3.20 (Factoring n from n, e, and d) *One considers an RSA cryptosystem (n, e, d). Let $s = \max\{v \in \mathbb{N}, \text{ such that } 2^v \text{ divides } ed - 1\}$ (In other words: $ed - 1 = t2^s$).*

1. *Show that there exists a variant of the Miller–Rabin algorithm that enables one to factorize n, that is, to determine p and q. The algorithm should perform only a single attempt and should return either the factors of n or an error.*
2. *What is the average number of calls of this algorithm that one should perform in order to find out the factorization of n?*

Solution on page 313.

Hence, breaking RSA by computing the private key d from the public key (e, n) is as difficult as factoring n (this problem is known to be difficult if p and q are very large). The confidence in RSA relies on this statement. Current factoring limits deal with numbers of approximately 232 decimal digits (so far, the current record [6] is held by Kleinjung, Aoki, Franke, Lenstra, Thomé, Bos, Gaudry, Kruppa, Montgomery, Osvik, te Riele, Timofeev, and Zimmermann, obtained in December 2009, during the RSA-768 challenge). Today, one considers that a modulo n of 2048 bits is secure.

---

[6] See http://www.loria.fr/~zimmerma/records/factor.html for the current factoring records.

3.4.2.2 *Attacks on* RSA The key generation which was presented previously is a simplified version, and in practice, one should be careful when generating the keys. These precautions are the results of attacks exploiting some relations between the RSA encryption parameters. Some attacks will be presented in the sequel in the form of exercises. Recommendations concerning the implementation of RSA-based cryptosystems (key generation, etc.) are summarized in the PKCS#1 standard. This standard is regularly updated (depending on the breakthroughs in the cryptanalysis of RSA).

Exercise 3.21 (Common Exponent Attack on RSA) *The RSA public keys of William, Jack, and Averell are, respectively, equal to $(3, n_W)$, $(3, n_J)$, and $(3, n_A)$. Joe sends the same message x to each one of them, with $0 \le x < \min(n_W, n_J, n_A)$, using their respective public keys.*
Prove that Lucky Luke, who is able to obtain $c_W = x^3 \mod n_W$, $c_J = x^3 \mod n_J$, and $c_A = x^3 \mod n_A$ on the network, can easily compute x.
Hint. *One recalls (or assumes !) that for a and k integers, the method of Newton–Raphson (convergence of the sequence $u_{i+1} = u_i(1 - \frac{1}{k}) - \frac{a}{k u_i^{k-1}}$) enables one to compute very quickly the value of $\lfloor a^{1/k} \rfloor$, with an arithmetic complexity bound of the order of $\mathcal{O}(\log^2 a)$.* *Solution on page 315.*

Exercise 3.22 (Common Modulus Attack on RSA)
An implementation of RSA gives the same modulus n (product of two prime numbers) to Alice and Bob but with two different pairs of keys (e_A, d_A) and (e_B, d_B). Moreover, one assumes that e_A and e_B are coprime (it is true in general). Then, one assumes that Alice and Bob receive the same message M encrypted using their respective public key. Oscar intercepts both messages $c_A = M^{e_A} \mod n_A$ and $c_B = M^{e_B} \mod n_B$, which are known to be two ciphertexts of the same plaintext. Show that Oscar is then able to easily recover the message M. *Solution on page 316.*

Exercise 3.23 (Well Chosen Ciphertext Attack on RSA)
Eve intercepts the ciphertext c sent by Bob to Alice: $c = m^{e_A} \mod n_A$. In order to decrypt c, Eve proceeds in the following way:

1. *Eve chooses an integer $0 < r < n_A$ randomly and computes $x := r^{e_A} \mod n_A$;*
2. *Eve computes $y = x.c \mod n_A$;*
3. *Eve asks Alice to sign y using her private key; Alice sends $u = y^{d_A} \mod n_A$ to Eve.*

Show that Eve is now able to recover the message m sent by Bob. Morality? *Solution on page 316.*

Exercise 3.24 (Factorial Attack or Pollard p-1 Attack) *Let p and q be the two prime numbers that are used to build the modulus $n = pq$ of an RSA public key. The integer $p - 1$ is even; let B be the smallest integer such that $B!$ (factorial of B) is a multiple of $p - 1$. In other words, there exists an integer μ such that: $\mu(p - 1) = B!$*

1. Let p_1 be a prime factor of $(p - 1)$. Show that $p_1 \leq B$.
2. Let $a < n$ be an integer. Show that $a^{B!} = 1 \mod p$.
3. Let $A = a^{B!} \mod n$; deduce that $(A - 1)$ is a multiple of p.
4. Let k be an integer; what is the cost of computing $a^k \mod n$?
5. Deduce a bound on the cost of computing $A = a^{B!} \mod n$ with respect to B and $\log n$.
6. If $p - 1$ is a divisor of $B!$, with B small, then an attacker who knows n but neither p nor q is able to perform the following attack: assuming that C is a small upper bound of B ($C \geq B$), he computes

$$A = 2^{C!} \mod n \quad et \quad G = \gcd(A - 1, n).$$

Prove that, if G is neither equal to 1 nor n, then an attacker has necessarily broken RSA with the modulo n.

7. One assumes that $p - 1$ is a divisor of $B!$ with $B = \alpha \log n$; moreover, one assumes that α is small (for instance $\alpha \leq 1000$).
   Show that this attack enables one to break RSA. Give an upper bound on the cost of this attack.
8. What is the counter-measure ?

Solution on page 316.

3.4.3 El Gamal Encryption

While RSA relies on the problem of factoring integers, El Gamal encryption exploits the Discrete Logarithm Problem (DLP), which was studied in Section 1.3.3.3. The key generation is performed in the following way:

- Let p be a prime number for which the DLP is difficult in $\mathbb{Z}_p^*$.
- Let $g \in \mathbb{Z}_p^*$ be a primitive root.
- Let s be an integer and $\beta = g^s$.
- Then, the public key is the triplet $K_e = (p, g, \beta)$.
- The corresponding private key is $K_d = s$.

El Gamal encryption: Let M be the plaintext one wishes to encrypt and let $k \in \mathbb{Z}_{p-1}$ be a secret random number. One has

$$E_{K_e}(M) = (y_1, y_2) \text{ with } \begin{cases} y_1 = g^k \mod p \\ y_2 = M.\beta^k \mod p. \end{cases}$$

El Gamal decryption: For $y_1, y_2 \in \mathbb{Z}_p^*$, one defines

$$D_{K_d}(y_1, y_2) = y_2.(y_1^s)^{-1}$$

Indeed $y_2.(y_1^s)^{-1} = M.\beta^k.(g^{k.s})^{-1} = M.g^{s.k}.(g^{k.s})^{-1} = M$.

Therefore, it is possible to easily encrypt a message using modular exponentiation. Decryption without the private key is equivalent to solving the discrete logarithm.

However, when one has the private key, it is enough to perform a modular exponentiation, followed by the extended Euclidean algorithm to find the inverse of an element in $\mathbb{Z}_p^*$. The main interest of this kind of encryption is that, for a given level of security, it can work with smaller numbers – hence quicker – than RSA. Indeed, the complexity of the attacks performed on RSA and DLP make it that the size of the RSA parameters must be roughly twice as large as those required for an El Gamal encryption.

Besides, as DLP can be applied in any group, one is able to extend El Gamal to other groups in which the Discrete Logarithm Problem is much more difficult. For instance, this is the case for the group of points on an elliptic curve, see Section 1.3.6, in which index calculus attacks do not succeed. On the basis of the conjectured complexity bound of the currently known attacks on RSA and Elliptic Curve Cryptography (ECC), the NESSIE[7] project as well as the U.S. NIST thus proposed the equivalence guide of Table 3.12.

Indeed, the only known attacks for the discrete logarithm in elliptic curve groups are of baby-step/giant-step or Pollard's rho type, with complexity bound $O(\sqrt{n})$, where n is the number of points in the curve. Thus, the recommended number of points in the elliptic curve (and therefore the cardinal number of the underlying finite field) should be around 2^{2t}, where t is the required security.

3.5 AUTHENTICATION, INTEGRITY, NONREPUDIATION, SIGNATURES

In addition to secrecy, cryptographic ciphers are also used to insure message authentication. The recipient must be able to determine whether the message was actually sent by the person who maintains he has sent the message or not. Therefore, one must also insure an integrity check, that is to say verify that the message arrives in the way it was issued. For this, one uses hash functions. Section 1.4.2.2, on page 74, has introduced such functions. Now, we will give some more specific analysis, notably of the most famous cryptographic hash functions. We will also introduce the construction of Message Authentication Code (MAC), which enable one to check both the integrity and the authentication of the source of a data. Finally, the concept of digital signature will be presented with the main signature schemes that are in use nowadays.

TABLE 3.12   Conjectured Compared Security of Block Ciphers

bits	80 Skipjack	112 3-DES	128 AES-small	196 AES-medium	256 AES-large
RSA	1024	2048	3072	7168	13312
ECC	192	224	256	384	521

[7] https://www.cosic.esat.kuleuven.be/nessie/

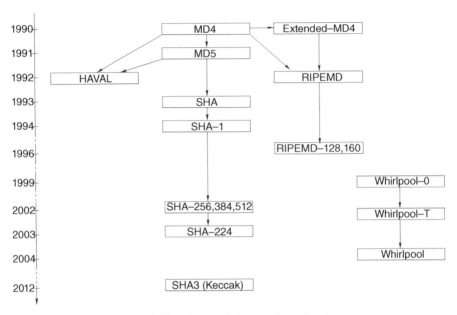

Figure 3.17   History of the main hash functions

3.5.1   Cryptographic Hash Functions

Hash functions have already been introduced in Chapter 1, on page 74. Figure 3.17 summarizes briefly the main cryptographic hash functions and shows the details of how they are built.

The most famous cryptographic hash functions are the Secure Hash Algorithm (SHA) (in versions SHA-1, SHA-256, etc.), the Message-Digest Algorithm 5 (MD5), and Whirlpool. They do not use any key and one can hardly predict their behavior (inputs and outputs are almost independent). The property of resistance to collisions (see page 75) is essential to insure cryptographically secure signature schemes or encryption schemes. Hence, a hash function is considered to be *broken* if there exists an algorithm that enables one to find collisions for this function with a better complexity than the Yuval attack (with $\mathcal{O}(2^{\frac{n}{2}})$ successive fingerprint computations, n being the size of the fingerprint – see Section 1.4.3.4).

Exercise 3.25 (Construction of a Hash Function Resistant to Collisions)
In this exercise, we are going to build a hash function, $h : \{0, 1\}^{2m-2} \longrightarrow \{0, 1\}^m$, resistant to collisions.

For this, one uses a one-way function (here the discrete logarithm with $m = 1024$ bits = 64 bytes). A Merkle-Damgård-like construction will provide a hash function resistant to collisions. We proceed in the following way:

1. *We choose two prime numbers p and q such that $q = \frac{p-1}{2}$. In other words, $p = 2q + 1$. We assume that p has m bits (thus q has $m - 1$ bits).*

2. *Then we consider the multiplicative groups $\mathbb{Z}_p^*$ and $\mathbb{Z}_q^*$. Let α and β be two generators of $\mathbb{Z}_p^*$ ($\alpha \neq \beta$). That is to say:*

$$\mathbb{Z}_p^* = \{\alpha^0, \alpha^1, \alpha^2, \ldots, \alpha^{p-2}\} = \{\beta^0, \beta^1, \beta^2, \ldots, \beta^{p-2}\}.$$

We set $\lambda = \log_\alpha(\beta)$ (therefore $\alpha^\lambda = \beta \mod p$). We assume that λ is unknown and extremely difficult to compute.

3. *α, β, and p are assumed to be publicly known and we define*

$$h : \begin{array}{ccc} \mathbb{Z}_q \times \mathbb{Z}_q & \longrightarrow & \mathbb{Z}_p \\ (x_1, x_2) & \longrightarrow & \alpha^{x_1} \beta^{x_2} \mod p. \end{array}$$

a. *Numerical application: for $p = 83$, $q = 41$, $\alpha = 15$, and $\beta = 22$, compute the fingerprint of $(12, 34)$. On what computation does the function h rely on for resisting to collisions?*

In order to prove that h is resistant to collisions, we use the following proof by contradiction:

- *Let us assume that a collision is given. In other words, let us suppose that one is given $x = (x_1, x_2) \in \mathbb{Z}_q^2$ and $y = (y_1, y_2) \in \mathbb{Z}_q^2$ (with $x \neq y$) such that $h(x) = h(y)$*

- *Then, let us prove that one is able to compute λ easily.*

In the sequel, we set $d = \gcd(y_2 - x_2, p - 1)$.

b. *What are the divisors of $p - 1$? Deduce that $d \in \{1, 2, q, p - 1\}$.*

c. *Show that $-q < y_2 - x_2 < q$ and deduce that $d \neq q$.*

d. *Show that $\alpha^{x_1 - y_1} = \beta^{y_2 - x_2} \mod p$.*

e. *Assuming that $d = p - 1$, prove that $x = y$. Deduce that $d \neq p - 1$.*

f. *Assuming that $d = 1$, prove that $\lambda = (x_1 - y_1)(y_2 - x_2)^{-1} \mod p - 1$.*

g. *Suppose that $d = 2 = \gcd(y_2 - x_2, 2q)$. Deduce that $\gcd(y_2 - x_2, q) = 1$. Set $u = (y_2 - x_2)^{-1} \mod q$.*

  1. *Prove that $\beta^q = -1 \mod p$ and deduce that: $\beta^{u(y_2 - x_2)} = \pm\beta \mod p$.*

  2. *Prove that either $\lambda = u(x_1 - y_1) \mod p - 1$ or $\lambda = u(x_1 - y_1) + q \mod p - 1$.*

h. *Conclude and give an algorithm that takes collisions $x = (x_1, x_2) \in \mathbb{Z}_q^2$ and $y = (y_1, y_2) \in \mathbb{Z}_q^2$ as inputs and returns λ. Give an upper bound on the cost of such an algorithm and deduce that h is resistant to collisions.*

Solution on page 316.

Now, let us give the details of the most famous hash functions, including the status of their cryptanalysis.

3.5.1.1 Message-Digest Algorithm 5 (MD5)

MD5 was first submitted by Rivest in 1991. Here, we focus on the compression function used in MD5. This function processes a block M of $b = 512$ bits and produces a fingerprint of $n = 128$ bits (using the notation introduced in Figure 1.14 on page 76).

Each block M is first split into 16 subblocks $\{M_i\}_{0 \leq i \leq 15}$ of 32 bits. MD5 also uses 64 constant values $\{K_i\}_{0 \leq i \leq 63}$. The algorithm processes a state of 128 bits, which is divided into 4 words of 32 bits: A, B, C, and D (which are initialized with constant values). Then, 64 rounds are performed and produce a fingerprint as the result of the compression function.

The details of a round in MD5 are shown in Figure 3.18. The rounds are divided into 4 packets of 16 subrounds in which the function F takes the following successive values:

Security of MD5. The size of the fingerprint is 128 bits in MD5. Therefore, finding collisions with a brute force attack (Yuval's attack) requires 2^{64} fingerprint computations. Yet, several algorithms have been submitted to find collisions in MD5 with only 2^{42} computations or even 2^{30} computations.

This is the reason why, nowadays, **MD5 is no longer considered to be secure**.

3.5.1.2 SHA-1

SHA-1 was first issued in 1995 by the NIST in the form of a standard. The compression function used in SHA-1 processes a block M of $b = 512$ bits and produces a fingerprint of $n = 160$ bits (using the notations introduced in Figure 1.14 on page 76). As for MD5, the block M is first split into 16 subblocks $\{M_i\}_{0 \leq i \leq 15}$ of 32 bits that are then extended into 80 new blocks $\{W_i\}_{0 \leq i \leq 79}$. Besides, four constant values $\{K_i\}_{1 \leq i \leq 3}$ are set.

Therefore, the algorithm processes a state of 160 bits divided into 5 words of 32 bits: A, B, C, D, and E (which are initialized with constant values). 64 rounds are performed and produce a fingerprint as the result of the compression function. The details of a round in SHA-1 are shown in Figure 3.19.

The rounds are divided into 4 packets of 16 subrounds in which the function F takes the following successive values:

1. $F = (B \text{ AND } C) \text{ OR } (\bar{B} \text{ AND } D)$

2. $F = (D \text{ AND } B) \text{ OR } (\bar{D} \text{ AND } C)$

3. $F = B \oplus C \oplus D$

4. $F = C \oplus (B \text{ OR } \bar{D}))$

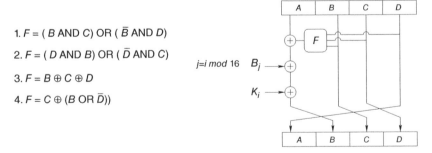

Figure 3.18 Rounds 1, 2, 3, and 4 in MD5 ($0 \leq i \leq 63$)

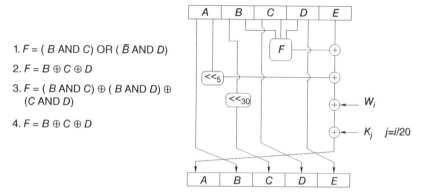

1. $F = (B \text{ AND } C) \text{ OR } (\bar{B} \text{ AND } D)$

2. $F = B \oplus C \oplus D$

3. $F = (B \text{ AND } C) \oplus (B \text{ AND } D) \oplus (C \text{ AND } D)$

4. $F = B \oplus C \oplus D$

Figure 3.19 Round i in SHA-1 $(0 \leq i \leq 79)$

Security of SHA-1. The size of the fingerprint is 160 bits in SHA-1. Therefore, finding collisions with a brute force attack (Yuval's attack) requires 2^{80} fingerprint computations. Recently, a technique which is similar to the one used against MD5 had enabled one to obtain collisions with only $\mathcal{O}(2^{63})$ fingerprint computations. Finally, a new theoretical attack requiring only $\mathcal{O}(2^{51})$ calls to the core SHA-1 was presented in 2008.

Thus, one considers that **SHA-1 has been broken**, even if the attack remains difficult to perform. As the first standard, this hash function is however still widely used (notably in signature schemes, or for the copy prevention of the Xbox MS, etc.).

3.5.1.3 SHA-256 SHA-256 is a more robust improvement (supporting a larger size of fingerprint) of SHA-1, which was published in 2000. It is based on a block cipher symmetric encryption (SHACAL-2) and it processes a block M of $b = 512$ bits to produce a fingerprint of $n = 256$ bits (see Figure 1.14 on page 76). Here, we are not going to give the details of the inner mechanisms of SHA-256.

Security of SHA-256. The size of the fingerprint is 256 bits in SHA-256. Therefore, finding collisions with a brute force attack (Yuval's attack) requires 2^{128} fingerprint computations. Currently, there is no **effective known attack against SHA-256**. Therefore, it is still considered to be secure.

3.5.1.4 Whirlpool Whirlpool is one of the hash functions, which was recommended by the NESSIE project in 2004. Its compression function is based on the Miyaguchi–Preneel construction (see Section 1.4.2.2). The underlying symmetric block cipher, which is used is W, a variant of Rijndael (one recalls that Rijndael is the symmetric encryption algorithm at the origin of the AES standard – see page 151). Table 3.13 summarizes the main differences between these two encryption functions.

The compression function in Whirlpool contains 10 rounds and processes a block M of $b = 512$ bits to produce a fingerprint of $n = 512$ bits (always using the notation introduced in Figure 1.14 on page 76). Here, we are not going to give the details of its implementation.

TABLE 3.13   Main Differences between W and Rijndael

	Rijndael	W
Block size	128, 160, 192, 224 or 256	512
Number of rounds	10, 11, 12, 13 or 14	10
Irreducible	$X^8 + X^4 + X^3 + X + 1$	$X^8 + X^4 + X^3 + X^2 + 1$
on $\mathbb{F}_{256}$	**(0x11B)**	**(0x11D)**
Origin of the SBox	$t : a \longrightarrow a^{-1}$ on $\mathbb{F}_{256}$	Recursive structure
Origin of the	Polynomials x^i on $\mathbb{F}_{256}$	Successive inputs
round constants		of the SBox

Remark: The names of the hash functions and the encryption functions often have a mysterious origin. For instance, Whirlpool is the name of the first galaxy whose spiral structure was discovered.

Security of Whirlpool. Looking for collisions in Whirlpool requires 2^{256} fingerprint computations. Currently, there is **no known efficient attack against Whirlpool**. Therefore, it is still considered to be secure.

3.5.1.5   Keccak (SHA-3)   Then, on November 2007, NIST announced a public competition to develop a new cryptographic hash algorithm, SHA-3. On December 2010, five finalists were selected (BLAKE, Switzerland-UK; Grøstl, Danemark-Austria; JH, Singapore; **Keccak**, ST micro-electronics; and Skein, USA) and the SHA-3 standard (Keccak) has been revealed in October 2012. Apart from security issues, Table 3.14 gives the respective speed attained on software for long messages hashing with these routines.

Keccak-512 uses an internal state of 5×5 words of 64 bits ($5 \times 5 \times 2^6 = 1600$ bits). Then, it iterates a function f on this internal state. This function uses a *sponge* construction (as it first *absorbs and then extracts hashes by* pressure) with parameters $c = 2 \times 512$ bits and $r = 1600 - c = 576$ bits, as shown in Figure 3.20. The output is included in the 576 bits of z_0, and more generally in the iterates $z_0, \ldots, z_i$ whenever more bits are required, as, for example, for a Mask Generating Function (MGF).

The internal function f uses $12 + 2 \times 6 = 24$ rounds of five steps each (θ, parity computations; ρ, bitwise rotations; π, permutations; χ, bitwise linear combination; and ι, an LFSR) :

θ :   XOR of the parity of two consecutive columns: $a[i][j][k]\oplus = \text{parity}(a[0..4][j - 1][k]) \oplus \text{parity}(a[0..4][j + 1][k - 1])$.

TABLE 3.14   SHA-3 Candidates Speed (Cycles/Byte) on an Intel i7

	SHA-2	Whirlpool	BLAKE	Grøstl	JH	Keccak	Skein
256-bits	17.44		8.24	13.73	13.71	**13.68**	9.65
512-bits	11.65	24.11	7.95	18.29	13.75	**12.80**	7.82

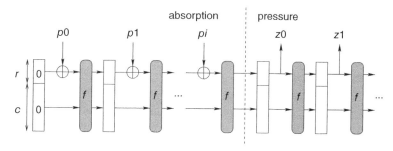

Figure 3.20 Keccak's sponge construct (SHA-3)

ρ : circular shifts: $a[i][j][k] = a[i][j][k - (\mathbf{r} + 1)(\mathbf{r} + 2)/2]$ with $\mathbf{r}$ satisfying $[i, j] = [0, 1] \cdot \begin{bmatrix} 3 & 1 \\ 2 & 0 \end{bmatrix}^{\mathbf{r}}$ mod 5.

π : word permutations: $a[j][2i + 3j] = a[i][j]$.

χ : nonlinear combination: $a[i][j][k]\oplus = (!a[i][j + 1][k]) \,\&\, (a[i][j + 2][k])$.

ι : XOR and LFSR: at round n, for $0 \le m \le 6$, $a[0][0][2m - 1]\oplus = b_{m+7n}$ where b_i is the ith bit of LFSR$_{X^8+X^6+X^5+X^4+1}$ mod 2.

On multicore processors, Keccak exhibits very good performance, roughly five to six cycles per byte, and is the fastest among the SHA-3 finalists on dedicated hardware. Moreover, Keccak's security is based on proven parts (the sponge construct) and quire conservative parameters (for instance 13 rounds should be sufficient, where 24 have been specified). Several years after its presentation, Keccak is still resisting the world's cryptanalists.

3.5.1.6 Status of the Resistance to Collisions for the Main Hash Functions
As we have seen before, one of the main criteria of robustness of a hash function is its resistance to collisions: it is considered secure if there exists no attack that enables one to find collisions with a better complexity than Yuval's attack. Table 3.15 summarizes the resistance to collisions for the most famous hash functions. It is a survey

TABLE 3.15   Resistance to Collisions for the Most Famous Hash Functions

Function	Fingerprint	Birthday Attack	Resistance to Collisions	Complexity of the Attack
MD5	128 bits	$\mathcal{O}(2^{64})$	Broken	$\mathcal{O}(2^{30})$
SHA-1	160 bits	$\mathcal{O}(2^{80})$	Broken	$\mathcal{O}(2^{51})$
HAVAL	256 bits	$\mathcal{O}(2^{128})$	Broken (2004)	$\mathcal{O}(2^{10})$
SHA-256	256 bits	$\mathcal{O}(2^{128})$	**Secure**	
Whirlpool	512 bits	$\mathcal{O}(2^{256})$	**Secure**	
SHA-3 (Keccak)	512 bits	$\mathcal{O}(2^{256})$	**Secure**	

performed at the time of writing this book; therefore, it is likely to evolve depending on further cryptanalysis.

One may also notice that the resistance to collisions is not always sufficient. Hence, one also considers other properties that might be required for hash functions. For instance, one may consider:

- the *resistance to close collisions*: it must be difficult to find collisions (x, x') for which the Hamming distance (defined in Chapter 4) between the fingerprints $d(H(x), H(x'))$ is small.
- the *resistance to pseudo-collisions* in which one allows the modification of the initialization vector IV of the hash function to find collisions.
- finally, the *pseudo-random behavior*: it concerns making the distinction between H and a random function difficult.

3.5.1.7 Integrity Check for Hash Functions   The integrity of the data which is transmitted on an insecure channel may be insured by error correction codes (see Chapter 4) but also by hash functions. One distinguishes three different methods:

1. Use a secure channel to transmit the fingerprint in a secure way, the message being transmitted on the insecure channel. Then one is able to check the conformity between the fingerprint of the received message and that which was received through the secure channel. Such a layout is illustrated in Figure 3.21.
2. Use an encryption function E (and the related decryption function D) to encrypt both the message and the fingerprint before sending them on the insecure channel. Such a layout is illustrated in Figure 3.22.
3. Use an authentication code. The details of such approach are given in the following section.

Exercise 3.26 (RSA-OAEP)   *OAEP is a padding scheme providing a nondeterministic encryption of block ciphers. It requires a random source and two standard cryptographic hash functions.*

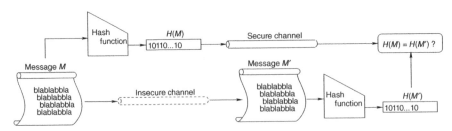

Figure 3.21   Integrity check with hash functions using a secure channel

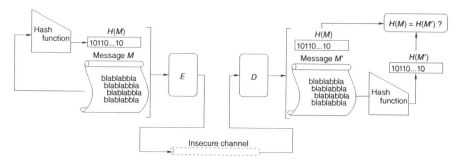

Figure 3.22   Integrity check with hash functions using an encryption function

OAEP works as follows, where the message to be padded is M, r is a vector of random bits, G and H are the two hash functions, '||' is concatenation, and $\oplus$ is XOR:

$$OAEP(M) = [(M \oplus G(r))||(r \oplus H(M \oplus G(r)))].$$

In the following, we note $s = M \oplus G(r)$ and $t = r \oplus H(M \oplus G(r)) = r \oplus H(s)$ so that $OAEP(M) = [s||t]$.

1. **Sizes**

   (a) *Let m be the output size and k_0 the size of r. Give the sizes of M, s, and t and the caracteristics of G and H.*

   (b) *For given s and t show how to find r then M.*

2. **RSA-OAEP**: *OAEP is in general a preliminary step for an RSA encryption, we then speak of RSA-OAEP. An advantage of RSA-OAEP is that with good parameters it can be proved secure in an ideal model, the random oracle model. This version is recommended by the PKCS* (Public Key Cryptography Standard). *We note E_{pub} the RSA encryption function with pub = (e, N) and D_{priv} the decryption function with priv = (d, N). RSA − OAEP just applies the encryption function to the OAEP-padded result so that $RSA − OAEP(M) = E_{pub}(OAEP(M))$.*

   (a) *With N = 77, recall why we can choose e = 7 and what is the associated private key.*

   (b) *We let m = 7 bits and k_0 = 3 bits and define $G(r) = -r \mod 16$ and $H(s) = \lfloor s/2 \rfloor$. For the sake of simplicity, in this exercise, we clearly chose a hash function H, which is not collision resitant. Give some collision for H.*

   (c) *Compute $E_{pub}(OAEP(8))$ with the given parameters if the random value happens to be r = 5.*

3. **Integrity check**: *In practice, to form M, one adds k_1 zeros to the right of the useful information, as shown in Figure 3.23. This allows to detect badly crypted/transmitted blocks at decipher time.*

   (a) *Why would this addition of zeros allow this partial verification ?*

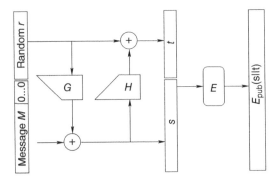

Figure 3.23 Optimal Asymmetric Encryption Padding (OAEP)

(b) In practice, suppose that modifications of M are uniformly distributed and that preimages of G and H are also uniformly distributed for uniformly distributed outputs. What would then be the probability that such a modification goes undetected?

Solution on page 317.

3.5.1.8 Message Authentication Code (MAC) One is able to use hash functions to perform both the authentication and the integrity check of the message. Then, one talks about an MAC: it is a one-way hash function customized with a secret key K (thus, one will denote $H_K(x)$ the value of the fingerprint of x), which satisfies the following additional property:

$$\text{For all } K \text{ unknown and for all set of pairs } \left\{ \begin{array}{l} (x_1, H_K(x_1)) \\ (x_2, H_K(x_2)) \\ \vdots \\ (x_i, H_K(x_i)) \end{array} \right. ,$$

it is impossible to compute (in reasonable time) another valid pair $(x, H_K(x))$ for $x \notin \{x_1, x_2, ..., x_i\}$.

To summarize, only the legitimate owners of the secret key K are able to compute (and thus to check) the fingerprint:

- Alice and Bob share a key K.
- Alice sends M and $r = H_K(M)$ to Bob.
- Bob receives M' and r and he checks that r is actually equal to $H_K(M')$.

Such a layout is illustrated in Figure 3.24. An MAC enables one to insure both the integrity of the transmitted message (all possessors of K are able to check whether M

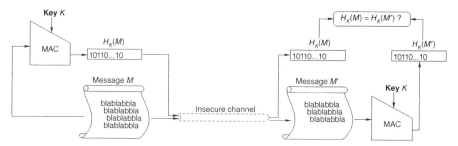

Figure 3.24   Principle of the use of an MAC

has been modified or not as it corresponds to the fingerprint r) and the authenticity of the source of the data: assuming that only Alice and Bob share the key K, they are the only ones who are able to generate the fingerprint $H_K(M)$.

In practice, one tries to make the breaking of an MAC as difficult as the breaking of the hash function itself.

Construction of an MAC. Basically, there are two ways to set up an MAC:

- Using a symmetric block cipher in CBC mode or CFB mode (then, the fingerprint is the last cipher block), or in CTR mode as shown in Algorithm 3.3. For the CBC mode, this operation is illustrated in Figure 3.25.
  On a Pentium III 500 MHz, a software implementation of the CBC-MAC-AES (hence a CBC-MAC in which the encryption E_K is performed using the standard AES based on the Rijndael algorithm) can produce message signatures with a rate up to 234 Mbits/s. The same implementation of the AES alone runs at up to 275 Mbits/s. Therefore, the cost of the fingerprint computation is very close to the cost of the encryption.

- Using a one-way hash function. Then, the idea is to include the key K in the fingerprint computation. Several solutions are possible but not all of them can be

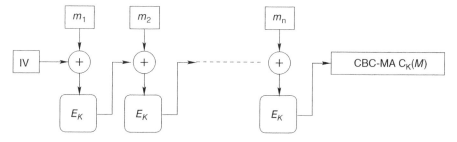

Figure 3.25   MAC using symmetric encryption

applied here. For instance, in a Merkle–Damgård model for the hash function, **one may not use** the following construction:

🏆 $H_K(M) = H(K||M)$

🏆 $H_K(M) = H(M)$ with $IV = K$

🏆 $H_K(M) = H(M||K)$.

Exercise 3.27 *Explain why these three constructions do not provide a valid* MAC.
Solution on page 318.

Therefore, one will prefer the following constructions, each one of them using two keys K_1 and K_2:

- Envelope: $H(K_1||M||K_2)$
- NMAC: $H_{K_1}(H_{K_2}(M))$
- Hybrid: $H_{K_1}(x||K_2)$

Remark: Although an MAC provides both authentication and integrity, it obviously does not insure the confidentiality of the message. For this purpose, one has to use other additional techniques such as the Galois Counter Mode (GCM), which combines the counter mode CTR of Section 1.3.1 and the Galois hashing of Section 1.4.2.2:

Algorithm 3.3 Galois Counter Mode

Input A plaintext message M.
Input An authentication data A.
Input A key K and a symmetric block cipher E.
Output The ciphertext C, and the associated authentication tag T.
 1: $C = CTR - E_K(M)$;
 2: Let $h = E_K(0)$;
 3: $S = GHASH_h(A||C||length(A)||length(C))$;
 4: **return** $(C, T = CTR - E_K(S))$.

3.5.2 Public Key Authentication

When receiving it, B will use his private conversion function D_B for decrypting. As the function D_B is secret, if A's transmission is eavesdropped, the intruder will not be able to decode C. Therefore, confidentiality is preserved. However, as E_B is public, B has no means of knowing the sender's identity. Similarly, the message sent by A can be tampered with. Thus, the authentication and integrity features are not included in the system. For them to be so, the conversions must satisfy the property $E(D(M)) = M$. Indeed, let us suppose that A wants to send an authenticated message M to B.

This means that B must be able to check that the message was indeed sent by A and that it has not been modified on the way. For this, A will use his private conversion function D_A, compute $M' = D_A(M)$, and send M' to B. B can then use the public conversion function E_A to compute $E_A(M') = E_A(D_A(M)) = M$.

Assuming that M is a "valid" text (in the sense of the protocol used), B is sure that the message was sent by A and was not tampered with during its transmission. This comes from the single-direction nature of E_A: if an attacker could use a message M to find M' such that $E_A(M') = M$, it would mean that he could compute the inverse of the function E_A, which is a contradiction.

However, in this case, secrecy would not be ensured because anyone can have access to E_A and therefore decode the message. The following exercise incorporates the public key authentication principle. It is simple enough for you to discover it at this stage, based on the constraints that we have just described.

Exercise 3.28 (Principle of Public Key Authentication)   *Using the functions E_A, D_A, E_B, and D_B, find a pair of encryption/decryption functions providing both secrecy and authentication.*   *Solution on page 318.*

Exercise 3.29 (RSA Cryptography and Authentication)   *A teacher sends his marks to the secretarial staff of the school by mail. The teacher's public key is $(e_P, n_P) = (3, 55)$, whereas the secretarial staff's is $(e_S, n_S) = (3, 33)$.*

1. *Find the private keys of the teacher and the school's secretarial staff.*
2. *To ensure the confidentiality of his messages, the teacher encrypts the marks with the secretarial staff's RSA key. What encrypted message corresponds to mark the 12?*
3. *To ensure the authenticity of his messages, the teacher signs each mark with his private key and encodes the result with the secretarial staff's RSA key. The secretarial staff receives message 23. What is the corresponding mark?*

Solution on page 318.

3.5.3   Electronic Signatures

For a long time, handwritten signatures have been used to prove the identity of the author or at least to insure the agreement of the signatory to the content of a document. With digital documents, one has to set up protocols to replace handwritten signatures. First, one will notice that an electronic signature must depend on both the signatory **and** the document. Otherwise, a simple copy/paste (which is particularly easy with a digital document) would enable one to obtain a valid signature.

Hence, an electronic signature has to be:

- *authentic*: it must convince the recipient that the signatory has actually deliberately signed a document;
- *nonforgeable*;

- *nonreusable*: it is attached to a given document and it cannot be used on a different document;
- *nonmalleable*: any modification of the document can be detected; and
- *nonrepudiable*: the signatory cannot repudiate the signed document.

Let us consider the functions offered by cryptography (3.1.2). One notices that electronic signatures provide integrity, authentication, and also nonrepudiation.

As for encryption algorithms, one distinguishes two types of signature:

1. Symmetric signatures that use a symmetric cryptosystem. In this case, one must either consider a referee or a secret key, which will be used in an MAC in CBC or CFB mode (as presented in the previous section).
2. Asymmetric signatures that use a public key cryptosystem and a public hash function (without key) like SHA-256 or Whirlpool.

The main principle of the latter approach is shown in detail in Figure 3.26 (This figure does not give the explicit details of the signature and verification algorithms used; the details of the best-known ones are given in the sequel). Indeed, one would rather sign a constant size fingerprint of a document that is small enough to be efficiently processed by a public key cryptosystem. Hence, when Alice signs a document M, she uses the fingerprint of M, $h_M = H(M)$, her private key K_d, and finally the decryption function D. Hence, she generates the signature $s(M) = D_{K_d}(h_M)$ (one will

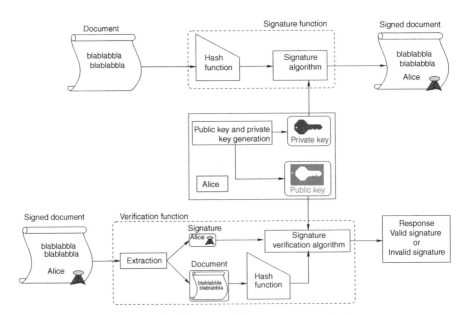

Figure 3.26 Principle of public key signatures and verification

notice that only Alice can generate $s(M)$). Therefore, the signed document consists of the couple $[M, s(M)]$.

This document can be verified by Bob from Alice's public key K_e and the encryption function E (also public). It is enough to compute the fingerprint h_M of the document and to check that $E_{K_e}(s(M)) = h_M$.

Now let us give the details of the two most common signature schemes.

3.5.3.1 RSA Signature

Indeed, it is possible to use RSA system to define a digital signature. For this, it is enough to apply the inverse RSA.

The parameter generation is the same as in RSA. Therefore, let $K_e = (e, n)$ be Alice's public key and let d be her secret exponent.

When Alice wishes to sign a document M, it is enough for her to perform the following operations:

- She computes the fingerprint $h_M = H(M)$. One will assume that $0 \le h_M < n$.
- She generates the signature $s(M) = (h_M)^d \mod n$ (once again, one notices that only Alice is able to generate such a signature as she only has the secret exponent d).
- Then, the signed document sent to Bob is the couple $[M, s(M)]$.

Hence, Bob has received a signed document $[\widetilde{M}, s(M)]$ from Alice. This document might have been modified or even forged by a malicious third party. Therefore, Bob recovers Alice's public key (e, n) (Section 3.6.2 is dedicated to key exchange protocols). Then he computes $\widetilde{h}_M = H(\widetilde{M})$ and checks the equality

$$s(M)^e = \widetilde{h}_M \mod n.$$

Indeed, $s(M)^e = (h_M)^{e.d} \mod n = h_M \mod n = h_M$ and, if the document is authentic, one has $h_M = \widetilde{h}_M$.

Thus, the security of such a signature scheme relies on the security of the RSA cryptosystem. One will notice that this presentation remains quite simple and is still subject to attacks.

3.5.3.2 Digital Signature Standard (DSS)

This signature scheme is based on the discrete logarithm problem. Such a system includes some shared parameters q, p, and g as well as a public key y and a private key x, which are generated in the following way:

1. Choose q prime with 160 bits.
2. Find $p = kq + 1$ prime with 512 or 1024 bits.
3. While $a = 1$, choose g and compute $a \leftarrow g^{\frac{p-1}{q}} \mod p$. *(The order of g is at most q).*

4. Choose x on 160 bits.
5. $y \leftarrow g^x \mod p$.

Once the parameters are built, the signature is performed in the following way:

1. Alice chooses k lower than q randomly.
2. Alice computes and sends the signature of her message m using a hash function h (for DSS, it is SHA-1):

$$r = (g^k \mod p) \mod q \ \text{ and } \ s = (k^{-1}[h(m) + xr]) \mod q.$$

3. Bob checks that the signature is valid if and only if $v = r$ for
   - $w = s^{-1} \mod q$;
   - $u_1 = h(m)w \mod q$;
   - $u_2 = rw \mod q$;
   - $v = (\left[g^{u_1}y^{u_2}\right] \mod p) \mod q$.

Theorem 25 *The DSS verification is correct.*

Proof. The parameter s is built in such way that $k = (s^{-1}[h(m) + xr]) \mod q$. Yet we have $g^{u_1}y^{u_2} = g^{u_1 + xu_2}$. Therefore, given u_1 and u_2, and as $g^q = 1 \mod p$ by construction, one has $g^{u_1}y^{u_2} = g^{h(m)w + xrw}$. Yet, as $w = s^{-1}$, the remark at the beginning of the proof gives $g^{u_1}y^{u_2} = g^k$, hence $v = r \mod q$. $\square$

Exercise 3.30 *While DSS was being developed in the United States, the Russians developed their own signature scheme: GOST. The parameters p, q, g, x, and y are the same except that q is a prime number of 254–256 bits and p is a prime number of 509–512 bits (or between 1020 and 1024 bits). Only the s part of the signature is different:*

1. *Alice computes and sends*

$$r = (g^k \mod p) \mod q \ \text{ and } \ s = (xr + kh(M)) \mod q.$$

2. *Bob checks that the signature is valid if and only if $u = r$ for*
   - $v = h(M)^{q-2} \mod q$.
   - $z_1 = sv \mod q$.
   - $z_2 = ((q - r)v) \mod q$.
   - $u = ((g^{z_1}y^{z_2}) \mod p) \mod q$.

Prove that the verification is correct. *Solution on page 318.*

Exercise 3.31 (Elliptic Curve Digital Signature Algorithm (ECDSA)) *ECDSA is a standardized protocol for electronic signature using elliptic curves. Let H be a cryptographic hash function. The protocol is as follows.*

Key generation	1. *Choose an elliptic curve* $\mathbb{E}(\mathbb{F}_q; a, b)$ *with a prime number* $p > 2^{160}$ *of points;* 2. *Choose a point* $G \in \mathbb{E}$ *on this curve;* 3. *Choose an integer* $s \neq 0 \mod p$; 4. *Compute* $Q = [s]G \in \mathbb{E}$.
Public key	$\mathbb{E}, G, Q$
Private key	s
Key validation	1. *Check that* $Q \neq \mathcal{O}$; 2. *Check that* $Q \in \mathbb{E}$; 3. *Check that* $[p]Q = \mathcal{O}$.
	For a message m
Signature	1. *Randomly choose* $k \neq 0 \mod p$; 2. *Compute* $M = (x, y) = [k]G$; 3. *Compute* $z = k^{-1}(H(m) + sx) \mod p$; 4. *The signature is the pair* (x, z).
Verification	1. *Compute* $u = H(m)z^{-1} \mod p$; 2. *Compute* $v = xz^{-1} \mod p$; 3. *Compute* $M' = (x', y') = [u]G \oplus [v]Q$; 4. *Check that* $x = x'$.

1. *Prove that the verification is correct.*

2. *How could* $[p]Q$ *be the infinite point* $\mathcal{O}$?

3. *To compute* $[k]P$ *for a point on an elliptic curve, one uses the double-and-add algorithm. Now to compute* $[u]G \oplus [v]Q$ *one could use this algorithm twice, to get* $[u]G$ *and* $[v]Q$, *and then add the results.*

   (a) *Give the number of doublings and bound the number of additions to compute* $[u]G \oplus [v]Q$ *this way.*

Algorithm 3.4 Shamir's Trick for Simultaneous Double-And-Add

Input P, Q and $R = P \oplus Q$, points on an elliptic curve $\mathbb{E}$ of order n;
Input u and v non negative integers lower than n.
Output $([u]P) \oplus ([v]Q)$.
 1: **If** $u = 0$ **then return** $[v]Q$ **End If**
 2: **If** $v = 0$ **then return** $[u]P$ **End If**
 3: Recursively compute $T = \left(\lfloor \frac{u}{2} \rfloor P \right) \oplus \left(\lfloor \frac{v}{2} \rfloor Q \right)$;
 4: Compute $M = [2]T$;
 5: **If** u is odd **and** v is odd **then return** $M \oplus R$ **End If**
 6: **If** u is odd **and** v is even **then return** $M \oplus P$ **End If**
 7: **If** u is even **and** v is odd **then return** $M \oplus Q$ **End If**
 8: **If** u is even **and** v is even **then return** M **End If**

(b) A. Shamir proposed to speed up this computation by precomputing $P \oplus Q$ and performing the double-and-add simultaneously as shown in Algorithm 3.4. Compare its number of curve operations with the previous algorithm.

Solution on page 319.

3.6   KEY MANAGEMENT

Each step of a process of interchanging encrypted messages is crucial because it is likely to be the target of attacks. In particular, while symmetric systems are good cryptographic systems, their weakness lies largely in the key exchange system. Protocols have been invented to ensure the security of these exchanges.

3.6.1   Generation of Cryptographically Secure Bits

We have looked at various pseudo-random generators in Section 1.3.7, and at different attacks which allow one to predict the behavior of some of these generators (see Sections 1.4.3.1 and 1.4.3.2). An example of a secure generator is that of Blum, Blum, and Shub. Let p and q be two fairly large prime numbers congruous to 3 modulo 4 prime numbers. Let x_0 be the square of some random number modulo $n = pq$. This generator computes the sequence of successive squares $x_{i+1} = x_i^2$ mod n. Yet, discovering the least significant bit of x_0 subsequent to the least significant bits of these x_i is as difficult as breaking the factorization. More generally, it is possible to use RSA to produce cryptographically secure pseudo-random sequences, as presented in the following exercise:

Exercise 3.32 (RSA Pseudo-Random Bit Generator)   *Let n and e be the modulus and the exponent of an RSA code. Let $k = \mathcal{O}(\log(\log n))$ be an integer. Then knowing $c = x^e$ mod n, finding the k first bits of x is as difficult as finding the secret key associated with n and e.*
Describe a process taking k as an input that generates a sequence of l cryptographically secure pseudo-random bits. *Solution on page 319.*

3.6.2   Public Key Infrastructure (PKI)

A PKI (for *Public Key Infrastructure*) is a set of infrastructures allowing one to effectively perform secure communication. Indeed, once one has defined complex algorithms, using public keys for example, the first practical problem is "how do you assign a public key to its owner?" First of all, the idea of PKIs is to avoid broadcasting the keys but rather to distribute digital certificates containing these keys and identity data (civil status, postal address, e-mail address, domain name or IP address for a server, etc.). Then, PKIs are precise structures that handle, in particular, the creation and management of such certificates.

Exercise 3.33 (Throwaway Credit Card Numbers)   *A bank has a one-time-card number mechanism. A user has received a code by postal mail for generating such numbers on his bank's Web site.*

1. *When the user asks to generate a throwaway number, what kind of authentication is employed?*
2. *Find an attack that lets you retrieve the code.*
3. *How can the bank counter this attack?*

Solution on page 319.

3.6.2.1   General Principle   To authenticate itself, an entity seeks to prove that it has a secret information item that only it can know. In the case of a PKI, an entity (Alice, for instance) generates a pair public key/private key. Alice keeps the private key (either in a folder only accessible to her or, better still, on a smart card or a USB memory stick). Then, the public key has to be made available to any person wanting to exchange information with her.

For this, Alice uses a *trusted third party* (a Certification Authority (CA): see the next paragraph) to generate a *certificate*.

A certificate is a digital document containing at least Alice's personal contact information, together with her public key. This document is signed by the CA. This signature is used to certify the origin of the certificate, as well as its integrity. Figure 3.27 illustrates the different stages of the creation of a certificate. We still have to ascertain how to check the authenticity of the trusted third party. In practice, this third party also has a certificate signed by another third party and so on. The last party in this *chain of certificates* will have to sign for himself. Then, one talks about a self-signed or a root certificate. To increase the trust that a user can place in them, these root certificates must be cross-certificated with other CAs.

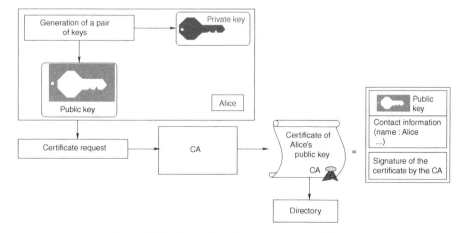

Figure 3.27   Principle of the creation of certificates

Therefore, a PKI is a set of technologies, organizations, procedures, and practices compatible with the implementation and usage of certificates based on public key cryptography. Thus, it is a set of systems providing services pertaining to digital certificates. It provides the means of using these certificates for authentication between entities. There is a standard for this mechanism, which is shown in Figure 3.33.

3.6.2.2 Elements of the Infrastructure A PKI must first provide a number of functions, the main ones of which are the following:

send certificates to previously authenticated entities; revoke certificates; maintain them; establish, publish, and comply with certification practices to create an area of trust; make certificates public by means of directory services; and possibly, manage keys and provide archiving services. In the latter case, there are three types of services to be provided to the users:

1. *Key management.* An architecture can handle the management of creation, distribution, storage, usage, recovery, archiving, and destruction of the keys (public/private pairs or symmetrical encryption secret keys).
2. *Pooling of keys.* This is accomplished, for example, via the Diffie–Hellman protocol discussed in Section 3.3.1.
3. *Key transmission.* This is done, for example, via RSA, as discussed in Section 3.5.2.

For example, the issuing procedure is standardized and must follow the various steps shown in Figure 3.28.

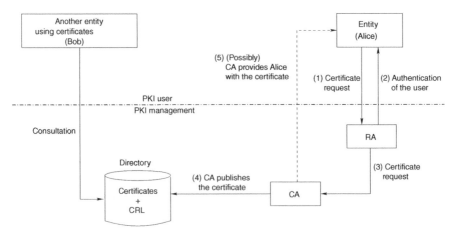

Figure 3.28 Issuing a certificate

The players in a PKI. We begin with a description of the various entities in a PKI:

- The *certificate holder*: this is an entity that possesses a private key and is the subject of a digital certificate containing the corresponding public key. It may be a physical person, a Web server, a network installation, and so on.
- The *certificate user*: this user recovers the certificate and uses the public key it contains in the transaction with the holder of the certificate.
- The Certification Authority (CA): this is a set of resources (software and/or hardware) and people identified by name and public key, which
  - generates certificates
  - sends and maintains information concerning the Certification Revocation List (CRL);
  - publishes certificates that have not yet expired;
  - maintains archives concerning expired and revoked certificates.

  It is also the legal and moral entity of a PKI.
- The Registration Authority (RA): This is the intermediary between the key holder and the CA. It checks users' requests and forwards them to the CA (the degree of verification depends on the security policy applied). Each CA has a list of accredited RAs. An RA is known to a CA by its name and its public key – the latter checking the information items supplied by an RA through its signature.
- The *CRL issuer*: the issuing of revocation lists can be delegated to a special entity different from the CA.
- The *repository* or *directory*, which deals with
  - disseminating certificates and CRLs
  - accepting certificates and CRLs from other CAs and making them available to the users.

  It is known by its address and access protocol.
- The *archive*, which handles long-term storage of information on behalf of a CA. This enables disputes to be settled, by knowing which certificate was valid at what period of time.

In this organization, the central component of a PKI is the Certification Authority. Therefore, a legitimate question is "Why do we need registration authorities?" Two types of factors are involved:

1. Technical factors
   - Efficient algorithms are necessary for the creation and management of keys. An RA can provide such implementations – software or hardware – to the users that do not have such possibilities.

- The users are not necessarily capable of publishing their certificates.
- The RA can issue a *signed* revocation, even if a user has lost all his/her/its keys (the RA is supposed not to lose its own!)

Therefore, the RA is a secure intermediary.

2. A simplified organization
- It is cheaper to equip one RA than all users.
- The number of CAs necessary is reduced by grouping simple functions.
- Closeness to users is enhanced.
- *Previously existing* structures can often act as an RA.

However, separating the CA and the RA is generally less secure than centralizing everything within one CA: a user and an RA can strike an agreement, *but* the RA then has to send it to the CA. The CA – which has the final decision – may tamper information. Therefore, security relies on the trust in the CA.

3.6.2.3 Electronic Certificates There are several standards for PKIs – most of which are evolving. Examples of public key infrastructures currently undergoing standardization by the IETF (*the Internet Engineering Task Force*) are PKIX, Simple Public Key Infrastructure (SPKI), and Simple Distributed Security Infrastructure (SDSI). Each infrastructure has its own format of certificate. In the following, we describe the main format used: the X.509 standard.

Figure 3.29 shows what a certificate in X.509 format looks like.

This diagram illustrates by means of examples the entries in the main fields composing this certificate. One may notice, in the examples of "Distinguished Name"

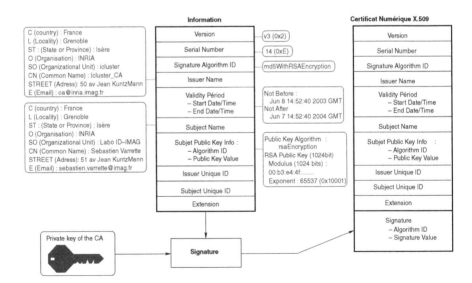

Figure 3.29 Generation and content of an X.509 certificate

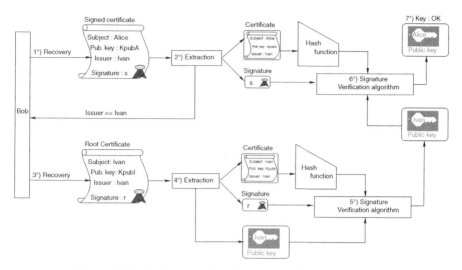

Figure 3.30 Verification of certificate and public key extraction

(DN) ("Issuer Name" and "Subject Name" fields), the list of subfields composing these Dns. They permit the related entities to be located very precisely. Once a certificate has been issued and deposited in a directory, other users are able to come and query the directory to recover and verify these certificates, as illustrated in Figure 3.30 for instance, or consult the CRLs.

There have been several versions of the X.509 standard, due to feedback from experience (v1: 1988, v2: 1993, v3: 1996). It also specifies the format of Certificate Revocation Lists. It is very similar to the format of certificates: a version number, the type of algorithms used, the sender's name, the validity dates, the invalid certificates list, and the CAs signature.

X.509 certificates and CRLs are written in a specification language called ASN.1 (*Abstract Syntax Notation*).

Among the main ASN.1 types used for X.509 certificates, one may find

- "OID" (*Object Identifier*): numbers separated by dots. The US Department of Defense is, for example, designated by {1.3.6}.
- "*Algorithm Identifier*": an algorithm descriptive name. For instance, 1.2.840.113549.3.7 corresponds to *DES − EDE*3 − *CBC*, 1.2.840.113549.1.1.4 corresponds to *md5withRSAEncryption*, 1.2.840.10045.1 corresponds to a signature based on elliptic curves with SHA-1 *ecdsawithSha*1, etc.
- "*Directory String*": text information.
- "*Distinguished Names*," "*General names*," "*Time*": for instance, dates are specified by "Time:=CHOICE { UTCTime, GeneralizedTime }," where "UTCTime" is valid between 1950 and 2049 and "GeneralizedTime" after 2050.

Exercise 3.34 (Electronic Certificates)

1. *Describe the key components of a digital certificate. What does it incorporate, and why?*
2. *Explain the benefits of digital certificates.*
3. *What is a certification policy?*

Solution on page 320.

3.6.2.4   The PKIX Model   The IETF's Public Key Infrastructure for X.509 certificates (PKIX) workgroup was set up in autumn 1995 to develop the Internet standards necessary for an infrastructure based on X.509 certificates.

The first standard produced, RFC-2459, describes version 3 of X.509 certificates and version 2 of CRLs. RFC-2587 describes CRL storage, RFC 3039 certification policy, and RFC 2527 the practical framework of certificates followed. Finally, the protocol for certificate management (RFC 2510), the status of online certificates (RFC 2560), the certificate management request format (RFC 2511), certificate dating (RFC 3161), certificate management messages (RFC 2797), and the use of FTP and HTTP for transmission of PKI operations (RFC 2585) are the other standards developed by the group. All in all, every administration function for a public key infrastructure has been specified. Figure 3.31 shows the structures adopted by the group.

The main function of a PKI is to use certificates to authenticate people, with no third party and without any risk of being subjected to an attack of *man-in-the-middle* type.

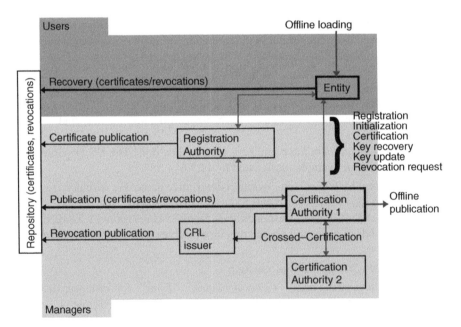

Figure 3.31   PKI model for X-509 certificates

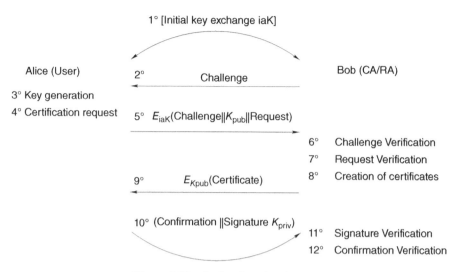

Figure 3.32   Authenticated registration

In particular, the initial registration of an entity with the creation and signature of the associated certificate is governed by the following mechanism, shown in Figure 3.32.

In this process, each certificate verification is performed by extraction of the information items concerning the sender and the verification of signatures, using his public key, as shown in Figure 3.30.

Once this registration has been completed, subsequent authentications are easier. Figure 3.33 shows the various steps in mutual authentication (unilateral authentication does not contain the last message) in the FIPS 196 protocol.

1. Alice sends Bob an authentication request.
2. Bob generates a random number R_b, which he stores and thereby creates the token $TokenBA_1$ by means of

$$TokenBA_1 = R_b.$$

Bob sends it to Alice, possibly with an identification token.

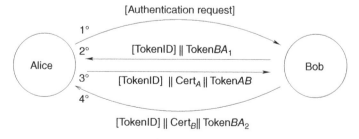

Figure 3.33   Authentication via public key cryptography

3. Alice generates a random number R_a, which she stores. Then, she generates an authentication token *TokenAB* in the form:

$$TokenAB = R_a||R_b||B||Sign_a(R_a||R_b||B).$$

This token contains the message and the signature with the private key. Alice sends it to Bob coupled with her certificate (which therefore contains her public key, which permits the signature to be verified) and, possibly a token identifier (actually, even sending the certificate is optional).

4. Bob starts by verifying Alice's certificate (Figure 3.30). Then, he can verify the information items enclosed in *TokenAB* using Alice's public key, which is contained in the certificate. After checking Alice's signature, she has been authenticated with Bob. Now he needs to authenticate himself by also generating, in his turn, an authentication token *TokenBA*$_2$ by means of:

$$TokenBA_2 = R_b||R_a||A||Sign_b(R_b||R_a||A)$$

Bob sends it to Alice with his certificate and possibly a token identifier (the same comment as above applies).

5. Alice follows the same steps for authenticating Bob. At the end, mutual authentication has been completed.

Once the two parties have been authenticated, they can then use their public keys to encrypt and sign messages, without fearing of a Man-in-the-middle attack.

Exercise 3.35 (OpenSSL – Exercise to be Done on a Computer) *OpenSSL is a set of cryptography utilities implementing Secure Sockets Layer (SSL) v2/v3, Transport Layer Security (TLS) v1 and the standards they require (notably those for PKIs).*

1. Creating a file of random characters: *under Linux (version 1.3.30 onwards), there is an entropy pool file (/dev/urandom, created from different hardware random sources). Using* dd, *how do you create a random* .rand *file of at least 16kb in size, with 16 separate blocks?*

2. Creation of a CA[8]: *Create a directory demoCA and subdirectories called private, certs, crl, and newcerts. Enter a serial number in the file demoCA/serial and create a file called demoCA/index.txt. Define the access rights for all of these directories and files.*

   (a) *Using* openssl genrsa, *how do you create a new pair of 4096-bit keys using your random file? This key will be stored in a file called* cakey.pem *in the* demoCA/private *directory and encrypted on the disc with AES-256 bits.*

---

[8]All the following names can be edited in the file openssl.cnf.

   (b) With `openssl req`*, how do you create a new self-signed root certificate using the preceding key? This certificate must be in X.509 format, stored in the file* `demoCA/cacert.pem`*, and valid for 365 days.*

3. User certificate.

   • *Using* `openssl`*, how do you create a 1024-bit* RSA *key pair?*

   • *How do you produce a certificate query with* `openssl req` *using this key? This query must also contain the key and be valid for 2 months.*

   • *Using* `openssl ca`*, how to you ask the* CA *to reply to your query? This query must create a certificate file* `newcert.pem` *and specify the default security policy* `policy_anything`*.*

4. Application to the sending of secure e-mail messages. *E-mail clients (such as Thunderbird) tend to use the PKCS12 format for certificates rather than X.509 format. How do you add a certificate created above to a client of this type? What happens if the private key associated with this certificate is lost? In particular:*

   (a) Can you still send encrypted e-mail messages? Can you receive such e-mails?

   (b) Can you still sign e-mail messages that you send? Can you check the signatures of e-mail messages received?

Solution on page 320.

3.6.2.5   *Nonhierarchical Architectures, PGP* In contrast with PKIX, PGP was designed to provide secure messaging. It came into being before the proliferation of CAs accessible via the Internet. PGP had to solve the problem of trust delegation within a nonhierarchical model. Instead of relying on different CAs, PGP makes each user his/her own CA.

Having the equivalent of one CA per user is impossible! PGP then added the concept of trust: if a user knows that the certificate of user B is valid, then he/she can sign B's certificate. Thus, PGP allows an unlimited number of users to sign a given certificate. Therefore, a true network of acquaintances is set up and creates mutual trust.

In this model, the difficulty is to find the chain of trust that links two users. The elegant solution offered by PGP is partial trust: a signature on a certificate only instils a fraction of the trust in this certificate. Therefore, several trust signatories are required to establish a certificate, see Figure 3.34. The other difficulty of this system is to distinguish between granting one's trust to a user's certificate and granting one's trust to a third party for signing other certificates. One single untrustworthy or simply negligent user can destroy the whole trust network.

Lastly, one may notice that the latest versions of the PGP trust model introduce a "meta" entity that finally also plays the role of a root CA so as to emulate hierarchical operation.

Exercise 3.36 *In a PGP exchange model, you receive a message signed by a so-called Oscar. Oscar's certificate is signed by Bob, whose certificate is signed by Alice, in whom you have complete trust to sign certificates. What do you think of the message you have received?* *Solution on page 321.*

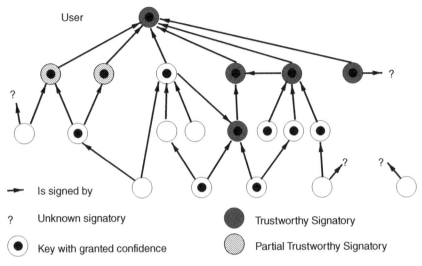

User

Is signed by

? Unknown signatory

Key with granted confidence

Trustworthy Signatory

Partial Trustworthy Signatory

Figure 3.34 An example of the PGP trust

3.6.2.6 Drawbacks of PKIs PKIs are not a panacea; some drawbacks can be described:

- Several people may have the same *"Distinguished Name."* This risk is reduced by the accumulation of information (country, locality, region, postal address, e-mail address, IP, DNS, etc.). However, one question remains: who certifies such additional information items?

- What exactly does one need to understand when a CA is pretending to be trustworthy? This problem is reduced by crossed certifications, but *all* the records have to be initiated *offline* (otherwise phrased as *"out-of-band"*), namely on a channel other than the current communication channel or in a nonelectronic way.

- The security policy of all CAs is therefore that of the weakest!

- Lastly, a dating authority is lacking.

Exercise 3.37 *Carl M. Ellison and Bruce Schneier wrote an article called "What you're not being told about Public Key Infrastructure." In this article, they present 10 hazards linked to the use of PKIs. Comment on the following four risks:*

1. *Risk n°1: "Who do we trust, and for what?" More precisely, the question is to ascertain who gave a CA the authority to sign certificates, and what is the concept of trust.*
   Comment on the following scenarios: PKI within a single company; PKI between one company and its clients/subsidiaries; PKI managed by a

specialized company (VeriSign, RSA Security, etc.) for an outside company; CAs preloaded in browsers or operating systems.

2. Risk n°2: "Who is using my key?" More exactly, how do you protect secret keys?

3. Risk n°4: "Which John Robinson is he?" More precisely, how do you deal with the various John Robinsons known by a CA?

4. Risk n°9: "How secure are the certificate practices?" For instance:

   (a) What criteria should one use to establish the validity period of keys?

   (b) How does one decide on the lengths of keys and hashing?

   (c) Should one implement CRLs?

   (d) More generally, how does one figure out the certification practices of an authority?

Solution on page 321.

To conclude, one needs to carefully specify the security policy and, in the end, all the drawbacks of PKIs are almost solved if a PKI is restricted to one single administrative entity (e.g., one single company) and they remain reasonable when some of these entities interact.

3.6.3 Securing Channels with the SSH Tool

Despite the relative simplicity of functions D and E within the scope of RSA or El Gamal, they are not as fast for computing as their equivalents for DES: modular exponentiation is a more time-consuming operation than permutations or searches in a table when p is large. This makes it more complicated to design an electronic component intended to quickly cipher and decipher using this approach. An algorithm of RSA type is around 10,000 times slower than a DES.

The solution for efficient encryption lies in the joint use of symmetric and asymmetric cryptosystems. Hence, the PGP system encrypts a message with the following protocol:

1. The source text is enciphered with a key K of 3-DES type.

2. The key K is enciphered according to the RSA principle, using the public key of the recipient.

3. A message, composed of the key K encrypted with RSA and a text enciphered using an algorithm of 3-DES type, is sent.

The recipient will then perform the following decrypting operations:

1. Decode the key K using his/her RSA private key D.

2. Decode the text using 3-DES (or using another algorithm called IDEA) with the key K.

For authentication, the principle is slightly different:

- Generate a code identifying the text by a number of fixed size – a hashing function, for instance.
- Encrypt this code using RSA with the private key of the sender.

This enables the recipient to verify the validity of the message and the sender's identity, using the public key of the sender.

Exercise 3.38 *A group of n people want to use a cryptographic system to exchange confidential information items on a two-by-two basis. The information items to be exchanged between two members of the group must not be readable by another member.*

1. *What is the minimum number of symmetric keys which are required?*
2. *What is the minimum number of asymmetric keys which are required?*
3. *What are the reasons for which the group finally uses a hybrid system for encryption?*

Solution on page 321.

As an application of the PGP system, let us cite the Secure SHell (SSH) program used in networks for logging in to another hardware system, performing file transfers and starting applications.

3.6.3.1 SSH, a Hybrid Protocol SSH is a secure remote lognalyse-in protocol for secure sessions via insecure channels, within a Client–server model.

It is composed of three parts:

1. a transport layer, which permits server authentication, confidentiality, and integrity;
2. a user authentication layer; and
3. a session protocol that permits the use of several logical channels.

Moreover, this protocol ensures: confidentiality of the data using strong encryption; integrity of communications; entity authentication; privileges control; and implementation of a secure channel for subsequent communications.

Similar to PGP, it uses a public key protocol for exchanging the secret keys that are used by the faster enciphering algorithms adopted for the actual session traffic. Let us begin with version SSH-1.

3.6.3.2 Server Authentication Each server has its own public key identifying itself. The problem is disseminating this key to the clients. There are two strategies:

- the client maintains a database of public keys of servers to which he connects.

- there exists a trusted third party who is able to disseminate keys in a secure manner.

In practice, for the moment, the algorithm consists of the server sending its public key and, during the first session, the client storing it in his database (currently, in the file `~/.ssh/known_hosts`). The client compares this key with the keys he has previously received. However, this does allow a *Man-in-the-middle* attack, even if it becomes more complex. To improve the security, a signature of the key is computed and it can easily be exchanged by other means, such as over the telephone.

3.6.3.3 Setting Up a Secure Session This takes place in several phases, and it enables the server to securely provide a session key K, which will be used via a secret-key-based encryption algorithm:

1. *The client contacts the server.* The client simply sends a session request to the server's TCP port (port 22).
2. *The client and the server exchange the versions of the SSH protocol that they can use.* These protocols are represented by an ASCII string (for instance: `SSH-1.5-1.2.27`).
3. *The server and the client switch to communication using formatted packets.* The format of the packets is shown in Figure 3.35.
   Here is the purpose of each field in this packet:
   - **Length**: this is the packet size (without counting the "Length" and "Adjustment" fields) encoded as a 32-bit integer
   - **Adjustment**: these are randomly generated data items of which the length various from 1 to 8 bytes; more precisely, the length is given by the formula: $8 - (\text{Length mod } 8)$; This field make attacks with a chosen plaintext more difficult to perform
   - **Type**: specifies the type of packet
   - **Data**: the data sent
   - **Verification**: four bytes computed by Cyclic Redundancy Checks (CRC), see Section 4.2 for the building of a CRC.
   It is the "Adjustment," "Type," "Data," and "Verification" fields, which will be encrypted when a session key has been established.

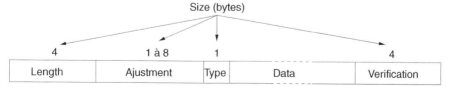

Figure 3.35 Format of an SSH packet

4. *The server identifies itself to the client and provides the session parameters.* The server sends the following information items to the client (still in clear):

   • a *host key* (public) H (which is the public key of the server);
   • a *server key* (public) S (a pair of RSA keys is regenerated every hour);
   • a sequence C of eight random bytes (check bytes): the client has to include these bytes in the next reply, or it will be rejected; and
   • the list of encryption, decompression, and authentication methods that can be used.

5. *The client sends a secret session key to the server.* The client chooses an encryption method M that can be used by both parties (for instance, IDEA in CFB mode, DES in CBC mode, and RC4 for SSH-1; 3-DES and AES in CBC mode for more-recent versions) and then randomly generates a session key K and sends $[M, C, E_H(E_S(K))]$. Thus, only the server will be able to decode K because only the server knows the private key associated with H. The second encryption using S ensures that the message has not been replayed, as S is only valid for 1 h.

   The client and the server also compute a session identifier (Id_S), which uniquely identifies the session and which will be used later.

6. *Each entity implements the encryption and completes the server authentication.* After having sent his session key, the client must wait for a confirmation message from the server (encrypted by means of the session key K), which will complete the authentication of the server with the client (only the expected server is able to decode the session key).

7. *A secure session has been established*: the client and the server have a secret session key that enables them to encrypt and decrypt their messages.

3.6.3.4 Client Authentication Once a secure session has been set up, the client can authenticate with the server. This authentication can be performed by using the host's name (using the file ~/.rhosts, a method which is not very satisfactory in terms of security), via a password or via a public key.

In the latter case, the client uses the ssh-keygen command to generate the files ~/.ssh/identity (which will contain the RSA secret key d and which is protected by a "passphrase") and ~/.ssh/identity.pub (which will contain the RSA public key (e, n)). The content of identity.pub is added on the server to the file ~/.ssh/authorized_keys.

Once this step has been completed, the client sends a query for an authentication via public key. The modulo n is passed as a parameter and used as an identifier. The server can reject the query if it does not allow authentication of this key (no associated entry in the file authorized_keys, for example).

Otherwise, it randomly generates a number C of 256 bits and sends C^e mod n to the client (RSA encryption with the public key of the client).

Then, using his private key d, the client decrypts C, appends it with the session identifier Id_S, computes the fingerprints of all these items with MD5, and sends them to the server in response. The server performs the same operation at its end and checks that the result agrees with what it receives. This latter verification completes the client authentication.

3.6.3.5 Security of the Algorithms, Data Integrity, and Compression

The algorithms for encryption, integrity and compression are chosen by both parties. The algorithms used are well-known and well-established. However, an algorithm can be changed if a failure occurs.

As we will see, the integrity checking is performed via a simple cyclical redundancy check code (see Section 4.2), which is not effective against some attacks (such as the Futoransky and Kargieman insertion attack). This weakness is partly at the origin of a new version of SSH, that is SSH-2. In SSH-2, the integrity of each packet is checked by adding signature bits (MAC, see Section 3.5.3). They are computed from the sequence number of the packet (which is not part of the packet) and its unencrypted content.

Finally, the data can be compressed, using the `gzip` utility, for example, which limits the bandwidth used for packet transmission.

3.6.3.6 Major Differences between SSH-1 and SSH-2

The new version of the SSH protocol, SSH-2, provides: a greater choice in algorithm negotiations between the client and the server (choice of the hashing, etc.); the management of X.509 certificates for public keys; a greater flexibility in authentication (including partial authentication); a better integrity check by encryption; a periodic replacement of the session key every hour; the secret keys are now of 128 bits; public keys are of 1024 bits; and several methods for exchanging keys, notably the Diffie–Hellman protocol.

Exercise 3.39 (OpenSSH Under Linux) *The* `ssh` *command under Linux starts a program to log onto a remote hardware system and to execute commands on this system, using the SSH protocol. In the* `.ssh` *directory, at the root of the user directory, this program maintains a file called* `known_hosts` *containing the servers with which the user has held sessions. The first session is considered to be secure, and subsequent sessions are authenticated using the public key stored in the file* `.ssh/known_hosts`.

1. *How can one make the server authentication more secure?*

2. *Several client authentication methods are possible (public key, password, and keyboard). How do you generate a public key/ private key pair of DSA type of 2048 bits with the* `ssh-keygen` *utility?*

3. *Add a public key, for instance, the one which has just been generated, to the file* `authorized_keys` *in the* `.ssh` *directory of a third party account. Log onto this account using* `ssh -v`. *What do you notice?*

4. *Delete the file* known_hosts. *Login again from another hardware system. What message would you expect to see?*

5. *Edit the* known_hosts *file and modify the public key. What message would you expect to see?*

Solution on page 321.

4

ERROR DETECTION AND CORRECTION

In the previous chapters, we have supposed that all communications were "without noise," namely that the message that was issued was systematically received as it is, or all distortions were due to a malicious third party that managed to hide them. In reality, one should also take the possible distortions on the message induced by the transmission channel into account.

The science enabling the correction of errors induced by such a noisy channel is thus called *channel coding* or simply *coding Theory*. To be more precise, we will rather denote it by error detection or error correction.

One calls *error rate* the probability that a bit that is received through the channel is different from the bit that was issued, that is, the number of erroneous bits with respect to the number of bits issued.

This error rate depends on the nature of the transmission line. Table 4.1 gives several orders of magnitude of the raw error rate depending on the channel that is used.

In the case of a phone call, whether it is local or international, the error rate depends on the number of repeaters and on the type of support (wire, satellite, etc.) and it can reach 10^{-4} (up to one error for 10,000 bits transmitted). Storage devices also contain errors. For instance, a numerical file that is recorded on a CD, a DVD, or a Blu-ray disk contains necessarily some errors owing to its burning, to the reading with a laser, and also to the defects on the support (dust, scratches, etc.). In a distributed storage server, the information is disseminated on several supports; it is crucial to be able to

Foundations of Coding: Compression, Encryption, Error Correction, First Edition.
Jean-Guillaume Dumas, Jean-Louis Roch, Éric Tannier and Sébastien Varrette.
© 2015 John Wiley & Sons, Inc. Published 2015 by John Wiley & Sons, Inc.
http://foundationsofcoding.imag.fr

TABLE 4.1   Order of Magnitude of Raw Error Rates

Line	Error Rate
Floppy disk	10^{-9}
	at 5 MB/s, 3 erroneous bits per minute
Optical CD-ROM	10^{-5}
	7 kB erroneous on a 700 MB CD-ROM
DAT audio	10^{-5}
	at 48 kHz, two errors per second
Blu-ray disk	$<2 \cdot 10^{-4}$
	about 1.6 MB erroneous on a 32 GB disk
Hard Disk Drives (HDD)	$>10^{-4}$
	$\sim 10^6$ errors in 10 GB
Flash technologies	$\approx 10^{-5}$
Solid-State Drives (SSD)	$<10^{-5}$
Semiconductor memories	$<10^{-9}$
Phone line	Between 10^{-4} and 10^{-7}
Infrared remote control	10^{-12}
Communication on optical fiber	10^{-9}
Spacecraft	10^{-6} (Voyager), 10^{-11} (TDMA)
ADSL	10^{-3} to 10^{-9}
Computer network	10^{-12}

recover the whole information even if some parts are missing; for instance, it may occur during a hard disk failure on a Redundant Array of Independent Disks (RAID) system or when two peers are unconnected in a peer-to-peer storage system.

Table 4.1 gives some raw error rates of such commonly encountered digital devices. Overall, after automatic error correction, the application data target error rate should be closer to 10^{-15}. This chapter thus deals with the algorithms optimizing the redundancy that has to be added in order to achieve this automatic correction.

With respect to an analogical information, the fundamental interest of a numerical information (hence, in the form of discrete symbols like bits) is that there exist some data representation formats that can enable one to recover the initial information, when the error rate is bounded. Developed in the XXth century from a seminal article of Shannon, the channel coding theory focuses on the study and the setup of such representations – error-correcting codes – with the best effectiveness.

The goal of this chapter is to introduce the main error-detecting codes and error-correcting codes which are used in practice: Cyclic Redundancy Checks (CRC) codes, Low Density Parity Check (LDPC) codes, Reed–Solomon codes, and turbo codes. The main principles that support error correction are presented in the first section and illustrated on everyday life examples, such as barcodes and bank account an credit card numbers, in Section 4.2. Then we need an additional theoretical formalization in Section 4.3, which deals, for example, with distance between codewords. This formalization is useful to construct more involved codes, in the last three sections, and to show their usefulness in technology.

4.1 PRINCIPLE OF ERROR DETECTION AND ERROR CORRECTION

4.1.1 Block Coding

In the following, a channel is a device transmitting some symbols (the characters) in an alphabet V. For a binary channel, each symbol is a bit: $V = \{0, 1\}$. Let $m \in V^+$ be a message one wishes to send in the form of a stream (one assumes that the source message is prior encoded in the form of a sequence of symbols in V, see Chapter 1). The *block coding* of size k consists of splitting the message $m \in V^+$ into blocks M_i on k symbols and processing each block one after the other.

When a sequence of k symbols $s = [s_1, \ldots, s_k]$ is issued on the channel, the sequence $s' = [s'_1, \ldots, s'_k]$ that is received by the recipient might differ; one speaks of a transmission error. If $s'_i \neq s_i$, one says that the symbol i is erroneous; if j symbols are erroneous, one says that there were j errors. In order to prevent one from such errors by detecting or even correcting them automatically, methods for *block coding* consist of adding some redundancy to the k symbols of information in the initial block.

Therefore, the encoding transforms the block one wishes to send $s = [s_1, \ldots, s_k]$ into a block on $n = k + r$ symbols, $\phi(s) = [c_1, \ldots, c_k, \ldots, c_n]$, which comprises r symbols of redundancy with respect to the k symbols of the initial message. The set $C_\phi = \{\phi(s) : s \in V^k\}$, image under ϕ of V^k, is called a *(n, k)-code*; its elements are called *codewords*. For the decoding to be able to recover the source message without ambiguity when there is no error, the encoding function ϕ must obviously be injective. The *code rate R* of a (n, k)-code is the rate of source symbols that are included in a codeword:

$$R = \frac{k}{n}.$$

Hence, the reception of a word not belonging to C_ϕ (i.e., a word in $\overline{C_\phi} = V^n \setminus C_\phi$) indicates an error. Error detection relies on this test of nonbelonging to C_ϕ. Following an error detection, the decoder may possibly perform a correction. One distinguishes two types of correction:

- direct correction: the erroneous signal that is received contains enough information for one to be able to recover the word that was issued;

- correction by retransmission, or Automatic Repeat reQuest (ARQ): when an error is detected but it cannot be corrected, the recipient asks for the sender to transmit the source message one more time.

In the following paragraphs, the principles of error detection and error correction are shown using two very simple codes.

4.1.2 A Simple Example of Parity Detection

In this section, one considers a binary channel: $V = \{0, 1\}$. One encodes the word $m = (s_1, \ldots, s_k)$ under $\phi(m) = (s_1, \ldots, s_k, c_{k+1})$ where $c_{k+1} = (\sum_{i=1}^{k} s_i) \mod 2$ (which is written with the exclusive or operator $c_{k+1} = \bigoplus_{i=1}^{k} s_i$). Therefore, one has

$$c_{k+1} \oplus \left(\bigoplus_{i=1}^{k} s_i \right) = 0.$$

In other words, $c_{k+1} = 1$ if and only if the number of 0 bits in m is even. This equality check is called a *parity control*. Obviously, this equality becomes false if, during the transmission, a odd number of bits in $\phi(m)$ change their value, as discussed in Section 1.4.2.1. Hence, adding a longitudinal parity bit enables one to detect an error on a odd number of bits (see Table 4.2).

This basic technique for detecting errors is still very often used at a hardware level, in particular for detecting errors in a memory. Parity codes are often used to check the correctness of many identification numbers.

Exercise 4.1 (Social Insurance Identification Number)
A French social insurance number is a number on $n = 15$ digits: an identification number K on $k = 13$ digits followed a key C on $r = 2$ digits that is computed in such way that $K + C$ is a multiple of 97.

1. *What is the key of the social insurance number 2.63.05.38.516.305?*
2. *What is the rate of this code?*
3. *How many errors on the digits can be detected by the key of the social insurance number?*

Solution on page 323.

4.1.3 A Simple Example of Direct Correction using Longitudinal and Transverse Parity

Still considering $V = \{0, 1\}$, one builds a $(n, k_1 k_2)$ binary code as follows. As $k = k_1 k_2$, a source word m can be represented in a bidimensional table of bits with k_1 lines and k_2 columns. The associated codeword $\phi(m)$ contains $(k_1 + 1)(k_2 + 1)$ bits including $k_1 + k_2 + 1$ parity bits: one for each line and each column and the other for the set of bits (see Table 4.3). This code enables one to not only to detect but also correct one error: it is enough to locate the line and the column where the error occurred by controlling the parity bit of each line and each column (see Exercise 4.2.)

TABLE 4.2   Encoding with a Parity Bit

m: source Word (7 bits)	$\phi(m)$ with a **Parity Bit** (8 bits)
0101001	01010011
0001001	00010010
0000000	00000000

TABLE 4.3   Error Correction using Parity Bits

m: source Word on $21 = 7 \times 3$ bits	$\phi(m)$ Encoded on 32 bits with parity bits	Word Received (1 error)	Word Corrected (1 correction)
0101001	0101001 **1**	01010011	01010011
0001001	0001001 **0**	00011010	00010010
0000000	0000000 **0**	00000000	00000000
	01000010	01000001	01000001

Exercise 4.2 (Longitudinal and Transverse Parity Code)   *One builds a longitudinal and transverse parity code for codewords on 9 bits.*

1. *What is the length n of the codewords $\phi(m)$?*
2. *Prove that one detects any error concerning an odd number of bits.*
3. *Prove that one detects up to 3-bit errors.*
4. *Give the example of two words containing four errors: one in which the error can be detected, the other one in which one is not able to detect the error.*
5. *Show that one is able to correct any word containing at most one error.*
6. *Give the example of one word received containing two errors that one is not able to correct.*

Solution on page 323.

4.1.4   Encoding, Decoding, and Probability of Error

More generally, with the injective encoding function $\phi : V^k \to V^n$ mapping any source word to a word of the (n, k) code, the complete block scheme C_ϕ operates in the following way:

1. The codeword $c = \phi(s)$ is computed and sent on the channel; the recipient receives a word $c' = [c'_1, \ldots, c'_n]$.
2. If the word c' which is received belongs to C_ϕ, the message is decoded into $\tilde{s}$ such that $\phi(\tilde{s}) = c'$.
3. Otherwise, $c' \notin C_\phi$ and one detects that there was an error. Several decoding strategies can be applied; here we present the *nearest-neighbor decoding*, sometimes called *Minimum Distance Decoding (MDD)*. In this case, the correction proceeds in the following way:
   (a) if there exists an integer i and a *unique* codeword $c'' \in C_\phi$ having at least $n - i$ bits equal to c', then one corrects c' into c'' and the message which is decoded is $\tilde{s}$ such that $\phi(\tilde{s}) = c''$.
   (b) otherwise, there exists at least two codewords having $n - i$ common digits with c', and no other codeword has $n - i + 1$ common digits with c'. Therefore, one cannot correct the error. Depending on the context, two

approaches are then considered: (i) perform a *complete* decoding. It means that a codeword *must* always be returned. Here, one of the possible codeword – let us say $\hat{c}$ – having $n - i$ common digits with c' is arbitrarily selected. If $\hat{c}$ is this codeword, then one corrects c' into $\hat{c}$ and the message which is decoded is $\tilde{s}$ such that $\phi(\tilde{s}) = \hat{c}$; (ii) alternatively, an *incomplete* decoding can be done. In this case, if a codeword cannot be determined (which is precisely the situation here), a specific symbol ∞ can be emitted, which could be read as "one or more errors were detected but were not corrected." Or a constant word $\tilde{s} = m$ on k bits may be returned, which is interpreted as an error signal.

Apart from the MDD, another strategy is often considered. It assumes that we know for each word $x \in V^n$ received, the (forward) probability $P(x \mid c)$ that c was sent for all codewords $c \in C_\phi$. Then the Maximum Likelihood Decoding (MLD) rule will conclude that c_x is the most likely codeword transmitted if c_x maximizes the forward probabilities $P(x \mid c)$, that is,

$$P(x \mid c_x) = \max_{c \in C_\phi} P(x \mid c).$$

Every decoding strategy exists in a complete or an incomplete version (the first one being the most difficult one, as one must always decode to some codeword). Note that as it will be seen in Exercise 4.14, MDD and MLD correspond to the same decoding rule in some circumstances.

In all cases, there is a *decoding error* if and only if $\tilde{s}$, which is finally decoded, is different from s: one denotes P_{C_ϕ} the probability of such error.

For the sake of efficiency, the code C_ϕ – and in particular the encoding function ϕ – is chosen in order to

- have a probability of error P_{C_ϕ} as arbitrarily small as one wishes;
- have the highest rate R;
- be computed with the least cost, thanks to the most efficient encoding (computation of ϕ) and decoding (membership to C_ϕ, computation of ϕ^{-1} and correction) algorithms.

For a given channel, the second theorem of Shannon shows that it is possible, with some constraints on the choice of k with respect to n, to build codes C_ϕ such that this probability of error P_{C_ϕ} is as small as one wishes.

4.1.5   Shannon's Second Theorem

Shannon is the author of an important theorem dealing with the possibility of building error correction codes on noisy channels. Here, we limit ourselves to the case of a noisy channel without memory. More precisely, the theorem we are going to describe can be applied to the *channel coding* in which each source word is transmitted through a theoretical channel transforming this word into another word between M values that are equally likely. In other words, the source is discrete and uniform.

4.1.5.1 Code Rate And Efficiency.

Let a given channel with its internal transmission error rates. Shannon's second theorem proves that there exist some codes with an arbitrary probability of error P_{C_ϕ}, but the rate of which is bounded with respect to the reliability of the channel, more precisely to its *capacity*. In other words, even on a distorted channel, it is possible to perform a transmission without error!

4.1.5.2 Channel Capacity.

Let a noisy channel without memory that transmits some symbols of the alphabet $V = \{s_1, \ldots, s_{|V|}\}$. Let X be a random source variable at the input of the channel, whose values are taken in the symbols of V. Likewise, let Y be the random variable at the output of the channel. One assumes that the values taken by Y are also symbols in V. Let the distribution $p_{j|i} = P(Y = s_j | X = s_i)$ of the probabilities of transition; $p_{j|i}$ is the probability of receiving s_j at the output of the channel knowing that s_i was issued on the input.

For instance, on a channel without error, $p_{i|i} = 1$ and $p_{j|i} = 0$ for $j \neq i$. Hence, the distribution $(p_{j|i})_{1 \leq i,j \leq |V|}$ characterizes the probabilities of the errors during the transmission on the channel without memory .

One denotes $p_i = P(X = s_i)$ the probability that X takes the value s_i. With the probabilities of transition, this distribution (p_i) of the source induces a probability distribution on the variable Y. With Bayes' equality (see Section 1.2.2.2), one has $P(Y = s_j) = \sum_{i=1}^{|V|} P(X = s_i, Y = s_j) = \sum_{i=1}^{|V|} P(X = s_i) \cdot P(Y = s_j | X = s_i)$; thus,

$$P(Y = s_j) = \sum_{i=1}^{|V|} p_i \cdot p_{j|i}.$$

The *channel capacity* $C(X, Y)$ is the maximum amount of information on the input that is actually transmitted on the channel, the maximum being taken on all the distributions of input $(p_i) \in \overline{p}$ satisfying $\sum_{i=1}^{|V|} p_i = 1$. Yet, the conditional entropy $H(X|Y)$ (see page 19) represents what is left to discover on the input X knowing the output Y, namely, the loss of information on the input. Therefore, the channel capacity is the maximum amount of information from the input decreased by this loss:

$$C = \max_{p \in \overline{p}} H(X) - H(X|Y).$$

Using the formulas of conditional entropy, it is possible to also rewrite this definition under the following forms:

$$C = \max_{p \in \overline{p}} H(Y) + H(X) - H(X, Y) = \max_{p \in \overline{p}} H(Y) - H(Y|X).$$

Therefore, the extreme cases correspond to

- $H(Y) = H(Y|X)$: if knowing the input does not influence the output, then the channel does never transmit any information of the input;
- $H(Y|X) = 0$: if the output can provide exactly the same information than the input, then the channel is, a priori, without error.

Computing this maximum is easy when the channel is *symmetric*. In this case, the probabilities of transition are independent from the symbol s_i one considers: for all $1 \leq i, j \leq |V|$ with $i \neq j$, then one has $p_{i|j} = p$ and $p_{i|i} = 1 - p$; then, the probability p is called the *probability of error of the channel*. The maximum is reached when the entropies $H(X)$ and $H(Y)$ have a maximum value, that is, for a uniform distribution of the probabilities of input $p_i = \frac{1}{|V|}$.

For instance, Exercise 4.3 shows that the capacity of a BSC (for which $|V| = 2$) with error probability p is equal to

$$C_{\text{BSC}} = 1 + p \log_2(p) + (1 - p) \log_2(1 - p).$$

This channel is illustrated on Figure 4.1.

Exercise 4.3   *A Binary Symmetric Channel (BSC) with error probability p is a channel for which $|V| = 2$ and*

- *the probability that the bit one receives is different from the bit which was issued is p: $p_{2|1} = p_{1|2} = p$;*
- *the probability of having the bit received equal to the bit which was issued is $1 - p$: $p_{1|1} = p_{2|2} = 1 - p$.*

1. *Show that the capacity of this channel is $C_{\text{BSC}} = 1 + p \log_2(p) + (1 - p) \log_2(1 - p)$.*
2. *Deduce that $C_{\text{BSC}} = 0$ if $p = \frac{1}{2}$ and $0 < C_{\text{BSC}} \leq 1$ otherwise.*

Solution on page 324.

4.1.5.3 Transmission without Error on a Constant Capacity Channel.

Thanks to the channel capacity, Shannon's theorem gives a necessary and sufficient condition in order to perform a transmission without error on a channel of capacity C.

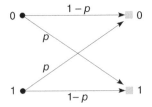

Figure 4.1   Binary Symmetric Channel (BSC) with error probability p

Theorem 26 (Shannon's Second Theorem) *Let a channel of capacity C. Let $\epsilon > 0$ arbitrary. Then, there exists at least one (n,k)-code of code rate $R = \frac{k}{n}$ with a probability of error $P < \epsilon$ if and only if*

$$0 \leq R < C.$$

For instance, in the case of a symmetric binary channel with a probability of error $p = \frac{1}{2}$, one has $C = 0$. Therefore, it is impossible for one to transmit some information correctly. However, if $p \neq \frac{1}{2}$, $0 < C \leq 1$; thus, there always exists a (n,k)-code that enables one to transmit without error, despite a constraint on its rate. More generally, it is always possible to transmit without error on a channel of nonzero capacity, but the code rate is bounded by the capacity of the channel.

Exercise 4.4 *One may find it intuitive for one to be able to transmit without error on a BSC channel for which the probability p of receiving a bit different from the one issued is lower than $\frac{1}{2}$.*
Then, justify without using Shannon's theorem that one is also able to transmit without error when $\frac{1}{2} < p \leq 1$. *Solution on page 324.*

This theorem gives a necessary condition on the minimum number r of redundancy digits one has to add:

$$r > k \left(\frac{1}{C} - 1 \right). \tag{4.1}$$

This bound does not depend on the rate of error correction but rather on the channel capacity.

The proof of Shannon's theorem is not that useful; the theorem proves the existence of such codes, but it does not indicate how to build them. Moreover, it is possible for the code rate to tend towards C when n tends towards infinity For instance, this can be achieved by setting the code as a subset of words chosen randomly in V^n and with the same cardinal number as V^k. However, to be practical, it is necessary for the encoding and the decoding to be performed efficiently, with reasonable time cost and material cost. Hence, the code must satisfy some additional properties that are not satisfied, a priori, by random codes.

This is why this theorem induced the research of efficient codes, especially in two directions:

- on one hand, for a given error correction rate, the construction of codes maximizing the code rate. In particular, this is the case of Reed–Solomon block coding;
- on the other hand, for a given code rate, the construction of codes maximizing the error correction rate; this is the case of convolutional codes and turbo codes.

Hybrid block/turbo codes then propose a trade-off between the two approaches.

The following sections introduce the main codes that are used for a binary source. After describing the model of the problem of error detection and giving the definition of the distance of a code (Section 4.3), linear block codes are defined in the Section 4.4. Also, specific classes of such codes are introduced, namely, LDPC codes and cyclic block codes, the later being illustrated with the Reed–Solomon codes. Interleaving techniques (Section 4.5) enable one to extend such codes for the correction of bursts of errors. Such techniques are illustrated with the practical example of the Cross-Interleaved Reed–Solomon Code (CIRC) for audio CDs, which is built from a Reed–Solomon code. Finally, this chapter concludes with the convolutional codes and the turbo codes that are built using interleaving.

Generally, these several codes are all related with polynomials. This representation using polynomials is first introduced in Section 4.2 with the error detection codes CRC; such codes appear in many practical cases in which the sender is able to resend a message that was badly received by the recipient.

4.2 ERROR DETECTION BY PARITY – CRC CODES

When the recipient is able to ask the issuer for a second transmission of the information item at low cost (ARQ, see Section 4.1.1), it is enough to be able to encode and decode quickly while detecting the errors efficiently, but without correcting them. Therefore, one is interested in building an *error-detecting code*.

To be efficient, error-detecting codes contain in each codeword the symbols of the related information items. One says that a (n, k)-code is *systematic* if there exist k indexes such that the restriction of any codeword $c = \phi(s)$ to these k indexes is equal to s. Such code is also said to be *separable* because one is able to extract directly the information items $s = [s_1, \ldots, s_k]$ from the codeword $c = \phi(s)$. These information items are often put on the correct order at the k first indexes. Then, the principle of systematic coding is to compute the $r = n - k$ redundancy symbols $[c_{k+1}, \ldots, c_n] = \phi_r([s_1, \ldots, s_k])$, where ϕ_r is the restriction of ϕ to the r last indexes. The generalization to a systematic code on any other k indexes is immediate.

In a systematic code, the redundancy symbols are called *parity symbols* or *control symbols* . Indeed, error detection is equivalent to a *parity check* (or *checksum*) as discussed in Section 4.1.2. Overall, one associates r redundancy symbols to each source word $[s_1, \ldots, s_k]$ such that the codeword $c = [s_1, \ldots s_k, c_{k+1}, \ldots, c_{k+r}]$ satisfies a predicate $f(c)$ (parity), with f easily computable.

After presenting several parity checks on integers that are used in common life fields largely overwhelming the single field of telecommunication, this section presents the Cyclic Redundancy Checks (CRC) that are used in computer networks.

4.2.1 Parity Check on Integers: ISBN, EAN, LUHN

As illustrated in the example of the social insurance number (see Exercise 4.1), parity-check codes are widely used. In such practical cases, the predicate $f(c)$ generally consists of checking whether a sum of integers c_i in the received message is a multiple of a given integer. ISBN (International Standard Book Number) code for the identification of books, bar codes for the identification of products (EAN, European Article Numbering) as well as their extensions – the Basic Bank Account Number (BBAN) key of a bank account or the PIN number of a smart card – are also some examples that are described in details in this section.

4.2.1.1 EAN Bar Code.

The EAN-13 code (*European Article Numbering*) is a bar code that is used in both the industry and the trading in order to identify some products or logistic units in a univocal way. It is composed of a 13 digits number $c_{12} - -c_{11}c_{10}c_9c_8c_7c_6 - -c_5c_4c_3c_2c_1c_0$ and a graphic pattern with black and white vertical stripes that can be read by an optical scanner. This code stems from the American code Universal Product Code (UPC-A) on 12 digits: the bars are identical but a zero is added on top of the UPC-A number (i.e., $c_{12} = 0$) in order to form the EAN-13 code. The 12 left digits $c_{12}, \ldots, c_1$ identify the product; c_0 is the parity digit that is computed in the following way. Let $a = \sum_{i=1}^{6} c_{2i}$ be the sum of all digits having a even index and $b = \sum_{i=1}^{6} c_{2i-1}$ the sum of all digits having an odd index. Then, one has $c_0 = 10 - (a + 3b) \mod 10$.

The graphical bar code encodes the same EAN-13 number: each column on 2.31 mm encodes one single digit. Each column is divided into seven subcolumns of width 0.33 mm but the EAN-13 code imposes that an element (a digit) is always encoded with a sequence of only four bars of different widths, but with an overall width equal to seven times the elementary width. For instance, the symbol 0 is encoded with a sequence of one white bar of width $3 * 0.33 = 0.99$ mm, one black bar of width $2 * 0.33 = 0.66$ mm, one white bar of width 0.33 mm, and one black bar of width 0.33 mm. One can summarize this coding scheme with $0 \rightarrow 000\ 11\ 0\ 1$. Symmetric representations must always encode the same digit. Therefore, one has also $0 \rightarrow 111\ 00\ 1\ 0$, $0 \rightarrow 1\ 0\ 11\ 000$, and $0 \rightarrow 0\ 1\ 00\ 111$.

Exercise 4.5 *Show that there are actually* 40 *possible combinations of four bars per column.* Solution on page 325.

The EAN-128 is an extension of the EAN-13 code, which enables one not only to encode digits but also to encode characters, as illustrated in Figure 4.2.

The EAN-13 code enables one to detect some errors but not to correct them. Some graphical bar codes enable one not only to detect but also to correct some errors;

Foundations of coding

Figure 4.2   The EAN-128 code for foundations of coding

for instance, PDF417 (*Portable Data File*), Aztec, datamatrix, or Quick Response code (QR-code). The latter are bidimensional multiline bar codes of small size, which enables one to encode up to 3000 characters, thanks to Reed–Solomon codes (whose details are given later on this chapter). These bidimensional codes are more suited to camera readers (e.g., on smartphones), as they not only use an error detection but also an error correction coding. We give more details on the QR-code in Section 4.4.6.3.

4.2.1.2 The ISBN Code.

The ISBN (for *International Standard Book Number*) is a number identifying all the books published worldwide. This number consists of 10 digits $c_{10}c_9c_8c_7c_6c_5c_4c_3c_2c_1$, which are structured in four segments $A - B - C - D$ separated with a dash. The first nine digits $A - B - C$ identify the book: A identifies the linguistic community, B the number of the publisher, and C the number of the book for the publisher. The control key $D = c_1$ is a parity symbol , which is either a digit between 0 and 9 or the character X, which represents 10. The key c_1 is such that $\sum_{i=1}^{10} i \times c_i$ is a multiple of 11; in other words, $c_1 = 11 - \left(\sum_{i=2}^{10} i \times c_i \right) \mod 11$.

The ISO 2108 standard, in effect from January 1st 2007, identifies the books with a EAN-13 bar code on 13 digits: the three first digits are equal to 978, the following nine digits are the first nine digits of the ISBN code (*ABC*), and the last digit is the EAN-13 control digit.

Exercise 4.6 (ISBN Code and EAN-13 Code) *Complete the sequence* $111 - 888 - 144$ *to obtain a valid ISBN. What is its associated EAN-13 bar code?*

Solution on page 325.

4.2.1.3 The Basic Bank Account Number (BBAN).

The BBAN $B - G - N - R$ consists of 23 characters. B and G are numbers on five digits identifying, respectively, the bank and the counter. N is composed of 11 alphanumeric characters, which are converted into a sequence S_N on 11 digits by replacing in a cyclic way the potential letters as follows: A and J by 1; B, K, S by 2; C, L, T by 3; D, M, U by 4; E, N, V by 5; F, O, W by 6; G, P, X by 7; H, Q, Y by 8; I, R, Z by 9. Finally, the BBAN R is a number on two digits such that the concatenation of B, G, S_N, and R is a number n on 23 digits, which is a multiple of 97. In other words, $R = 97 - ([BGS_N] \times 100) \mod 97$.

4.2.1.4 Credit Card: LUHN-10.

The 16-digits number $c_{15}c_{14}c_{13}c_{12} - c_{11}c_{10}c_9c_8 - c_7c_6c_5c_4 - c_3c_2c_1c_0$ of a credit card is a codeword of LUHN 10. In order to check the validity of the number, one multiplies the digits having an odd index by 2 and one subtracts 9 if the number one obtains is bigger than 9. All these digits are added up to the other digits having an even index. The overall sum is supposed to be a multiple of 10.

In addition to the number N on 16 digits, the validity of a credit card can also be checked from the 7 digits on the back of the card. The first four of these seven digits are actually the last four digits of the card number. The last three digits are the result of a computation involving N, and also the four digits mm/yy of its expiration date (N and *mmyy* are combined and enciphered by a 3DES-EDE with the *card verification key*; three digits of the result are then selected to form the Card Verification Value (CVV).

4.2.2 Cyclic Redundancy Checks (CRC)

The CRC are widely used in computer networks. In such codes, a binary word $u = [u_{m-1} \cdots u_0] \in \{0,1\}^m$ is represented using a polynomial $P_u(X) = \sum_{i=0}^{m-1} u_i X^i$ in $\mathbb{F}_2[X]$. For example, $u = [10110]$ is represented by the polynomial $P_u = X^4 + X^2 + X$.

A CRC code is characterized by a *generator polynomial* P_g of degree r: $P_g(X) = X^r + \sum_{i=0}^{r-1} g_i X^i$ in $\mathbb{F}_2[X]$. The binary source word $s = [s_{k-1} \cdots s_0]$ associated with the polynomial $P_s(X) = \sum_{i=0}^{k-1} s_i X^i$ is encoded by the binary codeword $c = [c_{n-1} \cdots c_0] = [s_{k-1} \cdots s_0 c_{r-1} \cdots c_0]$, where $[c_{r-1} \cdots c_0]$ is the representation of the remainder of the Euclidean division of $X^r \cdot P_s$ by P_g. Therefore, the multiplication of P_s by X^r being equivalent to a bit shift, the polynomial $P_c(X) = \sum_{i=0}^{n-1} c_i X^i$ checks

$$P_c = P_s \cdot X^r + (P_s \cdot X^r \mod P_g).$$

Example 4.1 Let $P_g = X^2 + 1$ be the generator polynomial, and let u denote the word $[10110]$. It is encoded by adding the redundancy bits of the polynomial $(X^4 + X^2 + X)X^2 \mod X^2 + 1 = X^6 + X^4 + X^3 \mod X^2 + 1 = X$ that corresponds to the redundancy bits $[10]$. Therefore, the word is encoded into $\phi(u) = [1011010]$.

4.2.2.1 CRC Encoding. Therefore, the encoding scheme is equivalent to implementing the computation of the remainder of the Euclidean division. This operation can be performed in time $O(n \log n)$ using an algorithm relying on the product of polynomials with DFT (see Section 1.4.2.7) or even in time $O(n)$ using the standard polynomial division algorithm in the practical case of a polynomial with a small number of nonzero coefficients ($O(1)$ in theory). Moreover, the hardware implementation of the standard algorithm is very efficient if one uses Linear Feedback Shift Registers (LFSRs) (see Section 1.3.7.2).

4.2.2.2 CRC Decoding. For the decoding, one notices that in $\mathbb{F}_2[X]$, one has also $P_c = P_s \cdot X^r - (P_s \cdot X^r \mod P_g)$; thus, the polynomial P_c is a multiple of P_g. This property enables one to perform a fast decoding, the latter also relies on a polynomial Euclidean division. After receiving $c' = [c'_{n-1} \cdots c'_0]$, it is enough for one to compute the remainder $R(X)$ of the polynomial $P_{c'}$ by the polynomial P_g. If this remainder is equal to zero, the word one has received is a codeword and one did not detect any error. Otherwise, if $R(X) \neq 0$, there were some errors during the transmission.

4.2.2.3 Number of Detected Bit Errors. Let us suppose that there was an error during the transmission. The coefficients of the polynomial $P_e = P_{c'} - P_c$ are equal to 0 for nonerroneous bits and equal to 1 for the bits c that have been modified. The error is detected if and only if P_e is not a multiple of P_g.

One deduces that if one multiple of P_g of degree at most $n-1$ has j monomials, then the CRC code generated by g can only detect at most $j-1$ errors. Reciprocally, for a CRC code to detect any error on at most j bits, a necessary and sufficient condition is for any polynomial of degree at most $n - 1$ and having at most j monomials not to be a multiple of P_g.

Besides, the error P_e equal to P_g, or multiple of P_g, cannot be detected. One deduces that the number of detected bit errors is at most $\omega(P_g)$, where $\omega(P_g)$ is the number of nonzero coefficients in P_g.

Property 13 *The CRC code of generator $P_g(X) = X^r + \sum_{i=1}^{r-1} g_i X^i + 1$ detects any error on at most $r - 1$ consecutive bits.*

Proof. A sequence of errors on at most $r - 1$ consecutive bits starting at the ith bit of the codeword is associated with a polynomial $P_e = X^i Q$ with Q of degree strictly lower than r; thus, Q is not a multiple of P_g. And because $g_0 = 1$, P_g is coprime with X; one deduces that P_e is not a multiple of P_g. Therefore, the error is very well detected.   □

This property is important; it explains why CRC codes are used in cases when the errors can affect several consecutive bits.

Exercise 4.7 (Condition on the Error Detection)   *Show that a necessary and sufficient condition for a CRC code to detect any error on a single bit is for its generator polynomial to admit at least two monomials.*   *Solution on page 325.*

Exercise 4.8 (Detection of an Odd Number of Errors)   *Prove that if the sum of the coefficients of the generator polynomial of a CRC code is null, then any error dealing with an odd number of bits is detected.*   *Solution on page 325.*

Exercise 4.9 (Detection of Two Errors)   *Show that if the generator polynomial of a CRC code admits one irreducible factor of degree d, then it detects any burst of errors (namely, some consecutive errors) dealing with at most d − 1 bits.*
Solution on page 325.

4.2.2.4   Examples of CRC Codes.   CRC codes are often used in computer networks. In addition to their good properties that were discussed above, they are also chosen for their efficiency in encoding and decoding. Table 4.4 gives several standardized examples; the standardization concerns not only the value of the polynomial but also the encoding and decoding algorithms.

4.3   DISTANCE OF A CODE

4.3.1   Error Correction Code and Hamming Distance

A (n, k)-code is said to be a *t-error-detecting code* (respectively, a *t-error-correcting code*) if it enables one to detect (respectively, correct) any error on t digits or less during the transmission of a codeword on n digits.

TABLE 4.4 Examples of CRC Codes

Name	Generator	Factorization	Examples of Use
TCH/FS -HS-EFS	$X^3 + X + 1$	Irreducible	GSM voice transmission
GSM TCH/EFS	$X^8 + X^4 + X^3 + X^2 + 1$	Irreducible	GSM channel precoding at full rate
CRC-8	$X^8 + X^7 + X^4 + X^3 + X + 1$	$(X + 1)(X^7 + X^3 + 1)$	GSM third generation
CRC-16	$X^{16} + X^{12} + X^5 + 1$	$(X + 1)(X^{15} + X^{14} + X^{13} + X^{12} + X^4 + X^3 + X^2 + X + 1)$	Protocol X25-CCITT; Layer control
X25-CCITT			PPP FCS-16 (RFC-1662)
CRC-24	$X^{24} + X^{23} + X^{18} + X^{17} + X^{14} + X^{11} + X^{10} + X^7 + X^6 + X^5 + X^4 + X^3 + X + 1$	$(X + 1)(X^{23} + X^{17} + X^{13} + X^{12} + X^{11} + X^9 + X^8 + X^7 + X^5 + X^3 + 1)$	Ultra High Frequency (UHF) communication and satellites (SATCOM); OpenPGP messages (RFC-2440)
CRC-24 (3GPP)	$X^{24} + X^{23} + X^6 + X^5 + X + 1$	$(X + 1)(X^{23} + X^5 + 1)$	GSM third generation
CRC-32	$X^{32} + X^{26} + X^{23} + X^{22} + X^{16} + X^{12} + X^{11} + X^{10} + X^8 + X^7 + X^5 + X^4 + X^2 + X + 1$	Irreducible	IEEE-802.3, ATM AAL5, PPP FCS-32 layer (RFC-1662); integrity checks for ZIP files and RAR files;
AUTODIN-II			

Example 4.2

- The addition of a bit in order to check the parity of the 7 previous bits is a systematic block code. It is a (8,7) code. It is a 1-error-detecting code and a 0-error-correcting code with a code rate equal to 87.5%.
- The longitudinal and transverse parity check on 21 bits (with the addition of 11 control bits) is a (32,21)-code. It is a 1-error-correcting code with a code rate equal to 65.625%.

In the sequel, we consider a code of length n; therefore, the codewords are elements in V^n. One calls *the Hamming weight* of $x = (x_1, \ldots, x_n) \in V^n$, denoted by $w(x)$, the number of nonzero elements in x:

$$w(x) = |\{i \in \{1, \ldots, n\}/x_i \neq 0\}|.$$

Remark 4 *If V is binary ($V = \{0, 1\}$), one denotes $x \oplus y$ the bitwise exclusive OR (or addition) of two words x and y. Then, the Hamming weight w satisfies the triangle inequality: $w(x \oplus y) \leq w(x) + w(y)$.*

One is able to obtain a notion of distance, the *Hamming distance* between x and y, denoted by $d_H(x, y)$, which is the number of elements differing between x and y, that is,

$$d_H(x, y) = |\{i \in \{1, \ldots, n\}/x_i \neq y_i\}|.$$

Exercise 4.10

1. *Show that d_H defined in this way is a distance over V^n.*
2. *Prove that if V is binary, $d_H(x, y) = w(x \oplus y)$.*

Solution on page 325.

The Hamming distance enables one to characterize the number of errors that can be corrected by a code C of length n. Indeed, let $m \in C$ be the word of n digits that is issued and let m' be the word that is received. One supposes that m' is different from m ($d_H(m, m') > 0$)

- for C to be able to detect an error, one must have $m' \notin C$ (otherwise, the word one has received is a word in C and it is considered to be correct).
- to be able to perform a correction (namely, to recover m from m'), m must be the unique word in C closest to m', namely,

$$\text{for all } x \in C, \text{ if } x \neq m \text{ then } d_H(x, m') > d_H(m, m').$$

This statement is described in detail in the following property.

Property 14   *Let C be a code of length n. C is a t-error-correcting code if*

$$\text{for all } x \in V^n, |\{c \in C/d_H(x,c) \le t\}| \le 1.$$

Remark 5   *The correction of an error can also be described by considering the balls $B_t(c)$ of radius t around $c \in C$: $B_t(c) = \{x \in V^n/d_H(c,x) \le t\}$. When receiving m', one is able to correct m' to m if one has $B_{d_H(m,m')}(m') \cap C = \{m\}$.*

Remark 6   MDD *(introduced in Section 4.1.4) can now be formalized as follows: when a word $x \in V^n$ is received, an* MDD *strategy will decode x to c_x if $d_H(x, c_x)$ is minimal among all the codewords of C, that is,*

$$d_H(x, c_x) = \min_{c \in C} d_H(x, c).$$

The correction capacity of a code C is, therefore, bonded to the minimum distance between two elements in C.

The *minimum distance* (or simply the *distance*) of the code C, denoted by $\delta(C)$, is defined by

$$\delta(C) = \min_{c_1, c_2 \in C \; ; c_1 \ne c_2} d_H(c_1, c_2) . \tag{4.2}$$

The Property 14 and the Remark 5 are at the origin of the following theorem giving the characteristics of a *t*-error-correcting code.

Theorem 27   *Let C be a code of length n. The following properties are equivalent. Therefore, each of them implies that C is a t-error-correcting code*

 (i) for all $x \in V^n$, $|\{c \in C/d_H(x, c) \le t\}| \le 1$;
 (ii) for all $c_1, c_2 \in C$, $c_1 \ne c_2 \Longrightarrow B_t(c_1) \cap B_t(c_2) = \emptyset$;
 (iii) for all $c_1, c_2 \in C$, $c_1 \ne c_2 \Longrightarrow d_H(c_1, c_2) > 2t$;
 (iv) $\delta(C) \ge 2t + 1$.

Proof.

- $(i) \Longrightarrow (ii)$: Let us suppose that there exists $x \in B_t(c_1) \cap B_t(c_2)$; hence, c_1 and c_2 are at a distance $\le t$ from x. According to (i), this can be achieved for at most one codeword; therefore, $c_1 = c_2$.
- Now $(ii) \Longrightarrow (iii)$: by contradiction. Suppose that $d_H(c_1, c_2) \le 2t$ and let $i_1, \ldots, i_d$ with $d \le 2t$ the indexes of the digits differing between c_1 and c_2. Let x be the word in V^n such that $x = c_2^{(i_1)} \cdots c_2^{(i_{d/2})} c_1^{(i_{d/2+1})} \cdots c_1^{(i_d)}$. Then $d_H(x, c_1) = d/2 \le t$. Thus, one has $x \in B_t(c_1)$. The same way, $d_H(x, c_2) = d - (d/2) \le t$. Thus, one has $x \in B_t(c_2)$. Hence, $x \in B_t(c_1) \cap B_t(c_2)$ with contradicts (ii).
- For $(iii) \Longrightarrow (iv)$: it is immediate.

- Finally, for $(iv) \Longrightarrow (i)$: let us assume that there exists $x \in V^n$ such that $|\{c \in C / d_H(x, c) \le t\}| \ge 2$. Then there exist $c_1 \ne c_2$ such that $d_H(x, c_1)$, $d_H(x, c_2) \le t$. As the Hamming distance d_H satisfies the triangle inequality, $d_H(c_1, c_2) \le d_H(c_1, x) + d_H(x, c_2) \le 2t$, one has $\delta(C) \le 2t$.

$\square$

Exercise 4.11 *Prove that if C is a t-error-correcting code then C is a s-error-detecting code with $s \ge 2t$. In what cases is the converse proposition true?*   *Solution on page 325.*

Exercise 4.12 *We consider a repetition code C over $V = \{0, 1\}$, namely, a (mk, k)-code in which each group of k bits is simply repeated m times.*

1. *What is the minimum distance between two codewords?*
2. *Propose a 2-error-correcting repetition code.*
3. *What is the rate of this code?*

We consider a $(n = 5k, k)$ repetition code and wish to set up a decoding process returning as output the decoded word s and a Boolean e, which is true if s can be considered to be correct (no errors or corrected errors) and false otherwise (some errors were detected but not corrected).

4. *How many errors can be detected? Write down the decoding algorithm to detect a maximum number of errors without correcting any of them.*
5. *How many errors can be corrected? Write down the decoding algorithm to correct a maximum number of errors. How many errors are detected but not corrected?*
6. *Write down the decoding algorithm that corrects a single error and detects up to three errors.*

Solution on page 326.

Exercise 4.13 (Naive Computation of the Distance of a Code) *Let C be a (n, k)-code over some alphabet V. Write down a process computing the detection and correction rates of this code; give the complexity of the algorithm with respect to k and n. Is this algorithm efficient?*
Practical application: let us consider the binary code

$$C = \{0000000000, 0000011111, 1111100000, 1111111111\}.$$

What are the values of n and k for this code? Compute its code rate and its detection and correction rates.   *Solution on page 327.*

Exercise 4.14 (MLD Versus MDD Strategies on a BSC Channel) *Let us suppose that the codewords of a binary code C of length n are sent over a BSC channel with error probability $0 < p < \frac{1}{2}$ (see Exercise 4.3).*

1. *Show that for any word $x \in \{0,1\}^n$ received, the (forward) probability that $c \in C$ has been sent is $P(x \mid c) = (1-p)^n \left(\frac{p}{1-p}\right)^e$, where $e = d_H(x,c)$.*

2. *Let $x \in \{0,1\}^n$ be the received word. Let $c_1, c_2 \in C$ be two codewords such that $d_H(x,c_1) = d_1$ and $d_H(x,c_2) = d_2$. Show that*

$$P(x \mid c_1) \leq P(x \mid c_2) \Longleftrightarrow d_1 \geq d_2$$

3. *What can you deduce from this result as regards the MLD and MDD decoding strategies in this context?*

Solution on page 328.

4.3.2 Equivalent Codes, Extended Codes, and Shortened Codes

As the distance characterizes the number of errors that can be corrected by a code, it is an important characteristic, complementary to its rate. In order to choose trade-offs between the rate and the distance, several methods enable one to modify a code in order to build another code with different properties.

4.3.2.1 Equivalent Codes. Let $x_1 x_2 \cdots x_n$ and $y_1 y_2 \cdots y_n$ be two codewords:

- let π be a permutation of the indexes $\{1, \cdot, n\}$; one has

$$d_H(x_1 x_2 \cdots x_n, y_1 y_2 \cdots y_n) = d_H(x_{\pi(1)} x_{\pi(2)} \cdots x_{\pi(n)}, y_{\pi(1)} y_{\pi(2)} \cdots y_{\pi(n)}) \,;$$

- let $(\pi_i)_{i=1,\cdots,n}$ be n permutations of the symbols in V (which are possibly distinct), one also has

$$d_H(x_1 \cdots x_n, y_1 \cdots y_n) = d_H(\pi_1(x_1) \cdots \pi_n(x_n), \pi_1(y_1) \cdots \pi_n(y_n)).$$

Consequently, neither the order of the symbols in V one has chosen nor the order of the indexes in the codewords modifies the distance. Therefore, two codes are said to be *equivalent* if one code can be obtained from the other through a permutation π of the indexes or through permutations $(\pi_i)_{i=1,\ldots,n}$ of the values of the symbols. Two equivalent codes have the same distances between corresponding elements, thus they have the same detection and correction rates.

For instance, for a binary code, with a permutation of the symbols in the first position and the third position, and with a substitution of the 0 with 1 (and reciprocally) in the second position, one obtains an equivalent code.

Property 15 *Two equivalent codes have the same code rate and the same distance.*

4.3.2.2 Extended Codes. Let C be an (n,k)-code; one calls an $(n+1,k)$-code C' that is obtained by adding a parity-check digit to C an extended code of C.

For instance, if an addition operator is defined over V,

$$C' = \left\{ c_1 c_2 \cdots c_n c_{n+1} \mid c_1 c_2 \cdots c_n \in C, \sum_{i=1}^{n+1} c_i = 0 \right\}.$$

The distance d' of the extended code obviously satisfies the relation $d \leq d' \leq d + 1$.

Exercise 4.15 (Extension of a Code) *Let C be a binary code of distance d odd. Show that the distance of the extended code C' is $d + 1$.*   *Solution on page 329.*

*4.3.2.3 **Punctured Codes.*** Let C be a (n, k)-code of distance d. *Puncturing* consists of removing all the symbols at m constant positions in the code C. The code C' one obtains is called a *punctured code* of C; then, the distance d' of C' satisfies $d' \geq d - m$.

*4.3.2.4 **Shortened Code.*** Let C be a code of length n and distance d, and let $s \in V$ be a symbol and $i \in \{1, \ldots, n\}$ an index. One *shortens* the code C by taking into account only the codewords having their ith symbol equal to s and by removing this symbol. The code C' one obtains is called a *shortened code*; thus, its length is $n - 1$ and its distance d' satisfies $d' \geq d$.

Example 4.3 The binary code $C = \{0000, 0110, 0011, 1010, 1110\}$ is of length 4 and distance 1. The shortened code C' one obtains with the symbol 0 at the first position 1 is $C' = \{000, 110, 011\}$; its length is 3 and distance is 2.

Hence, shortening a code enables one not only to increase the rate without decreasing the distance but even to increase possibly the distance as shown in the previous example. Therefore, this operation is often used in the construction of codes or as a tool for proofs.

Exercise 4.16 (Shortened Code) *Let C be a code of length n, cardinal number M, and distance d. Show that C is the shortened code of a code of length $n + 1$, cardinal cardinal $M + 2$, and distance 1.*   *Solution on page 329.*

Exercise 4.17 ((9,4) Longitudinal and Transverse Parity Code) *The longitudinal and transverse parity check on 4 bits leads to the following $(9,4)$-code: the codeword associated with the source word $b_0 b_1 b_2 b_3$ is*

$$[b_0, b_1, b_2, b_3, (b_0 + b_1), (b_2 + b_3), (b_0 + b_2), (b_1 + b_3), (b_0 + b_1 + b_2 + b_3)].$$

Hence, one obtains $C = \{000000000, 000101011, 001001101, 001100110, \ldots\}$.

1. *Prove that C is exactly a 1-error-correcting code.*
2. *Give an example of a word containing two errors that cannot be corrected.*
3. *Show that C is a 3-error-detecting code but not a 4-error-detecting code.*

4. *Give the characteristics of the punctured code of C at the first position.*

5. *Give the characteristics of the shortened code of C at the first position.*

Solution on page 329.

4.3.3   Perfect Codes

A t-error-correcting code enables one to correct any error e of weight $w(e) \leq t$; but there might still remain some errors that are detected but not corrected (see the previous exercise). One says that a code is *perfect* (one should not make a confusion with the perfect or unconditionally secure ciphers described in Section 1.2.5) if any detected error is corrected. This section discusses several properties of perfect codes. A t-*perfect* code is a t-error-correcting code in which any error being detected can be corrected. If C is a t-perfect code and one receives a word $m' \notin C$, then there exists a unique codeword m in C such that $d(m, m') \leq t$. Moreover, because C is a t-error-correcting code, the balls of radius t around the codewords in C are pairwise disjoint; hence, the following theorem.

Theorem 28   *The code (n, k)-code C over V is a t-perfect code if the balls of radius t around the codewords in C define a partition of V^n, that is,*

$$\biguplus_{c \in C} B_t(c) = V^n.$$

Obviously, such partition is possible only for some specific values of n and k, depending on the cardinal number of V. The following theorem gives the necessary conditions for the existence of t-error-correcting and t-perfect codes.

Theorem 29   *Let C be a (n, k) t-error-correcting code over V. Then, one has*

$$1 + C_n^1(|V| - 1) + C_n^2(|V| - 1)^2 + \cdots + C_n^t(|V| - 1)^t \leq |V|^{n-k}. \tag{4.3}$$

Moreover, in case of equality, then $C(n, k)$ is a t-perfect code.

Proof.   The proof relies on the computation of the cardinal number of $\biguplus_{c \in C} B_t(c)$, the balls being pairwise disjoint for a t-error-correcting code. Indeed, the cardinal number of a ball of radius t in V^n is

$$|B_t(x)| = 1 + C_n^1(|V| - 1) + C_n^2(|V| - 1)^2 + \cdots + C_n^t(|V| - 1)^t.$$

As a code (n, k)-code has exactly $|V|^k$ elements in V^n associated with pairwise disjoint balls whose union is included in V^n, one has

$$|V|^k \left(1 + C_n^1(|V| - 1) + C_n^2(|V| - 1)^2 + \cdots + C_n^t(|V| - 1)^t \right) \leq |V|^n;$$

hence, the first inequality. In case of equality, the cardinal number of the union is equal to $|V|^n$; moreover, because the code is a t-error-correcting code, the balls are disjoint. Thus, their union is equal to V^n and the code is perfect.   □

Exercise 4.18 *Show that any 1-error-correcting binary code on words of $k = 4$ bits requires at least 3 bits of redundancy. Prove that if there exists a 1-error-correcting code with 3 redundancy bits, then it is actually a perfect code.*

Solution on page 330.

4.3.4 Binary Hamming Codes

Binary Hamming codes (1950) are 1-error-correcting codes with minimum redundancy. Indeed, let $x \in \mathbb{F}_2^n$; then, the binary Hamming weight of x is given by the formula $w(x) = |\{i \in \{1, \ldots, n\}/x_i \neq 0\}| = \sum_{i=1}^{n} x_i$.

However, in $\mathbb{F}_2$, the addition and the subtraction are the same operator ($0 = -0$ and $1 = -1$); thus, one has the following properties.

Property 16 *Let $x, y \in \mathbb{F}_2^n$ and $\wedge$ the bitwise operator AND. Then*

- $w(x) = d_H(x, 0)$;
- $d_H(x, y) = w(x + y) = w(x) + w(y) - 2w(x \wedge y)$.

Exercise 4.19 *Let us consider a (n, k) 1-error-correcting binary code.*

1. Show that

$$k \leq 2^r - r - 1. \tag{4.4}$$

2. Deduce a bound on the maximum rate of a 1-error-correcting code with 3 control bits, then with 4 bits, with 5 bits, and finally with 6 bits.

3. Does there exist a 1-perfect code of length $n = 2^m$ with $m \in \mathbb{N}$?

Solution on page 330.

Knowing k, inequality (4.4) (written as $2^r \geq n + 1$) enables one to determine the minimum number of control bits one must add in order to obtain a 1-error-correcting code. Thus, binary Hamming codes are systematic codes reaching this theoretical bound: for n bits, the number of control bits is $\lfloor \log_2 n \rfloor + 1$ (hence, if $n + 1$ is a power of 2, $\lfloor \log_2 n \rfloor + 1 = \log_2(n + 1)$). Therefore, the Hamming codes are perfect codes for $n = 2^r - 1$; in other words, they are $(n, n - \lfloor \log_2 n \rfloor - 1)$-codes.

4.3.4.1 Description of an Encoding Scheme for a Binary Hamming Code $(n, n - \lfloor \log_2 n \rfloor - 1)$

A codeword $c = c_1 \cdots c_n \in \{0, 1\}^n$ in the binary Hamming code is such that all bits c_i with i being a power of 2 ($i = 2^l$ with $l = 0, 1, \ldots$) are the control bits and all other bits contain the data. The control bit of index $i = 2^l$ is the sum modulo 2 of all databits c_j whose index j written in the binary basis has its $(l + 1)$th bit (starting from the left) equal to 1. That is to say

$$c_{2^l} = \sum_{j=2^l+1}^{2^{l+1}-1} c_j.$$

For example, in a $(7,4)$ Hamming code, a source message $[s_1, s_2, s_3, s_4]$ corresponds to the codeword $[c_1, c_2, c_3, c_4, c_5, c_6, c_7]$, which is given by

$$\begin{cases} c_3 = s_1 \\ c_5 = s_2 \\ c_6 = s_3 \\ c_7 = s_4 \\ c_1 = c_3 + c_5 + c_7 \\ c_2 = c_3 + c_6 + c_7 \\ c_4 = c_5 + c_6 + c_7. \end{cases}$$

Hence, the message 1000 is encoded into 1110000.

To be able to correct in a Hamming code, the parity check is performed in the following way. All control bits of index $i = 2^l$ are checked; an error is detected if one of these bit is erroneous (wrong parity). Then, let e be the sum of the indexes i of all the erroneous control bits. If there is a single error, then it comes from the bit of index e.

Theorem 30 *The Hamming code $(n, n - \lfloor \log_2 n \rfloor - 1)$ is a 1-error-correcting code requiring a minimum number of control bits among all (n, k)-codes that are 1-error-correcting codes.*
In particular, the Hamming code $(2^m - 1, 2^m - 1 - m)$ is a 1-perfect code.

The proof comes directly from the previous properties. Besides, one has also immediately the following property:

Property 17 *The minimum distance of a Hamming code is 3.*

Proof. This is a 1-error-correcting code; therefore, one has $\delta(C) \geq 2t + 1 = 3$. It is enough to show that there are two codewords at a distance 3; for any word, by changing only the first bit of data (c_3), only the first two control bits are changed.   □

4.3.4.2   Example of Correction with the (7,4) Binary Hamming Code   Let us take back the previous example. Let us assume that one receives the word 1111101. The source message should be 1101 but the parity check indicates that bits 2 and 4 are erroneous; then, the correction of a single error is performed by modifying the bit at the index $4 + 2 = 6$. Therefore, the corrected codeword is 1111111, and it corresponds to the source word 1111.

Exercise 4.20 *One considers the Hamming code $(15,11)$ of distance 3.*

1. *What is the rate of this code?*
2. *Check that the Hamming code $(15,11)$ is equivalent to the the code $C(15,4)$ that is defined by some function $\phi_C : \mathbb{F}_2^{11} \to \mathbb{F}_2^{15}$ in the form $\phi_C(s) = s \cdot [I_{11}R]$, where I_{11} is the 11×11 identity matrix and R is the matrix in $\mathcal{M}_{4,11}(\mathbb{F}_2)$ to be determined.*

3. *Give the encoding algorithm.*

4. *Give an algorithm for detecting up to two errors.*

5. *Give an algorithm for correcting one error. What happens if there are two errors?*

Solution on page 331.

For some applications having a small error rate, a Hamming code can be used. For instance, the Minitel[1] system uses a 1-error-correcting Hamming code (128,120): the message is split into blocks on 15 bytes, that is, 120 bits; a sixteenth byte is added, which contains 8 control bits in order to locate 1 erroneous bit among the 128 bits. Besides, a seventeenth byte – called the *validation byte* – containing only 0's is used to detect large perturbations. Therefore, the final code is a 1-error-correcting binary code of parameters (136,120).

However, the development of cyclic codes – and notably the conception of very efficient encoding and decoding processes – has encouraged the involvement of error-correcting codes in many applications having large error rates. The following paragraphs present some of these codes that are used, for instance, in CDs and for the transmission of images through spacecraft communications.

4.4   LINEAR CODES AND CYCLIC CODES

4.4.1   Linear Codes and Minimum Redundancy

We have seen that a (n, k) error-correcting code is characterized by a map $\phi : V^k \to V^n$. The analysis of a general function ϕ is tricky; as a consequence, we will only consider the case where ϕ is linear. Such a restriction offers advantages in terms of computational time: both encoding and decoding are performed quite quickly, in polynomial time with respect to n. To be able to study this case, V^k and V^n have to be equipped with a vectorial structure. Namely, V must be equipped with the structure of a field $\mathbb{F}$ (in addition to the restrictions that were discussed concerning the cardinal number of V; see the mathematical revision in Chapter 1). In the sequel, we will suppose that the alphabet V and the finite field $\mathbb{F}$ have the same cardinal number.

Let C be a (n, k) code with symbols in the field $\mathbb{F}$. One says that C is a *linear code* of length n and rank k if C is a vector subspace of $\mathbb{F}^n$ of rank k.

As two vector spaces having the same rank over the same field are isomorphic, a (n, k)-code over $\mathbb{F}$ is a linear code if and only if there exists a linear map $\phi : \mathbb{F}^k \longrightarrow \mathbb{F}^n$ such that $\phi(\mathbb{F}^k) = C$.

For a given basis of the vector subspace C, the linear map ϕ is described by its matrix G of dimension $k \times n$ with coefficients in $\mathbb{F}$. Such matrix G is called a *generator matrix* of the code C.

Remark 7   *As codewords are often represented in the form of row vectors, one chooses to represent ϕ with a rectangular matrix whose rows are generator vectors of $Im(\phi)$.*

---

[1]The Minitel was a French videotex pre-World Wide Web online service accessible through telephone lines, developed in the eighties.

For a given linear code C, there are as many generator matrices as possible choices for a basis of C. Moreover, if G is a generator matrix of C, then for any invertible (square) matrix A of rank k with elements in $\mathbb{F}$, the matrix $G' = A \cdot G$ is a generator matrix of C.

Proof. $Im(G') = \{x^t \cdot A \cdot G / x \in \mathbb{F}^k\} = \{y^t \cdot G / y \in Im((A)^t)\} = \{y^t \cdot G / y \in \mathbb{F}^k\} = C$. □

Example 4.4 Let us consider the $(4, 3)$ parity code over $\mathbb{F}_2$. Then, the codeword associated with the information word $x^t = [x_0, x_1, x_2]$ is $b^t = [b_0, b_1, b_2, b_3]$ defined by

$$\begin{cases} b_0 = x_0 \\ b_1 = x_1 \\ b_2 = x_2 \\ b_3 = x_0 + x_1 + x_2 \quad \text{mod } 2. \end{cases}$$

This code is a linear code over $\mathbb{F}_2$ whose generator matrix is

$$G = \begin{bmatrix} 1 & 0 & 0 & 1 \\ 0 & 1 & 0 & 1 \\ 0 & 0 & 1 & 1 \end{bmatrix}$$

Then one has $b^t = x^t G$.

Theorem 31 *Let C be a (n, k) linear code, and let $d = \min_{c \in C \ ;c \neq 0} w(c)$. Then, one has*

$$\delta(C) = d,$$

that is, C is a $(d-1)$-error-detecting code and a $\left\lfloor \frac{d-1}{2} \right\rfloor$-error-correcting code. The code C is called a (n, k, d)-code.

Proof. C is a vector subspace of $\mathbb{F}^n$. Therefore, $0 \in C$ (0 is the vector having n zero elements). Hence, for all $c \in C$ with $c \neq 0$, $\delta(C) \leq d(c, 0) = w(c)$, and so one has $\delta(C) \leq \min_{c \in C, c \neq 0} w(c)$.

Reciprocally, let c_1 and c_2 be two elements in C such that $\delta(C) = d(c_1, c_2) = w(c_1 - c_2)$. As C is a vector subspace, $c = c_1 - c_2$ belongs to C; $\delta(C) \geq \min_{c \in C} w(c)$. Finally, $\delta(C) = \min_{c \in C, c \neq 0} w(c)$. □

Theorem 32 (Singleton Bound) *The minimum distance d of a (n, k) linear code is bounded by*

$$d \leq n - k + 1.$$

Proof. Let C be a linear (n, k) code. Let us consider the subspace E of $\mathbb{F}^n$ composed by all vectors having their last $k - 1$ elements equal to zero: $\dim(E) = n - k + 1$.

Hence, E and C are two vector subspaces of $\mathbb{F}^n$ and $\dim(C) + \dim(E) = n + 1 > n$. Thus there exists a nonzero element a in $C \cap E$. As $a \in E$, $w(a) \leq n - k + 1$; because $a \in C$, $\delta(C) \leq w(a) \leq n - k + 1$. □

Therefore, the Singleton bound implies that a (n, k) linear code of distance d should have at least $r \geq d - 1$ redundancy digits. A code reaching this bound $d = r + 1$ is called a Maximum Distance Separable (MDS) code.

Example 4.5 The $(7, 4)$ binary Hamming code is a linear code having the following generator matrix:

$$G = \begin{bmatrix} 1 & 1 & 1 & 0 & 0 & 0 & 0 \\ 1 & 0 & 0 & 1 & 1 & 0 & 0 \\ 0 & 1 & 0 & 1 & 0 & 1 & 0 \\ 1 & 1 & 0 & 1 & 0 & 0 & 1 \end{bmatrix}. \tag{4.5}$$

Its distance being equal to 3, it is a $(7, 4, 3)$ linear code.

More generally, the binary Hamming code of length n is a $(n, n - 1 - \lfloor \log_2 n \rfloor, 3)$ code (we have seen that such code is a 1-error-correcting code). Although its distance is 3, it does not reach the Singleton bound because $d = 3 < 2 + \lfloor \log_2 n \rfloor$ except for the case $(n, k) = (3, 1)$. Nevertheless, we have seen that it is a perfect code and that there does not exist a binary code of distance 3 with less redundancy digits when n is not a power of 2.

Theorem 33 *Any punctured code of an MDS code is an MDS code.*

Proof. Let C be a (n, k) linear MDS code and G a generator matrix of C. Let C' be the punctured code of C one obtains by removing u indexes in the codewords. The code C' is a $(n - u, k)$ linear code because the submatrix G' one obtains by removing the columns of G at the u corresponding indexes is a generator matrix of C'. Moreover, the distance d' of C' is greater or equal to $d - u$. As C is an MDS code, $d = n - k + 1$; hence, $d' \geq (n - u) - k + 1$. Therefore, $C'(n - u, k)$ reaches the Singleton bound $n - u - k + 1$ and C' is an MDS code.   □

Exercise 4.21 (An MDS Code is a Systematic Code) *MDS Let G be a generator matrix of an MDS code, and let $\phi(x) = x^t G$ be the associated encoding. Show that for any codeword $c = \phi(x)$, it is possible to recover x in a unique way given any k coefficients in c.* *Solution on page 331.*

Exercise 4.22 *Show that any shortened code of an MDS code is an MDS code.* *Solution on page 331.*

4.4.2 Encoding and Decoding of Linear Codes

If a code has no particular structure, decoding and error correction can be quite long, and even impossible for some very large codes. It would consist of comparing each received word with all codewords in C and identifying the closest one. In practice, the linear structure of codes leads to quite efficient encoding and decoding algorithms when the number of errors corrected by the code t is small.

To study the encoding and decoding processes of a linear code C, one can limit oneself to considering only a generator matrix G written in its *systematic* form:

$$G = \left[\quad L \quad \middle| \quad R \quad \right], \tag{4.6}$$

where L is a $k \times k$ invertible square matrix and R is a $k \times r$ matrix.

Indeed, if G is in such a form, one permutes the columns in G until one obtains L invertible; this is possible because $\mathrm{rg}(G) = k$. Then, one obtains a generator matrix G_σ of a linear code C_σ, which is equivalent to C. After the decoding and the correction from C_σ, one recovers the initial message by reapplying the permutation matrix.

Thus, one builds $G' = L^{-1}G$, namely,

$$G' = \left[\quad I_k \quad \middle| \quad T = L^{-1}R \quad \right].$$

The matrix G' is also a generator matrix of C, according to the Remark 7.

The matrix G' is called a *normalized* (or canonical) generator matrix of the code C. Any linear code has a canonical generator matrix.

Moreover, this canonical matrix is unique. Indeed, let $[I_k|T_1]$ and $[I_k|T_2]$ be two generator matrices of C. Thus, for all $x \in \mathbb{F}^k$, $[x^t, x^t T_1]$ and $[x^t, x^t T_2]$ are in C. As C is a vector subspace, their difference $[0, x^t(T_1 - T_2)]$ is also in C. Yet, the only element in C having its k first elements equal to zero is 0. Thus, for any $x \in \mathbb{F}^k$, one has $x^t(T_1 - T_2) = 0$, that is, $T_1 = T_2$.

4.4.2.1 Encoding by Matrix-Vector Multiplication

One deduces from the previous statement on encoding method for C: any source word $u \in \mathbb{F}^k$ (row vector) is encoded by $\phi(u) = uG' = [u, u \cdot T]$. Hence, one writes u followed by uT containing all the redundancy digits.

Using this scheme, it follows that any source word is encoded into its corresponding codeword using $O(kn)$ field operations.

4.4.2.2 Decoding by Matrix-Vector Multiplication

The method of error detection and decoding uses the following property.

Property 18 *Let H be the $r \times n$ matrix $H = \left[\; T^t \; \middle| \; -I_r \; \right]$. Then $x^t = [x_1, \ldots, x_n] \in C$ if and only if $Hx = 0$. H is called the* control matrix *of C.*

Proof. Let $x \in C$. There exists $u \in \mathbb{F}^k$ such that $x^t = u^t[I_k|T]$. Hence, $x^t H^t = u^t[I_k|T] \begin{bmatrix} T \\ -I_r \end{bmatrix}$. However, $[I_k|T] \begin{bmatrix} T \\ -I_r \end{bmatrix} = [T - T] = [0]$; thus, for all x, one has $Hx = 0$.

Reciprocally, if $Hx = 0$, then $[x_1, \ldots, x_n] \begin{bmatrix} T \\ -I_r \end{bmatrix} = [0, \ldots, 0]_r$.

Then, the jth element $(1 \leq j \leq r)$ gives $[x_1, \ldots, x_k] \begin{bmatrix} T_{1,j} \\ \vdots \\ T_{k,j} \end{bmatrix} - x_{k+j} = 0.$

Hence, we have $x_{k+j} = [x_1, \ldots, x_k] \begin{bmatrix} T_{1,j} \\ \vdots \\ T_{k,j} \end{bmatrix}.$ Therefore, $[x_{k+1}, \ldots, x_{k+r}] = [x_1, \ldots, x_k]T$ and one has $[x_1, \ldots, x_n] = [x_1, \ldots, x_k][I_k|T] = [x_1, \ldots, x_k]G'$, which, finally, proves that $x \in C$. $\qquad\qquad\square$

Therefore, when one receives a word y, one detects an error by computing Hy, called the *error syndrome*. One detects an error if and only if $Hy \neq 0$. Then, given y, one wishes to compute the word x which was issued. For this, one computes the error vector $e = y - x$. Such vector e is the unique element in $\mathbb{F}^n$ with a minimum Hamming weight $w_H(e)$ such that $He = Hy$. Indeed, if C is a t-error-correcting code, then there exists a unique codeword $x \in C$, such that $d_H(x, y) \leq t$. As $d_H(x, y) = w_H(x - y)$, one deduces that there exists a unique element $e \in \mathbb{F}^n$, such that $w_H(e) \leq t$. Moreover, $He = Hy - Hx = Hy$ because $Hx = 0$.

Then, one builds a table with $|\mathbb{F}|^r$ entries in which each entry i corresponds to a unique element z_i in $\text{Im}(H)$; in the entry i, one stores the vector $e_i \in \mathbb{F}^n$ of minimum weight and such that $He_i = z_i$.

Then, correction is trivial. When one receives y, one computes Hy and the entry i in the table such that $z_i = Hy$. Then, one finds e_i in the table and one returns $x = y - e_i$.

Example 4.6 Let us consider the Hamming code $(7,4)$ whose generator matrix G is given by Relation (4.5). In this case, one has

$$L = \begin{pmatrix} 1 & 1 & 1 & 0 \\ 1 & 0 & 0 & 1 \\ 0 & 1 & 0 & 1 \\ 1 & 1 & 0 & 1 \end{pmatrix} , \quad R = \begin{pmatrix} 0 & 0 & 0 \\ 1 & 0 & 0 \\ 0 & 1 & 0 \\ 0 & 0 & 1 \end{pmatrix},$$

$$\text{and} \quad T = L^{-1}R = \begin{pmatrix} 0 & 1 & 1 \\ 1 & 0 & 1 \\ 1 & 1 & 0 \\ 1 & 1 & 1 \end{pmatrix}.$$

The canonical generator matrix G' and the control matrix H are given by

$$G' = \begin{pmatrix} 1 & 0 & 0 & 0 & 0 & 1 & 1 \\ 0 & 1 & 0 & 0 & 1 & 0 & 1 \\ 0 & 0 & 1 & 0 & 1 & 1 & 0 \\ 0 & 0 & 0 & 1 & 1 & 1 & 1 \end{pmatrix} \quad \text{and} \quad H = \begin{pmatrix} 0 & 1 & 1 & 1 & 1 & 0 & 0 \\ 1 & 0 & 1 & 1 & 0 & 1 & 0 \\ 1 & 1 & 0 & 1 & 0 & 0 & 1 \end{pmatrix}.$$

If one receives the word $y = 1111101$, then the computation of $Hy = \begin{pmatrix} 0 \\ 1 \\ 0 \end{pmatrix}$ shows that

there is an error. In order to correct the error, it is sufficient to notice that the vector $e = 0000010$ has a minimum Hamming weight and that $He = Hy$ (the table containing $2^3 = 8$ entries is not necessary for this simple example). Therefore, the correction of y is $x = y + e = 1111111$.

Exercise 4.23 (Dual Code)   *Let C be a linear code (n,k) over $\mathbb{F}$. The dual code of C, denoted by $C^\perp$, is the set of all words in $\mathbb{F}^n$ orthogonal to C:*

$$C^\perp = \{x \in \mathbb{F}^n, \text{ such that for all } c \in C \ : \ x \cdot c^t = 0\}.$$

Show that $C^\perp$ is a linear code $(n, n-k)$ over $\mathbb{F}$ generated by the control matrix H of the code C. Solution on page 332.

Exercise 4.24 (Golay Code)   *One considers the compound (i.e., over $V = \mathbb{F}_3$) Golay code $\mathcal{G}_{12}$ of distance 6 and generator matrix $G = [I_6 | R]$ with*

$$R = \begin{bmatrix} 0 & 1 & 1 & 1 & 1 & 1 \\ 1 & 0 & 1 & 2 & 2 & 1 \\ 1 & 1 & 0 & 1 & 2 & 2 \\ 1 & 2 & 1 & 0 & 1 & 2 \\ 1 & 2 & 2 & 1 & 0 & 1 \\ 1 & 1 & 2 & 2 & 1 & 0 \end{bmatrix}.$$

1. *Give the characteristics of $\mathcal{G}_{12}$ and its control matrix.*
2. *One easily checks that if r and s are any lines in G, then $r \cdot s = 0$. Deduce that $\mathcal{G}_{12}$ is auto-dual, that is, $\mathcal{G}_{12} = \mathcal{G}_{12}^\perp$.*
3. *Show that $\mathcal{G}_{12}$ is not a perfect code.*
4. *Let $\mathcal{G}_{11}$ be the code one obtains from $\mathcal{G}_{12}$ by removing the last element; give the control matrix associated with $\mathcal{G}_{11}$. What is the distance of this code?*
5. *Show that $\mathcal{G}_{11}$ is a perfect code.*

Solution on page 332.

Exercise 4.25 (McEliece Cryptosystem)
McEliece cryptosystem is a code-based asymmetric cipher: it uses a secret code and secret masking matrices. It has several advantages:

- *For equivalent sizes, encryption and decryption are faster than those of RSA or ECC;*
- *Extending the security requires also less key size extension;*
- *As of today, there is still no polynomial time algorithm breaking this code, even in a quantum computer model. Therefore, this kind of cryptosystem is sometimes called* post-quantic.

Now, as we will see afterwards, the major drawbacks of these systems is the size of the public and private keys. The system works as follows:

Key generation	1. *Consider a (n, k, d) code, with generator matrix G, correcting up to t errors.* 2. *Randomly choose an invertible $k \times k$ matrix S.* 3. *Randomly choose an $n \times n$ permutation matrix P (a single nonzero entry 1 in each row and column).*
Public key	$(\mathcal{G} = S \cdot G \cdot P, t)$
Private key	(S, G, P)
Encryption	*For a message m,* 1. *randomly choose e of Hamming weight less than t;* 2. *compute $c = m \cdot \mathcal{G} + e$.*
Decryption	1. *Compute $a = c \cdot P^{-1}$;* 2. *Decode b from a with the error-correcting code C;* 3. *Solve for m, $b = m \cdot S$.*

1. *Explain why the decryption is correct.*

2. *Current typical code size required to obtain a security equivalence to 128-bit symmetric cryptography are close to $(2960, 2288)$. compare the size of the keys in this setting to those of other codes, as in Table 3.12.*

3. *With the same parameters compare the complexity of encryption and decryption with those of an RSA system.*

Solution on page 332.

Thus, by focusing on linear codes, we have greatly improved the performance of encoding and decoding with error correction (in polynomial time with respect to n). There exists several classes of linear codes, which improves further the easiness of computation:

- LDPC codes, which provide near channel capacity performance (see Section 4.1.5.2) while simultaneously offering linear time decoding schemes. Such codes are discussed in the following section.

- Cyclic codes, which provide the possibility of an easy hardware implementation on electronic circuits. Moreover, thanks to cyclic codes, we will also see some simple methods for building codes while ensuring a given correction rate. These aspects are presented in Section 4.4.4.

4.4.3 Low Density Parity Check (LDPC) codes

LDPC codes are a class of powerful linear block codes that are able to approach channel capacity performance (see Theorem 26, Section 4.1.5.2) while offering extremely fast decoding – actually linear time decoding for the so-called *Expander codes* that derive directly from LDPC codes. These peculiarities have significantly contributed to make LDPC codes integrated in the latest communication standards (i.e., DVB-S2 for digital television broadcast by satellite and IEEE 802.16e for wireless communications). First proposed by Gallager in his 1960 Ph.D dissertation, LDPC codes were largely forgotten in the 30 years that followed. This was probably due to the introduction of Reed–Solomon codes (see Section 4.4.6) and the fact that concatenated Reed–Solomon and convolutional codes (presented in Section 4.6) were considered perfectly suitable for error control coding. Their comeback in the mid-1990s is mostly due to the work of MacKay and others who noticed the advantage of linear codes that possess sparse (i.e., low-density) parity-check matrices H.

Although LDPC codes can be generalized to nonbinary alphabets, only *binary* LDPC codes will be considered in the sequel for the sake of simplicity.

4.4.3.1 LDPC Codes Description.
A *LDPC* code is a linear code whose control matrix H (often referred to as the *parity-check matrix*) is sparse, that is, has very few nonzero elements in each row and column. More precisely, a *regular* binary LDPC code is a linear code for which the $r \times n$ control matrix H has exactly w_c ones in each column and $w_r = w_c \dfrac{n}{r}$ ones in each row, where $w_c \ll r$ or, equivalently, $w_r \ll n$.

Exercise 4.26 (Regular LDPC Code Rate)   *Assuming that H is full rank, show that the code rate for a regular LDPC code with parity matrix H and row (respectively, column) weight w_r (respectively, w_c) is $R = 1 - \dfrac{w_c}{w_r}$.*   *Solution on page 333.*

If w_r and w_c are not constant, then the code is an *irregular* LDPC code. It is worth noticing that irregular codes generally outperform regular LDPC codes. In all cases, in order to satisfy the low-density constraints, the parity-check matrix is usually very large, therefore, leading to very long codewords. This is confirmed by the actual constructions of LDPC codes that perform close to the channel capacity limit at a bit error rate of 10^{-6}, yet using a block length of 10^7.

4.4.3.2 Encoding of LDPC Codes.
Until now, linear block codes were defined by means of their generator matrix G. By defining an LDPC code in terms of the parity matrix H, alone, what constitutes the set C of codewords is not obvious. Hopefully, a straightforward approach for doing this is to first reduce H to its systematic form

$$H_{\text{sys}} = \left[\; T^t \;\middle|\; -I_r \;\right] = \left[\; T^t \;\middle|\; I_r \;\right].$$

This operation is typically performed by Gaussian elimination and column reordering, as it was done in Section 4.4.2 for the generator matrix G. As long as H is full (row) rank, H_{sys} will have r rows. Otherwise, some of the rows of H are linearly dependent and the resulting H_{sys} will be in systematic form, albeit with fewer rows.

In all cases, once in its systematic form, a valid canonical generator matrix for the LDPC code is

$$G_{canonical} = \left[\begin{array}{c|c} I_k & T \end{array} \right].$$

It is interesting to note that H_{sys} has no longer fixed column and row weight. Moreover, with high probability, T is dense. The denseness of T can make LDPC encoder quite complex, as illustrated in Exercise 4.27. It follows that LDPC design approaches often target efficient encoding, typically via algebraic or geometric methods. This leads to "structured" codes that can later be encoded with shift register circuits.

Exercise 4.27 *Let C be a (10,000, 5000) binary regular LDPC code, defined by its sparse parity-check matrix H with $w_c = 3$.*

1. **LDPC decoding**: *how many binary operations ($\oplus$) are required to compute the error syndrome?*
2. **LDPC encoding**: *assuming that H is in systematic form H_{sys} and that the density of ones in T is $\frac{1}{2}$, how many binary operations ($\oplus$) are required to encode one codeword using the canonical generator matrix derived from H_{sys}?*
3. *Assuming that C is no longer a regular LDPC code but a "simple" binary linear block code where the density of 1's in H is $\frac{1}{2}$, how many binary operations ($\oplus$) are required to compute the error syndrome?*

Solution on page 333.

4.4.3.3 *LDPC Code Representation by Tanner Graphs.*

Tanner introduced an effective graphical representation of LDPC codes (and actually of any linear code) into the form of a bipartite graph, now called a *Tanner graph*. Such a graph not only provides a complete representation of the codes but also helps the comprehension of iterative LDPC decoding techniques as explained in the sequel. A bipartite graph is an undirected graph whose nodes may be split into two distinct classes, where edges only connect two nodes residing in different classes. In the context of Tanner graphs, the two types of nodes are the *message* nodes (also called *variable* nodes depending on the literature) and the *check* nodes (also called *function* nodes).

A Tanner graph $\mathcal{G}$ of a code whose parity-check matrix is $H = \left(h_{i,j} \right)_{0 \le i < r, 0 \le j < n}$ is drawn according to the following principle: check node j is connected to message node i whenever the element $h_{i,j}$ of H is 1. It follows that there are n message nodes, each of them associated to the n coordinates of the codewords y_i. There are also r check nodes, one for each parity-check equation in H. Furthermore, the r rows of H specify the r check nodes connections, while the n columns of H define the n message nodes connections. Note that $\mathcal{G}$ is not uniquely defined by the code.

For instance, Figure 4.3 illustrate a (10,5) regular LDPC code defined by the parity-check matrix H where $w_c = 2$ and $w_r = w_c \frac{n}{r} = 4$, together with its associated Tanner graph. In this example, the check node f_0 (that corresponds to the first row of H) is connected to the message nodes y_0, y_1, y_2, and y_3 owing to the fact that

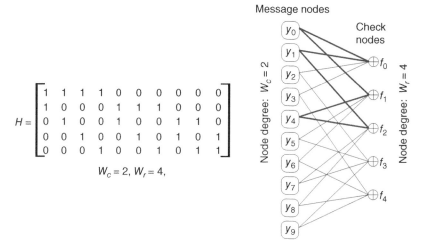

$$H = \begin{bmatrix} 1 & 1 & 1 & 1 & 0 & 0 & 0 & 0 & 0 & 0 \\ 1 & 0 & 0 & 0 & 1 & 1 & 1 & 0 & 0 & 0 \\ 0 & 1 & 0 & 0 & 1 & 0 & 0 & 1 & 1 & 0 \\ 0 & 0 & 1 & 0 & 0 & 1 & 0 & 1 & 0 & 1 \\ 0 & 0 & 0 & 1 & 0 & 0 & 1 & 0 & 1 & 1 \end{bmatrix}$$

$W_c = 2, W_r = 4,$

Figure 4.3 Example of a (10,5) regular LDPC code and its representation by a Tanner graph. The six bold edges show a length-6 cycle in the graph

$h_{0,0} = h_{0,1} = h_{0,2} = h_{0,3} = 1$. Analogous situations hold for the other check nodes. Also, as $Hy = 0$, the bit values connected to the same check node must sum to zero, that is, $f_0 = y_0 \oplus y_1 \oplus y_2 \oplus y_3 = 0$ and $f_1 = y_0 \oplus y_4 \oplus y_5 \oplus y_6 = 0$. Finally, one can notice that each message node has degree w_c (number of connected edges) while each check node has degree w_r.

Remark 8 *In the case of irregular LDPC codes, the parameters w_c and w_r are no longer constant and other quantities are generally used to characterize such codes. More precisely, one often consider for each type of nodes their respective degree distribution polynomials $D_d(x) = \sum_{i=1}^{d} \alpha_i x^{i-1}$, where α_i denotes the number of nodes with degree i and d the maximum node degree.*

Another important characteristic for the design of LDPC codes is the *girth* γ of a Tanner graph $\mathcal{G}$ representing the code. This quantity is defined as the minimum cycle length[2] in $\mathcal{G}$. As it will be made clearer in the sequel, short cycles in Tanner graphs have a negative impact on decoding

Exercise 4.28

1. *What is the length of the shortest possible cycle in a Tanner graph?*
2. *How do such cycles manifest themselves in the matrix H? Propose a method when designing the parity-check matrix of an LDPC code to avoid such cycles.*
3. *What is the girth of the graph proposed in Figure 4.3?*

Solution on page 333.

[2] A cycle of length *l* corresponds to a path containing *l* edges that starts and ends at the same vertex in the graph and does not traverse any other vertex more than once.

4.4.3.4 Iterative Decoding of LDPC Codes. The approach seen for decoding generic linear codes of Section 4.4.2.2 can be used in the context of LDPC codes. Now for LDPC, there is a more efficient general class of decoding techniques based on Message Passing Algorithm (MPA). This technique makes use of the graphical representation of the code by Tanner graphs. MPA is an iterative process involving several rounds during which information is exchanged (passed) along the edges of the graph (i.e., between the two types of nodes of the graph). On the one hand, if, at some point of the iterative process, the syndrome of the estimated decoded vector is the all-zero vector at the level of the check nodes, then this estimated vector is output. On the other hand, if the algorithm has not converged to a solution after a predetermined number of iterations, then a decoding failure is raised.

One important aspect of MPA is its running time: because the algorithm traverses the edges in the graph, and the graph is sparse, the number of traversed edges is small. Moreover, if the algorithm runs for a constant number of iterations, then each edge is traversed a constant number of times, and the algorithm uses a number of operations that is linear in the number of message nodes.

The Bit-Flipping Algorithm. When considering the number of exchanged messages, the simplest MPA that was proposed in the literature for decoding LDPC codes is called the *bit-flipping* algorithm. It operates on BSC channels (see Section 4.1.5.2) and the information passed between message and check nodes consists of 0 and 1. In this case, one often speaks of a *hard-decision decoder*, as opposed to soft decision decoders that use a larger range of values for the exchanged messages, as we will see later.

The bit-flipping algorithm is detailed in Algorithm 4.1, where the following notations are used:

- $q_{i,j}^{(r)}$ is the message sent from the message node y_i to the check node f_j on round r;
- $r_{j,i}^{(r)}$ is the response message sent by the check node f_j to the message node y_i on round r;
- $C(i)$ is the set of check nodes connected to the message node y_i.

The principle is quite simple: each message node i reports to its neighboring check nodes its current value (0 or 1), that is, y_i. Then using the messages received, each check node computes whether or not its parity-check equation is satisfied, in which case 1 is returned to its neighboring message node (or 0 otherwise). If *all* parity checks are satisfied, the algorithm terminates and y is returned: it means that $Hy = 0$ such that y is correct. Otherwise, some bit of the message nodes should be flipped in the hope that, later, all parity checks are satisfied. This is done in the following way: for each message node, if the majority of parity-check equations reported are not satisfied, it flips its current value, otherwise the value is retained. This process is repeated until

---

Algorithm 4.1 Hard-Decision Decoder by Bit-Flipping Algorithm

---

Input $\mathcal{G}$, a Tanner graph representing the LDPC code C;

Input $H = \left(h_{i,j}\right)_{0 \leq i < r, 0 \leq j < n}$ the associated parity-check matrix;

Input $y \in \{0, 1\}^n$ the received binary word of length n to be decoded;

Input R_{max} the maximum number of rounds.

Output $c \in C$ the corrected word, or ∞ to state a decoding failure.

    // Initialization

1: Assign each bit value of y to the n message nodes of $\mathcal{G}$

2: **For all** i, j such that $h_{i,j} = 1$ **do**

3:     $y_i \rightarrow f_j$: $q_{i,j}^{(0)} = y_i$

4: **End For**

5: **For** $r = 1$ to N_{max} **do**

    // Step 2: First half round iteration – Parity-checks

6:     **For all** j, i such that $h_{i,j} = 1$ **do**

7:         $f_j \rightarrow y_i$: $r_{j,i}^{(r)} = 1 \bigoplus_i q_{i,j}^{(r-1)}$

8:     **End For**

    // Stop here if all parity-check equations are satisfied

9:     **If** $r_{j,i} = 1$ $\forall i, j$ s.t. $h_{i,j} = 1$ **then return** y **End If**

    // Step 3: Second half round iteration – Codeword update

10:     **For** index i from 0 to $n - 1$ **do**

11:         **If** MAJORITY$_{j \in C(i)}\left(r_{j,i}^{(r)} = 0\right)$ **then** $y_i = \overline{y_i}$ **End If** *// bit-flipping*

12:         Send to all neighboring check nodes j: $q_{i,j} = y_i$

13:     **End For**

14: **End For**

15: **return** ∞ *// Decoding failure*

---

all the parity-check equations are satisfied or if the maximum number of allowed iterations is reached.

Example 4.7 To illustrate the operation of the bit-flipping decoder, we will again consider the Hamming code (7,4). Its parity-check matrix was determined in Section 4.4.2.2. The corresponding Tanner graph is depicted in Figure 4.4, together with a run of the decoding algorithm for the received word $y = 0011101$. Each subfigure (a), (b), and (c) illustrates the decisions made at each step of the algorithm. A cross ($\times$) indicates that the parity check operated at the step 2 failed while a tick ($\sqrt{}$) represents a satisfied parity check. For the edges, a dashed arrow corresponds to the messages "bit = 0" or "parity-check failed" (depending on the direction), while a solid arrow represents the message "bit = 1" or "parity-check is satisfied."

The Belief-Propagation Algorithms. Apart from the bit-flipping decoding algorithm described previously, one important subclass of message-passing algorithms is

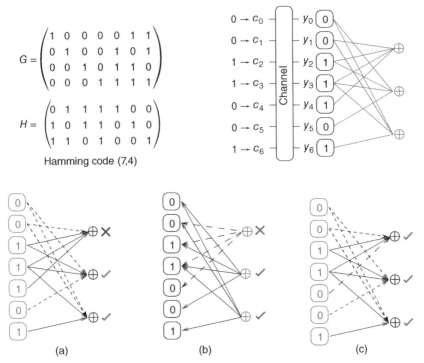

Figure 4.4 Example of the bit-flipping decoding over the Hamming code (7,4) for the received word $y = 0011101$ when the codeword $c = 0011001$ has been transmitted. (a) Step 2: parity checks, (b) step 3: codeword update, and (c) stopping criteria (success)

the Belief Propagation Algorithm (BPA), also called *Sum-Product Algorithm (SPA)*. For this variant, the messages passed along the edges are probabilities or beliefs, possibly represented as specific likelihood values.

More precisely, the aim of BPA is to compute the A posteriori probability (APP) that a given bit, in the transmitted codeword $c \in C$, is equal to 1, given the received word $y \in \{0, 1\}^n$. Therefore, focusing on the decoding of the bit c_i, we are interested in computing the APP, $p_i = P(c_i = 1 \mid y)$, or the APP ratio, also called the Likelihood Ratio (LR), $l(c_i)$ or, for reasons that will become clearer in a few paragraphs, the Log-APP ratio is also known as the log-Likelihood Ratio (LLR) $L(c_i)$. These values are defined as follows:

$$l(c_i) = \frac{P(c_i = 0 \mid y)}{P(c_i = 1 \mid y)} \text{ and } L(c_i) = \ln\left(l(c_i)\right) = \ln\left(\frac{P(c_i = 0 \mid y)}{P(c_i = 1 \mid y)}\right).$$

The BPA in itself is quite similar to the bit-flipping algorithm and is detailed in its generic form in Algorithm 4.2. Depending on the targeted measure (APP, LR or LLR), the semantic of the messages differ – Table 4.5 highlights these differences. The algorithm proceeds as shown in Algorithm 4.2.

Algorithm 4.2 Generic Belief Propagation Algorithm for LDPC Code Decoding

---

Input $\mathcal{G}$, a Tanner graph representing the LDPC code C;

Input $H = \left(h_{i,j}\right)_{0 \le i < r, 0 \le j < n}$ the associated parity-check matrix;

Input $y \in \{0,1\}^n$ the received binary word of length n to be decoded;

Input $R_{\max}$ the maximum number of rounds.

Output $c \in C$ the corrected word, or ∞ to state a decoding failure.

1: Assign each bit value of y to the n message nodes of $\mathcal{G}$
   // Step 1: Initialization

2: **For all** i, j such that $h_{i,j} = 1$ **do**

3:     $y_i \to f_j$: $q_{i,j}^{(0)} = \mathtt{InitFromChannel}(y_i)$

4: **End For**

5: **For** $r = 1$ to $N_{\max}$ **do**
   // Step 2: First half round iteration – Parity-check extrinsic beliefs

6:     **For all** j, i such that $h_{i,j} = 1$ **do**

7:         $f_j \to y_i$: $r_{j,i}^{(r)} = \mathtt{ParityCheckBelief}\left(\left\{q_{i,j}^{(r-1)}\right\}_{i \in \mathcal{M}(j)}\right)$

8:     **End For**
   // Step 3: Second half round iteration – Codeword extrinsic belief

9:     **For all** i, j such that $h_{i,j} = 1$ **do**

10:        $y_i \to f_j$: $q_{i,j}^{(r)} = \mathtt{CodewordExtrinsicBelief}\left(\left\{r_{j,i}^{(r)}\right\}_{j \in C(i)}\right)$

11:    **End For**

12:    **For** index i from 0 to $n-1$ **do**
   // Step 4: Soft decision – codeword belief quantification

13:        $Q_i^{(r)} \leftarrow \mathtt{EstimatorConfidence}()$
   // Step 5: Hard decision – possible bit-flipping / codeword update

14:        $y_i \leftarrow \hat{c}_i = \begin{cases} 1 & \text{if } Q_i^{(r)} > 0.5 \\ 0 & \text{otherwise} \end{cases}$

15:    **End For**
   // Stopping criteria

16:    **If** $Hy = 0$ **then return** y **End If**   *// as it means that $y \in C$*

17: **End For**

18: **return** ∞ *// Decoding failure*

The major steps in Algorithm 4.2 are

Step 1: *Initialization.* Initialization. The initial messages $q_{i,j}^{(0)}$ sent from the message nodes i to the check nodes j correspond to the APP (or LR or LLR) of the ith received symbol y_i, given the knowledge of the channel properties. Exercise 4.29 proposes to detail this initial message assuming that a BSC channel with error probability p is used.

Step 2: *Parity-Check Extrinsic Beliefs.* In one half iteration, each check node j processes its input messages and sends the results to its neighboring message node i, as

TABLE 4.5   Comparison of MPAs

Message	Bit-flipping	BPA-APP	BPA-LR	BPA-LLR
Type	bit	APP	LR	LLR
Range $q_{i,j}$ is	$\{0,1\}$ c_i	$[0,1] \times [0,1]$ For $b \in \{0,1\}$, $P(c_i = b \mid y)$	$\mathbb{R}^+$ $l(c_i) = $ $\dfrac{P(c_i = 0 \mid y)}{P(c_i = 1 \mid y)}$	$\mathbb{R}$ $L(c_i) = \ln\left(l(c_i)\right)$
$r_{j,i}$ is	check f_j OK	$P(f_j \text{ OK} \mid y)$	$l(f_j) = $ $\dfrac{P(f_j \text{ KO} \mid y)}{P(f_j \text{ OK} \mid y)}$	$L(f_j) = \ln\left(l(f_j)\right)$

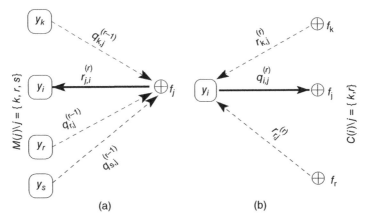

Figure 4.5   Illustration of the extrinsic information passed to compute the messages $r_{j,i}^{(r)}$ (a, step 2) and $q_{i,j}^{(r)}$ (b, step 3)

illustrated on the Figure 4.5(a). The information transmitted concerns the *extrinsic* APP that the parity-check equation conducted on f_j is satisfied assuming that the ith bit of the codeword is 1. In practice, this extrinsic APP is defined at round r by the following equations (that will be made explicit in the Exercise 4.30):

$$r_{j,i}^{(r)}(0) = \frac{1}{2} + \frac{1}{2} \prod_{i' \in \mathcal{M}(j)\backslash i} (1 - 2q_{i',j}^{(r-1)}) \quad \text{and} \quad r_{j,i}^{(r)}(1) = 1 - r_{j,i}^{(r)}(0),$$

where $\mathcal{M}(j)\backslash i$ denote the set of message nodes connected to the check node f_j yet without the message node y_i. This pair of values is, therefore, sent along the edges of the graph for the APP version of the BPA decoding. The LR and the LLR versions of the algorithm derive the above quantities to send the following messages:

$$\text{LR: } l\left(r_{j,i}^{(r)}\right) = \frac{r_{j,i}^{(r)}(0)}{r_{j,i}^{(r)}(1)} \qquad \text{LLR: } L\left(r_{j,i}^{(r)}\right) = \ln\left(\frac{r_{j,i}^{(r)}(0)}{r_{j,i}^{(r)}(1)}\right).$$

Step 3: *Codeword Extrinsic Belief.* In the other half iteration, each message node i updates its current estimation of the extrinsic APP for the ith bit of the codeword, based on the received messages from the check nodes and the previous events. This is illustrated on Figure 4.5(b). At round r, this is done via the following equations:

$$q_{i,j}^{(r)}(0) = \alpha_{i,j}(1 - p_i) \prod_{j' \in C(i)\setminus j} r_{j',i}^{(r)}(0)$$

and, similarly,

$$q_{i,j}^{(r)}(1) = \alpha_{i,j} p_i \prod_{j' \in C(i)\setminus j} r_{j',i}^{(r)}(1),$$

where $C(i)\setminus j$ denotes the set of check nodes connected to the message node y_i yet without the check node f_j. The constants $\alpha_{i,j}$ are chosen to ensure that $q_{i,j}^{(r)}(0) + q_{i,j}^{(r)}(1) = 1$. Again, this pair of values is sent along the edges of the graph for the APP version of the BPA decoding. Also, the LR and the LLR versions of the algorithm derive the above quantities to send the following messages:

$$\text{LR: } l\left(q_{i,j}^{(r)}\right) = \frac{q_{i,j}^{(r)}(0)}{r_{i,j}^{(r)}(1)} \qquad \text{LLR: } L\left(q_{i,j}^{(r)}\right) = \ln\left(\frac{q_{i,j}^{(r)}(0)}{q_{i,j}^{(r)}(1)}\right).$$

Step 4: *Soft Decision – Codeword Belief Quantification.* Now each message node i can update its local estimation of the APP for the ith bit $\hat{c}_i$ of the codeword, this time, based on all information available (i.e., not only extrinsic). This is done via the following equations, similar to the one of the previous steps except that this time, the information of all neighbor check nodes $\mathcal{N}(i)$ are taken into account:

$$Q_i^{(r)}(0) = \beta_i(1 - p_i) \prod_{j \in C(i)} r_{j,i}^{(r)}(0)$$

and, similarly,

$$Q_i^{(r)}(1) = \beta_i p_i \prod_{j \in C(i)} r_{j,i}^{(r)}(1),$$

where the constants β_i are chosen to ensure that $Q_i^{(r)}(0) + Q_i^{(r)}(1) = 1$. This step is often called the *soft decision* step as it quantifies, at a given moment of time, the confidence (or belief) one can have on the fact that the ith bit of the codeword is a 1. At this level, the LR and the LLR versions of the algorithm determine the following values:

$$\text{LR: } l\left(Q_i^{(r)}\right) = \frac{Q_i^{(r)}(0)}{Q_i^{(r)}(1)} \qquad \text{LLR: } L\left(Q_i^{(r)}\right) = \ln\left(\frac{Q_i^{(r)}(0)}{Q_i^{(r)}(1)}\right).$$

Step 5: *Hard Decision.* Following the previous step and based on the confidence metric Q_i, one can now decide about the actual value of the codeword bit $\hat{c}_i$. Note that this may result in a particular bit-flipping. This is done in the following way:

$$\text{APP} : \hat{c}_i = \begin{cases} 1 & \text{if } Q_i^{(r)}(1) > Q_i^{(r)}(0), \text{ or equivalently if } Q_i^{(r)}(1) > \frac{1}{2} \\ 0 & \text{otherwise} \end{cases}$$

$$\text{LR} : \hat{c}_i = \begin{cases} 1 & \text{if } l\left(Q_i^{(r)}\right) < 1 \\ 0 & \text{otherwise} \end{cases} \qquad \text{LLR} : \hat{c}_i = \begin{cases} 1 & \text{if } L\left(Q_i^{(r)}\right) < 0 \\ 0 & \text{otherwise,} \end{cases}$$

Remark 9 *The above BPA decoding algorithm has been presented for pedagogical purposes and some elements may be adjusted to optimize the number of computations. For instance, steps 4 and 5 can be done prior to the step 3, such that step 3 can be done with the following equation:*

$$q_{i,j}^{(r)}(b) = \alpha_{i,j}\frac{Q_i^{(r)}(b)}{r_{j,i}^{(r)}(b)}, \text{ for } b \in \{0,1\}.$$

Exercise 4.29 *We consider here that a codeword has been transmitted over a BSC channel with error probability p (see Section 4.1.5.2). Detail the content of the initial messages $q_{i,j}^{(0)}$ that are computed at step 1 of the BPA decoding process, Algorithm 4.2, for each versions of the algorithm (APP, LR, or LLR).* *Solution on page 333.*

Exercise 4.30 (Step 2 of the BPA Decoding Algorithm)

1. *Consider a sequence $\{x_i\}_{0 \leq i < n}$ of n independent binary digits for which $P(x_i = 1) = p_i$. Show that the probability that the whole sequence contains an even number of 1's is*

$$\frac{1}{2} + \frac{1}{2}\prod_{i=0}^{n-1}(1 - 2p_i).$$

2. *Use this result to justify the expression of $r_{i,j}^{(r)}$ at the step 2 of Algorithm 4.2.* *Solution on page 334.*

Exercise 4.31 (Step 3 of the BPA Decoding Algorithm)   *Let S_i denote the event that the parity-check equations involving y_i are satisfied. We also denote by* $\text{MSG}_c(\backslash j)$ *the set of messages coming from all check nodes except f_j. Then* $q_{i,j}^{(r)}(b) = P(c_i = b \mid y_i, S_i, \text{MSG}_c(\backslash j))$, *where $b \in \{0, 1\}$.*
Justify the expression of $q_{i,j}^{(r)}(b)$ given at the step 2 of the BPA decoding algorithm.

Solution on page 334.

The BPA assumes that the messages passed are statistically independent. As the y_i are assumed independent, this assumption holds as soon as the Tanner graph has no cycle: for a graph with girth γ, the independence assumption is true up to the $(\frac{\gamma}{2})$th iteration, after which the messages loop back on themselves on the various graph cycle throughout the decoding process. It follows that on a cycle-free Tanner graph, the MPA would yield the exact APP (or LR or LLR, depending on the chosen decoding algorithm) and lead to an optimal MLD (see Section 4.1.4). Otherwise, one should ensure that the maximum number of rounds satisfy $N_{\max} \leq \frac{\gamma}{2}$. Notwithstanding this limitation, in practice, simulations have shown that the approach seems to remain valid and very effective provided that length-4 cycles are avoided.

4.4.3.5   *Practical Applications of LDPC Codes.*   As it was said at the beginning of this section, LDPC codes have been largely ignored after their initial discovery in the 1960s. Again, this was simply due to the fact that BCH codes (presented in Sections 4.4.5 and 4.4.6) and, most importantly, Turbo codes (see Section 4.6) were simply considered as better alternatives.

Yet the recent advances in the analysis and the design of "good" LDPC codes (with linear time decoding scheme) make them more and more popular and integrated in the latest communication standards. Besides, several open-source libraries that implement LDPC codes (among them, we can cite the Coded Modulation Library (CML) Matlab library) can now be found.

For instance, the Digital Video Broadcasting (DVB) project (started in 1993 to standardize digital television services) has its latest DVB-S2 standard integrate a LDPC code. More precisely, it uses a concatenation of an outer BCH code and an inner LDPC code, where the codeword length can be either $n = 64, 800$ for normal frames or $n = 16, 200$ for short frames). LDPC codes are also at the heart of the IEEE 802.16e (WiMAX) standard for wireless communications, or the 802.3an (10 GB/s Ethernet over Twisted pair) standard, just to cite a few of them.

Now, LDPC codes share their capacity to closely approach the Shannon limit with turbo codes, for instance (see Section 4.6). On the one hand, among the various reasons for the new success of LDPC codes over turbo codes, one can cite the fact that the BPA allows for a parallel implementation of the LDPC decoder. Also they seem to offer higher performance against bursts of errors (which will be analyzed in Section 4.5). Furthermore, a single LDPC code can be universally good over a collection of channels.[3] Finally, the BPA of some good LDPC codes is able to detect an uncorrected codeword with near-unity probability (see steps 4 and 5 of Algorithm 4.2).

On the other hand, the main drawbacks of LDPC codes are first, the complexity of the encoders and second, their relatively slow speed, when compared to turbo codes, for short length codes.

Another important class of linear codes is the class of cyclic codes. This class adds a circular structure to the generating matrices and, therefore, a polynomial representation. We show in the next section that this additional structure eases the computations and offers a great flexibility with simple methods to build codes with a given correction rate.

4.4.4 Cyclic Codes

One calls *cyclic shift operation* the linear map σ from V^n onto itself defined by

$$\sigma([u_0, \dots, u_{n-1}]) = [u_{n-1}, u_0, \dots, u_{n-2}].$$

The operation σ is linear and has as matrix

$$\Sigma = \begin{bmatrix} 0 & 0 & \cdots & \cdots & 1 \\ 1 & 0 & \cdots & \cdots & 0 \\ 0 & 1 & 0 & \cdots & 0 \\ 0 & \ddots & \ddots & \ddots & \vdots \\ 0 & \cdots & 0 & 1 & 0 \end{bmatrix}.$$

A *cyclic code* is a linear code that is constant with respect to the cyclic shift operation. In other words, a linear code C in V^n is cyclic when

$$\sigma(C) = C.$$

Example 4.8   The parity code $(n, n-1)$ is a cyclic code. Indeed, if $c = (c_0, \dots, c_{n-1})$ is a codeword, then one has $c_{n-1} = \sum_{i=0}^{n-2} c_i \mod 2$. But then, one also has $c_{n-2} = c_{n-1} + \sum_{i=0}^{n-3} c_i \mod 2$; hence, $\sigma(c) = (c_{n-1}, c_0, \dots, c_{n-2})$ is also a codeword. Therefore, the parity code is cyclic. This statement can also be seen directly on the matrices: indeed, one can associate the generator matrix G to the parity code, where

$$G = \begin{bmatrix} 1 & 0 & \cdots & 0 & 1 \\ 0 & 1 & \ddots & \vdots & 1 \\ \vdots & \ddots & \ddots & 0 & \vdots \\ 0 & \cdots & 0 & 1 & 1 \end{bmatrix}.$$

Then, Remark 7 gives that ΣG and G generate the same code because Σ is invertible.

---

[3] In this book, we limited ourselves to the presentation of the BSC channel, yet other models exist such as the Binary Erasure Channel (BEC) or the Binary-input Additive White Gaussian Noise Channel (BI-AWGNC).

4.4.4.1 Characterization: Generator Polynomial.

Any element $U = [u_0, \dots, u_{n-1}]$ in V^n can be represented by some polynomial of degree $n - 1$ in $V[X]$ (see Section 1.3.4.5)

$$P_U = \sum_{i=0}^{n-1} u_i X^i.$$

As $X^n - 1$ is a polynomial of degree n, V^n is isomorphic to $V[X]/(X^n - 1)$. Then, in $V[X]/(X^n - 1)$, one has

$$P_{\sigma(U)} = X \cdot P_U(X) - u_{n-1} \cdot (X^n - 1) = X \cdot P_U \quad \text{mod } (X^n - 1).$$

In others words, the shift operation σ of a vector is equivalent to the multiplication of its associated codeword by X in $V[X]/(X^n - 1)$. This property is at the origin of the following theorem giving an algebraic characterization of a cyclic code.

Theorem 34 *Any cyclic code $C = (n, k)$ admits a generator matrix G_C of the form:*

$$G_C = \begin{bmatrix} m \\ \sigma(m) \\ \dots \\ \sigma^{k-1}(m) \end{bmatrix}$$

with $m = [a_0, a_1, \dots, a_{n-k}] = [1, 0, \dots, 0]$ such that $g(X) = \sum_{i=0}^{n-k} a_i X^i$ is a unitary divisor of $(X^n - 1)$ of degree $r = n - k$.
The polynomial g is called the generator polynomial *of the cyclic code .*
Reciprocally, any divisor g of $(X^n - 1)$ is a generator polynomial of a cyclic code.

Proof. First, one may use the following lemma.

Lemma 4 *Let $C(X)$ be the set of polynomials associated with the codewords of the cyclic code C. Then $C(X)$ is an ideal of $V[X]/(X^n - 1)$.*

Indeed, $C(X)$ is obviously a group. Then, for all P_U in $C(X)$, $P_{\sigma(U)} = XP_U$ is in $C(X)$ because C is cyclic. In the same way, all the $X^i P_U$ are also in C. Finally, by linearity, all linear combinations of the previous polynomials are also in C. In other words, for all $A(X) \in V[X]/(X^n - 1)$, $A(X)P_U$ is in C.

Let us go back to the proof of the theorem. The ring $V[X]/(X^n - 1)$ is a principal ring (see Section 1.3.4), thus $C(X)$ is generated by some polynomial $g(X)$ of minimum degree r.

Let us show that $r = n - k$. As $g(X)$ is a generator polynomial, all the codewords are written $A(X)g(X)$. Modulo $X^n - 1$, $A(X)$ is, therefore, of degree $n - r - 1$; thus, there are exactly $|V|^{n-r}$ distinct elements of the code. This can be achieved only if $n - r = k$.

Now, one has to prove that the polynomial g is a divisor of $X^n - 1$. One writes the Euclidean division $X^n - 1 = Q(X)g(X) + R(X) = 0 \mod X^n - 1$ with $\deg(R) < \deg(g)$. However, 0 and $Q(x)g(X)$ are in the ideal $C(X)$; therefore, by linearity, so is $R(X)$. But g is a generator of $C(X)$ of minimum degree, thus $R(X) = 0$ and g divides $X^n - 1$.

Finally, for the converse proposition, one writes

$$
G_C = \begin{bmatrix} g(X) \\ Xg(X) \\ \cdots \\ X^{n-r-1}(m) \end{bmatrix}.
$$

This is a $(n, n - r)$ linear code, thus $k = n - r$. Then, it is a cyclic code because any codeword is written UG_C or $\sum_{i=0}^{n-r-1} u_i X^i g(X)$. Therefore, $\sigma(UG_C) = \sum_{i=0}^{n-r-1} u_i X^{i+1} g(X) = u_{n-r-1} g(X) + \sum_{i=0}^{n-r-2} u_i X^{i+1} g(X) \mod X^n - 1$ is actually a linear combination of powers of g and it belongs to the code generated by the powers of g.   □

This property enables one to build directly an error-correcting code, given a divisor polynomial of $X^n - 1$. To recognize such divisors, it is possible to factorize $X^n - 1$. This can be performed in reasonable time, for instance, using the Cantor–Zassenhaus algorithm given in the following exercise.

Exercise 4.32 (Cantor–Zassenhaus Probabilistic Factorization)
The complexity (in number of arithmetic operations on a prime field $\mathbb{Z}/p\mathbb{Z}$) of the addition of two polynomials of degree at most d will be denoted by $A_d = O(d)$, the complexity of the multiplication or the division will be denoted by M_d, and the complexity of the extended Euclidean algorithm will be denoted by E_d. The purpose of this exercise is to estimate the complexity of the factorization of polynomials without squares over a finite field.

1. *By adapting Algorithm 1.8, deduce an algorithm Distinct Degree Factorization (DDF) that factorizes a polynomial P into $P = P_1 \cdots P_k$ where P_i is a product of irreducible polynomials of degree i.*

2. *What is the maximum value of k? Deduce the complexity of the DDF.*

3. *If $p = 2$, how can one factorize P_1?*

4. *Therefore, in the sequel, we will assume that p is odd and $i \geq 2$. Now, one has only to separate the irreducible factors of the P_i. Show that for any polynomial $T = \sum a_j X^j$, $X^{p^i} - X$ divides $T^{p^i} - T$ in $\mathbb{Z}/p\mathbb{Z}$.*

5. *Deduce that for all T, the irreducible factors of P_i are shared between T, $T^{\frac{p^i-1}{2}} - 1$, and $T^{\frac{p^i-1}{2}} + 1$.*

6. *In practice, Cantor and Zassenhaus proved that if T is any polynomial of degree $< 2i$, there is approximately a one in two chance that the factors of P_i are not all in the same polynomial among the three polynomials described above. Deduce a probabilistic factoring algorithm FS (Factor Separation).*

How can one reduce the size of the polynomials and then, what is the average complexity?

Solution on page 335.

The link between a cyclic code and a generator polynomial is important; it is at the origin of efficient encoding and decoding algorithms that avoid the multiplication by the generator matrix G_C (of cost $O(nk)$) replacing it with a multiplication by the polynomial g of cost $O(n \log n)$. Besides, the practical interest is that both encoding and decoding can be quite easily implemented in circuits, for instance, using LFSR.

4.4.4.2 Encoding Process. Let C be a cyclic code of generator polynomial g; let G be a generator matrix of C built from g according to Theorem 34. Let $a = [a_0, \ldots, a_{k-1}] \in V^k$ be a source word, and let $P_a = \sum_{i=0}^{k-1} a_i X^i$ be its associated polynomial. The codeword associated with a is $\phi(a) = aG$ with polynomial P_{aG}. Using the representation of G from the coefficients of $g(X)$ (Theorem 34), one has

$$P_{aG} = \sum_{i=0}^{k-1} a_i (X^i g(X) \mod X^n - 1)$$

$$= [g(X)(\sum_{i=0}^{k-1} a_i X^i)] \mod X^n - 1$$

$$= [g(X) \cdot P_a(X)] \mod X^n - 1 .$$

Therefore, the encoding process corresponds to a product of polynomials, the degrees of the monomials being taken modulo n: indeed, the computation modulo $X^n - 1$ boils down to considering that $X^n = 1 = X^0$.

Example 4.9 We consider the cyclic code (7,4) associated with the polynomial $g = (1 + X^2 + X^3)$. Let $a = [a_0, a_1, a_2, a_3]$ be a source word; then, the codeword of a is equal to aG; it is obtained from the right multiplication by the matrix G. The same word is obtained by computing the coefficients of the polynomial:

$$(a_0 + a_1 X + a_2 X^2 + a_3 X^3)(1 + X^2 + X^3) \mod X^7 - 1 .$$

Hence, for $a = [1001]$, $g \cdot P_a \mod X^7 - 1 = (1 + X^2 + X^3)(1 + X^3) = 1 + X^2 + 2.X^3 + X^5 + X^6 = 1 + X^2 + X^5 + X^6$. Therefore, $\phi(a) = [1010011]$.

4.4.4.3 Error Detection and Decoding Process. The previous encoding shows that any codeword is a multiple of $g(X)$. Let $m \in V^n$ be a message one receives and let P_m be its associated polynomial. During the decoding process, one first computes $P_e = P_m \mod g$;

- if $P_e = 0$, the polynomial one has received is actually a multiple of g: thus, it corresponds to a codeword. One recovers the message that was issued by computing the quotient P_m/g.

- otherwise, $P_e \neq 0$, the word one has received is not a codeword and there were some errors during the transmission.

Therefore, error detection is performed via the computation of $P_e = P_m$ modulo g; P_e is the *error syndrome*.

If P_e is nonzero, one can make a correction. The brute-force manner is consists in storing in a table all the words in V^n and associate to each word the closest codeword corresponding to the corrected message. Then, correction is performed with a simple reading of the table.

The link between cyclic codes and polynomials implies the existence of less costly algorithms (in terms of memory storage) to correct an erroneous message. Meggitt's method and its variants are examples of such algorithms.

Therefore, error detection is a division of polynomials, which is equivalent, as for encoding, to a multiplication of polynomials of cost $O(n \log n)$. The Berlekamp–Massey algorithm (see the description on page 85) enables one to perform the correction in a cyclic code with a similar cost.

Exercise 4.33 *We have shown that any cyclic code is characterized by a given generator polynomial, which is a unitary divisor of degree $r = n - k$ of $X^n - 1$. Therefore, the code C is determined, given only $r = n - k$ coefficients $g_0, \ldots, g_{n-k-1}$. Reciprocally, justify that given a polynomial g, which is a unitary divisor of degree $n - k$ of $X^n - 1$, then one can define a unique cyclic code (n, k).*   Solution on page 335.

4.4.5   Bose–Chaudhuri–Hocquenghem (BCH) Codes

The error rate of a cyclic code is hard to compute. Nevertheless, this section presents a theorem that enables one to ensure a lower bound on the distance of a code and, consequently, (according to Theorem 31) a lower bound on the detection rate.

4.4.5.1   *Minimum Distance of a Code*   Let us consider a finite field $\mathbb{F}_q$, and let us recall the notion of an nth primitive root of unity , which was discussed in Section 1.4.2.6: this is a simple root of the polynomial $X^n - 1$ of order n (in general, the order of any nth root of unity γ is the smallest integer o such that $\gamma^o = 1$ and its value is *at most n*).

One reason for studying nth roots of unity is that one may use them to find codes having a given minimum distance.

Theorem 35 *Let C be a (n, k) cyclic code of generator polynomial $g \in \mathbb{F}_q[X]$ with n coprime with q and let β be a nth primitive root of unity. If there exist two integers l and s such that $g(\beta^l) = g(\beta^{l+1}) = \cdots = g(\beta^{l+s-1}) = 0$, then*

$$\delta(C) \geq s + 1.$$

Therefore, the code C is at least a s-error-detecting code and a $\lfloor s/2 \rfloor$-error-correcting code.

Proof. As the code is linear, it is enough to prove that no codeword has a Hamming weight lower than $s + 1$. By contradiction, let us assume that there exists a codeword $m = m_0 + m_1 X + \cdots + m_{n-1} X^{n-1}$ of weight w such that $1 \leq w < s + 1$. As m is a multiple of g, m also satisfies $m(\beta^l) = m(\beta^{l+1}) = \cdots = m(\beta^{l+s-1}) = 0$. This can also be written in the following matricial form (only the lines satisfying $m_{i_k} \neq 0$ are kept):

$$
\begin{bmatrix}
\beta^{l i_1} & \cdots & \beta^{l i_w} \\
\beta^{(l+1) i_1} & \cdots & \beta^{(l+1) i_w} \\
\vdots & \ddots & \vdots \\
\beta^{(l+w-1) i_1} & \cdots & \beta^{(l+w-1) i_w}
\end{bmatrix}
\begin{bmatrix}
m_{i_1} \\
m_{i_2} \\
\vdots \\
m_{i_w}
\end{bmatrix}
=
\begin{bmatrix}
0 \\
0 \\
\vdots \\
0
\end{bmatrix}.
$$

This linear system is a square linear system, and it exists only if $w \geq s$ since there are only s roots of g of the form β^{l+i} giving a second member of the equation equal to zero. As the m_{i_k} are nonzero, this system has a solution only if the matrix is singular. However, this is a Vandermonde matrix and its determinant is equal to $\beta^{l(i_1 + \cdots + i_w)} \prod_{i_j < i_k} (\beta^{i_j} - \beta^{i_k})$. The latter being nonzero (because β is an nth primitive root); this concludes the contradiction and w is strictly greater than s.   □

4.4.5.2 Construction of BCH Generator Polynomials
As an application of this theorem, Bose, Chaudhuri, and Hocquenghem proposed a method for building cyclic codes having any error rate.

One assumes that n is coprime with q. Then, one considers an nth primitive root of unity β. Finally, one writes the relation $X^n - 1 = \prod (X - \beta^i)$. One can also write the factorization $X^n - 1 = P_1(X) \cdots P_k(X)$ using irreducible polynomials in $\mathbb{F}_q[X]$. Yet, because n is coprime with q, all roots of $X^n - 1$ are distinct (hence, the roots of one single irreducible polynomial P_i). One denotes i_k, the index of the irreducible polynomial having the root β^k. Then, Bose, Chaudhuri, and Hocquenghem suggested using the following generator polynomial of a code

$$
g(X) = \text{ppcm}\{P_{i_{k+1}}(X), \ldots, P_{i_{k+s}}(X)\}.
$$

Such code is called a *BCH code*.

Corollary 3 *A BCH code has a minimum distance greater than $s + 1$ and, hence, a minimum correction rate greater than $\lfloor s/2 \rfloor$.*

Proof. In an extension, one notices that $g(X) = H(X) \cdot \prod_{i=1}^{s}(X - \beta^{k+i})$ for some polynomial H. Then, Theorem 35 provides us with the lower bound on the distance.   □

Example 4.10 In order to build a 2-error-correcting code in $\mathbb{F}_5$, let us consider $\mathbb{F}_5[X]$ and, for instance, $X^8 - 1$. Then, one computes, for example, using the algorithm presented in Exercise 4.32:

$$
X^8 - 1 = (X^2 + 2)(X^2 + 3)(X + 1)(X - 1)(X - 2)(X - 3) \quad \text{mod } 5.
$$

Obviously, 1, 2, 3, -1 have an order lower than 5 and they cannot be eighth prim-
itive roots of unity. In an extension of the field, one denotes β a root of $X^2 + 2$.
Then $\beta^2 = -2 = 3$ and thus $\beta^3 = 3\beta$, $\beta^4 = 4$, $\beta^5 = 4\beta$, $\beta^6 = 2$, $\beta^7 = 2\beta$, and $\beta^8 =$
$6 = 1$. Here one is lucky because there exists an eighth root of unity in $\mathbb{F}_5$. Other-
wise, one would have had to try other polynomials of the form $X^n - 1$ with $n \neq 8$.
Then, if one wishes to build a 2-error-correcting code, one has to find some irreducible polynomials having the roots β^i (for i from 1 to 4, for instance). β is a root of
$X^2 + 2$, $\beta^2 = 3$ is a root of $X - 2$, $\beta^3 = 3\beta$, and $(3\beta)^2 = 4 * 3 = 2$; thus 3β is a root
of $X^2 + 3$ and finally, $\beta^4 = 4 = -1$ is a root of $X + 1$. Therefore, one can consider
$g(X) = (X^2 + 2)(X^2 + 3)(X + 1)(X - 3)$. However, one may notice that one obtains a
2-error-correcting code with seven redundancy characters out of eight and, hence, a
code rate of only 0.125.

Exercise 4.34 (BCH Code with a Better Rate)

1. *Find a sixteenth primitive root of unity modulo* 5 *using* $X^{16} - 1 =$
   $(X^4 + 2)(X^4 + 3)(X^8 - 1) \mod 5$.

2. *How can one build a 2-error-correcting code with a better rate than the code
   presented in the previous example?*

Solution on page 335.

On this example, one clearly sees that one is able to build codes having any chosen
correction rate; yet, for this, one must manage to find an appropriate primitive root.

In practice, the most common BCH codes correspond to $n = q^t - 1$; such codes
are called *primitive codes*. Among those codes, the BCH codes having $n = q - 1$ are
called *Reed–Solomon codes* and we are going to see that they have a better code rate
and that they are easier to build.

4.4.6 Optimal BCH Codes: Reed–Solomon Codes

Any primitive BCH code has a length $n = q^t - 1$. Thus, one must have n coprime
with q. Besides, Reed–Solomon codes satisfy more precisely $n = q - 1$. In this case,
there always exist nth primitive roots of unity, namely, the primitive roots in $\mathbb{F}_q$ (see
Section 1.3.5.3). Then, we will see that it is always possible to choose only irreducible
polynomials over $\mathbb{F}_q[X]$ of degree 1 to be the minimal polynomials for each of the β^{k+i}.
Then, the generator polynomial has a minimum overall degree, and thus the code has
a minimum redundancy for a given correction rate.

There are two interests in these codes. First, they are optimal with respect to the
number of redundancy digits for a given correction capacity. Moreover, they are particularly fast for encoding and decoding.

Thus, let us build a Reed–Solomon generator polynomial. Indeed, the polynomial
$X^{q-1} - 1$ can be factorized very easily over $\mathbb{F}_q$: its roots are all the nonzero elements
in $\mathbb{F}_q$.

$$X^{q-1} - 1 = \prod_{\lambda \in \mathbb{F}_q - \{0\}} (X - \lambda).$$

The multiplicative group $\mathbb{F}_q - \{0\}$, being cyclic, has a primitive root α. Then, one has $\alpha \in \mathbb{F}_q$ and no splitting extension is required in order to have

$$X^{q-1} - 1 = \prod_{i=1}^{q-1}(X - \alpha^i).$$

The construction of a Reed–Solomon code with r redundancy digits relies on the choice of a generator polynomial of degree r, whose roots are consecutive:

$$g(X) = \prod_{i=s}^{s+r-1}(X - \alpha^i).$$

Therefore, the Reed–Solomon code one obtains is a $(n = q - 1, k = n - r)$ code for any r.

The correction rate of this code is optimal. Indeed, being a BCH code, the minimum distance δ of a Reed–Solomon code is at least $\delta \geq r + 1$. Yet, the Singleton bound (Theorem 32) shows that $\delta \leq n - k + 1 = r + 1$; hence, the distance is $\delta = r + 1$ and the code reaches the Singleton bound.

Reed–Solomon codes are commonly used in practice, for instance, in spacecraft communications.

Example 4.11 (The Galileo Unmanned Spacecraft) *Galileo*, an unmanned spacecraft that studied the planet Jupiter and its moons, uses the Reed–Solomon code (255,223) of distance 33. This is a 16-error-correcting code over the field $\mathbb{F}_{2^8}$. If α is a primitive root of $\mathbb{F}_{2^8}$ (here, α is any root of the primitive polynomial $T^8 + T^7 + T^2 + T + 1$ that is used to generate $\mathbb{F}_{2^8}$), the generator polynomial of degree $r = 32$ of the chosen Reed–Solomon code (255,223,33) is:[4] $g = \prod_{j=12}^{43}(X - \alpha^{11j})$.

4.4.6.1 Decoding of Reed–Solomon Codes. The decoding of Reed–Solomon codes can be performed very quickly because the error syndrome computation is equivalent, in this case, to a fast Fourier transform calculus! Indeed, the control matrix H defined in Section 4.4.2 of a Reed–Solomon code can be easily expressed as follows:

$$H = \begin{bmatrix} 1 & \alpha & \alpha^2 & \dots & \alpha^{n-1} \\ 1 & \alpha^2 & (\alpha^2)^2 & \dots & (\alpha^2)^{n-1} \\ \vdots & \vdots & \vdots & & \vdots \\ 1 & \alpha^r & (\alpha^r)^2 & \dots & (\alpha^r)^{n-1} \end{bmatrix} = \begin{bmatrix} L_\alpha \\ L_{\alpha^2} \\ \dots \\ L_{\alpha^r} \end{bmatrix}.$$

[4] $g = X^{32} + [96]X^{31} + [E3]X^{30} + [98]X^{29} + [49]X^{28} + [B2]X^{27} + [82]X^{26} + [28]X^{25} + [32]X^{24} + [F1]X^{23} + [64]X^{22} + [C2]X^{21} + [70]X^{20} + [F0]X^{19} + [72]X^{18} + [4C]X^{17} + [76]X^{16} + AFX^{15} + [20]X^{14} + [65]X^{13} + [9F]X^{12} + [6B]X^{11} + [8B]X^{10} + [69]X^9 + [29]X^8 + [57]X^7 + [D3]X^6 + [6A]X^5 + [7F]X^4 + [C4]X^3 + [90]X^2 + [D6]X + [7C].$

The reason for this is that if G is the generator matrix of the code, then GH^T is the map of the polynomial g onto the different coefficients of H, the α^i, shifted by X at each line:

$$GH^T = \begin{bmatrix} \overline{g(X)} \\ \overline{Xg(X)} \\ \vdots \\ \overline{X^{r-1}g(X)} \end{bmatrix} \cdot [\ L_\alpha^T \mid L_{\alpha^2}^T \mid \cdots \mid L_{\alpha^r}^T \ ] \tag{4.7}$$

$$GH^T = \begin{bmatrix} g(\alpha) & g(\alpha^2) & \cdots & g(\alpha^{r-1}) \\ \alpha g(\alpha) & \alpha g(\alpha^2) & \cdots & \alpha g(\alpha^{r-1}) \\ \vdots & \vdots & & \vdots \\ \alpha^{r-1}g(\alpha) & \alpha^{r-1}g(\alpha^2) & \cdots & \alpha^{r-1}g(\alpha^{r-1}) \end{bmatrix}. \tag{4.8}$$

However, this matrix GH^T is zero because all α^i are roots of the polynomial $g(X)$; besides, the rank of H is equal to r because α is a primitive root. Therefore, H is *the* control matrix of the code.

Then a codeword $b = b_0 + b_1 X + \cdots + b_{n-1} X^{n-1}$ is a multiple of g ($b(X) = u(X)g(X)$, where u is the initial message), because a Reed–Solomon code is cyclic. The dual interpretation in the particular case of a Reed–Solomon code is that a codeword is characterized by the r first coefficients of its Discrete Fourier Transform (DFT) being equal to zero:

$$bH^T = \sqrt{n}\mathrm{DFT}_{1..r}(b).$$

This follows formula (1.14), as well as the fact that $0 = ugH^T = bH^T$, because H is the control matrix of the code.

The decoding is performed as follows. Let b be the codeword that was issued, c be the word one receives and e be the error vector, Namely, $c = b + e$. As b is a codeword, its multiplication with the control matrix gives the null vector. Thus the first coefficients of its Fourier transform are equal to zero. Consequently, the first coefficients of the DFT of c and e are equal $\mathrm{DFT}_{1..r}(c) = \mathrm{DFT}_{1..r}(e)$.

Then, the problem that remains is to recover e, given only the first coefficients of its Fourier transform. The trick is that the coefficients of the DFT of c are linearly generated by some polynomial whose degree is equal to the Hamming weight of e (the number of errors $w(e)$, see Section 4.3.1).

Theorem 36 (Blahut) *The DFT coefficients of e are linearly generated by some polynomial of degree $w(e)$.*

Proof. First, let us complete the series E associated with the DFT of the polynomial $e(T) = \sum_{j=0}^{n-1} e_j T^j$: one has $E(X) = \sum_{i=0}^{\infty} E_i X^i$.

As α is a primitive root, its order is $n = q - 1$ in $\mathbb{F}_q$. Therefore, one has $\alpha^i = \alpha^{i \bmod n}$, and for $i \geq n$, $E_i = \frac{1}{\sqrt{n}}e(\alpha^i) = \frac{1}{\sqrt{n}}e(\alpha^{i \bmod n}) = E_{i \bmod n}$. Hence, $E(X) =$

$\frac{1}{\sqrt{n}} \sum_{i=0}^{\infty} e(\alpha^i) X^i$ and even $E(X) = \frac{1}{\sqrt{n}} \sum_{i=0}^{\infty} \left(\sum_{j=0}^{n-1} e_j \alpha^{ij} \right) X^i = \frac{1}{\sqrt{n}} \sum_{j=0}^{n-1} e_j \sum_{i=0}^{\infty} (\alpha^j X)^i$.

Yet, the latter formula includes the power series of $\frac{1}{1-\alpha^j X}$. Thanks to this remark, one is able to write

$$E(X) = \frac{1}{\sqrt{n}} \sum_{j=0}^{n-1} e_j \frac{1}{1 - \alpha^j X} = \frac{1}{\sqrt{n}} \sum_{j=0 \text{ and } e_j \neq 0}^{n-1} e_j \frac{1}{1 - \alpha^j X} = \frac{R(X)}{\Pi(X)}.$$

Therefore, $E(X)$ is the simple element expression of a rational fraction $\frac{R(X)}{\Pi(X)}$, with degree(R) < degree(Π) and $\Pi(X) = \prod_{j=0 \text{ and } e_j \neq 0}^{n-1} (1 - \alpha^j X)$. Thus, we have that degree(Π) = $w(e)$ and Π is the minimal generator polynomial of the sequence $E(X)$ computed using the Berlekamp–Massey algorithm, as illustrated in Equation (1.16). $\square$

From this constructive proof, one immediately deduces the correction rate as well as the decoding algorithm of a Reed–Solomon code.

Algorithm 4.3 Decoding of a Reed-Solomon code

Input c a word containing less than $\frac{r-1}{2}$ errors.
Output b the corrected codeword.
  1: $[E_0, \ldots, E_{r-1}] = \mathrm{DFT}_{1..r}(c)$
  2: $\Pi(X) = \mathrm{Berlekamp\text{–}Massey}(E_{0..r-1})$
  3: $E = \mathrm{LFSR}_\Pi(E_0, \ldots, E_{r-1})$
  4: $e = \mathrm{DFT}^{-1}(E)$
  5: **return** $b = c - e$

Corollary 4 *A Reed–Solomon code is a ($\frac{r-1}{2}$)-error-correcting code.*

Proof. By definition, it has the maximum possible rate. Then, if $2w(e) < r - 1$, the proof of the previous theorem shows that the Berlekamp–Massey algorithm has enough coefficients to find a generator of degree $w(e)$ and complete the error syndrome. $\square$

Corollary 5 *A Reed–Solomon code can be decoded is almost linear time.*

Proof. If n is the size of the codeword, $q = n + 1$ is the size of the field. Thus, there exist nth roots of unity in this field because $n = q - 1$ (thanks to Theorem 17). Therefore, the DFT is possible with an nth root of unity in this field.

The complexity bound of the DFT calculus or that of its inverse is almost linear in $O(n \log(n))$ operations for the fastest algorithms. Likewise, the Berlekamp–Massey algorithm for the synthesis of LFSR requires $4r^2$ operations or $O(r \log^2(r))$ with a fast Euclidean algorithm stopped in the middle of the computation. Finally, applying the

LFSR requires $2(n-r)w(e) < 2nr$ operations or $O(n \log(n))$ with a fast polynomial multiplication.   □

One may notice that in order to directly apply the fast DFT Algorithm 1.12, n should be a power of 2. But in the Reed–Solomon case, one often uses $q = 2^8$ and thus $n = 255$! Nevertheless, there exist fast truncated transform algorithms when n is not a power of two, but such algorithms go beyond the scope of this book; it is also possible to perform fast transforms not using two transforms of size $n/2$ but rather k transforms of size n/k. For $n = 255$, one may use, for instance, 17 transforms of size 15.

Exercise 4.35 (Correction of Erasures)   *When reading a CD-ROM, a laser beam can return three symbols: '0', '1', and '?'. The symbol '?' corresponds to an invalid zone on the disk (this might be due for instance to dust or a scratch); then, one says that there is an* erasure. *More generally, the presence of a symbol '?' in the output of a channel indicates that the corresponding symbol is missing. Contrary to an error, an erasure gives the position of the erroneous bit.*

1. *Show that any (n, k)-code of distance d enables one to correct $d - 1$ erasures.*

2. *One considers a binary channel on which one wishes to correct up to 1% of erasures (of bytes) using a Reed–Solomon code over $\mathbb{F}_{256}$. Give the details (n, k, d) of such code.*

3. *One assumes that the word one receives contains some erasures, but no errors. Propose a method for correcting at most $d - 1$ erasures.*

4. *Let C be a (n, k)-code of distance $d = 2t + s + 1$. Deduce a method for correcting simultaneously t errors and s erasures.*

Solution on page 336.

4.4.6.2 *PAR-2 Protocol*   Reed–Solomon codes are widely used for the correction of errors and erasures in distributed file systems, such as RAID systems or peer-to-peer systems; in such systems, data-storage resources might disappear. Then, the use of error-correcting codes enables one to recover the missing blocks, thanks to redundancy.

For instance, the PAR-2 protocol is used for the storage of a file on a peer-to-peer system; it is based on the Reed–Solomon code over $\mathbb{F}_{2^{16}}$ with the primitive polynomial $X^{16} + X^{12} + X^3 + X + 1$.

In practice, PAR-2 enables one to rebuild a file when blocks are missing; thus, it does not correct errors but only erasures. The number of blocks that can be recovered can be parameterized and it is denoted by r in the example above.

Consider a source file of $2km$ bytes one wishes to store; PAR-2 divides this file into k files $D_1, \ldots, D_k$ whose common size is equal to m words of 16 bits. In addition to these files, r redundant files $C_1, \ldots, C_r$, also containing m words of 16 bits, are added. Besides, in their headers, the files C_i contain some additional information items, such as a MD5 summary of all files and their sizes; these information items are used to detect corrupted files. In the sequel, the word composed of the $n = k + r$

16-bit digits in the position i in the files $D_1, \dots, D_k, C_1, \dots, C_r$ is considered to be a codeword. It is denoted by $d_1, \dots, d_k, c_1, \dots c_r$ in a generic way, for any i.

The redundancy digits $c_1, \dots, c_r$ are computed using a Reed–Solomon (n,k)-code, which is the shortened code of the standard Reed–Solomon code of length 65,535 over $\mathbb{F}_{16}$, generated by the polynomial $g(x) = \prod_{i=1}^{r}(X - \alpha^i)$; thus, its distance is equal to $r + 1$.

To read the data, one wishes to recover the n files $D_1, \dots, D_k, C_1, \dots, C_r$ but one stops as soon as one obtains k complete and noncorrupted files (checks on the MD5 hashes and on the sizes). To recover the d_i, one only keeps the k corresponding files by puncturing the r other positions. Now, let y be one of the m received words. Let G' be the submatrix of G that is built by removing the columns of the erasures. Then, G' has a rank k (Theorem 33); therefore, the system $x \cdot G' = y$ admits a unique solution x, which is computed by solving the linear system and is the corrected codeword.

4.4.6.3 *Quick Response codes (QR-codes)*

QR-codes also use shortened Reed–Solomon codes for their error correction. QR-codes are bidimensional multiline bar codes where black pixels represent a 1 and white pixels represent a 0 on a binary alphabet. These pixels are set on a matrix of dimension from 21×21 up to 177×177 (40 different formats available, with 4 pixel increase per dimension between formats). Each of these formats comprises three 8×8 position detection patterns, four 8×1 format information zones, two $6 \times 0..3$ version information zones, one row and column for timing pattern, and from zero to 46 alignment patterns as shown, for example, on the second 25×25 format on Figure 4.6. This leaves between 208 and 29648 pixels for data encoding.

Then for each of the 40 possible formats, there are four possible levels of error correction: from level L (about 7% correction), level M (about 15% correction), and level Q (about 25% correction) to level H (about 30% correction) see for instance an example of compression of level L on (Figure 4.7).

In all the cases, error correction is performed via a CIRC over the field $\mathbb{F}_{2^8}$ with 256 elements represented as binary polynomials modulo 2 and modulo the primitive polynomial $x^8 + x^4 + x^3 + x^2 + 1$. Thus the codewords consist of 8 pixels, most of them being represented as regular 2×4 blocks in the QR-code matrix.

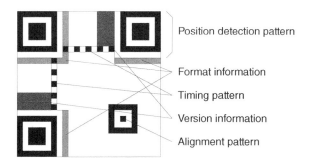

Position detection pattern

Format information

Timing pattern

Version information

Alignment pattern

Figure 4.6 25×25 QR-code and pattern locations

Figure 4.7   3-L, 29 × 29, QR-code for http://foundationsofcoding.imag.fr

Exercise 4.36   *On the second format,* 25×25, *described on Figure 4.6, there is actually no version information zone.*

1. *What is the number of data codewords in this QR-code?*
2. *From the required correction rate of the different levels of error correction, give the characteristics of the shortened Reed–Solomon codes with optimal minimal distance for this number of codewords.*
3. *In practice, those are the codes chosen for level 2-H and 2-Q, but two other codes have been chosen:* $(44, 34, 4)$ *for level 2-L and* $(44, 28, 8)$ *for level 2-M. What could be the reasons for these choices?*

Solution on page 336.

4.5   BURSTS OF ERRORS AND INTERLEAVING

4.5.1   Packets of Errors

In most channels, the errors do not occur in an isolated way (they do not follow a uniform random distribution) but they can occur, for example, in several consecutive symbols; one speaks of *packets of errors*. For instance, it is the case for CDs (dust, scratches) or satellite links (electromagnetic disruptions).

The *length* of a packet is its size in number of symbols. For instance, after issuing the binary sequence …10010110011…, if the received sequence is …10111011011…, then, the error vector is …00101101000… that contains four errors in a packet of length 6.

Most of the time, the length of the packet has a random value and even the average length may change during the transmission.

Exercise 4.37 (Linear Code and Detection of a Packet of Errors)   *Let* C *be a linear* (n, k)-*code over* $\mathbb{F}_q$ *that detects any packet of length at most* l. *Show that* C *does not contain any word being a packet of length lower or equal to* l. *Deduce that* $l \leq n - k$. *Solution on page 337.*

Exercise 4.38 (Distance of a Code and Length of a Packet) *On a binary channel, one uses a block code $C(n, k)$ over $\mathbb{F}_{256}$ of distance d. What is the maximum length l of a binary packet of errors corrected by this code?*

Solution on page 337.

For a given code and a given correction rate, interleaving and cross-interleaving techniques enable one to increase the length of the packets of errors that can be corrected.

4.5.2 Interleaving

Instead of transmitting the codewords consecutively, the interleaving technique consists of mixing them so that two consecutive digits of a single word will not appear consecutively in the transmitted sequence.

In the sequel, C is a (n, k)-code. There exist several methods for interleaving and transmitting a message $M = [a, b, c, ...]$ composed of a sequence (of any length) of codewords. The principle is the following. Let us assume that one wishes to transmit a message M composed of three codewords $[a, b, c]$ of length 5. The transmission without interleaving of M consists of sending on the channel the sequence $a_1 a_2 a_3 a_4 a_5 b_1 b_2 b_3 b_4 b_5 c_1 c_2 c_3 c_4 c_5$. Using matrices, the message M is written as

$$M = \begin{bmatrix} a_1 & a_2 & a_3 & a_4 & a_5 \\ b_1 & b_2 & b_3 & b_4 & b_5 \\ c_1 & c_2 & c_3 & c_4 & c_5 \end{bmatrix}$$

and, without interleaving, this matrix is sent line by line. The drawback of this method is that a packet of errors of length 2 can cause two errors in the same codeword and the latter will not be corrected if the code is only a 1-error-correcting code.

Using interleaving, the matrix is sent column by column; thus, the corresponding sequence is $a_1 b_1 c_1 a_2 b_2 c_2 a_3 b_3 c_3 a_4 b_4 c_4 a_5 b_5 c_5$. Therefore, any packet of errors of length of at most 3 can cause at most one error in the same word; thanks to interleaving, the packet can be corrected even with a 1-error-correcting code.

One generalizes the previous interleaving by processing the message by blocks of p words; such interleaving is said to have a *depth p*. If the initial code corrects packets of length l, the interleaving of depth p enables one to correct packets of length $p.l$ (see Exercise 4.39).

Exercise 4.39 (Interleaving Depth and Length of Corrected Packets) *Let C be a (n, k)-code over V of distance d that corrects packets of length l. Let p be an integer, and let C_p be the (np, kp)-code over V composed of the set of all interleavings of p codewords in C. The code C_p is called the* interleaved code of C of depth p. *Show that the distance of C_p is d and also that C_p enables one to correct any packet of errors of length l_p.*

Solution on page 337.

4.5.3 Interleaving with Delay and Interleaving Table

As encoding is often performed on-the-fly, one does not know in advance the size of the message M to be sent; Therefore, M is a sequence of unknown size of codewords in a (n, k)-code. Thus, one performs an *interleaving with delay* of M, on-the-fly. Such interleaving uses the common technique of the *interleaving table* ; in fact, the table is used as a cyclic buffer that is read line by line.

Such a table is characterized by its delay r. For the sake of simplicity, we will assume that the table has n lines and $r.n$ columns. During the initialization, one stores the first r words (hence, nr symbols) in the table as follows: the symbol of index i in the word j is stored on line i and column $j + (i - 1)r$. In other words, the first r words are stored in the r first columns; then, for $i = 1, \ldots, n$, the line i is shifted $(i - 1).r$ positions to the right. The final result is given in Table 4.6. After this initialization, and in order to send the different words of the message, one iterates the three following operations on each block of p words:

1. one first sends on the channel the sequence composed of the first r columns of the table, one after the other;
2. then one shifts the columns r positions to the left; thus, the column $r + 1$ becomes the first column and r new columns are added on the right;
3. finally, one stores the next r words of the message in the table in the same way as for the r previous words: the symbol of index i of the word j is stored once again in line i and column $j + (i - 1)r$.

Table 4.7 illustrates the state of the table after one round.

TABLE 4.6 Initial Interleaving Table with Delay 2 for Codewords of Length 5

To be Sent									
a_1	b_1								
		a_2	b_2						
				a_3	b_3				
						a_4	b_4		
								a_5	b_5

TABLE 4.7 Interleaving Table with Delay 2 After One Round

To be Sent									
c_1	d_1								
a_2	b_2	c_2	d_2						
		a_3	b_3	c_3	d_3				
				a_4	b_4	c_4	d_4		
						a_5	b_5	c_5	d_5

One notices that when the table is full, each transmitted symbol corresponds to a symbol of the message M. This is not the case at the beginning and at the end of the communication because noninitialized symbols of the table are sent. That is why one removes some symbols not corresponding to the symbols of the source during the beginning and the end of the decoding of the sequence; for instance, one removes the positions 2 to n if $r \geq 1$.

Thanks to this interleaving with delay, two consecutive characters of the same codeword are separated by at least $rn + 1$ characters in the sequence transmitted on the channel. Therefore, if the initial code corrects packets of length l, the interleaving with delay r enables one to correct packets of length $l(rn + 1)$.

Remark 10 *The length of the corrected packets is bounded by the delay. For this reason, this technique does not enable one to correct packets whose average length may vary during the transmission. Moreover, choosing a too large value for the delay induces a proportional overhead (transmission of useless characters at the beginning and at the end of the messages). This is inefficient for small messages. Thus, other interleaving techniques have been proposed, notably for turbo codes. For instance,* Golden *interleavings are based on an interleaving whose depth varies according to an arithmetic progression with a common difference equal to the golden ratio.*

4.5.4   Cross-Interleaved codes

Cross-interleaved codes are based on the composition of two codes, one of them being in charge of detecting packets of errors and the other of correcting them.

More precisely, let $C_1(n_1, k_1)$ and $C_2(n_2, k_2)$ be two codes of respective distances d_1 and d_2. The principle of the encoding of a source message M of m symbols is the following:

1. One first encodes the message M split into blocks of k_1 symbols using C_1, to obtain a message M' of $\left\lceil \frac{m}{k_1} \right\rceil$ words; hence, $m_1 = n_1 . \left\lceil \frac{m}{k_1} \right\rceil$ symbols;
2. The codewords in C_1 are interleaved, for example, using a delay; one obtains a message M'' having the same size m_1 (for the sake of simplicity, one does not take the additional symbols of the interleaving – at the beginning and at the end of the message – into account);
3. Then, the message M'' is split into blocks of k_2 symbols and encoded using C_2 to give a message M''' of $m_2 = n_2 . \left\lceil \frac{m_1}{k_2} \right\rceil$ symbols.

Eventually, the words in M''' can also be interleaved but this case is not discussed in the sequel.

For the decoding, the code C_2 is used to detect the errors, and the code C_1 is used to correct them. Hence, the correction capacity of the code C_2 is not fully exploited, the accent being put on its detection capacity. In practice, one sets $d_2 = 2.t_2 + u_2 + 1$, with t_2 small enough. The maximum correction capacity of C_2 would be $t_2 + \lfloor \frac{u_2}{2} \rfloor$, but one only uses a correction capacity of t_2 errors. Hence, if one detects more than t_2 errors, one does not correct them with C_2 for it would decrease the capacity of correcting large packets of errors; on the contrary, these errors are only marked for the code C_1 to deal with them. More rigorously, the principle of decoding is the following:

1. One first decodes each block M_i''' of n_2 symbols of M'''. One distinguishes two cases. Either the word can be decoded with at most t_2 corrections, and one recovers the source sequence M_i'' of k_2 symbols encoded by C_2. Otherwise, one detects the presence of more than t_2 errors, which is the case if the word is corrupted by a packet of errors; in this case, one marks the sequence M_i'' of k_2 symbols as an erasure.

2. One uninterleaves the obtained symbols to recover the words M_i' encoded by C_1;

3. Owing to the uninterleaving, the word M_i' may contain some erased symbols, but no erroneous symbols. Consequently, the distance d_1 of C_1 enables one to correct up to $d_1 - 1$ erased symbols in M_i' in order to recover the k_1 source symbols of M_i (see Exercise 4.35).

4.5.4.1 Cross-Interleaved Reed–Solomon Code (CIRC) Reed–Solomon codes are often used as the basis codes of a cross-interleaved code; then, one talks about a CIRC. For example, the code used for encoding sound frames on audio CDs is a CIRC. A scratch of 1 mm destroys around 3300 bits on the track of a CD; the code enables one to correct up to 28, 224 consecutive bits on the track, which corresponds to a length of around 8.2 mm on the disk!

On an audio CD, the source digital information is encoded by blocks called *frames*. A frame corresponds to six stereo samples of 32 bits (16 bits on the left and 16 bits on the right) and, hence, 24 bytes or 192 source bits with the addition of 8 parity bytes as well as 1 control byte. Each of these bytes is physically represented with 17 bits: a word of 14 bits (EFM, which stands for *Eight-to-Fourteen Modulation* encoding) followed by a 3-bit merging word. Moreover, 27 bits are also added between each frame. Finally, 192 bits of digital information become $(24 + 8 + 1) \times (14 + 3) + 27 = 588$ bits on the physical track (actually, the information is stored in the form of lands or pits that are burnt on the CD and detected by the laser), which corresponds to around 0.17 mm on the track. The digital signal is converted into an analogical sound with a frequency of 44,100 Hz; thus 1 s of music is encoded with $44, 100 \times 588/6 = 4, 321, 800$ bits on the track, namely, about 1.2 m.

The CIRC used is built with the cross-interleaving of two codes, $C_1(28, 24)$ and $C_2(32, 28)$. These two codes have a distance 5 over $\mathbb{F}_{256}$, and they are obtained from the shortened code of a (255, 251) Reed–Solomon code (cf. Exercise 4.40). They have, respectively, the canonical generator matrices $G_1 = \begin{bmatrix} I_{24}, R_1 \end{bmatrix}$ and $G_2 = \begin{bmatrix} I_{28}, R_2 \end{bmatrix}$, where R_1 is a 24×4 matrix and $R_2 = \begin{bmatrix} T \\ \hline R_1 \end{bmatrix}$ is a 28×4 matrix (i.e., T is a 4×4 matrix). The encoding process is the following:

- Each frame x of 24 bytes is encoded with C_1 into a word y of 28 bytes: $y = [x, x \cdot R_1]$. Hence, one obtains a sequence of codewords in C_1 of 28 bytes;
- The codewords in C_1 are interleaved in a table with a delay of 4 bytes; after the interleaving, one obtains a sequence of words of 28 bytes, each word y' corresponding to a column of the table;
- Each word y' is encoded with C_2 into a word z of 32 bytes: $z = [y', y' \cdot R_2]$.

This encoding has a rate $\frac{3}{4}$ and the decoding process is performed as follows (cf. Exercise 4.41):

- Each block z of 32 bytes is decoded with C_2 into a word y' of 28 bytes correcting at most one error. If more than one erroneous digit is detected, then no correction is performed and the word is classed as erased. In the sequel, we will write '?' for erasure (this symbol does not belong to $\mathbb{F}_{256}$); for instance, one returns the word y' composed by 28 '?'s.
- The blocks y' of 28 symbols are uninterleaved. Hence, one recovers a sequence of blocks y of 28 symbols. In a block y, one may find some bytes in $\mathbb{F}_{256}$ and some '?'s, each '?' corresponding to an erasure owing to an error detected by C_2.
- Each block y of 28 symbols is decoded using C_1. Having a distance 5, C_1 enables one to correct up to four erasures in a block y. If one manages to correct these erasures, one returns the 24 first bytes of the corrected codeword; otherwise, one returns an error message.

This decoding process enables one to correct up to 15 consecutive frames (see Exercise 4.42), namely, $15 \times 32 \times 8 = 3840$ bits of signal or $588 \times 15 = 8820$ bits corresponding to a scratch of around 2.5 mm.

Besides, it is possible to guess the sound of a missing sample given the previous and the next samples. Consequently, at the output of the code C_1 – before the interleaving with delay – one performs a preliminary permutation. At the output of C_1, the 28 bytes correspond to 14 words of 16 bits: $l_1 \ r_1 \ l_2 \ r_2 \ l_3 \ r_3 \ l_4 \ r_4 \ l_5 \ r_5 \ l_6 \ r_6 \ p_1 \ p_2$, where each word g_i and d_i refers to the 16 left or right bits of a stereo sample of 32 bits and p_1, p_2 refer to the 4 redundancy bytes. To separate two consecutive samples of 16 bits, one permutes them into $l_1 \ l_3 \ l_5 \ r_1 \ r_3 \ r_5 \ p_1 \ p_2 \ l_2 \ r_2 \ l_4 \ r_4 \ l_6 \ r_6$. Hence, thanks to interleaving with delay, a packet of errors affecting 48 frames of 32 bytes can prevent one from recovering a sample of 16 bits (g_3 for instance) but one is sure to have the previous and the next samples at the output of C_1 (l_2 and l_4 for l_3). With this extrapolation, it is possible to correct $48 \times 32 \times 8 = 12{,}288$ bits of information, hence $48 \times 588 = 28{,}224$ bits or around 8.2 mm on the track.

Another additional interleaving is performed at the output of C_2: one splits the frames of 32 bytes into blocks of 16 bytes and one permutes the blocks having an even index with those having an odd index. With this permutation, two consecutive errors will affect two distinct codewords in C_2 instead of one. As C_2 corrects at most one error per block, this method increases its probability of correction during the decoding process by avoiding some erasures.

Exercise 4.40 (Construction of C_1 and C_2) *Give a construction for the generator matrices G_1 and G_2 from a (255,251) Reed–Solomon code over $\mathbb{F}_{256}$. Justify that the codes C_1 and C_2 have a distance 5.* Solution on page 338.

Exercise 4.41 (Decoding of a CIRC on an Audio CD) *We now consider the codes $C_1(28, 24)$ and $C_2(32, 28)$ over $\mathbb{F}_{256}$ of the CIRC on audio CDs. The purpose of this exercise is to give the details of the steps of decoding.*

  1. When one receives a block of 32 bytes, explain how to erase a block or to correct at most one error with the code C_2 using the calculus of the error syndrome.
  2. During the decoding with C_1, explain how to correct at most four erasures.

Solution on page 338.

Exercise 4.42 (Correction Rate of the CIRC) *Prove that the preceding CIRC enables one to correct 15 consecutive frames.* Solution on page 338.

The serial interleaving technique used in CIRC enables one to correct large packets of errors by mixing the symbols coming from a given number of distinct blocks. It is also possible to perform an interleaving of unbounded size by reconsidering the notion of blocks; convolutional codes are examples of such a method.

4.6 CONVOLUTIONAL CODES AND TURBO CODES

Convolutional codes do not process blocks but rather a stream of data: they extend the preceding interleavings by encoding each bit issued by a source with a set of bits. They provide an easy decoding process and good performance.

4.6.1 Encoding by Convolution

In general, a convolutional code processes blocks of k bits and applies operations to the last m blocks via a matrix of $k \times n$ polynomials in $\mathbb{F}_2[X]$ of maximum degree m. Thus, such code encodes each block into a block on n bits.

Therefore, the parameters of the code are the size k of the input blocks, the size n of the output blocks, the number of blocks m, and the $k \times n$ polynomials.

To simplify this presentation, we are going to explain the mechanisms of a convolutional code encoding all bits of the source message one by one, that is, $k = 1$. Thus, one considers n generator polynomials of maximum degree m.

The source is represented by an infinite sequence of bits $(S_i)_{i \geq 0}$. The bits of negative index are considered to be null to indicate the beginning of the message.

The set of the n generator polynomials can be written in the form of a matrix G over $\mathbb{F}_2$: $G = (g_{ij})$ has a size $m \times n$.

For each source bit of index l, one denotes $S(l)$ the line vector $S_l \cdots S_{l-m}$. Then, the bit S_l is encoded with the n bits

$$C(l) = S(l)G. \tag{4.9}$$

Therefore, each bit j of the code corresponds to the convolution $\sum_{i=0}^{m}(g_{ij}S_{l-i})$; hence, the name of convolutional codes.

Example 4.12 If the generator polynomials are $P_1 = X$ and $P_2 = X + 1$, one has $G = \begin{bmatrix} 0 & 1 \\ 1 & 1 \end{bmatrix}$. In this case, the message 100110100 will be encoded by 110100111001110100000.

Relation (4.9) gives – to encode the source $(S_i)_{i\geq 0}$ – the relation $C = SG_\infty$, where G_∞ is the infinite matrix

$$\begin{bmatrix} & & & 0 & 0 & 0 & 0 & 0 & 0 & \cdots \\ & G & & & & & 0 & 0 & 0 & \cdots \\ & & & G & & & & & & \cdots \\ 0 & 0 & 0 & & & & G & & & \cdots \\ 0 & 0 & 0 & 0 & 0 & 0 & & & & \cdots \\ \vdots & \vdots & \vdots & 0 & 0 & 0 & 0 & 0 & 0 & \cdots \\ \vdots & \vdots & \vdots & \vdots & \vdots & \vdots & 0 & 0 & 0 & \cdots \\ \vdots & \vdots & \vdots & \vdots & \vdots & \vdots & \vdots & \vdots & & \cdots \end{bmatrix}.$$

Thus, a convolutional code is a linear code, cyclic, on an infinite matrix (for a finite message of size N, the size of the matrix is nN).

One can also consider the code as the product of the message – represented by a list of coefficients of a polynomial – with each of the generator polynomials, followed by an interleaving. One recognizes the principle of stream encoding, where the bitwise encoding of a message on-the-fly corresponds to a linear operation on the whole message.

Exercise 4.43 *Check in the previous example that the encoded message can be obtained by products of polynomials.* *Solution on page 339.*

4.6.2 Shortest Path Decoding

Convolutional code are error-correcting codes. Thus, for the decoding, one assumes that one receives a message R, namely, the encoded message with errors. The decoding algorithm recovers the closest codeword to the received word with respect to the Hamming distance and gives the corresponding source message.

The principle of decoding is similar to the principles of dynamic programming and to the shortest path problem. The decoding algorithm is known as the *Viterbi's algorithm*.

4.6.2.1 State Diagram The *state diagram* of a convolutional code is an oriented graph having its nodes equal to the 2^m binary words of size m, corresponding to all the possible states of the input. Then, for any word $a_0 \cdots a_{m-1}$, one adds two edges corresponding to the two possible values of the next bit in the input: one towards $a_1 \cdots a_{m-1}0$ and the other towards $a_1 \cdots a_{m-1}1$.

Then, one tags each edge with the code produced by the corresponding input (a codeword of n bits).

Each codeword corresponds to a path running along the graph, that is to say a set of consecutive edges that can appear several times. In the same way, any path corresponds to a codeword.

Example 4.13 (Sequel of the Preceding Example) The state diagram for the code of generator polynomials $P_1 = X$ and $P_2 = X + 1$ is illustrated in Figure 4.8.

4.6.2.2 Encoding Lattice The *encoding lattice* follows the principle of the state diagram by extending it to all the stages of the practical encoding. Namely, the lattice contains, for each bit received in the input, a set of 2^m nodes as for the state diagram, and each edge links a word $a_0 \cdots a_{m-1}$ at stage i to the words $a_1 \cdots a_{m-1}0$ and $a_1 \cdots a_{m-1}1$ at stage $i + 1$. Each codeword corresponds to a path in this graph and reciprocally.

Example 4.14 (Sequel of the preceding example) The lattice of the code of generator polynomials $P_1 = X$ and $P_2 = X + 1$ is illustrated in Figure 4.9.

4.6.2.3 Viterbi's Algorithm Viterbi's algorithm consists of finding the path corresponding to the codeword closest to the received word. This is a common algorithm for finding the shortest path in an oriented graph without cycles, using dynamic programming. The weight of the edges corresponds to the Hamming distance between the received words and the codewords corresponding to the tags of the edges.

Exercise 4.44 *For the code of generator polynomials $P_1 = X$ and $P_2 = X + 1$, give the codeword closest to* 10010010011101111010 *and give the associated source message.*   *Solution on page 339.*

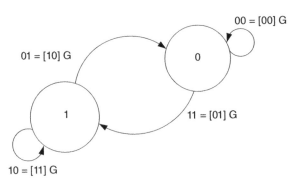

Figure 4.8 State diagram of the convolutional code of generator polynomials $P_1 = X$ and $P_2 = X + 1$

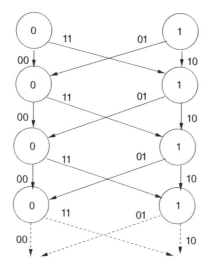

Figure 4.9   Lattice of the convolutional code generated by $P_1 = X$ and $P_2 = X + 1$

Algorithm 4.4 enables one to recover the correct codeword from the whole received word. In practice, in a convolutional code, it is more interesting to decode on-the-fly because the code may have an infinite length (actually, it could be a very long code). The idea is to consider that an error has an impact on a bounded number of codewords: this bound is called the *constraint length* of the code and it is equal to km. Hence, to decode on-the-fly, one applies Viterbi's algorithm to $T = km$ received words. Then, it is possible to decide that the first source word no longer depends on the last visited node. One restarts Viterbi's algorithm with the next received word and so on.

Now, let us look at the correction capacity of a convolutional code. One also uses the notion of the distance between two codewords, but because these code-words may have an infinite length, one speaks of a *free distance* of the code. As the code is linear, the free distance is the minimum weight of a sequence not completely null.

A sequence not completely null is obtained by starting from the sequence 000 ..., by passing through nonnull characters and then by ending with a sequence of zeros. In other words, the minimum weight of a sequence not completely null is exactly the minimum weight of a cycle starting and ending at zero. For the example in Figure 4.9, one notices that the shortest cycle passes through state 1 only once for the edges 11|01. Therefore, the free distance of the code is 3.

As a convolutional code is linear, Theorem 31 can be applied and the free distance gives the correction rate. Therefore, in the preceding example, the convolutional code is a 1-error-correcting code.

This means that this convolutional code is able to correct 1 error in each block of codewords of size equal to the constraint length.

Algorithm 4.4 Viterbi's Algorithm (Decoding of Convolutional Codes)

Input A binary word r of length T

Output The codeword c closest to r with respect to the Hamming distance

1: Mark with $m(v) \leftarrow \infty$ all the nodes v of the lattice.
2: Mark with $prec(v) \leftarrow \emptyset$ all the nodes v of the lattice.
3: For all nodes v at stage 0, $m(v) \leftarrow 0$.
4: **For** index i from stage 1 to stage T **do**
5:    **For** all nodes v of the lattice at stage i **do**
6:      **For** all edges uv towards the node v **do**
7:         Let d be the Hamming distance between the received word at stage i and the tag of the edge uv
8:         **If** $d + m(u) < m(v)$ **then**
9:            $m(v) \leftarrow d + m(u)$
10:           $prec(v) \leftarrow u$
11:        **End If**
12:      **End For**
13:    **End For**
14: **End For**
15: Let v be the node s. t. $m(v)$ has a minimum value among all nodes at stage T.
16: **For** index i from stage T to stage 0 **do**
17:    Let uv be the edge such that $prec(v) = u$
18:    Write on the left of the preceding word the codeword corresponding to the tag of uv.
19: **End For**

4.6.2.4 Systematic Convolutional Codes, Rate, and Puncturing

We have seen that a convolutional code processes a stream of data, or in *serial*, by interleaving several bits. Therefore, this mechanism induces an interleaving called a *serial interleaving*. As for block codes, a convolutional code is called *systematic* if the source bits directly appear in the output bits. In other words, the matrix G contains the identity matrix give or take a permutation of the columns. On the contrary, in a Nonsystematic Convolutional code (NSC), any output bit is the combination of several input bits.

Thus, in the output of a systematic convolutional code, one has a sequence of bits being the alternation between two sequences: on one hand, one has the input bits X and on the other hand, one has the bits Y computed by the encoder. The rate of such a convolutional code is – a priori – far worse than the rate of a block code. To increase the rate of the code while keeping a systematic code that enables one to decode the input, the *perforation* or *puncturing* consists of removing one part of the bits Y. For instance, let us assume that the code has a rate $\frac{1}{3}$; for each bit X_i in the input, one has 3 bits in the output and, hence, a sequence in the form $\ldots, X_i, Y_i, Y_i', X_{i+1}, Y_{i+1}, Y_{i+1}', \ldots$ By puncturing the bits at positions 2 and 5 modulo 6, one obtains the sequence $\ldots, X_i, Y_i', X_{i+1}, Y_{i+1}, \ldots$ The code one obtains is a systematic convolutional code of rate $\frac{1}{2}$ working as a punctured code.

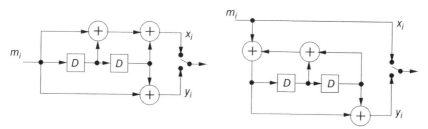

Figure 4.10 Systematic convolutional code of constraint length 3 transformed into a RSC code

4.6.2.5 *Recursive Convolutional Codes* A convolutional code is said to be *recursive* if some bits at the output of the encoder are reinjected into the input. A Recursive Systematic Convolutional codes (RSC) can be built from a systematic code by reinjecting into the input one of the outputs (see Figure 4.10, where D is a shift register or an LFSR). RSC are at the origin of the construction of turbo codes.

4.6.3 Turbo Codes

Turbo codes use the combination of two codes with interleaving. They often use RSC in which the output bits are reinjected into the input of the encoder; the decoding makes good use of this property and, hence, the name *turbo*.

Reinjecting the output bits into the input bits is an iterative process and then, the correction is performed round by round, each round correcting more and more errors. More precisely, only the corrections dealing with a small number of bits are performed during each round, the corrected word then being reinjected by the turbo code. From the latter, a new correction round is initiated. As the word has already been corrected, the old errors deal with a smaller number of bits and they can be corrected more efficiently. On the theoretical level, the guaranteed number of corrected errors in the worst case is not improved with respect to block codes. However, on the practical level, the number of badly corrected errors and even undetected errors is largely reduced. Besides, if some very particular words are able to avoid the correction, the interleaving system enables one to spread the errors in a pseudo-random way, uniformly among all the codewords. Hence, the *average* practical behavior of turbo codes on any inputs is very good. Now, we are going to give more details concerning the turbo technique.

4.6.3.1 *Parallel Composition* Contrary to cross-interleaved codes that use the serial interleaving of two codes, turbo codes generally use the parallel interleaving of two encoders C and C' (see Figure 4.11). The code C remains an RSC, and generally so does the code C'. Besides, in practice, one often has $C' = C$.

As the code C (respectively, C') is systematic, its output is an alternation of two sequences: on the one hand, one has the bits X of the source and on the other hand,

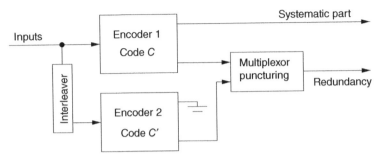

Figure 4.11   Parallel composition and interleaving of two RSC encoders

one has the bits Y (respectively, Y') computed by the convolutional encoder. A turbo encoding is performed in the following way:

- The source X is sent to the input of the encoder C whose systematic output is also the systematic output of the turbo encoder;
- The source X is interleaved before being sent to the input of the encoder C' whose output is Y';
- The outputs Y and Y' are used to build the output Z of the turbo code, also containing the bits of the source X.

With the code C and C' of rate $\frac{1}{2}$, one obtains a turbo code of rate $\frac{1}{3}$: at each clock cycle, three bits are generated in the output $Z = \ldots, X_i, Y_i, Y'_i, \ldots$
It is possible to increase the rate by multiplexing the outputs Y and Y' rather than concatenating them, which corresponds to a puncturing. For example, by multiplexing alternatively Y_i and Y'_i, the output becomes $Z = \ldots, X_i, Y_i, X_{i+1}, Y'_{i+1}, X_{i+2}, Y_{i+2}, \ldots$; one obtains a turbo code of rate $\frac{1}{2}$.

Exercise 4.45 (Parallel Turbo Code and Serial Turbo Code)   *Let C_1 and C_2 be two RSC codes of respective rates R_1 and R_2.*

1. *What is the rate of the turbo code obtained from a parallel composition of these two codes?*
2. *One can also build a serial turbo code by interleaving the output of C_1 and sending it to the input of C_2, as for cross-interleaved encoding. Then, the output of the serial turbo code is the output of C_2. What is the rate of a serial turbo code?*
3. *Compare the rate of the serial and parallel turbo codes when the rates are identical, that is, $R_1 = R_2 = r$. Study the case $r = \frac{1}{2}$.*

Solution on page 339.

4.6.3.2 Turbo Decoding From a practical point of view, it is difficult to decode a turbo code using the computation of the maximum of likelihood (Viterbi's algorithm): because of the interleaving, the complexity bound of this algorithm is prohibitive, in $O(2^L)$ where L is the size of a frame as well as the size of the interleaving. For this reason, the decoding of a turbo code uses the decoders of each of the two codes C and C' composing them, and it uses an iterative technique: the output of each decoder is reinjected into the input of the other decoder in order to compute the probability distribution of the input bits. As for a turbo engine, the fumes are reinjected to increase the performance.

For the decoding process, the demultiplexing and uninterleaving operators enable one to rebuild the sequences $\widetilde{X}$, $\widetilde{Y}$, $\widetilde{Y}'$ Corresponding, respectively, to the systematic output X – hence, the input – and to the outputs Y and Y' of the two encoders, but these sequences are potentially erroneous.

The correction is based on an iterative mechanism, and it uses the two decoders associated with the codes C and C' (see Figure 4.12). Each of the decoders computes at its end the APP of each source bit. This probability is used by the other decoder as information a priori on the value of the source bit. Hence, the decoder of C (respectively, C') computes the probability APP from the value $\widetilde{X}$ of the systematic input of the decoder, from the probability APP of the source computed by the decoder of C' (resp. C) and from its input $\widetilde{Y}$ (resp. $\widetilde{Y}'$). Hence, each decoder relies a priori on a probability distribution rather than on a predetermined value. For the decoding of each bit, this stage of reinjection/computation is iterated a given number of times (it is often 2). The decided value for the source bit at the end of the iteration is that having the highest probability.

4.6.3.3 Block Turbo Codes and Hybrid Turbo Codes It is possible to replace the convolutional encoders of a convolutional turbo code by block encoders. If the two encoders are block codes (for instance, two Reed–Solomon codes) one speaks about a *block turbo code*; if only one of the encoders is a block code and the other one is convolutional code, one speaks about an *hybrid turbo code*. The interest of replacing the convolutional codes by block codes is to increase the rate of the code. However, the block code must become probabilistic to make good use of the turbo effect. For this,

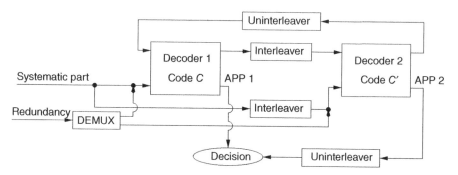

Figure 4.12 Iterative decoding of a turbo code

instead of correcting automatically with the closest codeword, one modifies the correction algorithm to rather indicate a set of close codewords with some weight (and a probability of being the correct codeword). Then, the final decision is made after the refinement of these weights as one goes along the turbo iterations.

4.6.3.4 *Performance and Practical Applications of Turbo Codes*   As a result of their efficiency, turbo codes have been integrated into many standards and, in particular, into spatial communications. The NASA has been using them since 2003 for all its spatial probes. The ESA (*European Space Agency*) used them also, for example, for the lunar probe Smart-1 (launched on September 27, 2003, in orbit around the Moon on November 15, 2004 and landing on it on September 3, 2006).

Turbo codes are intensively used for stream communications in general: cell phone industry (Asymmetric Digital Subscriber Line (ADSL) version 2, Universal Mobile Telecommunications System (UMTS), 3G, and 4G) or in the DVB-S2 standard for High-Definition Television (HDTV), normalized in 2005.

Among the parameters affecting the efficiency of a turbo code, the size of the interleaver plays a critical part; the performance decreases rapidly when this size decreases and inversely improves when it increases. Thus, one has to balance the trade-off between the cost and the performance depending on the application. Generally, the size L takes its value between 2^{10} and 2^{16}. Moreover, the interleaver is often built randomly, in order to avoid block interleavings. As for other codes, the rate also plays an important part. To obtain a code with a rate greater than $\frac{1}{3}$, a puncturing is necessary but it decreases the correction capacity. Finally, the number of iterations one has to perform during the decoding processes increases with respect to the size of the interleaving. Namely, one has to perform about nine iterations for a parallel turbo code with an interleaving of size $L = 16,384$ to have a good trade-off between the efficiency and the complexity.

The constraint length has a minor influence with respect to its impact on convolutional codes; that is why the turbo codes used in practice have a small constraint length, namely, 3 or 5.

COMPRESSION, ENCRYPTION, CORRECTION: AS A CONCLUSION

The encoding of messages over a readable alphabet through a channel enables one to optimize the size of the data sent, prevent the information from being affected by errors in the transmission, and ensure the confidentiality of the data. This section is a small practical conclusion to encoding in general.

Let M be the message issued, in the form of a string over some alphabet V, or, in an equivalent manner, in the form of a set of elements over V. One must be able to recover M from the message one has received (or possibly, one must receive an error alert if the message cannot be recovered). Let us assume that the issuer disposes of a compression utility $COMP$, a cipher $CRYPT$, and an error-correcting code $CORR$. The recipient disposes of the utilities $CORR^{-1}$, $CRYPT^{-1}$, and $COMP^{-1}$, which will enable him to recover the message. Then, what is the encoding process?

The message must be compressed before being encrypted. Indeed, if the message contains redundancy, this may not be removed by the encryption. Yet, a malicious third-party intercepting a message containing redundancy might use it as an angle of attack to find out the encryption method (the compression method is not secret). For the same reason, the message must be encrypted before undergoing the transformations meant to ensure its integrity (error detection and correction). Indeed, $CORR$ adds some organized and optimized redundancy, which must not be a weakness for the secret. Moreover, the error correction is necessarily the last part of the process: otherwise, a distorted message will not be corrected as soon as it is received and the error will be amplified by the first operators in the output of the channel (a decompression for instance). Finally, compression enables one to decrease the time of computation of the two other functions. Therefore, it is essential to perform the operations in this order.

Thus, the issuer generates the message

$$CORR(CRYPT(COMP(M)))$$

and sends it to the recipient. The received message M' corresponds to this

$$CORR(CRYPT(COMP(M))),$$

with potentially some distortion due to the transmission.

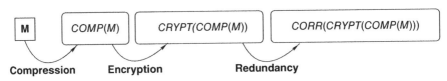

Figure 1   Encoding of a message M

The recipient applies

$$COMP^{-1}(CRYPT^{-1}(CORR^{-1}(M'))) = M.$$

If an error cannot be corrected, its detection might lead to an automatic return of the message to the issuer.

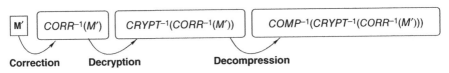

Figure 2   Decoding of a message $M' = CORR(CRYPT(COMP(M)))$

The message $CORR(CRYPT(COMP(M)))$ does not contain any information item which would enable one to recover M without having the correct functions. However, it must contain some information items to check its coherency and possibly to correct it. Finally, it must be as small as possible to minimize the length and the cost of the transmission.

These are the functions that were discussed separately in the preceding chapters. The first chapter ensures the cohesion of the whole book by providing a global method for using the different parts and by presenting the common theoretical basis.

Exercise 147 (The Casino)   *In a casino, one plays the number 421. The casino has a centralized server recording all the throws of dice on each table. On each table, a croupier sends the dice sequences to the server using infrared. The problem is to set up an architecture that enables one to perform a secure and reliable transmission of the information items.*

1. *Construction of a suitable Reed–Solomon code.*

   The infra-red contact is simulated using a symmetric binary channel of probability of error 0.001. Here, one wishes to ensure a reliable transmission over this channel.

   (a) *What is the error probability p when sending one byte?*

   (b) *To lesser the number of errors on the channel, when sending n bytes, one wishes to ensure the correction of $p \times n$ errors. Explain how to build a Reed–Solomon error-correcting code and specify:*

      i. *the ground field and the chosen value for n;*

      ii. *the degree of the generator polynomial and the rate of the code;*

      iii. *the maximum number of detected errors;*

      iv. *the dimension of a generator matrix of the code. How do you write this matrix from the coefficients of the generator polynomial?*

   (c) *For $d = 3, \dots, 10$, the following polynomials, with coefficients in $\mathbb{F}_2$, are primitive:*

TABLE 1   Several Primitive Polynomials in $\mathbb{F}_2[X]$

Degree d	Primitive Polynomial
3	$1 + \alpha + \alpha^3$
4	$1 + \alpha + \alpha^4$
5	$1 + \alpha^2 + \alpha^5$
6	$1 + \alpha + \alpha^6$
7	$1 + \alpha^3 + \alpha^7$
8	$1 + \alpha^2 + \alpha^3 + \alpha^4 + \alpha^8$
9	$1 + \alpha^4 + \alpha^9$
10	$1 + \alpha^3 + \alpha^{10}$

      i. *Give the polynomial which is used to implement the ground field and explain briefly how to perform the addition and the multiplication.*

      ii. *Give the expression of the generator polynomial with respect to α.*

   (d) *Compute the channel capacity. Compare it with the rate of the code.*

2. *Securing the communications.*

   How do you encode the sequences of dice in order to ensure that there is no cheating without the agreement of the croupier?

3. *Encoding throws.*

   One assumes that the dice of the casino are fair. One wishes to encode the sequences throws on the binary channel:

   (a) What is the entropy of a die ?

   (b) Propose an encoding algorithm with all the codewords having the same size.

   (c) Compute the average length of this encoding.

   (d) Propose a Huffman encoding.

   (e) Is it an optimal encoding ? If not, propose a more efficient encoding.

Solution on page 341.

PROBLEM SOLUTIONS

For several of the exercises, interactive solutions (using the free and open source mathematical software SAGE[1]) are available on the book's website. The general internet address is: http://foundationsofcoding.imag.fr. For the concerned exercises, the direct access to the associated SAGE worksheet is given in the beginning of the solution.

SOLUTIONS FOR CHAPTER 1

Exercise 1.1, on page 7.

- In this case, the code is not effective. The result can even be longer. For instance, if the message M is only composed of a sequence of alternating bits, that is, "01010101...01," then each sequence is encoded by "1 0 1 1." Certainly, this example is very unusual with faxes, but this demonstrates that the code has absolutely no guarantee of compression!

- In order to improve it, we could encode k consecutive "01" with "k01," and thus extend the code possibilities. Chapter 2 gives the keys for systematizing this kind of principle.

[1] http://www.sagemath.org/

Foundations of Coding: Compression, Encryption, Error Correction, First Edition.
Jean-Guillaume Dumas, Jean-Louis Roch, Éric Tannier and Sébastien Varrette.
© 2015 John Wiley & Sons, Inc. Published 2015 by John Wiley & Sons, Inc.
http://foundationsofcoding.imag.fr

Exercise 1.2, on page 9.
Trying all the possible keys is a reasonable method, as the space of possible keys is limited. We will see in Section 1.1.7 what size the key space must have to guarantee that such method is impossible.

Exercise 1.3, page 12 (foundationsofcoding.imag.fr/Ex/1.3.html).
CAESAR WOULD HAVE BEEN PROUD OF YOU!

Exercise 1.4, on page 14.
The complexity of this code is $O(n)$, where n is the number of pixels of the image. Indeed, the algorithm consists of passing through all the pixels, with a constant number of operations for the processing of each pixel.

Exercise 1.5, on page 16.
One can consider two possible attacks to justify the use of a new key for each message:

1. Assuming that one plaintext and its ciphertext are intercepted, one is able recover the key $K = \widetilde{M} \oplus M$.
2. Moreover, if $C_1 = M_1 \oplus K$ and $C_2 = M_2 \oplus K$ then $C_1 \oplus C_2 = M_1 \oplus M_2$. Notice that the key has disappeared. One can then analyze $M_1 \oplus M_2$ and determine fragments of M_1 and M_2.

Exercise 1.6, on page 16.
If the user does not have confidence in the machine used for the connection (it can capture a password typed in clear), he has to type the encrypted password. He acts in concert with the secured server to build a list of one-time-pad keys (for instance keys of eight characters if the password has eight characters) stored by the server. As for him, he will keep a printed version of this list. Each time he uses the system, the user has to manually encrypt his password with the next key on the list and send the encrypted password to the secured server, which will decrypt it and authenticate the user. Thus, the password is never transmitted in clear.

Exercise 1.7, page 18 (foundationsofcoding.imag.fr/Ex/1.7.html).

1. $P(C = 1) = 1/8; P(C = 2) = 7/16; P(C = 3) = 1/4; P(C = 4) = 3/16$.
2. $P(M = a|C = 1) = 1; \quad P(M = a|C = 2) = 1/7; \quad P(M = a|C = 3) = 1/4; \quad P(M = a|C = 4) = 0 \quad P(M = b|C = 1) = 0; \quad P(M = b|C = 2) = 6/7; \quad P(M = b|C = 3) = 3/4; P(M = b|C = 4) = 1$.
3. In this code, the knowledge of the ciphertext gives information about the plaintext, whereas a perfect encryption scheme should not give any information.

Exercise 1.8, on page 19.
We find an entropy of 0.469 (this is to be compared to the entropy of the uniform source 1). 0 will be a common character in the message. Hence, we can expect long sequences of 0. We can choose to encode these long sequences efficiently.

Exercise 1.9, on page 24.

The first, third, fourth, fifth, eleventh, and fourteenth spaces are larger. Suppose for instance that a single space encodes a 0 and a double space encodes a 1, then the number could be $10111000001001 = 11785$.

Exercise 1.10, on page 24.

1. As the messages M and the keys K are independent, we have directly $H(M, K) = H(M) + H(K)$ or else $H(M|K) = H(M)$ and $H(K|M) = H(K)$.

2. It follows from the construction of the Vernam code (with the xor) that: $H(M, K, C) = H(M, C) = H(M, K) = H(C, K)$. Indeed, knowing M and C we can recover the key $K = M \oplus C$. Similarly, knowing M and K, C does not add any information, and so on. Yet, for all X, Y, $H(X, Y) = H(Y) + H(X|Y) = H(X) + H(Y|X)$. We deduce that $H(C|K) = H(M|K)$, or else $H(K|C) = H(M|C)$.

3. If the source of the keys K is truly random, its entropy is maximal on the words of the same size using Property 1. Hence $H(K) \geq H(C)$, which proves that $H(K|C) \geq H(C|K)$. Combining the two previous results, we have then $H(M|C) \geq H(C|K) = H(M|K) = H(M)$. This proves that necessarily $H(M|C) = H(M)$. Thus, the knowledge of the ciphertext does not give any information about the plaintext.

Exercise 1.11, on page 25.

1. $0 = H(K|C_1 \ldots C_d) = H(K, C_1 \ldots C_d) - H(C_1 \ldots C_d)$ using Bayes equation. Thus $0 = H(K, M_1 \ldots M_d) - H(C_1 \ldots C_d)$. But the key is chosen uniformly at random, independently of the message. Therefore, using joint entropy, we have that $H(K, M_1 \ldots M_d) = H(K) + H(M_1 \ldots M_d)$. Finally, this shows that $H(K) + H(M_1 \ldots M_d) - H(C_1 \ldots C_d) = 0$.

2. $4.19 \cdot d$.

3. The entropy over a random 26 letters string is $-d \sum_a^z \frac{1}{26} \log_2 \left(\frac{1}{26} \right) \approx 4.70d$. So that a ciphertext entropy should approach this value for a good confusion and should be higher than that of a cleartext; therefore, a good cipher should satisfy $4.19 \cdot d \leq H(C_1 \ldots C_d) \leq 4.7 \cdot d$.

4. $d \geq \frac{H(K)}{4.70 - 4.19}$.

5. The key is a random permutation among the $26! \approx 4.033 \cdot 10^{26}$ possibilities. Therefore, $H(K) = \log_2(26!) \approx 88.382$ and $d > \frac{88.38}{4.70 - 4.19} \approx 173.15$: at least 174 letters of a ciphertext using a permutation of the alphabet are required to recover the used key.

Exercise 1.12, on page 30.

ECB: (and CTR) the blocks are independent.

OFB: C_1 is false, thus $M_1 = C_1 + Z_1$ is false, but this has no consequences on $M_2 = C_2 + Z_2$.

CFB: C_1 is false and $M_2 = C_2 + E(C_1)$, thus M_2 is false. But $M_3 = C_3 + E(C_2)$ only depends on C_2 and C_3 which are correct.

CBC: C_1 is false and $M_2 = C_1 + D(C_2)$, thus M_2 is false. But $M_3 = C_2 + D(C_3)$ only depends on C_2 and C_3 which are correct.

Exercise 1.13, on page 33.

Let a, b, and c be three integers in $\mathbb{Z}$. We have $\gcd(a, b) = 1$ and a divides bc. Bézout's theorem applied to a and b gives the existence of u and v in $\mathbb{Z}$, such that

$$ua + vb = 1.$$

This yields $uac + vbc = c$, and as a divides bc, there exists k, such that $bc = ka$, and in consequence $uac + vka = c$. This gives $(uc + vk)a = c$, which proves that a divides c.

Exercise 1.14, page 37 (foundationsofcoding.imag.fr/Ex/1.14.html).

Let us apply the extended Euclidean algorithm:

$$
\begin{array}{llllll}
(E_0): & 1 \times a & + & 0 \times b & = & a \\
(E_1): & 0 \times a & + & 1 \times b & = & b \\
(E_{i+1}) = (E_{i-1}) - q_i(E_i): & u_i \times a & + & v_i \times b & = & r_i
\end{array}
$$

We will only give the details of the computation of the first couple $(a, b) = (17, 50)$:

$(E_0):$	1×50	$+$	0×17	$=$	50	
$(E_1):$	0×50	$+$	1×17	$=$	17	$q_1 = 50/17 = 2$
						$r_1 = 50 \bmod 17 = 16$
$(E_2) =$	1×50	$+$	$(-2) \times 17$	$=$	16	$q_2 = 17/16 = 1$
$(E_0) - 2(E_1)$						$r_2 = 17 \bmod 16 = 1$
$(E_3) =$	$(-1) \times 50$	$+$	3×17	$=$	1	$q_3 = 16/1 = 16$
$(E_1) - (E_2)$						$r_3 = 16 \bmod 1 = 0$

For the two other couples, we have: $1 = 51 \times 11 + (-2) \times 280$ and
$5 = 3 \times 35 + (-2) \times 50$

Exercise 1.15, page 38 (foundationsofcoding.imag.fr/Ex/1.15.html).

1. As 17 and 50 are coprime, 17 is invertible modulo 50:

$$x = 17^{-1}.10 = 3.10 = 30 \quad \bmod 50$$

Thus $S = \{30 + 50.k, k \in \mathbb{Z}\}$.

NB: We compute the inverse using Bézout's algorithm: see previous exercise.

2. There exists $k \in \mathbb{Z}$ such that $35x = 10 + 50.k \iff 7x = 2 + 10k \iff 7x = 2$ mod 10.

As 7 and 10 are coprime, 7 is invertible modulo 10:

$$x = 7^{-1}.2 = 3.2 = 6 \quad \text{mod } 10.$$

Thus $S = \{6 + 10.k, k \in \mathbb{Z}\}$.

3. $\gcd(35, 50) = 5$ and 5 does not divide 11 hence $S = \emptyset$

Exercise 1.16, on page 38.

We use the class `mpz_class` of the C++ version of the GMP library[2] which implements integers with arbitrary precision.

```
#include <gmpxx.h>
typedef mpz_class My_Integer;

void AEE(const My_Integer a, const My_Integer b,
         My_Integer& d, My_Integer& x, My_Integer& y) {
    if ( b==0 )  {
        d = a;
        x = 1;
        y = 1;
    }
    else {
        AEE( b, a \% b, d, x, y );
        My_Integer tmp = x;
        x = y;
        y = tmp - (a / b) * y;
    }
}
```

Exercise 1.17, on page 39.

$x = 4.11.11^{-1 \bmod 5} + 5.5.5^{-1 \bmod 11}$ mod $55 = 44 - 25.2$ mod 55. Thus $x = -6$ mod $55 = 49$ mod 55 and hence $y = 49^{-1}$ mod 55 is projected into $4^{-1 \bmod 5} = 4$ mod 5 and into $5^{-1 \bmod 11} = 9$ mod 11. Thus we can recover

$$y = \left(4.11.11^{-1 \bmod 5} + 9.5.5^{-1 \bmod 11}\right) \quad \text{mod } 55.$$

To conclude, $y = 44 - 45.2$ mod $55 = -46$ mod $55 = 9$ mod 55.

Exercise 1.18, on page 39.

First of all, we only consider the system (3,4,5); Then $x = -1$ mod 3,4 and 5. Thus $x = -1$ mod 60. We have $x = 60.k - 1$.

Now let us verify the two other constraints modulo 2 and 6; $(60k - 1)$ mod $2 = -1$ mod $2 = 1$ and $(60k - 1)$ mod $6 = -1$ mod $6 = 5$. All constraints are satisfied thus $x = 60k - 1$.

[2]*Gnu Multiprecision package*, www.swox.com/gmp

Exercise 1.19, on page 40.

1. The only prime divisor of p^k is p. Hence, any number not coprime with p^k is a multiple of p. The form of such numbers is ap with $1 \le a < p^{k-1}$. Thus, there are $p^{k-1} - 1$ of them and we can conclude that $\varphi(p^k) = (p^k - 1) - (p^{k-1} - 1) = p^k - p^{k-1} = (p-1)p^{k-1}$.

2. We use a bijection between the set $\mathbb{Z}/m\mathbb{Z} \times \mathbb{Z}/n\mathbb{Z}$ and the set $\mathbb{Z}/mn\mathbb{Z}$: to $x \in \mathbb{Z}/mn\mathbb{Z}$ are associated two numbers $a = x \mod m$ and $b = x \mod n$. Reciprocally, using the Chinese Remainder Theorem with m and n coprime, if $(a, b) \in \mathbb{Z}/m\mathbb{Z} \times \mathbb{Z}/n\mathbb{Z}$, there exists a unique $x \le mn$ such that $x = a \mod m$ and $x = b \mod n$. As x is coprime with mn if an only if a is coprime with m and b is coprime with n, then the cardinal numbers of $\mathbb{Z}/m\mathbb{Z}^* \times \mathbb{Z}/n\mathbb{Z}^*$ and $\mathbb{Z}/mn\mathbb{Z}^*$ are equal.

3. From the previous questions, we can deduce that – having the prime factor decomposition $n = \prod p_i^{k_i}$ - we have $\varphi(n) = \prod (p_i - 1)p_i^{k_i-1}$.

Exercise 1.20, on page 40.

1. First, let us show that Ψ is a ring homomorphism:
   - $\Psi(0) = (0, \dots, 0)$, the neutral element for the operation "+" in $\mathbb{Z}/n_1\mathbb{Z} \times \dots \times \mathbb{Z}/n_k\mathbb{Z}$
   - $\Psi(1) = (1, \dots, 1)$, the neutral element for the operation "." in $\mathbb{Z}/n_1\mathbb{Z} \times \dots \times \mathbb{Z}/n_k\mathbb{Z}$
   - basic properties of modular arithmetic:

$$\begin{cases} a = b \mod n \\ c = d \mod n \end{cases} \implies \begin{cases} a + c = b + d \mod n \\ a.c = b.d \mod n \\ . \end{cases}$$

We deduce $\Psi(a + b) = \Psi(a) + \Psi(b)$ and $\Psi(a.b) = \Psi(a).\Psi(b)$

Now let us show that Ψ is injective. For this, as Ψ is a homomorphism, we show that $Ker(\Psi) = \{a \in \mathbb{Z}/N\mathbb{Z} \ / \Psi(a) = (0, \dots, 0)\} = \{0\}$.

We already have $\{0\} \subset Ker(\Psi)$. Reciprocally, let $a \in Ker(\Psi)$.

$\Psi(a) = (0, \dots, 0) \implies \forall i \in [1, k] : a$ a multiple of n_i. As the n_i are pairwise coprime, we deduce that a is a multiple of their product N. Thus $a = 0 \mod N$: $Ker(\Psi) \subset \{0\}$.

We compare the sizes of the spaces to conclude.

$$|\mathbb{Z}/N\mathbb{Z}| = N = \prod_{i=1}^{k} n_i = |\mathbb{Z}/n_1\mathbb{Z} \times \dots \times \mathbb{Z}/n_k\mathbb{Z}|$$

2. $\gcd(N_i, n_i) = 1$: there exists $u_i \in \mathbb{Z}$, such that $u_i N_i = 1 \mod n_i$. Then, let:

$$\Psi^{-1}(a_1, \dots, a_k) = a = \sum_{i=1}^{k} a_i u_i N_i \mod N$$

a satisfies the relation: $\forall i \in [1, k]$, $a = a_i u_i N_i = a_i \mod n_i$.

3. Ψ^{-1} is an isomorphism, a is unique (modulo N), and is the solution of the given system.

Exercise 1.21, on page 40.
This problem amounts to solving the following system

$$\begin{cases} x = 3 \mod 17 \\ x = 4 \mod 11 \\ x = 5 \mod 6. \end{cases}$$

17, 11 and 6 and pairwise coprime: according to the previous exercise, this system has a unique solution modulo $N = 1122$. Hence we have to compute $\Psi^{-1}(a_1, a_2, a_3)$ with $a_1 = 3$, $a_2 = 4$ and $a_3 = 5$.

- $N_1 = 11 \times 6 = 66$ and $u_1 = N_1^{-1} = 66^{-1} = 15^{-1} = 8 \mod 17$.
- $N_2 = 17 \times 6 = 102$ and $u_2 = N_2^{-1} = 102^{-1} = 3^{-1} = 4 \mod 11$.
- $N_3 = 17 \times 11 = 187$ and $u_3 = N_3^{-1} = 187^{-1} = 1^{-1} = 1 \mod 6$.

We can deduce that

$$\begin{aligned} \Psi^{-1}(a_1, a_2, a_3) &= a_1 u_1 N_1 + a_2 u_2 N_2 + a_3 u_3 N_3 \\ &= 8 \times 66 \times 3 + 4 \times 102 \times 4 + 1 \times 187 \times 5 \\ &= 4151 \\ &= 785 \mod 1122 \end{aligned}$$

Thus, the cook can expect at least 785 coins.

Exercise 1.22, on page 42.

1. We recall that in a finite commutative group $(G, \times, e)$ of cardinal number c, we have: for all $x \in G : x^c = e$ (Theorem 1). However, the cardinal number of the group of invertibles modulo n is $\varphi(n)$.
   After factoring of n, we compute $\varphi(n)$. Then we only need to compute $x^{-1} = x^{\varphi(n)-1} \mod n$ using exponentiation by squaring.
   - $63 = 3^2 \times 7$: $\varphi(63) = 3 \times 2 \times 6 = 36$.   Hence $22^{-1} \mod 63 = 22^{35} \mod 63 = 43 \mod 63$.

- $\varphi(24) = 2 \times 4 = 8$; thus $x^{8 \times u} = 1 \mod 24$. We deduce that $5^{2001} = 5 \mod 24$.

2. If $n_i = p_i^{\delta_i}$; then the n_i are pairwise coprime.
   - Algorithm 1: use the extended Euclidean algorithm.
   - Algorithm 2: use Euler's theorem and modular exponentiation. According to Euler's theorem, $y^{\varphi(n)} = 1[n]$. After the computation, we have $\varphi(n), y^{-1}[n] = y^{\varphi(n)-1}[n]$.

     NB: factoring N permits the computation of $\varphi(N)$.
   - Algorithm 3: use the Chinese remainder theorem and Euler's theorem on every prime number.

     Let $N = \prod p_i^{\delta_i}$ be the prime factor decomposition of N, and let $n_i = p_i^{\delta_i}$. First of all, we can compute the inverse of $y \mod n_i$ using Euler's theorem for all i. $y_i^{-1} = y_i^{\varphi(n_i)-1} \mod n_i$ with $\varphi(n_i) = n_i \left(1 - \dfrac{1}{p_i}\right)$. Thus, we compute the remainders of the inverses modulo n_i and we get the inverse using the Chinese remainder theorem. Let $N_i = N/n_i$. According to the Chinese remainder theorem,

$$
y^{-1}[N] = \left(\sum_{i=1}^{k} y^{-1} \mod n_i . N_i . N_i^{-1} \mod n_i \right) \mod N
$$

For example, let y be the inverse of 49 mod 55. Then $y = 4^{-1[5]} = -1[5]$ and $y = 5^{-1[11]} = -2[11]$. Hence $y = 9[55]$.

Exercise 1.23, on page 52.

First of all, one has $\Psi(0) = 0_K, \Psi(1) = 1_K, \Psi(n_1 + n_2) = \Psi(n_1) + \Psi(n_2)$. Then, since the multiplication of elements in K is distributive on the addition, one obtains

$$
\Psi(n_1) \times \Psi(n_2) = \underbrace{(1_K + 1_K + \dots + 1_K)}_{n_1} \times \underbrace{(1_K + 1_K + \dots + 1_K)}_{n_2}
$$

$$
= \underbrace{(1_K \times 1_K + \dots + 1_K \times 1_K)}_{n_1 n_2} = \underbrace{(1_K + \dots + 1_K)}_{n_1 n_2} = \Psi(n_1 n_2).
$$

Thus Ψ is a ring homomorphism. Since K is finite and $\mathbb{Z}$ is infinite, Ψ is non-injective. Thus, there exists $n \neq 0$ such that $\Psi(n) = 0_K$ (if $\Psi(j) = \Psi(i)$ for some $j \neq i$ then $n = |j - i|$ can be chosen). Now let $\tilde{n}$ be the smallest $n > 0$ such that $\Psi(n) = 0$. If $\tilde{n}$ is not prime, set $\tilde{n} = n_1 n_2$. One has $\Psi(n_1) \times \Psi(n_2) = 0_K$. Thus $\Psi(n_1) = 0_K$ or $\Psi(n_2) = 0_K$ (K is field. Hence all its nonzero elements are invertible). Therefore, there exists p prime such that $\Psi(p) = 0_K$.

As for the uniqueness of p: if p_1 and p_2 are prime numbers and $\Psi(p_1) = \Psi(p_2) = 0_K$. then, according to Bézout's theorem, there exist a, b such that $ap_1 + bp_2 = 1$. Hence $\Psi(1) = 0_K$, which is absurd.

Exercise 1.24, on page 52.

Let Ψ_p be the restriction of Ψ to $\mathbb{F}_p$. Set $k = \{\Psi_p(0), \Psi_p(1), \dots, \Psi_p(p-1)\}$; k is isomorphic to $\mathbb{F}_p$ (Ψ_p is injective and k and F_p have the same cardinal number); hence k is a subfield of K. K is a vector space over k; let m be its dimension. Since K is finite, m is finite and $|K| = k^m$.

Exercise 1.25, on page 52.

1. Necessary condition for P of degree $n \geq 2$ to be irreducible: P must be of the form $X^n + X^0 + \sum_{i=1}^{n-1} a_i X^i$ with $\sum_{i=1}^{n-1} a_i = 1 \mod 2$.
   This condition is sufficient for $2 \leq n \leq 3$. Hence
   if $n = 2$: $1 + X + X^2$ since neither 0 nor 1 is a root of this polynomial.
   if $n = 3$: $X^3 + X + 1$ and $X^3 + X^2 + 1$.

2. All polynomials satisfying the above condition which are not equal to $(1 + X + X^2)^2 = 1 + X^2 + X^4$. Hence:
   $X^4 + X^3 + X^2 + X + 1, X^4 + X^3 + 1, X^4 + X + 1$

3. Using polynomial $1 + X + X^2$, one has the elements $e_0 = 0$, $e_1 = 1$, $e_2 = X$, $e_3 = X + 1$. Then,

+	e_0	e_1	e_2	e_3
e_0	e_0	e_1	e_2	e_3
e_1	e_1	e_0	e_3	e_2
e_2	e_2	e_3	e_0	e_1
e_3	e_3	e_2	e_1	e_0

×	e_0	e_1	e_2	e_3
e_0	e_0	e_0	e_0	e_0
e_1	e_0	e_1	e_2	e_3
e_2	e_0	e_2	e_3	e_1
e_3	e_0	e_3	e_1	e_2

inverse	
e_0	−
e_1	e_1
e_2	e_3
e_3	e_2

Exercise 1.26, on page 55.

The calculation of the successive powers of X gives the following results:
$X^1 = X \mod P$; $X^2 = X^2 \mod P$; $X^3 = X^3 \mod P$; $X^4 = 1 + X^3 \mod P$; $X^5 = 1 + X + X^3 \mod P$; $X^6 = 1 + X + X^2 + X^3 \mod P$; $X^7 = 1 + X + X^2 \mod P$; $X^8 = X + X^2 + X^3 \mod P$; $X^9 = 1 + X^2 \mod P$; $X^{10} = X + X^3 \mod P$; $X^{11} = 1 + X^2 + X^3 \mod P$; $X^{12} = 1 + X \mod P$; $X^{13} = X + X^2 \mod P$; $X^{14} = X^2 + X^3 \mod P$; $X^{15} = 1 \mod P$.

So $P_1 \times P_2 = X^{12} \times X^{13} = X^{25 \mod 15} = X^{10} = X + X^3$. And $P_1 + P_2 = X^{12} + X^{13} = X^{12} \times (1 + X) = X^{12} \times X^{12} = X^{24 \mod 15} = X^9 = 1 + X^2$.

Exercise 1.27, page 59 (foundationsofcoding.imag.fr/Ex/1.27.html).

First for the non-2 and 3 characteristics: $b_2 = a_1^2/4 + a_2$; $b_4 = a_3 a_1/2 + a_4$ and $b_6 = a_3^2/4 + a_6$. Then $a = -b_2^2/3 + b_4$ and $b = 2b_2^3/27 - b_4 b_2/3 + b_6$.
Then, in characteristics 2 and 3, we have:

1. For $a_1 \neq 0 \in \mathbb{F}_{2^k}$: $b_0 = a_1^6$; $b_1 = a_1^3$; $b_2 = a_3 * a_1^3 + a_2 * a_1^4$; $b_4 = a_3^2 + a_4 * a_1^2$ and $b_6 = a_3^3/a_1^3 + a_2 * a_3^2/a_1^2 + a_4 * a_3/a_1 + a_6$. Then, with the second change of variable, one obtains $a_1^6 y^2 + a_1^6 xy = a_1^6 x^3 + b_2 x^2 - b_4^2/a_1^6 - b6$ so

that, after division by a_1^6, we have $a = b_2/a_1^6$ and $b = -b_4^2/a_1^{12} - b_6/a_1^6 = b_4^2/a_1^{12} + b_6/a_1^6$.

2. Using the change of variable one gets $y^2 + a_3 * y = x^3 + a_2^2 x + a_4 x + a_2 a_4 + a_6$ so that $c = a_3$, $a = a_2^2$ and $b = a_2 a_4 + a_6$.

3. One gets $b_2 = a_1^2 + a_2$; $b_4 = 2a_3 a_1 + a_4$ and $b_6 = a_3^2 + a_6$. Then, with the second change of variable, one obtains $a = b_2$ and $b = b_4^3/b_2^3 + 2b_4^2/b_2 + b_6$.

4. $a = 2a_3 a_1 + a_4$ and $b = a_3^2 + a_6$.

Exercise 1.28, on page 61.

1. For P, $1^2 = 1^3 - 1 + 1$; for Q, $(2 + T)^2 = 4 + 4T + T^2 = 4 + 4T - 2 = 2 + 4T$ and $(3 + T)^3 - (3 + T) + 1 = (27 + 3 \cdot 3^2 \cdot T + 3 \cdot 3 \cdot 3 \cdot T^2 + T^3) + 2 + 4T + 1 = (2 + 2T + 2 - 2T) + 3 + 4T = 2 + 4T$.

2. $(2 + T)(2 - T) = 4 - T^2 = 4 + 2 = 1$.

3. Let $\lambda = \frac{y_2 - y_1}{x_2 - x_1} = \frac{2 + T - 1}{3 + T - 1} = (1 + T)(2 + T)^{-1} = (1 + T)(2 - T) = 2 + T - T^2 = T - 1$. Then $x_3 = \lambda^2 - 1 - (3 + T) = T^2 - 2T + 1 - 4 - T = 2T$ and $y_3 = (T - 1)(1 - 2T) - 1 = T - 1 - 3T - 2T^2 - 1 = 2 + 3T$. To check that $R = (2T, 1 + 2T) \in \mathbb{E}$, we compute $(2T)^3 - 2T + 1 = 3(-2)T - 2T + 1 = 2T + 1$ and $(2 + 3T)^2 = 4 + 12T + 9T^2 = 1 + 2T$.

4. $\lambda = (3 - 1)/2 = 1$ and $(x_3 = 1^2 - 1 - 1 = 1, y_3 = 1(1 - 1) - 1 = -1)$ clearly belongs to the curve.

5. $\lambda = (3(3 + T)^2 - 1)2^{-1}(2 + T)^{-1} = (3(T^2 + 6T + 9) - 1)3(2 - T) = (3T)(1 - 3T) = 3T - 9T^2 = 3 + 3T$. So that $x_3 = (3 + 3T)^2 - 2(3 + T) = 4 + 3T + 4T^2 - 1 - 2T = T$ and $y_3 = (3 + 3T)(3 + T - T) - (2 + T) = 4 + 4T - 2 - T = 2 + 3T$. Now $T^3 - T + 1 = 1 - 3T = 1 + 2T$ and $(2 + 3T)^2 = 4 + 2T + 4T^2 = -4 + 2T = 1 + 2T$.

Exercise 1.29, on page 61.

$\lambda_1 = \frac{3-1}{2} = 1$, so that $[2]P = (1^2 - 2, 1(1 - (-1)) - 1) = (-1, 1)$. Then $\lambda_2 = \frac{3-1}{2} = 1$ and $[4]P = [2]([2]P) = (1^2 - 2(-1), 1(-1 - 3) - 1) = (3, 2)$. Finally $\lambda_3 = \frac{2-1}{3-(-1)} = \frac{1}{4} \equiv 2 \mod 7$, so that $[4]P \oplus [2]P = (2^2 - (-1) - 3, 2(-1 - 2) - 1) = (2, 0)$.

Exercise 1.30, on page 64.

Modulo 2, one has $1 = -1$, thus $x_4 = x_0 + x_2 + x_3 = 0 + 1 + 0 = 1$; $x_5 = x_1 + x_3 + x_4 = 1 + 0 + 1 = 0$; $x_6 = x_2 + x_4 + x_5 = 1 + 1 + 0 = 0$; $x_7 = x_3 + x_5 + x_6 = 0 + 0 + 0 = 0$; $x_8 = x_4 + x_6 + x_7 = 1 + 0 + 0 = 1$, etc.

Exercise 1.31, on page 68.

One has $p_i = 0, 1$ for all i, and $n = 21$. Then $e_0 = 3$, $e_1 = 2$, $e_2 = 6$, $e_3 = 3$, $e_4 = 2$, $e_5 = 2$, $e_6 = 1$, $e_7 = 0$, $e_8 = 1$, $e_9 = 1$. Set

$$K = \frac{0.9^2}{2.1} + \frac{0.1^2}{2.1} + \frac{3.9^2}{2.1} + \frac{0.9^2}{2.1} + \frac{0.1^2}{2.1} + \frac{0.1^2}{2.1} + \frac{1.1^2}{2.1} + \frac{2.1^2}{2.1} + \frac{1.1^2}{2.1} + \frac{1.1^2}{2.1}$$

Thus $K = 13.957$. As the alphabet is of size 10, the number of degrees of freedom is 9. With a probability 0.25 of error, one can then ensure that the obtained distribution is not uniform (The value of K is to be compared with 11.39). However, it is possible to reduce this probability of error since the other values in the table are greater than K. The probability of error being nonnegligible, one should not conclude anything concerning this test.

Exercise 1.32, on page 71.

1. The codeword for adbccab is 011110110110010, and the source word pour 1001101010 is bacbb.
2. One easily determines whether the code is instantaneous or not by comparing all codewords pairwise and by checking that none of them is a prefix of another one. Thus, it is an instantaneous code.
3. The entropy of the source is $H = 1.75$

Exercise 1.33, on page 72.

1. 0 is not a prefix of any other codeword, since all of them begin with a 1. All other codewords are of the same size, therefore, they can not be prefixes of one another.
   Another proof: one can draw a Huffman tree containing all the codewords (see Section 1.4.1.2).
2. $P(0\dots01) = P(0)\dots P(0)P(1) = p^k(1-p)$
3. For the codewords $(100, 101, 110, 111, 0)$, the ratios (number of bits of code per bit of the source) are $(3/1, 3/2, 3/3, 3/4, 1/4)$. Thus, the compression rate is $l = 3(1-p) + 3/2(1-p)p + (1-p)p^2 + 3/4(1-p)p^3 + 1/4p^4 = 3 - 3/2p - 1/2p^2 - 1/4p^3 - 1/2p^4$.

Exercise 1.34, on page 73.
($\Rightarrow$) One supposes that there exists an instantaneous code (that is to say it has the prefix property) whose words are of length $l_1, \dots, l_n$. We have shown that one can build its representation with a Huffman tree. The depth of the complete initial tree is l, and it has $|V|^l$ leaves.

One enumerates - at each cutting operation - the number of leaves of the initial complete Huffman tree which are removed. For a word of length l_i, it is the number of leaves of the complete tree of depth $l - l_i$, namely $|V|^{l-l_i}$ (one supposes that a leaf of a subtree of depth 0 is removed). For all these operations, one removes $\sum_{i=1}^n |V|^{l-l_i}$ leaves. However, one can not remove more leaves than the initial number, namely $\sum_{i=1}^n |V|^{l-l_i} \leq |V|^l$. Thus: $\sum_{i=1}^n \frac{1}{|V|^{l_i}} \leq 1$.

($\Leftarrow$) Reciprocally, one supposes that the inequality is satisfied. One wishes to build a Huffman tree whose codewords are of length $l_i, \dots, l_n = l$. All codewords are supposed to be sorted by increasing length.

One starts from a tree of depth l and then proceeds by induction.

To be able to choose a node in the tree, which corresponds to a word of lengths l_k, one needs to be able to find a complete subtree of depth $l - l_k$ in the tree. But all the previous cutting operations consist in removing subtrees of greater depth (corresponding to shorter words). Thus, if there remains at least $|V|^{l-l_k}$ leaves in the tree, the latter contains a subtree of depth $l - l_k$. Let us show that there actually remain $|V|^{l-l_k}$ leaves in the tree.

If one has already "placed" all words of length $l_1, \ldots, l_{k-1}$, then $\sum_{i=1}^{k-1} |V|^{l-l_i}$ leaves have been removed from the initial tree after the successive cutting operations. Hence, there remains $|V|^l (1 - \sum_{i=1}^{k-1} |V|^{-l_i})$ leaves. Yet, according to the Kraft inequality, we have:

$$\sum_{i=k}^{n} \frac{1}{|V|^{l_i}} \leq 1 - \sum_{i=1}^{k-1} \frac{1}{|V|^{l_i}}$$

Hence:

$$|V|^l \left(1 - \sum_{i=1}^{k-1} |V|^{-l_i} \right) \geq \sum_{i=k}^{n} |V|^{l-l_i} \geq |V|^{l-l_k}$$

Thus, one can place the words of length l_k and - by repeating the operations - build the Huffman tree. The Huffman code, whose codewords are of length $l_1, \ldots, l_n$, has the prefix property. This also proves the implication we postponed in the demonstration of Kraft's theorem.

Exercise 1.35, on page 75.

1. It is easy to find x such that $y = H(x)$. Hence, if one knows x, one computes $y = H(x)$. Then, one finds another x' such that $y = H(x')$.

2. It is easy to find x' knowing x, thus one chooses x randomly and generates x'.

Exercise 1.36, on page 75.
For example, let us take $x'_h = (x_h \oplus x_l)$ and $x'_l = 0$. Then, one has $x_h \oplus x_l = x'_h \oplus x'_l$, which is also true after having applied f.

Exercise 1.37, on page 76.
Let us suppose that H is not collision resistant. Then it is easy to find M and M' - distinct - such that $H(M) = H(M')$. One supposes that M is divided into $k \geq 1$ blocks of b bits and that M' is divided into $l \geq 1$ blocks, with $k \leq l$. Then, one sets $y_1 = h^{k-1}(M)$ and $y'_1 = h^{l-1}(M')$. Three cases are possible:

1. $M_1 \ldots M_{k-1} = M'_1 \ldots M'_{k-1} = u$. Then, $h(u||M_k) = h(u||M'_k \ldots M'_l)$ and a collision is found in h.

2. Otherwise, if $y_1 \neq y'_1$, a collision is found in h since $h(y_1) = H(M) = H(M') = h(y'_1)$.

3. Otherwise, $y_1 = y'_1$ and $M_1 \ldots M_{k-1} \neq M'_1 \ldots M'_{k-1}$. In the last case, one iterates the process with $y_i = h^{k-i}(M)$ and $y'_i = h^{l-i}(M')$ until $y_i \neq y'_i$.

Exercise 1.38, on page 77.

1. Let us suppose that h is not collision resistant. Then one is able to find y and y' such that $h(y) = h(y')$. Set $y = y_1||y_2$ and $y' = y_1'||y_2'$. Then, let $x = f(y_1)||f(y_2)$ and $x' = f(y_1')||f(y_2')$. One has $f(x) = f(x') = h(y)$. Thus f is not collision resistant.

2. The drawback of this strict construction is that it is extendable only to messages having a size a power of 2.

Exercise 1.39, on page 78.

1. Just swapping the blocks m_i and m_j gives: $GHASH_h(m_1, \ldots m_i, \ldots, m_j) = GHASH_h(m_1, \ldots m_j, \ldots, m_i)$.

2. The order of an element divides the ordre of the group of invertibles, 2^{128-1}. The latter has 9 distinct factors, therefore there are $2^9 = 512$ different possible values for the order of h.

3. If $h^i = h^j$ then $j - i$ is a multiple of o. Therefore, $j \geq o$ and the message must be at least this long.

4. It is better to choose a generator of the invertible group. Such an element would be of maximal order 2^{128-1} and therefore a collision would necessitate a message of 2^{95} GB.

5. It is equivalent to consider choosing a non zero element h or an index j with respect to a generator. Thus there is one chance over c_{14} that c_{14} divides a randomly chosen j, i.e. $\frac{1}{67280421310721} \approx \frac{1}{2^{46}}$, or that this happens only once every 64 quadrillion times.

6. If c_{14} divides j, or as shown previously, in every case occuring during say a human life, then the order of h is larger than c_{14}. Thus a collision would require more than c_{14} bits, i.e. be larger than 8000 GB.

Exercise 1.40, on page 83.

One first checks that there exists such a root: $31 - 1 = 2 \cdot 3 \cdot 5$ thus 6 divides 30. Then, one obtains $X^6 - 1 = (X^3 - 1)(X^3 + 1) = (X - 1)(X^2 + X + 1)(X + 1)(X^2 - X + 1)$. One looks for the roots of $X^2 + X + 1$ and $X^2 - X + 1$, if there exist such roots: these are respectively 5, -6, 6 and -5. Thus, one has six candidates for the 6th primitive roots, and only $\varphi(6) = \varphi(2)\varphi(3) = 2$ are valid: 1 is only a 1st primitive root. -1 is a 2nd primitive root. $5^3 = 5^2 \cdot 5 = -6 \cdot 5 = -30 = 1 \mod 31$. Thus 5 is a 3rd primitive root, and so is -6. Therefore, the two 6th primitive roots of unity modulo 31 are 6 and $-5 = 26$.

Exercise 1.41, on page 84.

4 does not divide 30, thus one has to consider an extension of $\mathbb{Z}/31\mathbb{Z}$.

One has $X^4 - 1 = (X - 1)(X + 1)(X^2 + 1)$ with $X^2 + 1$ irreducible modulo 31. Then, one considers the field $\mathbb{F}_{31^2} \simeq \mathbb{Z}/31\mathbb{Z}[X]/X^2 + 1$ in which 4 actually divides $31^2 - 1 = 960$.

One knows that the elements in $\mathbb{Z}/31\mathbb{Z}$ can not be 4th primitive roots. Thus, let us consider one root of $X^2 + 1$, denoted by i, which is known to be a 4th root. One checks that it is actually a primitive root: $i^2 = -1$, $i^3 = -i$ and $i^4 = -i^2 = 1$.

Exercise 1.42, page 85 (foundationsofcoding.imag.fr/Ex/1.42.html).

- The maximal period is $\varphi(p)$ and a is a primitive root.
- One gets $\varphi(p^e)$.
- $$\begin{bmatrix} x_n & 1 \\ x_{n+1} & 1 \end{bmatrix} \begin{bmatrix} a \\ b \end{bmatrix} = \begin{bmatrix} x_{n+1} \\ x_{n+2} \end{bmatrix} \quad \text{mod } m. \text{ Thus}$$

$$\begin{bmatrix} a \\ b \end{bmatrix} = (x_n - x_{n+1})^{-1} \begin{bmatrix} 1 & -1 \\ -x_{n+1} & x_n \end{bmatrix} \begin{bmatrix} x_{n+1} \\ x_{n+2} \end{bmatrix} \quad \text{mod } m.$$

- $x_{n+1} - x_n = a(x_n - x_{n-1})$ and $x_{n+2} - x_{n+1} = a(x_{n+1} - x_n)$. Thus $(x_{n+1} - x_n)^2 = (x_{n+2} - x_{n+1})(x_n - x_{n-1})$ if a is invertible modulo m. In the case where m is a factor of the difference of this equality, one is lead back to the previous case.
- $p = 1009$, $a = 238$, $b = 12$, $X_0 = 456$, $X_6 = 253$.

Exercise 1.43, on page 94.
By definition, t is a factor of $r - 1$. If $s \neq r$, then $s^{r-1} = 1 \mod r$ according to Fermat's theorem. Thus $m = 1 \mod r$, which implies that $p - 1 = 0 \mod r$. Then, $m = -1 \mod s$ by definition, and so $p + 1 = 0 \mod s$. Consequently, r divides $p - 1$, s divides $p + 1$ and t divides $r - 1$.

SOLUTIONS FOR CHAPTER 2

Exercise 2.1, on page 100.

1. 2^N files.
2. There is 1 file of size 0, 2 files of size 1, 4 files of size 2, ..., up to files of size 2^{N-1}. This gives an overall number of

$$\sum_{i=1}^{N-1} 2^i = \frac{2^N - 1}{2 - 1} = 2^N - 1$$

files of size strictly lower than N bits.

3. In such a compressor, at least two distinct files of N bits are compressed the same way. Therefore, there is a loss of information. Indeed, in this case, it will be impossible to determine which is the original message after compression. Otherwise, some compressed files need to contain more than N bits. In that case, there is no compression.

Exercise 2.2, on page 100.

From the previous exercise, we know that there are $2^{N-20} - 1$ files with strictly less than $N - 20$ bits. Therefore, among the 2^N files of N bits, not more than $2^{N-20} - 1$ of them can be compressed by more than 20 bits, without loss. This gives a ratio of

$$\frac{2^{N-20} - 1}{2^N} < \frac{2^{N-20}}{2^N} = 2^{-20} = \frac{1}{1,04,8576}.$$

Exercise 2.3, on page 105.

The code generated by the Huffman algorithm is

S	C
000	1
001	010
010	011
100	001
011	00011
101	00010
110	00001
111	00000

Its average length is $l = 1.05$. Hence, for each bit of the source, $l = 0.35$. This value is greater than the average length of the code in Exercise 1.33, but one has not necessarily to reconsider the optimal nature of the Huffman algorithm: one should compare with the fourth extension, which is better than the previous code.

The entropy S is

$$H(S) = 0.99 \log_2 \frac{1}{0.99} + 0.01 \log_2 \frac{1}{0.01} = 0.0808$$

Hence, the theorem is satisfied in all cases.

Exercise 2.4, on page 107.
The idea is to proceed by *rejection* (with a second toss if necessary) (Table 2).

TABLE 2   Die Simulation by Coin Toss

Coin toss	HHH	HHT	HTH	HTT	THH	THT
Throw of a die	1	2	3	4	5	6

If one gets TTH or TTT, the toss is rejected (thus, one can stop after two tosses as soon as he gets TT) and one restarts the three tosses (independent tosses).

Therefore, the average number of tosses N is

$$N = \frac{6}{8} * 3 + \frac{2}{8} * \left(2 + \frac{6}{8} * 3 + \frac{2}{8} \left(2 + \frac{6}{8} * 3 + \frac{2}{8} (\cdots) \right) \right) ;$$

hence,

$$N = \sum_{k=0}^{\infty} \left(\frac{2}{8} \right)^k \frac{6}{8} * 3 + \sum_{k=1}^{\infty} \left(\frac{2}{8} \right)^k 2 = \frac{6}{8} * 3 \frac{1}{1 - \frac{2}{8}} + \frac{2}{8} * 2 \frac{1}{1 - \frac{2}{8}} = 3 + \frac{4}{6}.$$

Thus, there is an average of $3(3 + \frac{2}{3}) = 11$ heads or tails for the three dice in the 421 game.

The entropy of the three fair dice being $3 * \left(6 * (\frac{1}{6}) * \log_2(6) \right) \approx 7.755$, this code is probably not optimal.

Indeed, the case of source extension with three dice enables one to build a code over eight coin tosses, because $6^3 = 216 < 256 = 2^8$. In this case, the average number of necessary tosses with rejection is closer to 8.5.

Exercise 2.5, on page 108.

1. $H(\text{fair die}) = \log_2(6) \approx 2.5850$; for this die, 2.5611.
2. Over $\{0,1,2\}$, using the Huffman procedure, we build the code, for example, (1-> 10 , 2-> 12 , 3-> 01 , 4-> 00 , 5-> 02 , 6-> 2) of (fixed) average length equal to $0.22 * 1 + (1 - 0.22) * 2 = 1.78$ digits. This is the optimal code (according to the theorem), and one can only obtain a better code (and still more than $\log_2(6)/\log_2(3) \approx 1.5850$) by encoding sequences of digits from the source.

3. Over $\{0,1\}$, a possible code is ($1\text{->}000$, $2\text{->}001$, $3\text{->}010$, $4\text{->}011$, $5\text{->}10$, $6\text{->}11$) of average length 2.6. This is also the optimal code.

Exercise 2.6, on page 109.

1. One encodes the sequences $\{1,2,3,4,51,52,53,54,55,56,61,62,63,64,65,66\}$ (there are 16 of them) with the 16 codewords of length 4.

2. Depending on the chosen code (and independently from the length of the sequences), one may obtain, for example, Tunstall($66\text{->}1111$ and $64\text{->}1100$): 11111100 and Huffman: $111|11|11|011$.

3. In order to encode two-digit long sequences, one needs 4 bits; hence, a yield of 2, and it is the same for one-digit long words; hence, a yield of 4. Thus, the average length per bit of the source is $2*0.22+2*0.18+4*0.60 = 3.2$.

Exercise 2.7, on page 113.

Number	Interval	Output
49991	$[40000; 59999]$	b
49991	$[48000; 51999]$	b
49991	$[49600; 50399]$	b
49916	$[46000; 53999]$	shift
49916	$[49200; 50799]$	b
49168	$[42000; 57999]$	Shift
49168	$[48400; 51599]$	b
49168	$[48400; 49679]$	a
91680	$[84000; 96799]$	Shift
91680	$[91680; 96799]$	c

Exercise 2.8, on page 114.

1. For example, $(a\text{->}0;b\text{->}10;c\text{->}110;d\text{->}111)$.

2. Thus a,b,c, and d require $4*8$ bits to be written and their codes require $1+2+3+3$ bits; hence, an overall of at least 41 bits.

3. In the case of the extension of a source on three characters, there are $4^3 = 64$ possible triplets, each of them written on 8 bits, and there are also 64 codes requiring an overall of at least $64*6$ bits.[3] Hence, one has to write at least $64*8+64*6 = 896$ bits in the compressed file.

---

[3]To see that this is a lower bound, one must consider a code of 64 words with some of these words of length strictly greater than 6 bits. Thus, this means that there are also words of length strictly lower than 6 bits. For instance, let us take a word of 8 bits and a word of 5 bits (e.g., 10101), and let us replace these two words with the two words of length 6 bits that directly extend the word of 5 bits in the code: 101010 and 101011. The code one obtains requires $8+5-6-6 = 1$ bit less in the table.

4. 18 ASCII characters: $8 * 18 = 144$ bits.

5. Compression by the Huffman: 0, 0, 0, 0, 0, 0, 0, 0, 0, 10, 110, 111, 10, 110, 111, 10, 110, 111; hence, $1 * 9 + 3 * (2 + 3 + 3) = 33$ bits, to which one adds the 41 bits of the table. In an extension of the source on three characters, the table (or the tree) would already require a memory space five times greater than the size of the initial file.

Exercise 2.9, on page 116.

1. $@a| 1| 0| 0| 0| 0| 0| 0| 0| @b| @c| @d$. Here the dynamic tree is $a->0$; $@->10$; $b->110$; $c->1110$; $d->1111$; thus the sequel of the compression process is 110| 1110| 1111| 110| 1110 and, just before the last character d, the tree has become $a->0$; $@->100$; $b->101$; $c->110$; $d->111$. Therefore, the last character d is encoded by 111. As a consequence, the full compression ignoring the first character $@$ is ASCII(a) 10000000 1ASCII(b) 10ASCII(c) 10ASCII(d) 110 1110 1111 110 1110 111, that is to say an overall of only $8 + 8 + 1 + 8 + 2 + 8 + 2 + 8 + 3 + 4 + 4 + 3 + 4 + 3 = 66$ bits (to be compared with the $33 + 41 = 74$ bits one gets using the static Huffman code).

2. When considering the groups of three characters, this gives the particular case $@aaa| 1| 0| @bcd| 10| 10$; thus ASCII(aaa)101ASCII(bcd)1010, which only requires an overall of $3 * 8 + 1 + 1 + 1 + 3 * 8 + 4 = 55$ bits.

Exercise 2.10, on page 118.

1. For example, 6801314131413141312222611, where 68 encodes the dimensions of the image (6×8 pixels), and each of the following digits encodes the number of consecutive pixels having the same color (alternation white–black).

2. Twenty five bytes (or 13 when restraining ourselves to blocks of length 16) instead of 6. This is quite a loss with small images!

3. One denotes a block using a bit concatenated with four other bits in hexadecimal (for instance, 0F = [0, 1, 1, 1, 1]). The first bit indicates whether one is encoding a color or a run. Therefore, one obtains 6, 8, 00, (13, 0F), 00, (14, 0F), 00, (13, 0F), 00, (14, 0F), 00, (13, 0F), 00, (14, 0F), 00, (13, 0F), 00, 0F, 0F, 00, 00, 0F, 0F, 00, 00, (16, 0F), 00, 0F. Here, one has $34 * 5 + 2 * 8 = 186$ bits = 24 bytes instead of $6 * 8 * 4 + 2 * 8 = 192$ bits = 26 bytes. One can also delete the bit set to 0 in the color following a run in order to obtain 6, 8, 00, 13F, 00, 14F, 00, 13F, 00, 14F, 00, 13F, 00, 14F, 00, 13F, 00, 0F, 0F, 00, 00, 0F, 0F, 00, 00, 16F, 00, 0F. This represents only $8 * 4 + 26 * 5 + 2 * 8 = 178$ bits = 23 bytes.

4. The repetition character is FF. One encodes black with "00" and white with "FE."
   Therefore, one has 6, 8, 00, (FF, 3, FE), 00, (FF, 4, FE), 00, (FF, 3, FE), 00, (FF, 4, FE), 00, (FF, 3, FE), 00, (FF, 4, FE), 00, (FF, 3, FE), 00, FE, FE, 00, 00, FE, FE, 00, 00, (FF, 6, FE), 00, FE. Hence, $8 * 4 + 34 * 8 + 2 * 8 = 320$ bits = 40 bytes instead of $6 * 8 * 8 + 2 * 8 = 400$ bits 50 bytes.

5. 6, 8, 00, (FF, 6, FE), 00, (FF, 6, FE), 00, FE, 00, (FF, 4, FE), 00, 00, FE, 00, (FF, 6, FE), 00, (FF, 6, FE), 00, FE, 00, 00, (FF, 3, FE), 00, 00, FE. Hence $6 * 4 + 29 * 8 + 2 * 8 = 272$ bits = 34 bytes instead of 50.

Exercise 2.11, on page 120.

1. "0123321045677654" and "0123456701234567."

2. "0123012345670123" and "0123456777777777." The second string clearly has a reduced entropy.

3. The frequencies are equal to $1/8$; therefore, entropy is maximal and 3 bits are necessary for each character. Thus one needs $3 * 16/8 = 6$ bytes.

4. For the first string, the entropy is $H = 4(\frac{3}{16}\log_2(\frac{16}{3})) + 4(\frac{1}{16}\log_2(16))$ $\approx 1.81 + 1 = 2.81$. Therefore, the Huffman code is 00, 01, 100, 101, 1100, 1101, 1110, 1111; hence, a code on only $2*3*2+2*3*3+4* 1*4 = 46 = 5.75$ bytes. For the second string, the result is even better: $H = 7(\frac{1}{16}\log_2(16)) + (\frac{9}{16}\log_2(\frac{16}{9})) = 1.75 + .47 = 2.22$. Then the Huffman gives 00, 01, 100, 101, 1100, 1101, 111, 1, that is to say only $2 + 2 + 3 + 3 + 4 + 4 + 3 + 1 * 9 = 30 = 3.75$ bytes!

5. Extended Huffman gives 000, 001, 010, 011, 1, respectively, for 12, 34, 56, 67 and 77. Hence, $4 * 3 + 4 * 1 = 16 = 2$ bytes are necessary, but with a table of size 256 bytes instead of eight triplets, hence, 3 bytes are necessary.

6. Thus, "move-to-front" followed by some statistical code is a "locally adaptive statistical code."

7. For $k = 1$, one gets "0123220345676644" and "0123456770123457" of respective entropies $H = 2.858$ and $H = 2.953$. For $k = 2$, one gets "0123112345675552" and "0123456777012347"; hence, $H = 2.781$ and $H = 2.875$.

Exercise 2.12, on page 122.

1. The initial string can be recovered from L and the primary index but not from F!!!

2. Here, $S = L =$"sssssssssh." Thus, the move-to-front strategy gives C=(1, 0, 0, 0, 0, 0, 0, 0, 1), which is also the output of the Huffman algorithm.

3. Practical implementation:

   (a) One can use the position of the first character of the source message.

   (b) **Input** A string S (of length n). Two integers i and j.
   Output "permutation i is before permutation j" or "permutation j is before permutation i"
   1: **While** No answer **do**
   2:   **If** $S[i] < S[j]$ **then**
   3:     Reply "permutation i is before permutation j"
   4:   **elsif** $S[i] > S[j]$ **then**

5:     Reply "permutation j is before permutation i"

6:    **else**

7:     $i \leftarrow (i + 1) \mod n$ and $j \leftarrow (j + 1) \mod n$

8:    **End If**

9: **End While**

(c) One has to store the source message S, the vector T containing the permutation indexes and eventually L, which is computed using $S[T[i] - 1]$.

(d) The primary index is the one for which $T[i] = 1$, because it is the location of the first line.

Exercise 2.13, on page 123.

1. One has to be careful to put the last letter ("f" in our case) in the last triplet and, therefore, to consider 10 of them. For the last triplet, the distance must obviously be greater than the length of the repetition. $(0, 0, a)$ $(0, 0, b)$ $(0, 0, c)$ $(0, 0, d)$ $(0, 0, e)$ $(0, 0, f)$ $(6, 6, a)$ $(12, 10, f)$.

2. Here, the distance and the length have to be encoded on 3 bits. Therefore, they are included between 0 and 7. Thus one must cut the last block in two parts: $(0, 0, a)$ $(0, 0, b)$ $(0, 0, c)$ $(0, 0, d)$ $(0, 0, e)$ $(0, 0, f)$ $(6, 6, a)$ $(6, 6, b)$ $(6, 3, f)$.

Exercise 2.14, on page 125.
Compression of "BLEBLBLBA" with LZW gives the following result:

String		Display		Dictionary		
B	⇝	42		BL	↔	80
L	⇝	4C		LE	↔	81
E	⇝	45		EB	↔	82
BL	⇝	80		BLB	↔	83
BLB	⇝	83		BLBA	↔	84
A	⇝	41				

If one uncompresses this output without treating the particular case, one obtains – because of the delay of setting up the dictionary – the following output:

Code		Display		Dictionary		
42	⇝	B				
4C	⇝	L		BL	↔	80
45	⇝	E		LE	↔	81
80	⇝	BL		EB	↔	82
83	⇝	???				

As code 83 is unknown, one is exactly faced with the particular case and the next group is necessarily the repetition of the previous one (*BL*) increased with the first letter of the group, namely, *BLB*. Here one clearly notices that treating the particular case enables one to update the dictionary one step earlier. Hence, any string repeated consecutively two times can be correctly treated during decompression.

Exercise 2.15, on page 126.

1. $(0, 0, a)$; $(0, 0, b)$; $(1, 1, a)$; $(0, 0, r)$; $(3, 3, b)$; $(4, 2, b)$; $(10, 5, a)$.

2. "0, 0, 1, 0, 3, 4, 10" becomes "1-0, 0, 1-1, 00, 1-3, 1-4, 1-10" with the dynamic Huffman. "a, b, a, r, b, b, a" becomes "1-a, 1-b, 00, 1-r, 010, 010, 010". Hence, the gzip code is $(10, 0, 1a)$; $(0, 0, 1b)$; $(11, 1, 00)$; $(00, 0, 1r)$; $(13, 3, 010)$; $(14, 2, 010)$; $(110, 5, 010)$.

3. f1.gz: $(0, 0, a)$; $(0, 0, b)$; $(1, 1, a)$; $(0, 0, r)$; $(3, 3, b)$,
   thus $(10, 0, 1a)$; $(0, 0, 1b)$; $(11, 1, 00)$; $(00, 0, 1r)$; $(13, 3, 010)$
   f2.gz: $(0, 0, b)$; $(0, 0, a)$; $(2, 1, b)$; $(3, 1, a)$; $(0, 0, r)$; $(3, 2, a)$,
   which becomes $(10, 0, 1b)$; $(00, 0, 1a)$; $(12, 1, 00)$; $(13, 1, 01)$; $(00, 0, 1r)$; $(011, 2, 010)$.

4. The first distance for the first character of a file is necessarily 0. Therefore, the first two characters of a gzip file are necessarily 10. Besides, because @ is forced with the bit 1, one can find the sequence 10 only at the beginning of a file. Therefore, anytime one meets the sequence 10 in the occurrence string of the file, one knows that it implies restarting all dynamic Huffman's encodings. This singularity implies that there is no structural difference between a single file compressed with gzip and a sequence of compressed files. If one uncompresses with gunzip f3.gz, one will get as a result a file whose content is identical to f1 appended with f2.

5. One can specify the maximum size of the window in LZ77. With a smaller window, the algorithm is faster but compression is less efficient.

Exercise 2.16, page 131 (foundationsofcoding.imag.fr/Ex/2.16.html).

1. From the definition in Figure 1.20, one can extract the formula for the DCT that yields $\begin{bmatrix} 102 & 3\sqrt{3} & -12 \\ -9/2\sqrt{3} & 0 & 0 \\ 3/2 & 3/2\sqrt{3} & -21/2 \end{bmatrix}$ and $\begin{bmatrix} 102 & 5 & -12 \\ -8 & 0 & 0 \\ 1 & 2 & -11 \end{bmatrix}$, after flooring.

2. The quantification matrix is $\begin{bmatrix} 4 & 3 & 2 \\ 3 & 3 & 2 \\ 2 & 2 & 2 \end{bmatrix}$ which yields $\begin{bmatrix} 25 & 1 & -6 \\ -3 & 0 & 0 \\ 0 & 1 & -6 \end{bmatrix}$ as the lossy compressed DCT.

Exercise 2.17, on page 132.

1. For $(4 : 2 : 2)$, there are two (U, V) pairs on the first row and two on the second row. This is thus a half horizontal resolution and a full vertical one for a total of eight values for Y and $2 + 2$ values for U and V. Thus the gain is $\frac{8+(2+2)2}{8*3} = \frac{2}{3}$.

2. $(4 : 2 : 0)$ is half horizontal and half vertical resolution, with a gain of $\frac{8+(2+0)*2}{8*3} = \frac{1}{2}$.

3. $(4 : 1 : 1)$ is quarter horizontal resolution and full vertical resolution with also a gain of $\frac{8+(1+1)*2}{8*3} = \frac{1}{2}$.

Exercise 2.18, on page 133.

1. One can compute the average value of a given coefficients and its neighbors as the expected distribution: $C^*_{i,j} = \frac{1}{9} \sum_{\delta=-1}^{1} \sum_{\epsilon=-1}^{1} C_{i+\delta,j+\epsilon}$ for a coefficient in the center of the 8×8 block. Border coefficients would consider only their neighbors within their 8×8 block.

2. Using this expected distribution, one can use a χ^2 test with the parameter K measuring the gap between the expected distribution and the observed distribution where the sum is over close 8×8 blocks of the picture:

$$K = \sum_i \sum_j \frac{(C^*_{i,j} - C_{i,j})^2}{C_{i,j}}.$$

Then Table 1.7 could reveal anomalous distributions.

Exercise 2.19, on page 134.

1. 720×576 pixels each with $3\frac{1}{2}$ bytes of color information and $25 \times 90 \times 60$ such images gives 78.21 *GB*.

2. The compression factor is $\frac{78.21 \times 1024}{800}$, more than a hundred times!

SOLUTIONS FOR CHAPTER 3

Exercise 3.1, on page 142.

1. $|\mathbb{Z}_{26}^*| = \varphi(26) = \varphi(13 \times 2) = 12$ and $\mathbb{Z}_{26}^* = \{1, 3, 5, 7, 9, 11, 15, 17, 19, 21, 23, 25\}$.

2. $15 \in \mathbb{Z}_{26}^*$. Therefore, the key is valid and one obtains the successive ciphertexts 7, 22 et 11.

3.
$$D_{(a,b)} : \begin{array}{ccc} \mathbb{Z}_n & \longrightarrow & \mathbb{Z}_n \\ y & \longrightarrow & D_{(a,b)}(y) = a^{-1}(y - b) \mod n. \end{array}$$

4. (a) Exhaustive search requires around $\mathcal{O}(|\mathbb{Z}_{26}^*|.|\mathbb{Z}_{26}|)$ tests for the key. Thanks to frequency analysis, one is able to propose some correspondences for the most common letters. Hence, one is almost certain that the letter 'e' is encrypted with 'o.' One deduces the equation:

$$E_{(a,b)}('e') = 'o' \iff 4a + b = 14 \mod 26.$$

From here, two methods are possible:

- One solves the Diophantine equation $4a + b = 14$ in $\mathbb{Z}$ and one deduces the set of possible solutions in $\mathbb{Z}_{26}$. Then, one checks the admissible keys (for $a \in \mathbb{Z}_{26}^*$) until one finds the right one. One recalls that, in order to solve this equation, one first solves the homogeneous equation $4a + b = 0$ (the set of solution is $S_H = \{(-k, 4k), k \in \mathbb{Z}\}$). Then, one finds a particular solution (a_0, b_0) (for instance$(0,14)$; one may also compute Bézout numbers using the extended Euclidean algorithm) and one deduces the set of solutions in $\mathbb{Z}$. Hence, one finds $S = \{(-k, 14 + 4k), k \in \mathbb{Z}\}$. One deduces the admissible values for k to find the solutions in $\mathbb{Z}_{26}$: $0 \le a < 26 \Rightarrow -25 \le k \le 0$. Then, one tries the corresponding admissible keys. One gets the following results:

  - $k = -25 \Rightarrow K = (a, b) = (1, 10)$. One decrypts using this key: `csqxre yirvesa, uar af srvre...` This is not the right key.

  - $k = -23 \Rightarrow K = (a, b) = (3, 2)$. One decrypts using this new key: `maitre corbeau, sur un arbre...` This makes sense in French: we have found the right key!

  Commonly, one has - at most - $\mathcal{O}(|\mathbb{Z}_{26}^*|)$ attempts.

- One extracts another probable relation (for the ciphertext related to 's,' which is the second most frequent letter after 'e') and one solves the corresponding system. Given the results of statistical analysis, one checks successively the following systems:

$$(1) \begin{cases} e_{(a,b)}('e') = 'o' \\ e_{(a,b)}('s') = 'b' \end{cases} \iff \begin{cases} 4a + b = 14 & \mod 26 \\ 18a + b = 1 & \mod 26 \end{cases}$$

$$(2) \begin{cases} e_{(a,b)}(\text{'e'}) = \text{'o'} \\ e_{(a,b)}(\text{'s'}) = \text{'c'} \end{cases} \iff \begin{cases} 4a + b = 14 \quad \text{mod } 26 \\ 18a + b = 2 \quad \text{mod } 26 \end{cases}$$

$$(3) \begin{cases} e_{(a,b)}(\text{'e'}) = \text{'o'} \\ e_{(a,b)}(\text{'s'}) = \text{'e'} \end{cases} \iff \begin{cases} 4a + b = 14 \quad \text{mod } 26 \\ 18a + b = 4 \quad \text{mod } 26. \end{cases}$$

$\vdots$

The last system is shown to be the right one.

Therefore, the encryption key is $K = (a, b) = (3, 2)$.

(b) One recovers the plaintext using the key:

> maitre corbeau, sur un arbre perche,
> tenait en son bec un fromage.
> maitre renard, par l'odeur alleche
> lui tint a peu pres ce langage:
> "he! bonjour, monsieur du corbeau,
> que vous etes joli! que vous me semblez beau!
> sans mentir, si votre ramage
> se rapporte à votre plumage,
> vous etes le phenix des hotes de ces bois."

Exercise 3.2, on page 146.

The two blocks L_i and R_i are obtained from the previous blocks and from the round key K_i by $L_i = R_{i-1}$ and $R_i = L_{i-1} \oplus f(R_{i-1}, K_i)$. Therefore, during decryption, one is able to recover L_{i-1} and R_{i-1} from the values of L_i, R_i and K_i simply by $R_{i-1} = L_i$, and $L_{i-1} = R_i \oplus f(L_i, K_i)$. Thus, one does not need to invert f. Besides, decryption is identical to encryption if one performs the rounds in the inverse order.

Exercise 3.3, on page 149.

- The knowledge of the key and the ciphertext enables one to decrypt; in other words, in general one has $H(K, C) \geq H(M, C)$, which yields $H(K|C) + H(C) \geq H(M|C) + H(C)$. The definition of perfect encryption gives $H(K|C) \geq H(M)$. Therefore, there are necessarily at least as many possible keys K as messages M.
- M and C are represented with words in $\{0, 1\}^{64}$, whereas the keys have only 56 bits. Thus, the number of keys is not sufficient to have a perfect encryption scheme.

Exercise 3.4, on page 152.

1. (a) We give the result in several representations:
   Using polynomials: $(X^6 + X^4 + X^2 + X + 1) + (X^7 + X + 1) = X^7 + X^6 + X^4 + X^2$.

Binary form: $[01010111] + [10000011] = [11010100]$

Hexadecimal form: $[57] + [83] = [D4]$

(b)

$$(X^6 + X^4 + X^2 + X + 1)(X^7 + X + 1) =$$

$$X^{13} + X^{11} + X^9 + X^8 + X^7 + X^7 +$$

$$X^5 + X^3 + X^2 + X + X^6 + X^4 + X^2 + X + 1 =$$

$$X^{13} + X^{11} + X^9 + X^8 + X^6 + X^5 + X^4 + X^3 + 1$$

and $(X^{13} + X^{11} + X^9 + X^8 + X^6 + X^5 + X^4 + X^3 + 1) \mod (X^8 + X^4 + X^3 + X + 1) = X^7 + X^6 + 1$.

As operations are performed modulo $g(X)$, one is sure that the result remains a binary polynomial of degree lower than 8 and that it can be represented with a byte. Therefore, one obtains $[57] \times [83] = [C1]$.

2. (a) Let $a \in \mathbb{F}_{256}$. In polynomial notation, $a(X) = a_7 X^7 + \ldots + a_1 X + a_0$.
Hence, $X.a(X) = a_7 X^8 + \ldots + a_1 X^2 + a_0 X$. For $X.a(X)$ modulo $g(X)$, two cases are possible:

- Either $a_7 = 0$; one directly obtains a reduced expression and $X.a(X) = a_6 X^7 + \ldots + a_1 X^2 + a_0 X$.

- Or $a_7 = 1$. In this case, one has $X.a(X) = X^8 + \ldots + a_1 X^2 + a_0 X$. Besides, $g(X)$ is necessarily zero modulo $g(X)$, which implies that $X^8 = X^4 + X^3 + X + 1 \mod g(X)$. Therefore, one has

$$X^8 + a_6 X^7 + \ldots + a_1 X^2 + a_0 X =$$

$$(a_6 X^7 + \ldots + a_1 X^2 + a_0 X) \oplus (X^4 + X^3 + X + 1).$$

In binary notation, this operation consists of shifting the byte of one position to the left followed – eventually – by a bitwise XOR with $\{1B\}$.

To sum up:

$$X * [a_7 a_6 a_5 a_4 a_3 a_2 a_1 a_0] =$$

$$\begin{cases} [a_6 a_5 a_4 a_3 a_2 a_1 b_0 0] & \text{if } a_7 = 0 \\ [a_6 a_5 a_4 a_3 a_2 a_1 b_0 0] \oplus [00011011] & \text{otherwise .} \end{cases}$$

(b) One iterates i times the previous algorithm.

3. We use the following representation: $\mathbb{F}_{256} \simeq \{0\} \cup \{w(X)^i \mod g(X)\}_{0 \le i < 255}$. This representation is called cyclic or exponential, or Zech's representation). There the multiplication of two nonzero elements a and b is an addition of

exponents:

$$a(X) = w(X)^i \tag{4.10}$$

$$b(X) = w(X)^j \tag{4.11}$$

$$a(X) \times b(X) = w(X)^{i+j \mod 255}. \tag{4.12}$$

One generates a table ExpoToPoly taking 256 values such that the kth value ExpoToPoly[k] gives the polynomial representation of $w(X)^k$ modulo $g(X)$. (By convention, the element 0 is mapped to $w(X)^0$ even if, mathematically speaking, one has $w^{255} = 1$). The table PolyToExpo corresponds to the inverse table. One uses these two tables to compute efficiently the multiplication of two elements a and b according to the previous relation: when a and b are nonzero, we have that $a \times b = ExpoToPoly[PolyToExpo[a] + PolyToExpo[b] \mod 255]$.

Exercise 3.5, on page 155.
InvSubBytes consists in performing the same manipulation, but from the inverse SBox S^{-1} denoted InvSBox.
Remark: As the function t is its own inverse, one has

$$\text{SBox}^{-1}[a] = t^{-1}\left(f^{-1}(a)\right) = t\left(f^{-1}(a)\right), \text{ for all } a \in \mathbb{F}_{256}.$$

The inverse affine function f^{-1} is defined by

$$b = f^{-1}(a) \Longleftrightarrow \begin{bmatrix} b_7 \\ b_6 \\ b_5 \\ b_4 \\ b_3 \\ b_2 \\ b_1 \\ b_0 \end{bmatrix} = \begin{bmatrix} 0 & 1 & 0 & 1 & 0 & 0 & 1 & 0 \\ 0 & 0 & 1 & 0 & 1 & 0 & 0 & 1 \\ 1 & 0 & 0 & 1 & 0 & 1 & 0 & 0 \\ 0 & 1 & 0 & 0 & 1 & 0 & 1 & 0 \\ 0 & 0 & 1 & 0 & 0 & 1 & 0 & 1 \\ 1 & 0 & 0 & 1 & 0 & 0 & 1 & 0 \\ 0 & 1 & 0 & 0 & 1 & 0 & 0 & 1 \\ 1 & 0 & 1 & 0 & 0 & 1 & 0 & 0 \end{bmatrix} \times \begin{bmatrix} a_7 \\ a_6 \\ a_5 \\ a_4 \\ a_3 \\ a_2 \\ a_1 \\ a_0 \end{bmatrix} + \begin{bmatrix} 0 \\ 0 \\ 0 \\ 0 \\ 0 \\ 1 \\ 0 \\ 1 \end{bmatrix}.$$

Exercise 3.6, on page 155.
By definition, SBox[a] $= f(t(a))$, for all $a \in \mathbb{F}_{256}$ with $t : a \longrightarrow a^{-1}$ over $\mathbb{F}_{256}$. However, $a = X + 1$ in polynomial notation. Thus, $t(a) = (1 + X)^{-1} = X^2 + X^4 + X^5 + X^7 \mod g(X) = [10110100] = [B4]$ with the Euclidean algorithm. Then, one performs the matricial operation to obtain $f([B4]) = [00011110] + [11000110] = [11011000] = [D8]$.

Exercise 3.7, on page 155.
Obviously, InvShiftrows consists in performing on line i a cyclic shift *to the right* C_i times.

Exercise 3.8, on page 157.

1. $[0B] + [A2] = [A9]$, $-[03] = [03]$, $[FD] - [F0] = [FD] + [F0] = [0D]$, $[23] + [45] = [66]$.
2. $X^8 + X^4 + X^3 + X + 1 = (X + 1)(X^7 + X^6 + X^5 + X^4 + X^2 + X) + 1$.
3. $X + 1 = [03]$, thus $[03]^{-1} = [F6]$.
4. The multiplication by X is equivalent to shifting the binary word to the left. Then, if X^8 is present, one has to replace it by $X^4 + X^3 + X + 1$ and to perform the sum. This is equivalent to performing a "eXclusive OR" (XOR) with 00011011. Therefore, with $X = [02]$, one obtains the following monomials: $X^8 = 00011011 = [1B]$, $X^9 = 00110110 = [36]$, $X^{10} = 01101100 = [6C]$, $X^{11} = 11011000 = [D8]$, $X^{12} = 10101011 = [AB]$, $X^{13} = 01001101 = [4D]$, and $X^{14} = 10011010 = [9A]$.
5. $(a_1 + a_2 + \ldots + a_n)^2 = a_1^2 + a_2^2 + \ldots + a_n^2 \mod 2$.
6. $[F6]^2 = X^{14} + X^{12} + X^{10} + X^8 + X^4 + X^2$. Hence, when additioning the binary values: $[F6]^2 = 01010010 = [52]$.
7. By Euclidean division, one obtains directly $Q = [F6]Y + [52]$ (for example, by identifying the coefficients).
8. $(U - VQ)c + VM = 1$.
9. MixColumn decoding is performed using the multiplication by the inverse of c, $(U - VQ)$, which is equal to $[OB]Y^3 + [0D]Y^2 + [09]Y + [0E]$. This stage amounts to performing the computation $b(X) = d(X) \times a(X) \mod (X^4 + 1)$, which can be written in a matricial way:

$$
\begin{bmatrix} b_0 \\ b_1 \\ b_2 \\ b_3 \end{bmatrix} = \begin{bmatrix} 0E & 0B & 0D & 09 \\ 09 & 0E & 0B & 0D \\ 0D & 09 & 0E & 0B \\ 0B & 0D & 09 & 0E \end{bmatrix} \times \begin{bmatrix} a_0 \\ a_1 \\ a_2 \\ a_3 \end{bmatrix}
$$

Exercise 3.9, on page 157.
It is actually the same operation as the addition and the subtraction over $\mathbb{F}_2$ are the same!

Exercise 3.10, on page 159.
The encryption routine can be inverted and reorganized in order to produce a decryption algorithm using the InvSubBytes, InvShiftRows, InvMixColumns, and AddRoundKey transformations. A formal model of the decryption algorithm is provided in Algorithm 1. In this version of the decryption, the sequence of the transformations differs from that of the encryption, the key expansion remaining unchanged. Several properties of the Rijndael algorithm enable one to implement an equivalent decryption routine respecting the sequence order of the encryption routine, the structure of the latter being the most efficient one. This equivalent version is not required here.

Algorithm 1 AES Decryption

Input A matrix State corresponding to the cipherblock, a key K
Output A matrix State corresponding to the plaintext block
  1: KeyExpansion(K, RoundKeys)
  2: AddRoundKey(State, RoundKeys[N_r]); // Preliminary addition
  3: **For** $r \leftarrow N_r - 1$ to 0 **do**
  4:     InvShiftRows(State);
  5:     InvSubBytes(State);
  6:     AddRoundKey(State, RoundKeys[r]);
  7:     InvMixColumns(State);
  8: **End For**
  9: // FinalRound
 10: InvShiftRows(State);
 11: InvSubBytes(State);
 12: AddRoundKey(State, RoundKeys[0]);

Exercise 3.11, on page 159.

1. Here is one example among many: a pay file:

   • The same cipherblock means the same salary

   • Exchanging the cipherblocks means exchanging salaries

2. (a) Triple DES processes 64 bits blocks, hence 8 bytes. Therefore, there are $2^{35-3} = 2^{32}$ blocks.
   Probability $\approx \frac{N(N-1)}{2H} = \frac{2^{32}(2^{32}-1)}{2*2^{64}} \approx 0.5$, one is two chance !

   (b) If $Y_i = Y_j$, then $X_i \oplus Y_{i-1} = X_j \oplus Y_{j-1} = S$. Therefore, $Y_{i-1} \oplus Y_{j-1} = X_i \oplus X_j = X_i \oplus S \oplus X_j \oplus S = Z$ and Z is the XOR of two plaintexts parts of the message. Thus, with several attempts of plaintexts M, one obtains a plaintext $X_i \oplus X_j \oplus M$.

   (c) With the AES processing 128 bits blocks, one only has

   $$\frac{N(N-1)}{2H} = \frac{2^{32}(2^{32}-1)}{2 \cdot 2^{128}}$$

   hence approximately 3.10^{-20} chances of collision. Therefore, the two parameters, key size and block size, are very important to obtain robust codes, the first one against brute force attacks and the latter against collisions.

Exercise 3.12, on page 160.

1. (a) Perform the XOR bit by bit for the eight positions to see that there is always an even number of 1.

(b) The key K is the same for all $X^{(m)}$. Therefore, XOR to K is an involution. `SubBytes` is also a bijection.

2. Let $a_1(x)$ and $a_2(x)$ be these two columns. As they differ on only a single coefficient, there exists $i \in \{0..3\}$ such that $a_2 = a_1 + \lambda x^i$. Now the MixColumn of $a(x)$ is $c(x)a(x)$ with $c(x)$ shown in Figure 3.12. Thus suppose by contraposition that the jth coefficients of both MixColumns are equal. Denote them by $(c \cdot a_1)_j = (c \cdot a_2)_j$. But $(c \cdot a_2)_j = (c \cdot a_1 + \lambda c \cdot x^i)_j$ so that the latter equation becomes $(\lambda c \cdot x^i)_j = \lambda(c \cdot x^i)_j = 0$. But as all the coefficents of $c(x)$ are nonzero, all the coefficents $c \cdot x^i \mod x^4 + 1$ are nonzero, and in particular $(c \cdot x^i)_j \neq 0$. Therefore, in a field, $\lambda = 0$.

3. The first `AddRoundKey`, `SubBytes` and `ShiftRows` only touch a single byte. The following `MixColumns` extends the active bytes to a whole column of which, by Question 2, each byte remains a permutation of 0..255. This column is splitted over the four columns by the second `ShiftRows`. By the second `MixColumns`, the active bytes extend to the whole matrix of which, by Question 2, each byte remains a permutation of 0..255. The fourth `AddRoundKey` and the third `SubBytes` and `ShiftRows` preserve these permutations and $\bigoplus_{m=0}^{255} L_{i,j}^{(m)} = 0 \, \forall i,j$.

4. $\forall i,j$ we have:

$$\bigoplus_{m=0}^{255} M_{i,j}^{(m)} = \bigoplus \left([02]L_{i,j} \oplus [03]L_{i+1,j} \oplus [01]L_{i+2,j} \oplus [01]L_{i+3,j}\right)$$

$$= \left([02]\bigoplus L_{i,j}\right) \oplus \left([03]\bigoplus L_{i+1,j}\right) \oplus \left([01]\bigoplus L_{i+2,j}\right) \oplus$$

$$\left([01]\bigoplus L_{i+3,j}\right)$$

$$= ([02]0) \oplus ([03]0) \oplus ([01]0) \oplus ([01]0) = 0.$$

Then $N_{i,j}^{(m)} = M_{i,j}^{(m)} \oplus K_{i,j}$ and therefore the sum is preserved also for N.

5. (a) $N_{i,j}^{(m)} = SubBytes^{-1}(Q_{i',j'}^{(m)} \oplus K4_{i,j})$.

   (b) It is thus sufficient to fix a coordinate (i,j) and compute every output of the AES for all the 256 possible first bytes. If $K4$ is the correct guess, then $N_{i,j}^{(m)} = 0$ and with high probability this is the only guess that yields 0.

6. 256 first bytes for every 256 bytes of the key, times $\frac{128}{8}$ key bytes, this is only 2^{20} AES computations.

Exercise 3.13, on page 161.

In order to deduce K, Oscar would have to recover a from A or b from B, to be able to compute either A^b or B^a. This is the discrete logarithm problem that we have seen in Section 1.3.3.3.

Exercise 3.14, page 161 (foundationsofcoding.imag.fr/Ex/3.14.html).

- Alice computes $A = 2^{292} \bmod 541 = 69$ and sends it to Bob.
- Bob computes $B = 2^{426} \bmod 541 = 171$ and sends it to Alice.
- Then, the secret key is $(171)^{292} \bmod 541 = 368 = (69)^{426} \bmod 541$.

Exercise 3.15, on page 167.

1. $Random_1$ gives to Alice the assurance at the end of step 2 that the key will not be reused.
2. $Random_2$ gives to Bob the assurance that step 3 was not reused. Alice sends $Random_2 - 1$ because sending back only $Random_2$ enciphered would be identical to what Bob has already sent.
3. Eve eavesdrops message 3. Once she has K, she is able to reuse this message and to easily pretend to be Alice by responding with K at step 5.
4. One must add a dating (a ticket). Kerberos was built as a response to this statement !
5. A Kerberos ticket is valid only for a given validity period (8 h in general) during which the user can present it to the TGS to obtain service tickets. The problem is that Kerberos does not include a revocation system. While the validity period is not over, one is also able to use a hacked session key.
6. Key theft, or even fingerprint theft enable one to pretend to be a client. Therefore, one must use a public key system in which the client possesses a private information item.

Exercise 3.16, page 170 (foundationsofcoding.imag.fr/Ex/3.16.html).

1. $p = 47$ and $q = 59$. One notices that the values suggested for p and q are small and that they obviously do not correspond to real keys.
   - one computes $n = p * q = 47 * 59 = 2773$.
   - one computes $\varphi(n) = (p-1)(q-1) = 46 * 58 = 2668$.
   - one checks that e is actually coprime with $\varphi(n)$ and one computes its inverse $d = e^{-1} \bmod \varphi(n)$. For this, one may use the extended Euclidean algorithm. Thus, one obtains $d = 157$.

   Finally, the public key is $K_e = (e, n) = (17, 2773)$. The private key is $K_d = (d, n) = (157, 2773)$.
2. The letter 'B' corresponds to the ASCII code $01000010 = 66$ (see Table 1.3 on page 27). Therefore, one is able to encrypt and to decrypt this value, which is indeed in the interval $[0, 2772]$.
   - Encryption: one computes $66^{17} \bmod 2773 = 872$.

- Decryption: one computes 872^{157} mod 2773 and one checks that it is actually equal to 66.

Exercise 3.17, on page 170.

1. $M' = 100^{11}$ (mod 319) = 265
2. One has to solve $11 * d = 1$ (mod 280). One finds $d = 51$
   - either using the extended Euclidean algorithm;
   - or trying "by hand"; indeed $51 = (280/11) * 2$: therefore, two attempts are enough to find the solution;
   - or using Euler's theorem, page 38, $d = 11^{-1}$ mod 280. This implies that $d = 11^{\varphi(280)-1}$ mod 280 $= 11^{\varphi(7\times5\times8)-1}$ mod 280 $= 11^{(6\times4\times4)-1} = 11^{95}$ mod 280. Thus $d = 11^{64+16+8+4+2+1} = 81.81.121.81.121.11 = 81.11 = 51$ mod 280.
3. One has to compute 133^{51} (mod 319). The hint gives $133^{25} = 133$ (mod 319). The result is $133 * 133 * 133$ (mod 319) = 12.
4. Obviously, it is impossible for both encryption and decryption as any message (plaintext or ciphertext) must belong to $\mathbb{Z}/n\mathbb{Z}$, namely $\mathbb{Z}/319\mathbb{Z}$ in this case.

Exercise 3.18, on page 171.

1. In a long message, if there are recurrent sequences of at least three letters, it is possible that this is not due to randomness. On the contrary, it may come from the same word in the message, which is encrypted several times using the same piece of key. Therefore, one might be able to determine the size of the key by computing the GCD of the distances between the recurrent sequences in the ciphertext (one calls this analysis Kasiski's test). Then, one has to regroup the characters of the ciphertext in the form of packets having the suggested size and to apply a frequential analysis on the position of the sequence.
2. $C = M^5$ mod 35. Then one computes
   $d = 5^{-1}$ mod $\varphi(7 \times 5) = 5^{-1}$ mod 24 = 5.
   One deduces that $M = 10^5$ mod 35. As $100 = -5$ mod 35, one has
   $10^5 = 25 \times 10 = 5 \times 50 = 5 \times 15 = 75 = 5$ mod 35.
   Therefore, the key has five characters.
3. One computes Oscar's private key:
   $d = 7^{-1}$ mod $\varphi(65) = 7^{-1}$ mod 48 = 7.
   Then $K_1 = 48^7$ mod 65 $= 48^2 \times 48^5 = 29 \times 3 = 87 = 22$ mod 65.
   As $4^3 = 64 = -1$ mod 65, one has
   $K_2 = 4^7$ mod 65 $= (-1)^2 \times 4 = 4$ mod 65.
4. One reorganizes the text in the form of a group of five characters.

H → J	W → A	Q → M	I → A	O → I
Q → S	V → –	P → L	I → A	F → –
T → V	D → I	I → E	H → –	T → N
Y → –	– → E	W → S	A → T	F → –
N → P	G → L	Y → U	– → S	F → –
C → E	O → T	M → I	V → N	I → C
C → E	G → L	E → A	V → N	Z → T
C → E	V → –	I → E	A → T	F → –
J → L	D → I	F → B	Z → R	K → E
Y → –	L → Q	Y → U	H → –	G → A
Y → –	G → L	E → A	H → –	R → L
S → U	H → M	M → I	M → E	X → R

C → E	V → –	H → D	B → U	F → –
A → C	J → O	Y → U	K → C	N → H
Z → A	I → N	X → T	H → –	P → J
Z → A	H → M	E → A	Q → I	Y → S
Y → –	J → O	R → N	H → –	T → N
Y → –	W → A	M → I	U → M	K → E
Y → –	K → P	P → L	B → U	Y → S
Y → –	G → L	E → A	H → –	A → V
G → I	– → E	D → –	Y → Q	– → U
Y → –	W → A	D → –	T → L	F → –
M → O	H → M	F → B	Z → R	K → E
Y → –	Z → D	Y → U	H → –	X → R
C → E	I → N	S → O	V → N	I → C
C → E	H → M	I → E	V → N	Z→ T

One performs a frequential analysis column by column:

- Column 1: 9 'Y' and 6 'C': one assumes that

$$\begin{cases} Y(24) \longleftarrow \_(26) \\ C(2) \longleftarrow E(4) \end{cases}$$

Encryption: shift of $-2 = 25 \mod 27$ (Z).
Decryption: shift of $+2$.

- Column 2: one already has the encryption key: $K_1 = 22 = -5 \mod 27$. Therefore, one must performs a shift of $+5$ to decrypt.

- Column 3: one also has the encryption key: $K_2 = 4 \mod 27$. To decrypt, one must perform a shift of $-4 = 23 \mod 27$.
- Column 4: 7 'H': one assumes that $H(7) \longleftarrow \_(26)$.
  Encryption: shift of $+8$ (I).
  Decryption: shift of $-8 = 19 \mod 27$.
- Column 5: 6 'F': one assumes that $F(5) \longleftarrow \_(26)$.
  Encryption: shift of $+6$ (G).
  Decryption: shift of $-6 = 21 \mod 27$.

Therefore, the plaintext is as follows:

JAMAIS_LA_VIE_N_EST_PLUS_ETINCELANTE_ET_LIBRE_
QU_A_LA_LUMIERE_DU_COUCHANT_
JAMAIS_ON_N_AIME_PLUS_LA_VIE_
QU_A_L_OMBRE_DU_RENONCEMENT

One is able to deduce the encryption key:

$$K_0 K_1 K_2 K_3 K_4 = (25, 22, 4, 8, 6) = \text{"ZWEIG"}.$$

Then, the decryption key is:

$$K_0^{-1} K_1^{-1} K_2^{-1} K_3^{-1} K_4^{-1} = (2, 5, 23, 19, 21) = \text{"CFXTV"}.$$

Exercise 3.19, on page 172.

1. As $\varphi(n)$ divides $ed - 1$ and $\varphi(n) = (p - 1)(q - 1) = n - (p + q) + 1$, there exists $k \in \mathbb{Z}$, such that $ed - 1 = k(n - (p + q) + 1)$.

2. One assumes that p and q are different from 2 and 3; hence, p and q are lower than $\frac{n}{4}$. Thus, one has $n \geq n - p - q + 1 \geq \frac{n}{2}$.
   Finally, with e and d positive, k satisfies $1 \leq k \leq \frac{2e.d}{n}$. Now, as $d < n$, finally one has $k \leq 2e$.

3. As e is small, one is able to enumerate all possible values between 1 and $2e$ to find the correct value for k. In this case, $n = pq$ and $S_k = n + 1 - \frac{ed - 1}{k} = p + q$ are the integer coefficients of the second degree equation whose roots are p and q: $X^2 - S_k \cdot X + n = 0$. As S_k must be equal to $p + q$, it also has to be positive. Thus, we can actually start with $k \geq \lceil \frac{ed - 1}{n + 1} \rceil$.
   The details of the method are given in Algorithm 2.

Exercise 3.20, on page 172.

1. One knows that $\varphi(n)$ divides $ed - 1$. There exists $k \in \mathbb{Z}$, such that $ed - 1 = k\varphi(n)$. Besides: $t = \frac{ed - 1}{2^s}$. Then, let us consider $a \in \mathbb{Z}$ coprime with n.

Algorithm 2 Factoring n from (n,e,d) in RSA (Special Case: e is Small)

Input (n, e, d).
Output p and q such that $n = pq$
   1: **For** $k \leftarrow \lceil \frac{ed-1}{n+1} \rceil$ to $2e$ **do**
   2:    $S_k \leftarrow n + 1 - \frac{ed-1}{k}$
   3:    **If** S_k is an integer **then**
   4:        Compute both roots p and q of the equation: $X^2 - S_k \cdot X + n = 0$
   5:        **If** p and q are integers **then**
   6:            **return** p and q.
   7:        **End If**
   8:    **End If**
   9: **End For**

One has $1 = a^{k\varphi(n)} = \left(a^t\right)^{2^s} \mod n$. Hence, the order of a^t in $\mathbb{Z}_n$ is necessarily in $\{2^j \; ; \; 0 \leq j \leq s\}$. In other words:

$$\text{there exists } i \in [0,s] \; / \; \begin{cases} a^{2^{i-1}t} \neq \pm 1 \mod n \\ a^{2^i t} = 1 \mod n \end{cases}$$

Set $u = a^{2^{i-1}t}$. Therefore, one obtains u such that

$$\begin{cases} u^2 - 1 = (u-1)(u+1) = 0 \mod n \\ (u-1) \neq 0 \mod n \\ (u+1) \neq 0 \mod n \end{cases}$$

Hence, $\gcd(u-1, n) = \gcd(a^{2^{i-1}t} - 1, n)$ is a non trivial factor of n. One gets the second factor with a simple division.

2. The average number of attempts (values for a) is 2 (the algorithm is immediate!) because if n is composite, at least half of the invertible elements do not satisfy the given relation.
   The proof of this statement can be divided into two parts. In the first part, one must show that there exists at least one value for a which satisfies these conditions. Then, one must prove that it is also the case for at least half of the invertible elements. Let us begin with the second part, which is easier.
   Set $m = 2^i t$. Let us assume that there exists a such that $a^m = 1$ and $a^{m/2} \neq \pm 1$. Let $\{b_1, \ldots, b_k\}$ be the set of b_i such that $b_i^{m/2} = \pm 1$ and $b_i^m = 1$. Then, necessarily, one has $(b_i a)^{m/2} \neq \pm 1$. Therefore, if there exists such a value for a, then there exists at least $\frac{\varphi(n)}{2}$ of them, hence one out of two invertible elements.
   Now, one only has to prove that there exists at least one such value. This is not the case for any composite number, but we shall see that this is true if n is the product of two distinct prime numbers. One recalls that t is odd. Thus, $(-1)^t = -1 \neq 1 \mod n$. There exists one value for a (at worst, some power

---

Algorithm 3 Factoring n from (n, e, d) in RSA

Input (n, e, d).
Output (p and q such that $n = pq$) or ERROR.
  1: Let s and t such that $ed - 1 = t2^s$ (t odd)
  2: Let a be a random number between 0 and $n - 1$.
  3: $\alpha \leftarrow a^t \mod n$
  4: **If** $\alpha = 1$ or $\alpha = n - 1$ **then**
  5:   **return** ERROR;
  6: **End If**
  7: **For** $i \leftarrow 1$ to s **do**
  8:   tmp $= \alpha^2 \mod n$
  9:   **If** $tmp = 1 \mod n$ **then**
 10:     **return** $p = \gcd(\alpha, n)$ and $q = \frac{n}{p}$
 11:   **End If**
 12:   $\alpha \leftarrow$ tmp
 13: **End For**
 14: **return** ERROR;

---

of -1) which satisfies $u = a^{m/2} \neq 1 \mod n$ and $a^m = 1 \mod n$. According to the Chinese Remainder theorem $u^2 = 1 \mod p$ and $u^2 = 1 \mod q$. Hence, u is congruent to 1 or -1 modulo p and q. It cannot be equal to 1 modulo the two prime numbers because it would also be congruent to 1 modulo n. Therefore, one may assume that it is congruent to -1 modulo p. Then, if u is congruent to 1 modulo q, one has found a valid element.

Otherwise, u is congruent to -1 modulo n. However, in this case, one is able to build another element that satisfies the relation as $m/2$ does not divide either $p - 1$, nor $q - 1$ (otherwise u would be congruent to 1 modulo p or q). Indeed, one has $\frac{m}{2} = \frac{ed-1}{2^{s-i+1}} = \frac{k\varphi(n)}{2^{s-i+1}}$. As $m/2$ does not divide $p - 1$, one is able to set $\frac{m}{2} = v\frac{p-1}{2^j}$ with v odd and j between 0 and s. Then, one considers g, a primitive root modulo p, and one sets $\alpha = g^{2^j} \mod p$ and $\beta = a \mod q$. Then $\alpha^{m/2} = 1 \mod p$ (by construction) and $\beta^{m/2} = a^{m/2} = -1 \mod q$. One only has to apply the Chinese Remainder theorem to recover the element γ corresponding, respectively, to the remainders α and β modulo p and q. This element γ satisfies $\gamma^m = 1 \mod n$ and $\gamma^{m/2} \neq \pm 1 \mod n$. As there exists at least one such element, at least one invertible element out of two also satisfies the property and breaking RSA can be performed with two attempts on the average.

Exercise 3.21, on page 173.

Using the Chinese Remainder theorem, Lucky Luke can easily compute – in time $\mathcal{O}(\log^2(n_A + n_J + n_W))$ – the value of the integer $C = x^3 = \Psi^{-1}(c_W, c_J, c_A) \mod n_W . n_J . n_A$ i.e. $C = x^3$ (one recalls that $x < \min(n_W, n_J, n_A)$).
As x is an integer, it is enough to compute, in $\mathbb{R}$, $x = C^{1/3}$ with the Newton–Raphson method to obtain the value of x.

Exercise 3.22, on page 173.

Oscar knows (e_A, e_B, n) and (c_A, c_B). Using the Extended Euclidean algorithm, he easily computes (almost in linear time, with respect to the number of bits of n) Bézout numbers r and s such that $r e_A + s e_B = 1$.

Oscar is then able to compute $c_A^r . c_B^s \mod n$ with a fast modular exponentiation and to obtain $c_A^r . c_B^s = M^{r.e_A + s.e_B} \mod n = M$.

Morality: never use the same modulus n in a group of users.

Exercise 3.23, on page 173.

One just has to compute $u.r^{-1} \mod n_A$. Indeed, $u.r^{-1} = y^{d_A} . r^{-1} \mod n_A = c^{d_A} x^{d_A} r^{-1} \mod n_A$. However, $x^{d_A} = r^{e_A d_A} = r \mod n_A$. Therefore $u.r^{-1} = c^{d_A} r r^{-1} \mod n_A = c^{d_A} \mod n_A = m$. Computing $u.r^{-1} \mod n_A$ can be easily performed by Eve in time $\mathcal{O}(\log^2 n_A)$ and gives m.

Morality: never sign an unreadable message (random or encrypted); or sign only a summary of the message.

Exercise 3.24, on page 174.

1. $\mu p_1 k = B!$, therefore $p_1 \leq B$.
2. p is prime, thus the Fermat theorem gives $a^{p-1} = 1 \mod p$. One computes this equation to the power μ to get the result.
3. $(A - a^{B!}) = kn = kpq$, therefore $(A - 1) - (a^{B!} - 1) = (A - 1) - hp = kpq$.
4. $\log(k) \log^2(n)$.
5. $B \log(B) \log^2(n)$.
6. If $A - 1$ is a multiple of n, then $B!$ is a multiple of $\varphi(n) = (p - 1)(q - 1)$, thus B is greater than any factor of $p - 1$ and $q - 1$ from question 1. Yet B is small.
7. The cost: $\alpha \log^3(n) \log(\alpha \log(n))$ (one recalls that the cost of the GCD is equal to $\log^2(n)$).
8. One takes p and q such that $p - 1$ and $q - 1$ have large factors (strong prime numbers, see on page 94).

Exercise 3.25, on page 177.

a. $h(x_1, x_2) = 15^{x_1} 22^{x_2} \mod 83$. Hence, $h(12, 34) = 15^{12} 22^{34} \mod 83 = 63$. The resistance to collisions relies on the difficulty of finding λ such that $15^\lambda = 22 \mod 83$.

b. $p - 1 = 2q$ and q is prime. Thus, the divisors of $p - 1$ belong to the set $\{1, 2, q, 2q = p - 1\}$. By definition, d divides $p - 1$, therefore $d \in \{1, 2, q, p - 1\}$.

c. $-q < y_2 - x_2 < q$ as $y_2, x_2 \in \mathbb{Z}_q$. One deduces that $y_2 - x_2$ is coprime with q. Therefore, one has $d \neq q$.

d. $\alpha^{x_1} \beta^{x_2} = h(x) = h(y) = \alpha^{y_1} \beta^{y_2}$ implies that $\alpha^{x_1 - y_1} = \beta^{y_2 - x_2} \mod p$ as α and β are invertible.

e. If $d = p - 1 = 2q$ then, knowing that d divides $y_2 - x_2$, there exists $k \in \mathbb{Z}$ such that

$$-q < y_2 - x_2 = 2kq < q$$

One deduces that $k = 0$: $y_2 = x_2$.

Therefore, one has $\alpha^{x_1 - y_1} = \beta^{y_2 - x_2} = 1 \mod p$. However, α is a generator of $\mathbb{Z}_p^*$, $\alpha^u = 1 \mod p \Longleftrightarrow u = 0 \mod p - 1$: there exists $k \in \mathbb{Z}$ such that $x_1 - y_1 = k(p - 1)$. In the same way as in question 3, one proves that

$$-(p - 1) < -\frac{p - 1}{2} \leq -q < x_1 - y_1 < q \leq \frac{p - 1}{2} < p - 1.$$

In other words, $k = 0$: $x_1 = y_1$. Finally, $x = y$, which proves the contradiction.

f. If $d = 1$, one sets $u = (y_2 - x_2)^{-1} \mod p - 1$. Then
$\exists k \in \mathbb{Z}$ such that $u(y_2 - x_2) = 1 + k(p - 1)$. One deduces that

$$\beta^{u(y_2 - x_2)} = \beta^{1 + k(p-1)} = \beta = \alpha^\lambda = \alpha^{u(x_1 - y_1)} \mod p$$

and $\lambda = u(x_1 - y_1) \mod p - 1$.

g. 1. $u = (y_2 - x_2)^{-1} \mod q$. Then, there exists $k \in \mathbb{Z}$ such that $u(y_2 - x_2) = 1 + kq$. One deduces that $\beta^{u(y_2 - x_2)} = \beta^{1 + k.q} = \beta (\beta^q)^k$. Yet $q = \frac{p-1}{2}$ and β is a generator of $\mathbb{Z}_p^*$. Thus $\beta^{p-1} = 1 \mod p$ and $\beta^{\frac{p-1}{2}} = \beta^q = -1 \mod p$. Finally, $\beta^{u(y_2 - x_2)} = (-1)^k \beta \mod p = \pm \beta \mod p$.

   2. One deduces that $\beta^{u(y_2 - x_2)} = \pm \beta = (-1)^\delta \alpha^\lambda = (\alpha^q)^\delta \alpha^\lambda \mod p$ with $\delta \in \{0, 1\}$. In other words: $\alpha^{u(x_1 - y_1) - q\delta} = \alpha^\lambda \mod p$.
      - If $\delta = 0$: $\lambda = u(x_1 - y_1) \mod p - 1$
      - If $\delta = 1$: $\lambda = u(x_1 - y_1) - q = u(x_1 - y_1) + q \mod p - 1$ since $q = \frac{p-1}{2}$.

h. The algorithm is quite simple:
   - Compute $d = \gcd(y_2 - x_2, p - 1)$ using the Euclidean algorithm.
   - If $d = 1$, $u = (y_2 - x_2)^{-1} \mod p - 1$ and $\lambda = u(x_1 - y_1) \mod p - 1$.
   - If $d = 2$, $u = (y_2 - x_2)^{-1} \mod q$ and $\lambda = u(x_1 - y_1) \mod p - 1$. If $\beta^\lambda = -\beta \mod p$, then $\lambda = \lambda + q$.

This algorithm only performs basic or costless operations and computing λ is fast. Hence, this ends the proof by contradiction and one deduces that h is resistant to collisions.

Exercise 3.26, on page 184.

1. (a) G is a hash function with an output of size $m - k_0$, like M and s, where H is a hash function with an output of k_0 bits, like t.
   (b) $r = H(s) \oplus t$, then $M = s \oplus G(r)$.

2. (a) $E_{pub}(x) = x^e \mod N$; $\quad D_{priv}(y) = y^d \mod N$; $\quad e \cdot d = 1 \mod \varphi(N)$; $\varphi(77) = 60$ and 7 is coprime to 60; finally $2 * 60 - 17 * 7 = 1$ so that $d = 17$.

(b) For instance $H(7) = H(6)$.

(c) $G(r) = 11 = [1011]$, XOR $[1000]$ gives $s = [0011]$, then $H(s) = [001]$. the latter XOR $r = [101]$ gives $t = [100]$, so that $(s||t) = [0011100] = 16 + 8 + 4 = 28$. Then $28^2 = 14 \mod 77$, so that $28^3 = 392 = 7 \mod 77$, and $28^6 = 49 \mod 77$. Finally, we have $28^7 = -14 = 63 \mod 77$.

3. (a) There is no particular reason for badly deciphered s' and t' to be such that $s' \oplus G(H(s') \oplus t') = M'$ presents some zeros on the right.

(b) For a uniform draw, there is one chance over two for each bit to be zero. If the padding fixes k_1 zeros, the probability to have that number of zeros to the right is $\frac{1}{2^{k_1}}$.

Exercise 3.27, on page 186.

For the two first, the attacker (even without having the key K) is able to add a new block at the end of the process in order to get a valid MAC. For the last construction, a collision on H provides an MAC. Indeed, if $H(x) = H(x')$, then $H(x||K) = h(H(x)||K) = h(H(x')||K) = H(x'||K)$.

Exercise 3.28, on page 187.

To insure both the secrecy and the authentication, a common domain must exist between A and B or more precisely between E_A, D_A, E_B, and D_B.

Then, A sends $C = E_B(D_A(M))$ to B; at its end, B computes $E_A(D_B(C)) = E_A(D_A(M)) = M$.

As he does not possess D_B, a spy cannot decrypt C. Therefore, the secrecy is preserved. If a spy sends a message M' instead of C, M' will not be decrypted as a valid message M: indeed, for this, one would have to know D_A. This insures the authentication.

Exercise 3.29, on page 187.

1. For the teacher: $\varphi(55) = 40$ and $27 \times 3 = 81 = 1 \mod 40$.
   For the secretarial staff: $\varphi(33) = 20$ and $7 \times 3 = 21 = 1 \mod 20$.

2. The teacher sends $m = 12^3 \mod 33$. However $12^2 = 12 \mod 33$; therefore $m = 12 \mod 33$.

3. The teacher has computed $(x^{e_S} \mod n_S)^{d_P} \mod n_P$.
   The secretarial staff receives y and computes $(y^{e_P} \mod n_P)^{d_S} \mod n_S$.
   Hence the mark $(23^3 \mod 55)^7 \mod 33 = (12^7 \mod 33) = 12$.

Exercise 3.30, on page 190.

$g^{z_1} y^{z_2} = g^{sv} g^{xz_2} = g^{xrv+k} g^{xz_2} = g^{xrv+k} g^{xqv-xrv} = g^k \mod p$.

Exercise 3.31, on page 192.

1. We have $Q = [s]G$ so that $M' = [u + vs]G$, using the group law. Then $u + vs = (H(m) + xs)z^{-1} = (H(m) + xs)k(H(m) + sx)^{-1} \equiv k \mod p$.

2. p is the number of points of the curve, that is, the size of the group. By Lagrange Theorem 1, page 31, for any point Q of the group, $[p]Q$ is the neutral element of the group.

3. (a) $(\log_2(u) + \log_2(v))$ doublings and less than $(\log_2(u) + \log_2(v) + 1)$ additions.

   (b) Algorithm 3.4 performs only $\log_2(max\{u, v\})$ doublings and at most that number of additions if $R = P \oplus Q$ is precomputed. Thus if u and v have the same size, the overall number of operations can be divided by up to 2.

Exercise 3.32, on page 192.

The idea is to use some simple pseudo-random generators in order to build n, e, and x_0 (which will remain secret). Then, the process is described in Algorithm 4, on page 319.

Algorithm 4 RSA Cryptographic Pseudo-Random Generator

Input A size $b > 1024$.
Input An integer $k < \mathcal{O}(\log(b))$;
Output A sequence of l cryptographically secure pseudo-random bits.
1: Generate two robust prime numbers p and q on at least $\frac{b}{2}$ bits (see page 94);
2: $n = pq$;
3: Generate a pseudo-random exponent e such that $\gcd(e, (p-1)(q-1)) = 1$;
4: Generate a pseudo-random integer s (for instance, see page 62);
5: $x_0 = s^e \mod n$;
6: **For all** i from 1 to $\lceil \frac{l}{k} \rceil$ **do**
7:    $x_i = x_{i-1}^e \mod n$;
8:    z_i receives the k first bits of x_i;
9: **End For**
10: **return** the sequence $z_1 || z_2 || \ldots || z_l$;

Exercise 3.33, on page 193.

1. The authentication is unilateral: the bank authenticates the client.

2. A false web site!

3. The bank must also authenticate to the client. This is performed using the web site certificates and the related PKIs.

For instance, in France, such a system with throwaway numbers is mostly interesting for the bank: indeed, the true legal security of smart credit cards relies on the possibility of repudiation. By French law, it is up to the bank to prove that a given online purchase was actually performed by the owner of the bank account. Such a system with throwaway numbers reverses the legal responsibility as it is associated with a secret code received in the post. Hence, it is up to the user to prove that a throwaway number associated with his bank account was generated without his secret code.

Exercise 3.34, on page 198.

1. The main component of a digital certificate is the link between an identification and a public key.
2. This enables one to perform authentications without a third party (provided that an underlying PKI was set up) and without risking a Man-in-the-middle attack. Indeed, a Man-in-the-middle would have to possess a false identity certificate to pretend to be one of the parties.
3. A certification policy depends on a security policy. Notably, it must define the validity period of the certificates, who can be certified, and so on.

Exercise 3.35, on page 201.

1. `dd if=/dev/urandom of=demoCA/private/.rand bs=1k count=16`

2. First create the directories via `mkdir demoCA`;
   `mkdir demoCA/private demoCA/certs demoCA/crl demoCA/newcerts`;
   Then choose a first serial number (warning `openssl` recognizes only numbers in hexadecimal format with an even number of digits. So for instance:
   `echo "01" > demoCA/serial`;
   `touch demoCA/index.txt`;
   `chmod -R go-rwx demoCA`

   1. `openssl genrsa -aes256 -out demoCA/private/cakey.pem-rand demoCA/private/.rand 4096`
   2. `openssl req -new -x509 -key demoCA/private/cakey.pem-out ./demoCA/cacert.pem -days 60`

3. `openssl genrsa -aes256 -out luckyluke.key -rand demoCA/private/.rand 1024`
   `openssl req -new -key luckyluke.key -keyout newreq.pem -out newreq.pem -days 365`
   `openssl ca -policy policy_anything -out newcert.pem -infiles newreq.pem`

4. `openssl pkcs12 -export` enables one to convert certificates in X509 format into the pkcs12 format. Thus the command line is:
   `openssl pkcs12 -export -in cacert.pem -out cacert.p12-inkey private/cakey.pem`

(a) In order to send encrypted e-mails, one first has to recover the public key in the certificate of the recipient. This is always possible. On the contrary, it is impossible to decrypt the encrypted e-mails one has received as the key has been lost.

(b) In order to sign an e-mail, one must use one's private key, which has been lost. Therefore, it is impossible. On the contrary, it is still possible to check a signature as it only requires recovering the public key in the certificate of the sender.

Exercise 3.36, on page 201.
Since you have complete trust in Alice, you can be sure of Bob's certificate. However, you know nothing of Bob's certification policy. Therefore, you cannot be sure that the message was actually issued by Oscar.

Exercise 3.37, on page 203.

1. Within a company, there is no problem; between clients and subsidiaries, one already has to trust them; for specialized companies, their reputation is at stake so they should regularly check; for embedded CAs as well the reputation of the brower or operating system companies is at stake. The question is more that the trust assumptions are different in different settings.

2. In all cases: encrypted storage on a password-protected drive.

3. The other information items on a certificate (locality, e-mail address, etc.) are actually used to differenciate all the John Robinsons.

4. (a) Depending on the period required for breaking a key and on the probability of lost/theft of a private key based on the duration and the usage that is made of it.

   (b) Obtain some information on the algorithms and the attacks in order to define hard-to-break keys.

   (c) Yes, it enables one to manage key lost/theft.

   (d) An authority must describe all this in its certfication policy.

Exercise 3.38, on page 204.

1. One for each pair of persons: $\frac{n(n-1)}{2}$.
2. One pair of public/private keys for each of n persons.
3. Exchanging symmetric keys is difficult (for instance, it requires a pre-existing confidential channel). Moreover, a symmetric key does not allow directly non-repudiation (since both the recipient and the sender have the same key). On the other hand, asymmetric systems remain slower.

Exercise 3.39, on page 208.

1. One should use a PKI for instance.

2. `ssh-keygen -b 2048 -t dsa`

3. Now, the connection no longer uses the password associated with the login but rather the passphrase associated with the DSA key.

4. A message proclaiming that the server on which one wishes to connect is unknown. Therefore, one should check whether the public key which was submitted is correct:

```
The authenticity of host 'www.imag.fr' can't be established.
RSA key fingerprint is
3a:fa:9e:88:7f:13:89:8a:63:ad:18:45:5b:24:68:d6.
Are you sure you want to continue connecting (yes/no)?
```

5. The key which is sent by the server will not match the key stored locally. The connection must be1 rejected because different keys might indicate, for instance, that a Man-in-the-middle attack is being performed:

```
@@@@@@@@@@@@@@@@@@@@@@@@@@@@@@@@@@@@@@@@@@@@@@@@@@@@@@@@@@@@@@@@@@@
@ WARNING: REMOTE HOST IDENTIFICATION HAS CHANGED!              @
@@@@@@@@@@@@@@@@@@@@@@@@@@@@@@@@@@@@@@@@@@@@@@@@@@@@@@@@@@@@@@@@@@@
IT IS POSSIBLE THAT SOMEONE IS DOING SOMETHING NASTY!
Someone could be eavesdropping on you right now
(man-in-the-middle attack)!
It is also possible that the RSA host key has just been
changed.
The fingerprint for the RSA key sent by the remote host
is 13:bb:ae:c1:b2:df:19:2b:8f:ff:e1:b2:75:45:02:5c.
Please contact your system administrator.
Add correct key in .ssh/known_hosts to get rid of this message.
Offending key in .ssh/known_hosts:1
RSA host key for www.imag.fr has changed
and you have requested strict checking.
Host key verification failed.
```

SOLUTIONS FOR CHAPTER 4

Exercise 4.1, on page 212.

1. The key C is such that $2630538516305 + C$ is a multiple of 97; thus $C = 97 - 2630538516305 \mod 97 = 64$.

2. $R = \frac{13}{15} \simeq 86.67\%$.

3. The code enables one to detect an error in a single digit. Let $n = [K, C]$ be the integer of 15 digits associated with the social insurance number followed by the key. An error in a single digit c_i of index i gives $n' = n + e \cdot 10^i$ with $e \neq 0$ and $-c_i \leq e \leq 9 - c_i$. Then, one has $n' \mod 97 = e \cdot 10^i \neq 0$ because e and 10 are coprime with 97; the error is detected.

   On the contrary, an error in two digits is not detected. For instance, two errors in digits may transform the valid social insurance number 2.63.05.38.516.301.68 into the number 2.63.05.38.516.398.68, which is also valid.

Exercise 4.2, on page 213.

1. The word m is composed of three blocks of 3 bits; $\phi(m)$ contains 16 bits including seven parity bits.

2. If $\phi(m)$ contains an odd number of errors, then necessarily there exists at least one line or one column of 4 bits containing an odd number of errors. For these 4 bits, the fourth bit is the parity bit and it will necessarily differ from the binary sum of the 3 other bits.

3. Hence, the code detects one or three errors. If two errors appear, at least two parity bits will not be checked and the errors will then be detected. Therefore, this code detects up to 3-bit errors.

4. Let the codeword $\phi(m) = \begin{bmatrix} 0000 \\ 0000 \\ 0000 \\ 0000 \end{bmatrix}$. The word $\begin{bmatrix} 0100 \\ 0100 \\ 0100 \\ \mathbf{0010} \end{bmatrix}$ includes four errors

   with respect to $\phi(m)$; one detects that the word is erroneous by checking the parity bits in bold.

   The word $\begin{bmatrix} 1100 \\ 0000 \\ 0000 \\ 1100 \end{bmatrix}$ includes 4 errors with respect to $\phi(m)$ but these errors

   cannot be detected because all control bits are correct. In this case, the errors lead to a correct codeword.

5. Either the word one received does not include any error and one checks easily that all parity bits are checked or the word contains one error and the overall parity bit (which must correspond to the sum of all other bits) is obviously not checked. One distinguishes three cases depending on the number of the other parity bits that are not checked.

- Only the overall parity bit is not checked: it is sufficient to change it to correct the error.
- Another parity bit corresponding to line i (or column i) is not checked: it is sufficient to change this parity bit to correct the error.
- Two other parity bits are not checked; necessarily, one of them corresponds to a line i and the other one to a column j. It is sufficient to change the source bit of index (i, j) to correct the error.

6. The word $\begin{bmatrix} \mathbf{1001} \\ 0000 \\ 0000 \\ 0000 \end{bmatrix}$ includes two errors with respect to $\phi(m)$. Only the two

parity bits corresponding to the first and the fourth column are not checked. Even if one assumes that there were two errors, one cannot decide in which of the four lines they did appear. Therefore, one cannot correct without ambiguity: the first line could be equal to 0000, for instance, or the second, the third, or the fourth line could be equal to 1001 each (or all three of them), and so on.

Exercise 4.3, on page 216.

1. As the channel is symmetric, $H(Y|X) = H(Y|X = 0) = H(Y|X = 1) = -p \log_2(p) - (1 - p) \log_2(1 - p)$. Let p_1 be the probability of having the bit 0, respectively, $p_2 = 1 - p_1$ the probability of having the bit 1, at the input of the channel. Then the probability of having the bit 0 at the output is $y_1 = p_1 * (1 - p) + (1 - p_1) * p$, and the probability of having the bit 1 is $y_2 = (1 - p_1) * (1 - p) + p_1 * p$. As $H(Y|X)$ is independent of p_1, the maximum will correspond to the maximum of $H(Y)$. However, $H(Y)$ reaches its maximum when the probabilities y_1 and y_2 are equal, namely, when $y_1 = y_2 = 1/2$ (for instance, this happens when $p_1 = 1/2$). Then, one is able to compute $H_{max}(Y) = 1$, which gives the channel capacity $C_{BSC} = 1 + p \log_2(p) + (1 - p) \log_2(1 - p)$.

2. Then $1 - \frac{\log_2(2)}{2} - \frac{\log_2(2)}{2} = 0$ and $C'_{BSC} = \log_2(p) - \log_2(1 - p)$ so that we have the following variations and $0 < C_{BSC} \le 1$:

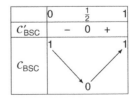

Exercise 4.4, on page 217.
If $p > \frac{1}{2}$, it is sufficient to turn each bit received into its opposite before decoding. This is equivalent to transforming the BSC channel of probability p into a BSC channel of probability $q = 1 - p$ with $q < \frac{1}{2}$.

Exercise 4.5, on page 219.

The number of different codes corresponds to the choice of three separators in a discrete interval from 1 to 7; hence, 3 among 6. This number is to be multiplied by 2: one can either start with a white bar or a black bar. Finally, there are actually $2 * C_3^6 = 40$ different possible codes per column, four per digit.

Exercise 4.6, page 220 (foundationsofcoding.imag.fr/Ex/4.6.html).

One obtains $c_1 = 11 - \sum_{i=2}^{10} c_i = 11 - (4 * 2 + 4 * 3 + 1 * 4 + 8 * 5 + 8 * 6 + 8 * 7 + 1 * 8 + 1 * 9 + 1 * 10 \mod 11) = 3$; Hence, the ISBN code is 111-888-144-3.

The EAN-13 code is 9-781118-88144c_0 with $c_0 = (10 - (9 + 8 + 1 + 8 + 8 + 4 + 3 * (7 + 1 + 1 + 8 + 1 + 4))) \mod 10 = 6$, namely, 9-781118-881446, as one can check on the cover of the present work.

Exercise 4.7, on page 222.

Any error not detected is associated with a polynomial P_e multiple of P_g. If the error deals with a single bit i, $P_e = X^i$. If P_g has at least two coefficients, it cannot divide X^i and the error is detected.

Reciprocally, if P_g has a single monomial $P_g = X^r$, it does not detect the error $P_e = X^{r+1}$.

Exercise 4.8, on page 222.

As $g_r = 1$, if $\sum_{i=0}^r g_i = 0$, then 1 is a root of P_g. Therefore, P_g is a multiple of $X + 1$. Any error not detected is associated with a multiple of $X + 1$. However, any multiple of $X + 1$ in $\mathbb{F}_2[X]$ has an even number of nonzero coefficients. Thus any error that is not detected deals necessarily with an even number of bits. Hence, the code detects any error dealing with an odd number of bits.

Exercise 4.9, on page 222.

For a burst of errors, $P_e = X^k + \cdots + X^i = X^k(1 + \cdots + X^{i-k})$. If $(i - k) < d$, then the irreducible factor of degree d will not divide P_e. Therefore, a fortiori P_g will not divide P_e either.

Exercise 4.10, on page 224.

1. Indeed, for all x, y, and z in V^n, one has
   - $d_H(x, y) \in \mathbb{R}^+$;
   - $d_H(x, y) = 0 \Leftrightarrow x = y$;
   - $d_H(x, y) = d_H(y, x)$;
   - $d_H(x, y) \leq d_H(x, z) + d_H(y, z)$.
2. The ith bit in $x \oplus y$ is equal to 1 if and only if $x_i \neq y_i$; thus $d_H(x, y) = w(x \oplus y)$.

Exercise 4.11, on page 226.

One receives the word m' with s errors with respect to the word m that was issued; the error will be detected if and only if $m' \notin C$. However, because C is a t-error-correcting code, one has for all $x \in C$, $d(m,x) \geq 2t + 1$. Thus there exists no word in C at a distance $\leq 2t$. Hence, if $d(m',m) = s \leq 2t$, then $m' \notin C$ and one detects the error. Therefore, C is a s-error-detecting code with $s \geq 2t$.

The reciprocal proposition is true: indeed, if C is an s-error-detecting code and $s \geq 2t$, then one has $\delta(C) > s$. Therefore, one has $\delta(C) \geq 2t + 1$. Consequently, C is at least a t-error-correcting code.

Exercise 4.12, on page 226.

1. Two distinct words have at least one distinct source bit; because this bit is repeated m times, one has, $\delta(C) \geq m$. Now let $\omega_0 = C(0^k) = 0^{mk}$ and $\omega_1 = C(10^{k-1}) = (10^{k-1})^m$; $d_H(\omega_0, \omega_1) = m$; therefore, $\delta(C) \leq m$. Finally, $\delta(C) = m$.

2. One must have $\delta(C) \geq 2 * 2 + 1 = 5$. Thus, $(5, 1)$ fits and so does $(5k, k)$.

3. $(5k, k)$ has a rate $\frac{k}{5k} = 0.2$.

4. The distance is 5; Algorithm 5 enables one to detect at least four errors (and even more if the errors occur in distinct source digits).

Algorithm 5 Repetition Code Decoding with Maximum Detection

1: error ← false
2: **For** $i \leftarrow 0$ to $k - 1$ **do**
3:    $s[i] \leftarrow$ readbit { Initialization of s}
4: **End For**
5: **For** $i \leftarrow k$ to $n - 1$ **do**
6:    **If** readbit $\neq s[i \mod k]$ **then**
7:       error ← true
8:    **End If**
9: **End For**

---

5. The distance is 5; Algorithm 6 enables one to correct two errors; it is sufficient to compute the number of 1's for each source symbol. If one obtains a majority of 1's (at least 3), one deduces that the source symbol is 1; otherwise the source symbol is 0. Hence, this algorithm is able to correctly deduce the source bit if at most two errors have been made on the 5 issued bits corresponding to the same source bit.

6. Algorithm 7 corrects only one error. Besides, it can detect two or three errors without correcting them (but not four!). The minimum distance is 5 and also if one receives four identical symbols (four '0' or four '1'), one assumes that there was a single error and performs the associated correction. If there are less than four identical symbols, one returns an error signal. One corrects all the simple errors and detects up to three errors corresponding to the block encoding a same source bit.

Algorithm 6 Repetition Code Decoding with Maximum Correction

1: **For** $i \leftarrow 0$ to $k - 1$ **do**
2:    $NbrOne[i] \leftarrow 0$ { Initialization }
3: **End For**
4: **For** $i \leftarrow 0$ to $n - 1$ **do**
5:    **If** readbit = 1 **then**
6:       Increase NbrOne[i mod k]
7:    **End If**
8: **End For**
9: **For** $i \leftarrow 0$ to $k - 1$ **do**
10:   **If** NbrOne[i] ≥ 3 **then**
11:     $s[i] \leftarrow 1$
12:   **else**
13:     $s[i] \leftarrow 0$
14:   **End If**
15: **End For**

Algorithm 7 Repetition Code Decoding with Detection and Correction

---

1: error $\leftarrow$ false
2: **For** $i \leftarrow 0$ to $k - 1$ **do**
3:    $NbrOne[i] \leftarrow 0$ { Initialization }
4: **End For**
5: **For** $i \leftarrow 0$ to $n - 1$ **do**
6:    **If** readbit() = 1 **then**
7:       Increase NbrOne[i mod k]
8:    **End If**
9: **End For**
10: **For** $i \leftarrow 0$ to $k - 1$ **do**
11:   **If** NbrOne[i] ≥ 4 **then**
12:     $s[i] \leftarrow 1$
13:   **elsif** NbrOnz[i] ≤ 1 **then**
14:     $s[i] \leftarrow 0$
15:   **else**
16:     error $\leftarrow$ true
17:   **End If**
18: **End For**

Exercise 4.13, on page 226.

One assumes that the words in the code C are stored in a table $C[1..|V|^k]$. Each word $C[i]$ is itself a table of size $k + r$ of digits in V. Then, one is able to compute the minimum distance between any two codewords: by enumerating all of them, one sees that there are $|V|^k$ words encoded with $n = k + r$ digits. The idea is then to consider all the possible pairs of words and to compute their distances.

Algorithm 8 Minimum Distance of a Code ($|V| = 2$)

1: delta ← +infinity
2: **For** $i \leftarrow 1$ to 2^k **do**
3:   **For** $j \leftarrow i + 1$ to 2^k **do**
4:     $d_{ij} \leftarrow 0$ { computation of the distance d_{ij} between $C[i]$ and $C[j]$ }
5:     **For** $l \leftarrow 1$ to $k + r$ **do**
6:       **If** $C[i][l] \neq C[j][l]$ **then**
7:         $d_{ij} \leftarrow d_{ij} + 1$
8:       **End If**
9:     **End For**{Update $\delta = \min(d_{ij})$ }
10:     **If** ($d_{ij} < \delta$) **then**
11:       $\delta \leftarrow d_{ij}$
12:     **End If**
13:   **End For**
14: **End For**
15: DetectionRate ← $\delta - 1$;
16: CorrectionRate ← $\frac{\delta - 1}{2}$;

Algorithm 8, implements this idea. It requires $O\left(\frac{|V|^k \cdot (|V|^k + 1)}{2}\right)$ comparisons and each comparison is performed on $n = k + r$ bits. Therefore, the overall binary cost of the algorithm is bounded by $O(n \cdot |V|^{2k})$. This is impracticable, even for $|V| = 2$, as soon as k and n are larger than a few dozens.

Now for the practical application, the number of source words is equal to the number of codewords $|C|$. Therefore, the number of bits that are necessary to encode these words is $k = \lceil \log_2(|C|) \rceil = 2$. This means that $r = 10 - 2 = 8$ and the code C is a $(10, 2)$-code. From inspection, it is easy to see that the minimal distance of this code is $\delta = 5$. Therefore, C is a 4-error-detecting code and a 2-error-correcting code.

Exercise 4.14, on page 227.

1. Let $x \in \{0, 1\}^n$ be the received word. As $d_H(x, c) = e$, we have $n - e$ bits transmitted correctly and e bits that are erroneous. It follows that by definition of a BSC channel, $P(x \mid c) = p^e (1 - p)^{n-e} = (1 - p)^n \left(\frac{p}{1-p}\right)^e$

2. As $p < \frac{1}{2}$,

$$1 = \left(\frac{p}{1-p}\right)^0 > \left(\frac{p}{1-p}\right)^1 > \left(\frac{p}{1-p}\right)^2 > \cdots > \left(\frac{p}{1-p}\right)^n > 0.$$

It follows that

$$P(x \mid c_1) \leq P(x \mid c_2) \iff (1-p)^n \left(\frac{p}{1-p}\right)^{d_1} \leq (1-p)^n \left(\frac{p}{1-p}\right)^{d_2}$$

$$\iff \left(\frac{p}{1-p}\right)^{d_1 - d_2} \leq 1$$

$$\iff (d_1 - d_2) \ln \left(\frac{p}{1-p}\right) \leq 0$$

$$\iff (d_1 - d_2) \geq 0.$$

3. Let c_x be the codeword decoded by an MDD strategy. From the previous result,

$$d_H(x, c_x) = \min_{c \in C} d_H(x, c) = \max_{c \in C} P(x \mid c) = P(x \mid c_x)$$

So c_x is also the codeword decoded by a MLD strategy. Conversely, the same reasoning leads to the conclusion that, finally, MLD and MDD rules are the same over a BSC channel with error probability $0 < p < \frac{1}{2}$.

Exercise 4.15, on page 228.

Let $x \in C'$, then one has $\bigoplus_{i=1}^{n+1} x_i = 0$. Thus all the codewords in C' have an even Hamming weight. Consequently, the distance d' between two codewords in C' is also even. As $d \geq d' \geq d + 1$ and d is odd, one deduces that $d' = d + 1$.

Exercise 4.16, on page 228.

As the cardinal number of V is at least 2, there exist two distinct symbols $a \neq b$. From C, one builds the code C' of length $n + 1$ as follows:

$$C' = \{c_1 \cdots c_n a \mid c_1 \cdots c_n \in C\} \cup \{aa \cdots ab, ba \cdots ab\}.$$

The cardinal number of C' is $M + 2$, and its distance is 1; moreover, C is a shortened code of C' built from the the codewords of C' ending with an a.

Exercise 4.17, on page 229.

1. It is sufficient to compute $\delta(C)$. Let $x \neq y$ be two codewords in C. There exist i such that $0 \leq i \leq 3$ and $x_i \neq y_i$. Let e be the number of such indexes i for which the digits in x and y differ.
   - If $e = 1$, then the bit in the position i appears in three other digits in x and y, namely, the bits $(b_i + b_k, b_i + b_l, b_0 + b_1 + b_2 + b_3)$. Thus $d(x, y) \geq 4$.
   - If $e = 2$, then x and y have exactly 2 bits in the positions i and j ($0 \leq i < j \leq 3$) differing. Then, because each bit b_i appears in two control digits in the form $b_i + b_l$ and $b_i + b_m$ (all the same for j), x and y differ at least in two of these bits. Hence, $d(x, y) \geq 4$.

- If $e = 3$, then x and y have three different bits. Thus x and y also differ in their last bit $(b_0 + b_1 + b_2 + b_3)$. Hence, $d(x, y) \geq 4$.
- If $e = 4$, then $d(x, y) \geq 4$.

Therefore, $\delta(C) \geq 4$. The two codewords $a = 000000000$ and $b = 110000110$ are in C and have a distance equal to 4: finally, one has $\delta(C) = 4$.

2. Let us return to the codewords. If $c = 100000010$, then $d(a, c) = d(b, c) = 2$ and no codeword is at a distance 1 from c. Thus, one cannot correct the error.

3. $\delta(C) = 4 \Longrightarrow C$ is a 3-error-detecting code $(\delta - 1 = 3)$.
   a is obtained from b by changing 4 bits; therefore, C is not a 4-error-detecting code.

4. The punctured code is of length 8 and its cardinal number is 16. As C is of minimum distance 4, the minimum distance of this code is ≥ 3. In particular, it contains the codewords $a' = 00000000$ and $b' = 10000110$ (the punctured codewords of a and b) that are at a distance of 3. Therefore, the minimum distance of this code is 3.

5. One considers that the code is shortened by taking the codewords in C having a 0 in the first position, that is, $b_0 = 0$ (the case $b_0 = 1$ is analogous). Then, the shortened code C' is a $(8, 3)$-code of cardinal number 8. Its minimum distance is at least that of C, that is, 4. The codewords $a = 000000000$ and $c = 001100110$ are in C; thus the words $a' = 00000000$ and $c' = 01100110$ are in C' at a distance equal to 4. Thus the minimum distance of the shortened code is 4.

Exercise 4.18, on page 230.

Let us consider a code with r redundancy bits, that is, $(n, 4)$ with $n = 4 + r$. In order to obtain a 1-error-correcting code, one must have $1 + n \leq 2^{n-4}$ (see Theorem 29); hence, $5 \leq 2^r - r$. The minimum number satisfying this condition is $r = 3$. Besides, for $r = 3$, one has equality. Therefore, a 1-error-correcting code $(7, 4)$ is perfect.

Exercise 4.19, on page 230.

1. The inequality in Theorem 29 with $t = 1$ is written $1 + n \leq 2^{n-k}$, or $1 + k + r \leq 2^r$.

2. The rate of the code is $\frac{k}{r+k}$; thus, maximizing the rate for a given r is equivalent to maximizing k. Then, the inequality given in Theorem 29 enables one to obtain a bound on the greatest possible value for k and thus a bound for the rate R.
   With $r = 3$, one has necessarily $k \leq 4$. Thus, $R \leq \frac{4}{7}$.
   With $r = 4$, $k \leq 11$ and $R \leq \frac{11}{15}$.
   With $r = 5$, $k \leq 26$ and $R \leq \frac{26}{31}$.
   With $r = 6$, $k \leq 57$ and $R \leq \frac{57}{63}$.

3. According to Theorem 29 (same computation as in a.), the length of a 1-perfect binary code is $n = 2^r - 1$. Therefore, there does not exist a 1-perfect code of length 2^m.

Exercise 4.20, on page 232.

1. $\rho = \frac{k}{n} = \frac{11}{15}$.

2. The code
$$
\begin{aligned}
b_1 &= b_3 + b_5 + b_7 + b_9 + b_{11} + b_{13} + b_{15} \\
b_2 &= b_3 + b_6 + b_7 + b_{10} + b_{11} + b_{14} + b_{15} \\
b_4 &= b_5 + b_6 + b_7 + b_{12} + b_{13} + b_{14} + b_{15} \\
b_8 &= b_9 + b_{10} + b_{11} + b_{12} + b_{13} + b_{14} + b_{15}
\end{aligned}
$$

To find the canonical form, one performs the permutation $s_1 = b_3; s_2 = b_5; s_3 = b_6; s_4 = b_7; s_5 = b_9; s_6 = b_{10}; s_7 = b_{11}; s_8 = b_{12}; s_9 = b_{13}; s_{10} = b_{14}; s_{11} = b_{15}; s_{12} = b_1; s_{13} = b_2; s_{14} = b_4; s_{15} = b_8;$ hence, the matrix R corresponding to the encoding ϕ_C

$$
R = \begin{bmatrix}
1 & 1 & 0 & 0 \\
1 & 0 & 1 & 0 \\
0 & 1 & 1 & 0 \\
1 & 1 & 1 & 0 \\
1 & 0 & 0 & 1 \\
0 & 1 & 0 & 1 \\
1 & 1 & 0 & 1 \\
0 & 0 & 1 & 1 \\
1 & 0 & 1 & 1 \\
0 & 1 & 1 & 1 \\
1 & 1 & 1 & 1
\end{bmatrix}.
$$

3. One computes the last four parity bits $[s_{12} ; s_{13} ; s_{14} ; s_{15}] = [s_1 ; \dots ; s_{11}].R$. Then the codeword is $[s_1 ; \dots ; s_{11} ; s_{12} ; s_{13} ; s_{14} ; s_{15}]$.

4. Let $[y_1 ; \dots ; y_{15}]$ be the word one receives; one computes $\sigma = [y_1 ; \dots ; y_{11}].R - [y_{12} ; y_{13} ; y_{14} ; y_{15}]$. One detects an error if and only if $\sigma \neq 0$.

5. As in the previous question, one computes $\sigma = [\sigma_1 ; \sigma_2 ; \sigma_3 ; \sigma_4]$. If $\sigma \neq 0$, let $j = \sum_{i=1}^{4} 2^i \cdot \sigma_i$. Then one corrects the error by modifying the jth bit y_j in y.

Exercise 4.21, on page 234.
Let n be the length of C. Given any k positions $1 \leq i_1 < \cdots < i_k \leq n$, one builds a (k, k) punctured code C' by removing in all codewords the $n - k$ other positions. Let ϕ' be the restriction of ϕ one obtains by keeping only the k positions $i_1, \dots, i_k$; ϕ' is the encoding function associated with C'.
As C' is a punctured code of an MDS code, C' is also an MDS code (see Theorem 33). Therefore, its minimum distance is $d' = k - k + 1 = 1$. Thus, for all $x \neq y \in \mathbb{F}^k$, one has $\phi'(x) \neq \phi'(y)$. Consequently, there exists a unique $x \in \mathbb{F}^k$ such that $\phi'(x)$ is equal to c in the k given positions $i_1, \dots, i_k$.

Exercise 4.22, on page 234.
Let C' be the shortened code $(n - 1, k')$ one obtains by taking in C all words having the symbol s in the position i and by removing the position i; one has $k' \geq k - 1$. From Section 4.3.2, C' has a minimum distance $d' \geq d = n - k + 1$; hence, according to the Singleton bound, one has $k' \leq n - d' \leq n - d = k - 1$. One deduces that $k' = k - 1$

and the shortened code is a $(n-1, k-1)$ code. As its minimum distance d' reaches the Singleton bound $n' - k' + 1 = n - k + 1$, it is an MDS code.

Exercise 4.23, on page 237.

The orthogonal set to a vector subspace of $\mathbb{F}^n$ of dimension k is a vector subspace of dimension $n - k$. Thus, $C^\perp$ is a linear code of length n and dimension $n - k$. Moreover, from Property 18, the $(n - k)$ row vectors of the control matrix H of C are orthogonal to C and linearly independent. One deduces that such vectors form a basis of $C^\perp$ and, hence, that H is a generator matrix of $C^\perp$.

Exercise 4.24, on page 237.

1. Code (12,6,6). One notices that R is symmetric.
2. One checks that if r and s are rows in G, then $r \cdot s = 0$; thus $\mathcal{G}_{12} \subset \mathcal{G}_{12}^\perp$.
   Also $\mathcal{G}_{12}$ and $\mathcal{G}_{12}^\perp$ have the same dimension (12,6); therefore, they are equal.
3. This code cannot be a perfect code because its minimum distance is even ($=6$). (Indeed, let x and y be two codewords at a distance 6 from each other; one easily builds a word in $\mathbb{F}_3^{12}$ at a distance 3 from both x and y which cannot be corrected in a unique way).
4. $G_{11} = [I_6 | R_5]$ with

$$R_5 = \begin{bmatrix} 0 & 1 & 1 & 1 & 1 \\ 1 & 0 & 1 & 2 & 2 \\ 1 & 1 & 0 & 1 & 2 \\ 1 & 2 & 1 & 0 & 1 \\ 1 & 2 & 2 & 1 & 0 \\ 1 & 1 & 2 & 2 & 1 \end{bmatrix}.$$

   As the minimum distance of $\mathcal{G}_{12}$ is 6 and that of $\mathcal{G}_{11}$ is at least 5. The first row is of weight 5 (because the first row of R_5 is of weight 4). However, all lines are codewords. One deduces that the code has one word of weight 5. Thus the minimum distance of this code is 5. Therefore, it is a (11,6,5) code.
5. As $\mathcal{G}_{11}$ is of distance 5, it is a 2-error-correcting code. Hence, all balls of radius 2 around the codewords in $\mathcal{G}_{11}$ are disjoint and they form a subset of $\mathbb{F}_3^{11}$ of cardinal number $3^6(1 + 2.C_{11}^1 + 2^2.C_{11}^2) = 177,147$.
   However, $\mathrm{card}(\mathbb{F}_3^{11}) = 3^{11} = 177,147$. Therefore, the union of all balls is equal to $\mathbb{F}_3^{11}$ and $\mathcal{G}_{11}$ is a perfect code.

Exercise 4.25, on page 238.

1. $a = c \cdot P^{-1} = m \cdot S \cdot G + eP^{-1} = (mS) \cdot G + e'$, where e' has the same Hamming weight as e, still less than t. Therefore, the error correction on a gives $b = m \cdot S$. Then $m = b \cdot S^{-1}$ is the sole solution of the system because S is invertible.
2. The generating matrix must then be $2288 \times 2960 = 6,772,480$ bits (roughly 6.5 MB) where an RSA key would be of 3072 bits and an ECC key of 256 bits.

3. Encryption is a matrix-vector multiplication of complexity bound $O(kn)$: this is about $2 \times 2288 \times 2960 \approx 13.5$ millions of operations. If an LU decomposition is precomputed for S, then decryption is a triangular system solving together with linear code decoding, both are of the same order of magnitude than matrix-vector multiplication. Now RSA encryption and decryption require a modular exponentiation of complexity bound $O(3072^3)$, that is, about 2000 times slower.

Exercise 4.26, on page 239.
Obviously, we have $R = \frac{k}{n} = 1 - \frac{r}{n}$ and $\frac{r}{n} = \frac{w_c}{w_r}$.

Exercise 4.27, on page 240.

1. The error syndrome is Hy and requires $r * w_r = n * w_c$ binary additions, leading to $3 * 10^4$ binary operations.
2. T is 5000×5000 and contains 12.5×10^6 nonzero elements, leading to $12.5 \times 10^6 - 5000$ binary additions.
3. H is $5000 \times 10,000$ and contains 25×10^6 ones, leading to roughly $25 \times 10^6 - 5000$ binary additions.

Exercise 4.28, on page 241.

1. The shortest possible cycle in a Tanner graph has length 4, as cycles necessarily have even lengths and length 2 is impossible. Note that this obviously holds for any bipartite graph.
2. Length 4 cycles correspond to 2×2 blocks filled with 1's on the corner of a submatrix of H. To avoid cycles of length 4, it is, therefore, sufficient to check that for any two columns, there is no more than one position that share a nonzero value.
3. Using the previous method, one can check that there is no cycle of length 4. Therefore, the girth of the graph is at least 6. Then, Figure 4.3 exhibits a cycle of length 6 and the girth of this graph is exactly 6.

Exercise 4.29, on page 248.
Over a BSC channel with error probability p, we have

$$P(c_i = b \mid y_i) = \begin{cases} 1 - p & \text{if } y_i = b \\ p & \text{if } y_i = \overline{b}. \end{cases}$$

Then, because $y_i \in \{0, 1\}$, we can note that

$$p_i = P(c_i = 1 \mid y_i) = (1-p)^{y_i} p^{1-y_i}$$
$$1 - p_i = P(c_i = 0 \mid y_i) = p^{y_i}(1-p)^{1-y_i}.$$

Therefore, the different expression of $q_{i,j}^{(0)}$ are as follows:

$$
q_{i,j}^{(0)} = \begin{cases} (1 - p_i, p_i) & \text{for the BPA-APP version} \\ \left(\frac{1-p}{p}\right)^{y_i} \left(\frac{p}{1-p}\right)^{1-y_i} & \text{for the BPA-LR version} \\ (-1)^{y_i} \ln\left(\frac{1-p}{p}\right) & \text{for the BPA-LLR version.} \end{cases}
$$

Exercise 4.30, on page 248.

1. We proceed by induction on n.
   The result holds for $n = 1$: $P(x_0 = 0) = 1 - p_0 = \frac{1}{2} + \frac{1}{2}(1 - 2p_0)$.
   We now assume that the result holds for a sequence of $\{x_i\}_{0 \le i < n}$ of n independent binary digits. Let $P_n = P(x_0 \oplus \cdots \oplus x_{n-1} = 0) = \frac{1}{2} + \frac{1}{2}\prod_{i=0}^{n-1}(1 - 2p_i)$.
   Consider now x_n a new independent digit with $P(x_n = 1) = p_n$. Then the sequence $\{x_i\}_{0 \le i < n+1}$ contains an even number of 1's if and only if $x_0 \oplus \cdots \oplus x_{n-1} \oplus x_n = 0$. It follows that (from the independence assumption):

$$
P_{n+1} = P_n \cdot P(x_n = 0) + (1 - P_n) \cdot P(x_n = 1)
$$

$$
= \frac{1}{2}\left[\left(1 + \prod_{i=0}^{n-1}(1 - 2p_i)\right)(1 - p_n) + \left(1 - \prod_{i=0}^{n-1}(1 - 2p_i)\right)p_n\right]
$$

$$
= \frac{1}{2}\left[1 + (1 - p_n - p_n)\prod_{i=0}^{n-1}(1 - 2p_i)\right] = \frac{1}{2}\left[1 + \prod_{i=0}^{n}(1 - 2p_i)\right].
$$

2. From this result and together with the correspondence $p_i \leftrightarrow q_{i,j}^{(r-1)}(1)$, we have

$$
r_{j,i}^{(r)}(0) = \frac{1}{2} + \frac{1}{2}\prod_{i' \in \mathcal{M}(j)\setminus i}(1 - 2q_{i',j}^{(r-1)}).
$$

Indeed, when $y_i = 0$, we consider the parity-check equation operated on the check node f_j: to satisfy this equation, the involved bits (i.e., the bits $\{y_{i'} : i' \in \mathcal{M}(j)\setminus i\}$) must contain an even number of 1's. In turn, this proves that

$$
r_{j,i}^{(r)}(1) = 1 - r_{j,i}^{(r)}(0).
$$

Exercise 4.31, on page 249.

From Bayes' rule (applied twice), with $p_i = P(c_i = 1 \mid y_i)$,

$$
q_{i,j}^{(r)}(0) = P(c_i = 0 \mid y_i, S_i, \text{MSG}_c(\setminus j))
$$

$$
= (1 - p_i)\frac{P(S_i \mid c_i = 0, y_i, \text{MSG}_c(\setminus j))}{P(S_i)}.
$$

As the messages, the digits, and the parity checks are assumed independent, we have

$$q_{i,j}^{(r)}(0) = \alpha_{i,j}(1 - p_i) \prod_{j' \in C(i) \backslash j} r_{j',i}^{(r)}(0).$$

Similarly,

$$q_{i,j}^{(r)}(1) = \alpha_{i,j} p_i \prod_{j' \in C(i) \backslash j} r_{j',i}^{(r)}(1).$$

Exercise 4.32, on page 253.

1. It is sufficient to keep all gcd not equal to 1 in the computation of the irreducibility test.
2. If P is reducible, then $k \le \frac{d}{2}$. Therefore, the Distinct Degree Factorization (DDF) has a complexity bound $\frac{d}{2}(\log(p)M_d + E_d)$.
3. If $p = 2$, the only possible factors of P_1 are X and $X - 1$.
4. $X^{p^i} = X \mod (X^{p^i} - X)$. Thus this property can be extended to any polynomial T by $T^{p^i} - T = \sum a_j(X^{jp^i} - X^j) = 0 \mod (X^{p^i} - X)$.
5. $T^{p^i} - T = T(T^{\frac{p^i-1}{2}} - 1)(T^{\frac{p^i-1}{2}} + 1)$.
6. One chooses T of degree $< 2i$ randomly and one computes $\gcd(T, P_i) \mod P_i$, then $\gcd(T^{\frac{p^i-1}{2}} - 1 \mod P_i, P_i)$, the powers being computed using fast square exponentiation modulo P_i at each step. The complexity is $2E_d + i\log_2(p)M_d$. On the average, the one in two chance of separating the factors gives an expected number of random draws for T of 2.

Exercise 4.33, on page 254.
Given $r = n - k$ coefficients of g, one defines a unique matrix G_C and thus a unique linear code. However, g is a divisor of $X^n - 1$; therefore, C is constant with respect to σ and C is cyclic.

Exercise 4.34, on page 256.

1. The roots of $(X^8 - 1)$ are not suitable because they are at most eighth roots of unity. So let us try γ, a root of $X^4 - 2$; hence, such that $\gamma^4 = 2$. The only possible orders for γ are 16, 8, 4, and 2. If $\gamma^2 = 1$, then $\gamma^4 = 1$, which is impossible because $\gamma^4 = 2$. γ^4 is obviously not equal to 1. $\gamma^8 = (\gamma^4)^2 = 2^2 = 4 = -1$ is also different from 1, thus γ is necessarily a sixteenth primitive root of unity.

2. Let us find the polynomial having the consecutive powers of γ as its roots:

γ	γ^2	γ^3	γ^4	γ^5	γ^6	γ^7	γ^8
$X^4 + 2$	$X^2 + 2$	$X^4 + 2$	$X + 2$	$X^4 + 3$	$X^2 + 3$	$X^4 + 2$	$X + 1$
γ^9	γ^{10}	γ^{11}	γ^{12}	γ^{13}	γ^{14}	γ^{15}	$1 = \gamma^{16}$
$X^4 + 2$	$X^2 + 2$	$X^4 + 2$	$X + 3$	$X^4 + 3$	$X^2 + 3$	$X^4 + 2$	$X + 4$

To be a 2-error-correcting code, the minimum degree of the generator polynomial is thus equal to 7. For instance, $g(X) = (X + 2)(X^4 + 3)(X^2 + 3)$ has the roots γ^4, γ^5, γ^6, and γ^7, which gives a code rate of $\frac{9}{16} = 0.5625$.

Exercise 4.35, on page 260.

1. Let $x \in C$; after $d - 1$ erasures, one obtains y with the symbol '?' at $d - 1$ positions. As the minimum distance of C is d, there exists at least one word at a distance $d - 1$ from y (the codeword x).
   Let us suppose that there exist two codewords $x_1 \neq x_2$ at a distance $d - 1$ from y. Then x_1 and x_2 are at a distance of at most $d - 1$ from each other because they can differ only in the positions of the erasures. But this is impossible because, the minimum distance of the code being equal to d, one has $d_H(x_1, x_2) \geq d$.
   Conclusion: x is the unique codeword in C which is equal to y in the nonerased positions in y. Hence, x is the only possible correction: the code enables one to correct up to $d - 1$ erasures.

2. The probability for a bit not to be erased is $p = 0.99$. In this case, if one considers the field $\mathbb{F}_{2^8}$, the probability for a digit not to be erased is $p^8 = 0.99^8 > 0.92$; therefore, with 1% of erased bits, one has between 7% and 8% of erased bytes. The length of the codewords in a Reed–Solomon code over $\mathbb{F}_{256}$ is $n = 255$. One has to be able to correct $0.08 \times 255 = 20.40 \leq 21$ erasures per word and, hence, a minimum distance of the code equal to 22: thus, one chooses $r = 21$. Let α be a primitive root of $\mathbb{F}_{256}$; for instance, one considers $g(X) = \prod_{i=1}^{21}(X - \alpha^i)$. One obtains a $(255, 234, 22)$-code over $\mathbb{F}_{256}$.

3. In the word one receives, one replaces the $s \leq d - 1$ erasures with s unknown values x_i; let x be the row vector one obtains. x must belong to the code. Thus, if H is the control matrix of the code, one has $H \cdot x^t = 0$, which is equivalent to a linear system of rank s with s unknown variables (the x_i). The resolution of this system gives the value of x.

4. Let x be the word containing s erasures one receives, and let x' be the word of length $n - s$ one obtains by removing in x the s erasures.
   Let C' be the punctured code of C one obtains by removing the s positions of the erasures. The code C' is a linear code of length $(n - s)$ and its minimum distance is equal to $d' \geq d - s = 2t + 1$. Therefore, it enables one to correct t errors in the word x'. Let $y' \in C'$ be the corrected word, and let y be the word of length n one obtains from y' by adding the erasures. Using the previous question, one corrects the s erasures in y with the control matrix of C. Hence, one obtains the unique codeword at a distance $s + t$ from x, which enables the correction.

Exercise 4.36, on page 262.

1. For instance, the second format of Figure 4.6 contains 25×25 pixels. Taking out $3 \cdot 8 \times 8$ position patterns, 5×5 alignment pixels, $2 \cdot 9$ timing pixels, and

$8 + 8 + 15$ format pixels leaves $625 - (192 + 25 + 18) - 31 = 359$ available bits. This is 44 codewords and 7 extra bits.

2. • For level 2-H, 30% of 44 is 13.2 so that the code needs to correct 14 codewords. This induces a minimal distance of 29 and $44 - (29 - 1) = 16$ data codewords for a $(44, 16, 14)$ shortened Reed–Solomon code.

   • For level 2-Q, 25% of 44 is 11 so that the shortened Reed–Solomon code is $(44, 22, 11)$.

   • For level 2-M, 15% of 44 is 6.6 so that the shortened Reed–Solomon code could be $(44, 30, 7)$.

   • For level 2-L, 7% of 44 is 3.08 so that the shortened Reed–Solomon code could be $(44, 36, 4)$.

3. • For level 2-M, this gives an extra error-correction capacity to $8/44 \approx 18.2\%$.

   • For level 2-L, this leaves 2 extra codewords, for instance, for an additional error detection that could reduce misdecodes, if more than four erroneous codewords are encountered.

Exercise 4.37, on page 262.

Let $w = 0 \cdots 0 e_1 \cdots e_l 0 \cdots 0 \in \mathbb{F}_q^n$ be a packet of errors of length at most l. As C detects any packet of length at most l, the word $0 + w$ is detected and it is erroneous. Therefore, $w \notin C$. One has $\dim(C) = k$ (see, e.g., the proof of the Singleton bound) and the set of all w has a dimension equal to l. If these two sets are completely disjoint, except for the word 0, one has necessarily $k + l < \dim(\mathbb{F}_q^n)$; hence, $l \leq n - k$.

Exercise 4.38, on page 263.

Let $t = \left\lfloor \frac{d-1}{2} \right\rfloor$; because this is a t-error-correcting code, it corrects any packet affecting at most t consecutive bytes. However, an error on $8.(t - 1) + 2$ consecutive bits can be spread to $t + 1$ consecutive bytes (all bits are erroneous in the $t - 1$ bytes in the middle and one single bit is erroneous in the extreme bytes) and it cannot be corrected. On the other hand, any packet of length $8.(t - 1) + 1$ is necessarily spread to t bytes and it can be corrected. Therefore, one has $l = 8. \left(\left\lfloor \frac{d-1}{2} \right\rfloor - 1 \right) + 1$.

Exercise 4.39, on page 263.

Any codeword in C_p is built from p words in C and it can be seen as an interleaved p-tuple of codewords in C. Hence, let us consider two different codewords in C_p; the two p-tuples differ in at least one codeword in C. Thus, the distance between them is at least d. Let us prove that it is the minimum distance: there exist two codewords u and v in C at a distance d. Let c be another codeword in C. Let the two words u' and v' be, respectively, the interleavings of the p-tuples $(u, c, \ldots, c)$ and $(v, c, \ldots, c)$; u' and v' differ for exactly d positions. Thus, C_p has a minimum distance equal to d.

One has clearly $l \leq d$. Let $v \in C_p$, and let e be a packet of errors of length $p * l$. The uninterleaved word of $v + e$ is a p-tuple in the form $v_1 + e_1, \ldots, v_p + e_p$ with $v_i \in C$ and e_i is a packet of errors of length at most l. As C corrects packets of length l, it enables one to correct the word in order to recover the p-tuple $(v_1, \ldots, v_p)$, which is associated with the word v in C_p. Therefore, C_p corrects at least the packets of length pl.

Exercise 4.40, on page 268.
Let α be a primitive root of $\mathbb{F}_{256}$ and let $g(X) = \prod_{i=1}^{4}(X - \alpha^i)$, for example. This polynomial defines a (255,251) Reed–Solomon code C over $\mathbb{F}_{256}$, of distance 5. The generator matrix of C associated with g has its k first columns linearly independent. Thus C admits a canonical generator matrix $G = [I_{251}, R_{251\times4}]$.

Let R_1 be the matrix formed by the last 24 rows of R, and let $R_2 = \left[\dfrac{T}{R_1}\right]$ be the matrix formed by the last 28 rows.

Let $G_1 = [I_{24}, R_1]$ (respectively, $G_2 = [I_{28}, R_2]$) be the 24×28 submatrix (respectively, 28×32 submatrix) formed by the last 24 (respectively, 28) rows and the last 28 (respectively, 32) columns.

The matrix G_1 generates the shortened code C_1 of C, formed by the codewords in C whose first 227 digits are null. Therefore, C_1 has a minimum distance d_1 greater than or equal to C and $d_1 \geq 5$. Moreover, according to the Singleton bound, one has $d_1 \leq 255 - 251 + 1 \leq 5$. Finally, C_1 has a minimum distance 5.

Exercise 4.41, on page 268.

1. The error syndrome is $s_2(z) = z \cdot H_2^t$, where H_2 is the control matrix of C_2.
   - If $s_2(z) = 0$, there is no error: one returns the first 28 bytes of z.
   - If $s_2(z)$ is collinear to a row of H_2^t: let $i \in \{1, 32\}$ and $\lambda \in \mathbb{F}_{256}$ such that $s_2(z) = \lambda \cdot e_i \cdot H_2^t = s_2(\lambda.e_i)$, where e_i is the ith canonical row vector. The correction $-\lambda \cdot e_i$ of weight 1 enables one to correct z; one returns the 28 first bytes y' of the vector $z - \lambda \cdot e_i$.
   - Otherwise, one detects that there were at least two errors. One does not perform any correction: one indicates that the word is erased. An erased symbol (hence, not belonging to $\mathbb{F}_{256}$) is denoted by '?'; therefore, one returns for instance the word y' composed of 28 symbols '?'.

2. One uses the calculus of the error syndrome of the code C_1. The decoding process is the following:
   - If the block y' does not contain any '?', one returns the 24 first bytes of y'.
   - If it contains at least five '?', the error cannot be corrected; one returns an error message.
   - Otherwise, one computes the values of the u unknown erasures ($1 \leq u \leq 4$) by solving the linear system of rank $u \times u$ defined by $y \cdot H_1^t = 0$, where H_1 is the control matrix of C_1. Then one replaces the erasures by their values in y and returns the 24 first bytes of y.

Exercise 4.42, on page 268.
Any word at the input of the C_1 decoding process containing less than four erasures is corrected. As the interleaving has a delay 4, this corresponds to at most 15

consecutive columns erased by C_2. A column is composed of 32 bytes; hence, it corresponds to one frame. Therefore, this code enables one to correct 15 consecutive frames.

Exercise 4.43, page 269 (foundationsofcoding.imag.fr/Ex/4.43.html).
The polynomial formed by the message 100110100 is $P = X^2 + X^4 + X^5 + X^8$. One has $P * P_1 = X^3 + X^5 + X^6 + X^9$, which corresponds to the binary word 1001101000, and $P * P_2 = X^2 + X^3 + X^4 + X^6 + X^8 + X^9$, which corresponds to the binary word 1101011100. By interleaving, one obtains 11010011100111010000, which actually corresponds to the message encoded on-the-fly in Example 4.12.

Exercise 4.44, on page 270.
One applies Viterbi's algorithm. The marks are illustrated in Figure 3. Let us give the details of the beginning of the decoding: at the beginning, all marks are equal to the infinity. At Stage 0, we have zeros everywhere. The first received codeword is 10 at a distance 1 from both the two possible edges starting at 0. Thus, the two marks at stage 1 are equal to 1. At stage 2 and all next stages, there are four possible edges. The second received word is 01, at a distance 0 from the edge 01, hence the mark 1 on the bit 0 and at a distance 1 from the edge 11, hence the mark 2 on the bit 1, and so on.

Therefore, the closest codeword is 11010011011101111010, at a distance 2 from the received word (mark on the last stage), and the associated source word according to the last part of the algorithm is 1001010111.

Exercise 4.45, on page 274.

1. For k bits in the input, one has $\frac{k}{R_1}$ bits in the output of the turbo code for C_1 and $\frac{k}{R_2} - k$ bits for C_2, because one does not keep the systematic output of C_2. Hence, a rate $R_P = \dfrac{1}{\frac{1}{R_1} + \frac{1}{R_2} - 1} = \dfrac{R_1 . R_2}{R_1 + R_2 - R_1 \cdot R_2}$.

2. For a serial encoding and k bits in the input, one has $\frac{k}{R_1}$ bits in the output of C_1 and in the input of C_2, hence $\frac{k}{R_1 \cdot R_2}$ bits in the output of C_2. Therefore, the rate is $R_S = R_1 \cdot R_2$.

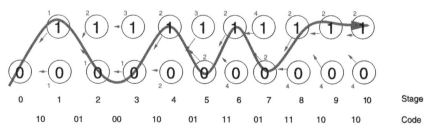

Figure 3   Viterbi's algorithm on the message 10010010011101111010

3. If $R_1 = R_2 = r$, the respective rates R_P and R_S of the parallel and serial codes are $R_S = r^2$ and $R_P = \frac{r}{2-r}$.

   As $0 < r < 1$ and $(r-1)^2 > 0$, one has $r < \frac{1}{2-r}$, thus $R_S < R_P$. The serial composition has a lower rate than the parallel composition.

   When $r = \frac{1}{2}$, one has $R_P = \frac{1}{3}$ and $R_S = \frac{1}{4}$.

SOLUTION FOR THE "CASINO" EXERCISE

Exercise 147, on page 280.

1. (a) $p_8 = 1 - 0.999^8 = 0.00797$

   (b) i As one sends bytes, one chooses the ground field $\mathbb{F}_{256}$, with $q = 256 = 2^8$ elements. Then, for a Reed–Solomon code, one must choose $n = q - 1 = 255$.

      ii To correct at least $0.0079n = 2.03$ errors, one must be able to correct 3 errors, hence one has to choose a code of minimum distance $\delta \geq 2 * 3 + 1 = 7$. With a Reed-Solomon code, the generator polynomial has a degree $r = \delta - 1 = 6$.

      iii The maximum number of detected errors is 6.

      iv Let $g = \sum_{i=0}^{6} g_i X^i$ be the generator polynomial. The code is $(255, 249, 7)$. The generator matrix has 249 rows and 255 columns. It is written in the form

$$\begin{bmatrix} g_6 & g_5 & \cdots & g_0 & 0 & \cdots & 0 \\ 0 & g_6 & g_5 & \cdots & g_0 & \cdots & 0 \\ & & & \cdots & & & \end{bmatrix}$$

   (c) i Thus, one chooses $P = 1 + \alpha^2 + \alpha^3 + \alpha^4 + \alpha^8$ to implement $\mathbb{F}_{256} = \mathbb{F}_2[\alpha]/P$. Let $X = \sum_{i=0}^{7} x_i \alpha^i$, with $x_i \in \{0, 1\}$; X is represented with the byte $(x_0, x_1, x_2, x_3, x_4, x_5, x_6, x_7)$.
   Let $Y = \sum_{i=0}^{7} y_i \alpha^i$ with $y_i \in \{0, 1\}$ be another element of the field. Then $X + Y$ is represented with the byte $(x_0 + y_0, \ldots x_7 + y_7)$.
   For $X \cdot Y$, one computes the product of polynomials $X \cdot Y \mod P$; the coefficients of this polynomial enable one to obtain the encoding of XY in the form of a byte.

      ii As P is primitive, α is a generator element of $\mathbb{F}_{256}^{\star}$ (a 255th primitive root of the unity). Therefore, it is sufficent to choose the generator polynomial $g = \prod_{i=1..6}(X - \alpha^i) \mod P = X^6 + \sum_{i=0}^{5} g_i X^i$, where each g_i is an element in $\mathbb{F}_{256}$ represented with a byte (cf. previous question).

   (d) The capacity of the symmetric binary channel with a probability of error $q = 0.001$ is $C = 1 + q \log_2 q + (1 - q) \log_2(1 - q) = 0.98859$. The code has a rate $249/255 = 0.97648$ and this rate is lower than the channel capacity (Second theorem of Shannon).

2. The problem is that each sequence of dice received by the server must be identified and associated with one croupier. Therefore, one uses a signature of the sequence by the croupier during the transmission.
   One may use a secret key signature (established between the casino and the croupier). But one would rather use a public key signature to enable the players to check that the sequence transmitted is correct. Each croupier has a private key and a public key (generated by the casino for instance). The croupier

encrypts the sequence with his private key: hence, the server and the player are able to check the correctness of the information using his public key.

To prevent a throw of dice encrypted by a true croupier from being intercepted and replayed later on by a false croupier (pretending to be a true croupier), each transmission is marked with the number of the throw (which is noted by the croupier after each throw) and possibly the date.

Finally, to minimize the cost of the encryption, the croupier may only encrypt the hash of the sequence (SHA-1 or Whirlpool for example).

To conclude: each croupier C has a public key Pub_C. He numbers each sequence and concatenates a header (date + number of the sequence) to obtain a plaintext m. Then he computes the hash $r = \mathrm{SHA1}(m)$ of m, he encrypts $D_{\mathrm{Priv}_C}(r) = r'$ with his private key, and he transmits the message (m, r') on the channel. Then, the players and the casino are able to check that the message was actually issued by the croupier: it is enough to check that $\mathrm{SHA1}(m) = E_{\mathrm{Pub}_C}(r')$.

3. (a) $H = \log_2(1/6) = 2.58$.

   (b) One encodes the six faces with three bits: I = 000, II = 001, III = 010, IV = 011, V = 100, VI = 101. The messages 110 and 111 remain unused.

   (c) $l = 3$. The length is always greater than the entropy, which is a lower bound for any binary encoding.

   (d) The entropy is a lower bound. One may obtain a better code than the previous one and come close to the entropy using a Huffman encoding. Then, one encodes V and VI on two bits: V = 10 and VI = 11. The encoding has an average length $= 4.3/6 + 2.2/6 = 2.67$.

   (e) This code is optimal; but one can still improve it by encoding several consecutive throws (extension of the source). Hence, if one encodes five consecutive throws, one has $6^5 = 7776$ possibilities. A block code of constant size can be performed with $\log_2 7776 = 12.92$, that is, 13 bits; this code has an average length per throw: $l = 13/5 = 2.6$. A Huffman code on these five throws is necessarily better (a Huffman code is optimal).

   Asymptotically, one tends toward $H = 2.58$. For instance, with 22 throws, one has $\log_2(6^{21}) = 56.8$; thus 22 throws can be encoded with a code of constant size $= 57$ bits, for an average length of the code per throw equal to 57/22=2.59.

BIBLIOGRAPHY

[1] Christos H. Papadimitriou. *Computational Complexity*. Addison-Wesley Longman, first edition, 1994. http://www.cs.berkeley.edu/~christos/.

[2] Jiri Adamek. *Foundations of Coding: Theory and Applications of Error-Correcting Codes, with an Introduction to Cryptography and Information Theory*. John Wiley & Sons, Inc., New York, 1991.

[3] Carlisle Adams and Steve Lloyd. *Understanding PKI: Concepts, Standards, and Deployment Considerations*. Addison-Wesley Professional, second edition, 2002.

[4] Gildas Avoine, Pascal Junod, and Philippe Oechslin. *Computer Systems Security*. CRC Press, 2007.

[5] Thomas Baignères, Pascal Junod, Yi Lu, Jean Monnerat, and Serge Vaudenay. *A Classical Introduction to Cryptography – Exercise Book*. Springer-Verlag, 2006.

[6] Richard P. Brent and Paul Zimmermann. *Modern Computer Arithmetic*, volume 18 of *Cambridge Monographs on Applied and Computational Mathematic*. Cambridge University Press, 2011.

[7] Johannes A. Buchmann. *Introduction to Cryptography*. Springer, 2004.

[8] David M. Burton. *Elementary Number Theory, International Series in Pure and Applied Mathematics*. McGraw-Hill, fourth edition, 1998.

[9] Lindsay N. Childs. *A Concrete Introduction to Higher Algebra*. Springer, third edition, 2009.

[10] Henri Cohen. *A Course in Computational Algebraic Number Theory*, volume 138 of *Graduate Texts in Mathematics*. Springer-Verlag, first edition, 1993.

Foundations of Coding: Compression, Encryption, Error Correction, First Edition.
Jean-Guillaume Dumas, Jean-Louis Roch, Éric Tannier and Sébastien Varrette.
© 2015 John Wiley & Sons, Inc. Published 2015 by John Wiley & Sons, Inc.
http://foundationsofcoding.imag.fr

[11] Henri Cohen and Gerhard Frey. *Handbook of Elliptic and Hyperelliptic Curve Cryptography, Discrete Mathematics and its Applications*. CRC, 2005.

[12] Jean-Guillaume Dumas, Jean-Louis Roch, Éric Tannier, and Sébastien Varrette. *Théorie des Codes: Compression, Cryptage, Correction*. Dunod, second edition, 2013.

[13] Joachim von zur Gathen and Jürgen Gerhard. *Modern Computer Algebra*. Cambridge University Press, third edition, 2013.

[14] Alain Glavieux. *Channel Coding in Communication Networks: From Theory to Turbo Codes, Digital Signal and Image Processing*. ISTE Pub. Company, 2007.

[15] Johannes Grabmeier, Erich Kaltofen, and Volker Weispfenning, editors. *Computer Algebra Handbook: Foundations, Applications, Systems*. Springer, 2003.

[16] Godfrey Harold Hardy and Edward Maitland Wright. *An Introduction to the Theory of Numbers, Oxford Science Publications*. Clarendon Press, fifth edition, 1998.

[17] Antoine Joux. *Algorithmic Cryptanalysis*. CRC, 2009.

[18] Donald E. Knuth. *Seminumerical Algorithms*, volume 2 of *The Art of Computer Programming*. Addison-Wesley, third edition, 1997. http://www-cs-faculty.stanford.edu/~knuth/taocp.html.

[19] Neal Koblitz. *Algebraic Aspects of Cryptography*, volume 3 of *Algorithms and Computation in Mathematics*. Springer-Verlag, 1998.

[20] Brian Komar. *Windows Server 2008 PKI and Certificate Security*. Microsoft Press, 2008.

[21] Rudolf Lidl and Harald Niederreiter. *Introduction to Finite Fields and their Applications*. Cambridge University Press, revised edition, 1994.

[22] David J. C. MacKay. *Information Theory, Inference and Learning Algorithms*. Cambridge University Press, 2003. http://www.inference.phy.cam.ac.uk/itprnn/book.pdf.

[23] James Massey. *Applied Digital Information Theory*. ETH Zurich, 1998. http://www.isiweb.ee.ethz.ch/archive/massey_scr.

[24] Alfred J. Menezes, Scott A. Vanstone, and Paul C. Van Oorschot. *Handbook of Applied Cryptography. Computer Sciences Applied Mathematics Engineering*. CRC Press, Inc., first edition, 1996. http://www.cacr.math.uwaterloo.ca/hac/.

[25] Bruce Schneier. *Applied Cryptography: Protocols, Algorithms, and Source Codes in C*. John Wiley & Sons, second edition, 1996.

[26] Bruce Schneier. *Secrets & Lies: Digital Security in a Networked World*. John Wiley & Sons, 2000.

[27] Victor Shoup. *A Computational Introduction to Number Theory and Algebra*. Cambridge University Press, second edition, 2009.

[28] Simon Singh. *The Code Book: The Science of Secrecy from Ancient Egypt to Quantum Cryptography*. Anchor, 2000.

[29] William Stallings. *Network Security Essentials: Applications and Standards*. Prentice Hall, third edition, 2007.

[30] Douglas R. Stinson. *Cryptography: Theory and Practice*. CRC Press, second edition, 2002. http://www.cacr.math.uwaterloo.ca/~dstinson/CTAP2/CTAP2.html.

[31] Serge Vaudenay. *A Classical Introduction to Cryptography: Applications for Communications Security*. Springer, 2005.

[32] Lawrence C. Washington. *Elliptic Curves: Number Theory and Cryptography*. CRC Press, second edition, 2008.

INDEX

Foundations of Coding: Compression, Encryption, Error Correction, First Edition.
Jean-Guillaume Dumas, Jean-Louis Roch, Éric Tannier and Sébastien Varrette.
© 2015 John Wiley & Sons, Inc. Published 2015 by John Wiley & Sons, Inc.
http://foundationsofcoding.imag.fr

Printed and bound by CPI Group (UK) Ltd, Croydon, CR0 4YY

27/10/2024

14580679-0001